D1344611

'Reading *Batavia's Graveyard* is a challenging experience . . . a lesser writer than Mike Dash might have wallowed in the lurid details of these atrocities or lingered over the ordeal endured by the women survivors who were forced into prostitution by Cornelisz's men. Instead, evidence gathered during years of research in the VOC archives and in Australia is presented here without invention or embellishment. Eyewitness accounts, selected and marshalled with as much care as they are here, are vivid enough. Dash identifies the issues which underpin the tragedy with clarity and insight, providing a superb reconstruction of the survivors' descent into anarchy. The text is fully sourced and supplemented by excellent notes'   *Times Literary Supplement*

'Truly thrilling . . . Dash has found a story big and exciting enough to hold anyone to the page . . . His account of Cornelisz's crimes is much like the man himself: horrific and mesmerising. You can't bear to read it but you can't bear not to. No history I have read in years places you so deeply inside a piece of the past'
                                                   National Geographic Adventure

'A shipwreck on a barren isle, a murderous heresy and a charismatic psychopath: all three intersected disastrously in the shipwreck of the Dutch trader *Batavia* on a coral islet in 1629 . . . Dash describes a mass descent into savagery with an unabashedly cinematic flair, and his account is backed by meticulous research'
                                                   New York Times

'[Dash] captures the reader with a narrative based on dogged research more richly evocative of character and place than any fiction, and so well crafted it is impossible to put down . . . *Batavia's Graveyard* shows how history, when it is well-written and researched, leaves today's trendy servings of fact mulched with fiction for dead'   *The Australian*

'The master story-teller of life in seventeenth-century Holland . . . The book reads like a thriller full of page-turning sub-plots'
                                                   Melbourne Herald-Sun

'This is what old-time baseball players liked to call a humdinger . . . a far better thriller than most fiction that passes for such these days'   Jonathan Yardley, *Washington Post*

Mike Dash is the author of the bestseller *Tulipomania*. A Cambridge-educated historian, he lives in London. This is his fourth book.

By Mike Dash

Batavia's Graveyard
Tulipomania
The Limit
Borderlands

BATAVIA'S GRAVEYARD

MIKE DASH

PHOENIX

A PHOENIX PAPERBACK

First published in Great Britain in 2002
by Weidenfeld & Nicolson
This paperback edition published in 2003
by Phoenix,
an imprint of Orion Books Ltd,
Orion House, 5 Upper St Martin's Lane,
London WC2H 9EA

A CIP catalogue record for this book
is available from the British Library.

ISBN 0 75381 684 9

Printed and bound in Great Britain by
Clays Ltd, St Ives plc

For Penny: my Creesje

Contents

Preface

Absolutely nothing in this book is invented. It is closely based on contemporary sources, and direct quotes, where they appear, are drawn from those same documents. In the few places where I have drawn my own conclusions about the thoughts and actions of the *Batavia*'s passengers and crew, I have indicated the fact in the notes.

Jeronimus Cornelisz and his companions sailed at a time when the use of surnames was still rare in the Dutch Republic, and when it was correspondingly common for names to be spelled and written in several different ways within a single document. I have taken advantage of this fact to avoid the possibility of confusion between two similarly named people, where there is contemporary authority for such usage. Thus Daniel Cornelisz, a mutineer, is referred to as 'Cornelissen' throughout, to prevent him being confused with Jeronimus; and of the two Allert Janszes who were on the ship, one has become Allert Janssen.

It is impossible to make accurate comparisons between prices in the Golden Age of the Dutch Republic and today's prices, but – roughly estimated – one guilder in 1629 bought the equivalent of £50 in 2001.

Place names are spelled as they were in the seventeenth century, thus Leyden rather than Leiden, and Sardam rather than Zaandam.

MIKE DASH, London, June 2001

THE UNITED
PROVINCES
c. 1628

Emden

AMELAND

TERSCHELLING   GRONINGEN

VLIELOROL   Groningen

                    Leeuwarden   Bergum   Winschoten

TEXEL   FRIESLAND

                                                        DRENTHE

            WEST
            FRIESLAND   Zuyder

                        Enkhuizen

                Hoorn   OVERIJSSEL

                            Zee

                        Monnickendam

            Sardam   Harderwijk
    Assendelft   Durgerdam
        Haarlem   Amsterdam

    Lisse

    Leyden   HOLLAND   Utrecht

The Hague   Woerden   GELDERLAND
        Delft   UTRECHT
            Gouola
        Rotterdam   Den Werd

                    Bommel
                        Bois-   Nijmegen
        Dordrecht   le-Duc   Rhine

                        Maas R.

Middelburg

    ZEELAND   BRABANT

        Scheldt R.   Antwerp

                                    Maastricht

SOUTHERN (SPANISH)

NETHERLANDS

            0   Miles   25

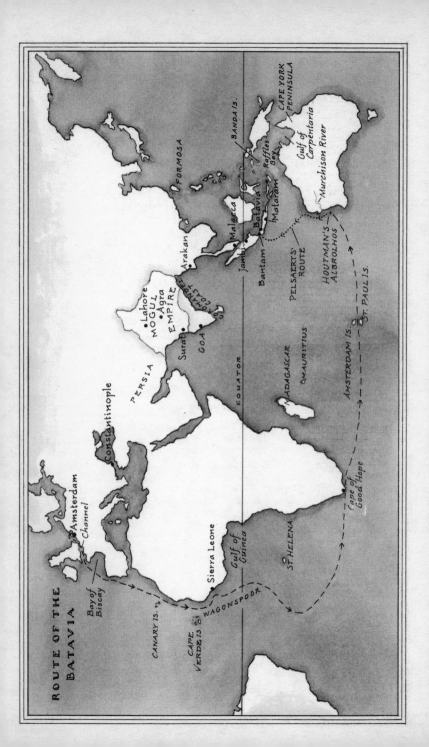

ROUTE OF THE
BATAVIA

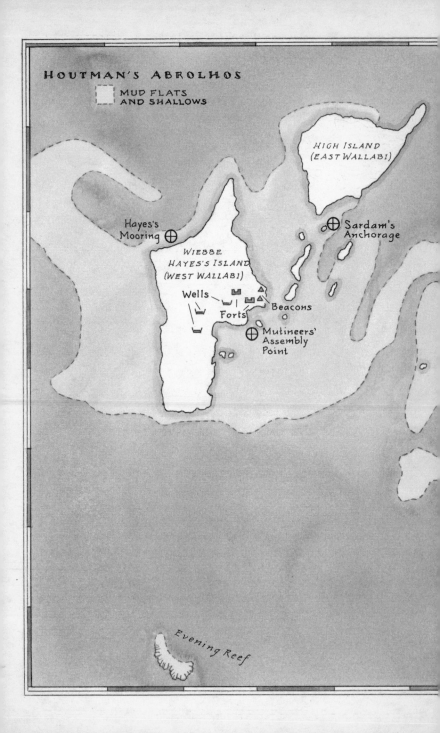

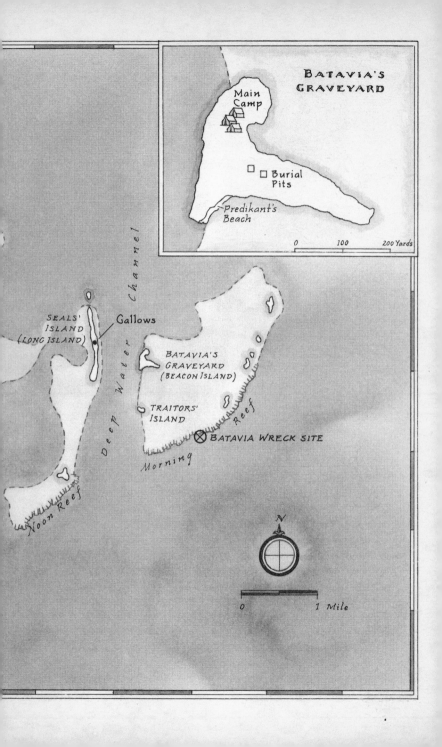

BATAVIA'S
GRAVEYARD

Main
Camp

Burial
Pits

Predikant's
Beach

0   100   200 Yards

Deep Water Channel

SEALS'
ISLAND
(LONG ISLAND)

Gallows

BATAVIA'S
GRAVEYARD
(BEACON ISLAND)

TRAITORS'
ISLAND

Reef

⊗ BATAVIA WRECK SITE

Morning

Noon Reef

N

0   1 Mile

'I looked at him with great sorrow: such a scoundrel, cause of so many disasters and of the shedding of human blood. Besmirched in every way not only with abominable misdeeds but also with damnable heresy … and still he had the intention to go on.'

From the interrogation of Jeronimus Cornelisz
by Francisco Pelsaert

BATAVIA'S
GRAVEYARD

Morning Reef

'The pack of all disasters has moulded together and fallen on my neck.'

FRANCISCO PELSAERT

The moon rose at dusk on the evening of 3 June 1629, sending soft grey shafts of light skittering across the giant swells of the eastern Indian Ocean. The beams darted their way from crest to crest, racing each other for mile after mile across the empty vastness of sea, until at last they caught and silhouetted something for an instant, a great black mass that wallowed in a trough between the waves.

In another second, the shape surged onward, rushing up the shifting wall of water in its path until it breasted the next swell. As it did so, it reared up momentarily and the moon fixed it as it slapped back into the water and sent plumes of fine white spray into the air on either side.

In the half-light of the southern winter, the black mass stood revealed as a substantial ship, steering north with the sting of a sharp wind at her back. She was built in the European style, squat and square-sailed, and she looked unbalanced, being considerably lower forward than she was aft. Her curved beak of a prow hung so close to the sea that it was frequently awash with a foam of dark water, but from there her decks curved sharply up like some massive wooden scimitar, rising so steeply that she towered almost 40 feet out of the water at the stern. As the ship came on, the moon was bright enough to pick out some of the larger details along the hull: her figurehead (a wooden lion springing upward), a tangled mass of rigging, the giant iron anchors lashed upside down along her sides. Her bows were blunt, and both the broadness of her beam and the fullness of her draught marked her as a merchant vessel.

Although the moon was bright that evening, there was too little light for the ship to be identified by the flags that writhed and snapped from all three of her masts, and there was little sign of activity on deck. The gunports had all been closed, and not even the quick glint of a lamp or two, shining through chinks in the hatches, hinted at life within. But an enormous lantern, five feet tall, hung over the stern, and its yellow glow illuminated the richly decorated woodwork beneath just well enough for a keen eye to pick out painted details that revealed the great ship's name and her home port.

She was the East Indiaman *Batavia,* seven months out of Amsterdam on her maiden voyage and still some 30 days' sailing from her destination, the Dutch trading settlements on the island of Java. Behind her, trailing in the phosphorescence of her wake, lay 13,000 miles of sea. Ahead were another 1,800 miles of uncharted ocean that had, by the end of the third decade of the seventeenth century, been crossed by only a handful of European vessels. There was rumour and speculation aplenty, among the geographers of England, the Netherlands, and Spain, about what might lie over the horizon in the immense blank that stretched south on their globes from the known waters of the Indies, but little information and no certain knowledge. The few charts of this unknown region that the *Batavia* carried were fragmentary in the extreme, and all but useless as navigational aids. So she sailed on blind into the gathering night, trusting to God and the skipper as the hourglass trickled away the minutes to midnight and the change of watch.

The ship had been brand-new when she left the Netherlands, but she was weathered now. Her upperworks, which had been painted pale green with embellishments in red and gold, were chipped and worn and scoured by sea salt. Her bottom, which had once been smooth and clean, was now festooned with so many barnacles and weeds that their drag slowed her progress north. And her hull, built though it was from oak, had been subjected to every conceivable extreme of temperature, so that it now shuddered as the ship rolled in the swell. First the *Batavia*'s timbers had swollen in the northern winter, for she had left Amsterdam late the previous October when the northern seas were already cold and stormy. Then they had been shrivelled by the sun as the ship sailed along the fever coasts of Africa, swung west on passing Sierra Leone, and crossed the equator headed for Brazil. Off the coast of

South America she had at last turned east, picking up a current that carried her to the Cape of Good Hope and then fierce easterlies that took her through the Roaring Forties and the Southern Ocean, where it was winter once again and perpetual gales hurried her onward, between the barren little islets of St. Paul and Amsterdam and into the unknown waters to the east.

At least it was warmer now, and the storms had abated as the *Batavia* headed north after more than seven long months at sea. But the endless discomforts of the voyage had if anything grown worse, and outweighed the slow improvement in the weather. The fresh food was long gone, the water was alive with worms, and below deck the ship herself stank of urine, unwashed bodies, and stale breath. Worst of all, in its own way, was the plodding monotony of the endless days at sea, which ate away the spirit of the passengers and undermined the efficiency of the crew.

At 12 the watch changed. The new watch, the midnight watch, was always acknowledged to be the most difficult and dangerous of all. Working conditions were at their worst, and the alertness of the men could not always be taken for granted. For these reasons it was customary for the skipper himself to be on deck by night, and as the last grains of sand slid through the glass, a small doorway opened on one of the upper decks and he came up.

The master of a Dutch East Indiaman was a man who enjoyed almost unlimited power in his small kingdom. He commanded a ship that had cost tens of thousands of guilders to build and contained a cargo that, in the Indies trade, was worth twice as much again. He was charged with the safe navigation of his vessel and responsible for the lives of all the hundreds of souls under his command. But, on the *Batavia* as on every other Dutch East Indiamen, the skipper was also the subordinate of an officer who typically had no experience of the sea and little understanding of how to manage a ship.

This man was the upper-merchant, or supercargo. He was, as his title implied, a commercial agent who bore the responsibility of ensuring that the voyage was a profitable one for his own masters, the directors of the *Verenigde Oost-indische Compagnie* – the United East India Company – which owned the ship. In the first half of the seventeenth century, the VOC was not only the most important organisation, and one of the largest employers, in the United Provinces of the Netherlands; it was also the wealthiest and most powerful company on Earth. It had become wealthy and powerful by putting trade and profit ahead of every other consideration.

Thus the supercargo and his deputy, the under-merchant, had the authority to order the skipper to make sail, or stay at anchor in some flyblown port until the holds were full, even if death and disease were striking down the crew.

The master of a Dutch East Indiaman was therefore in rather an unusual position. He was expected to combine the powers of seamanship and leadership that have always been demanded of any skipper with a degree of tact and even submissiveness that did not often come easily to men hardened by many years at sea. He had command of his ship from day to day, it is true, but he might at any moment be given an order he would be expected to obey. He could set a course but did not decide where his ship was heading. In port, he had very little power at all.

The skipper of the *Batavia* was a tough old seaman with considerable experience of the Indies trade, a man named Ariaen Jacobsz*. He came from Durgerdam, a fishing village just a mile or two northeast of Amsterdam, and he had been a servant of the VOC for two decades or more. The upper-merchant, who was called Francisco Pelsaert, was in many respects Jacobsz's opposite – not only in wealth and education, which was to be expected in this period, but in origin as well. For one thing, Pelsaert was no Dutchman; he came from Antwerp in the Southern Netherlands, the great rival of Amsterdam. Moreover, he had been born into a Catholic family at a time when the VOC required its officers to be Protestant; he lacked Jacobsz's powers of leadership; and despite long service in the Indies, he was as indecisive as the skipper was self-confident. The two men were not friends.

As for Ariaen Jacobsz, he was a veteran of several voyages to the East and probably in his middle forties, which would have made him one of the oldest men on board. That he was a superb sailor is beyond doubt; he had already skippered another large VOC merchantman with some success, and the East India Company was not in the habit of trusting its newest ships to indifferent officers. But the records of his service show that Jacobsz was also choleric, quick-tempered, and sensitive to any slight; that he sometimes drank to

*Surnames were still relatively uncommon in the United Provinces in the early seventeenth century. Most people identified themselves using patronymics – Ariaen Jacobsz would have been the son of a man named Jacob. Because it was unwieldy to spell out the full patronymic, which in this case is Jacobszoon, it was also common practice to abbreviate written names by omitting the 'oon' of 'zoon' (son) and shortening 'dochter' (daughter) to 'dr' When spoken, the name would have been pronounced in full.

excess; and that he was a lecher who was not above imposing his attentions on the female passengers whom he carried in his ships.

These, then, were the men charged with safeguarding the *Batavia* in the early hours of 4 June 1629. It was not a responsibility that weighed heavily on the skipper. For 211 days at sea, watch had followed watch with scarcely a noteworthy incident. The conditions on this night were good; the wind was blowing in gusts from the southwest, and with no sign of any storm or squall the weather was almost perfect for sailing. The ship was sound, and the noon position that Jacobsz had computed the previous day put the *Batavia* 600 miles distant from any known land. There seemed no need for particular vigilance from the men on watch, and since there was little or no real work to be done, some at least were able to talk and rest. Jacobsz himself stood gazing out to sea from a vantage point on the upper deck. A lookout watched beside him, and the steersman was stationed just below the skipper's post.

It was at some time after 3 A.M., when the alertness of the crew was at its lowest ebb, that the lookout, Hans Bosschieter, first suspected that all was not well. From his position high in the stern, the sailor noticed what appeared to be white water dead ahead. Peering into the night, Bosschieter thought he could make out a mass of spray, as though surf was breaking on an unseen reef. He turned to the skipper for confirmation, but Jacobsz disagreed. He insisted that the thin white line on the horizon was nothing more than moonbeams dancing on the waves. The skipper trusted to his own judgment, and he held the *Batavia*'s course, sailing on with all her canvas set.

When the ship struck, she therefore did so at full speed.

With a tremendous crash, the *Batavia* impaled herself on the half-hidden reef that had been lying in her path. In the first second of impact an outcrop of coral 15 feet beneath the surface tore the rudder half away; then, a moment later, the ship's bow hit the main body of the reef. Massive though she was, *Batavia*'s forward momentum brought her lurching out of the water, and her foreparts ground their way over the first few feet of the obstacle in a roar of shattered rock and splintered wood. The whole ship howled as shards of coral gouged their way along her sides, and her hull trembled from the blow.

Up on deck, Jacobsz and Bosschieter and the other men of the midnight watch were flung to the left and sent staggering against the *Batavia*'s sides and railings as the ship smashed into the reef.

Down below, in the dark and crowded living spaces, the rest of the ship's passengers and crew, another 270 people in all, were tipped from their hammocks and sleeping mats onto the deck. Lamps and barrels, crockery and ropes torn from their fastenings rained down on their heads, and in an instant the ordered, sleeping ship became a pitch-black pandemonium.

It took only a second or two for the *Batavia* to shudder to a halt. The coral cradle that the ship had torn out of the reef forced her stern down into the water and twisted her hull at an unnatural angle, like a human body broken in a fall. The noise of the initial collision rolled away into the darkness, to be replaced by the roar of breakers striking the hull and shouts of fear and panic from below.

The upper-merchant was the first on deck. Pelsaert had been lying half-asleep in his cabin in the stern, only a few feet from the spot where Jacobsz and Bosschieter had been standing, and the impact of the collision had thrown him out of bed. Picking himself up off the cabin floor, he hurried up, still clad in his nightclothes, to discover what had happened.

He found the ship in chaos. The *Batavia* had taken on a list to port and her timbers were shaking under the repeated pounding of the waves, which piled up under her stern and kept her bottom grating ominously against the coral. A cold veil of sea spray – thrown up by the impact of the surf against the hull – hung in the air all round the ship, and wind whipped the spume across the decks and into the faces of the half-naked men and women who now began to swarm up through the hatches from below, soaking and half-blinding them as they emerged.

Pelsaert fought his way onto the quarterdeck. The skipper was still there, yelling orders to the crew. Even the upper-merchant, with his limited knowledge of the sea, could tell immediately that the situation was serious. 'What have you done,' he screamed to Jacobsz over the general din, 'that through your reckless careless-ness you have run this noose around our necks?'

The *Batavia*'s position was indeed desperate. Not only was the ship stuck fast on the reef; her 10 great sails still billowed from the yards, pinning her ever more firmly to the coral. The timbers of the bow had been crushed in the collision, and though there were as yet no serious leaks below, it seemed from the groaning of the hull that her seams might burst at any moment. Worst of all, they were lost. The *Batavia* – at least in Jacobsz's opinion – was nowhere near any known shoal or coast. None of the other officers had had cause to question the skipper's estimate of their position. So no one had the least idea of where they were, what they had struck, or the nature and extent of the shallows they had blundered into.

The blustery southwesterly was whipping up the seas around them and the moon had almost set, but they set to work to try to save the ship. The most urgent need was to reduce the stress on the hull. Seamen were sent clambering up the masts to furl the *Batavia*'s 8,900 square feet of canvas, while down on the gun deck the ship's high boatswain* and his men ran back and forth, urging the rest of the crew to lighten the ship by throwing overboard almost anything that could be moved. They carried tarred rope 'starters' to lash the back of any man who shirked his duty, but there was little need to use them. Every sailor on the ship knew that without this urgent action he might not live to see daylight.

The *Batavia*'s gunners seized axes and swung at the cables that lashed their cannons to the deck. Freed from their constraints, the massive bronze and iron pieces – weighing around 2,200 pounds each – were manoeuvred out through the ports and into the sea, lightening the ship by up to 30 tons. A rain of boxes, rope, and other gear from the main deck followed the guns. While this was happening, another group of sailors took the smallest of the *Batavia*'s eight anchors and secured it to a good length of cable. When morning came, the anchor would be run out from the stern into deeper water and the cable attached to a capstan in the hope that the ship could be hauled backward off the reef.

By now it was nearly dawn. The wind scoured the decks with ever-greater savagery, and it began to pour with rain. Up on the poop, Pelsaert called for the sounding lead, a slim cylinder of metal on a long line used to determine the depth of the water around a vessel. As quickly as he could, the leadsman sounded all around the ship, finding no more than 12 feet of water around the bows and a maximum depth of 18 feet at the stern, only fractionally more than an East Indiaman's normal draught of 16 ½ feet.

This was a terrifying discovery. The chief hope was that they had had the luck to run aground at low water. If so, the *Batavia* might yet refloat herself as the tide rose. But if they had struck at high tide, there was so little water under the ship that the receding sea would quickly leave her stranded and make it impossible to

---

*The officer in day-to-day charge of the crew and – other than his commissioned rank – the equivalent of a modern-day bos'n.

wind her off with the anchor, adding to the stresses on the hull and perhaps even breaking her back by snapping the great keel in two.

With the work of lightening the ship complete, they waited, wondering if the tide was high. It was only at some time between five and six in the morning that it became clear that chance was against them: the waters under the hull were not rising but falling. Slowly the jagged tips of the reef on which they had been stranded began to emerge above the waves, and before long the people on the ship found themselves surrounded on three sides by raging surf and claws of coral. As the waters receded, the *Batavia* began to bump violently on the reef. It became impossible to stand or walk on deck; attempts at salvage had to be curtailed, and both passengers and crew could do little but sit in miserable huddles, listening to the awful grating of the hull.

Dutch East Indiamen were built strong. Their timbers were twice as thick as those of other merchantmen. But they were not designed to withstand stranding on a coral reef and, in particular, their bottoms were not made to take the full weight of the massive mainmast unsupported. This mast, 180 feet of Scandinavian pine, weighed well in excess of 15 tons with all its canvas, yards, and rigging, and ran down through all four decks to rest directly on the keel. Now, with the whole ship nearly clear of the water, fierce surf was thrusting the *Batavia* up off the reef six or seven times a minute, then ebbing rapidly away to let the hull crash back against the coral. And the mainmast had been turned into a gigantic pile driver, repeatedly smashing down onto the keel and threatening to grind right through the bottom of the ship.

Without her mainmast, the *Batavia* could scarcely sail. But with it, she would certainly founder there upon the reef. It was imperative to relieve the stress on the hull, and there was only one way to save the ship. Shortly after dawn, Jacobsz gave the order to fell the mast.

In the age of sail, cutting down a mainmast was an act of such dire significance that the skipper customarily accepted responsibility for the consequences by striking the first blow with his own axe. Jacobsz swung, then several others joined him in hacking at the mast where it passed down through the main deck. But, in their haste, they failed to calculate the necessary trajectory. Instead of falling overboard into the surf, the enormous mast with its spars and rigging thundered down onto the *Batavia* herself, crushing gear and railings, thoroughly entangling itself in the equipment left on deck, and causing a huge amount of damage.

By good fortune, no one was killed or even injured, but the ship's company surveyed the devastation with horror. The mast could not be moved, and it was obvious there was no longer any chance of saving the *Batavia*. The only hope for those on board was that there was at least some land in the vicinity that would not disappear beneath the waves by noon, when the tide was full.

The upper-merchant clambered as high into the stern as he was able and looked north. Now that the sun had come up and the tide had receded, he could see they had run onto the southern tip of a huge, crescent-shaped reef. A single line of breakers stretched for two miles to the east of them, and one mile to the north and west. But in the distance Pelsaert could see islands.

The largest – and the only ones of any size – appeared to him to be nearly six miles away. But several pancakes of broken coral lay much closer than that – three to the northwest and at least one more to the east. Breakers surrounded the islet on the eastern side of the reef, and it seemed unlikely they could land on it. But the merchant could see that half a mile to the west of their position, the reef was broken by a clear deep-water channel that led into the heart of the mysterious archipelago. With a modicum of care, it might be possible for the ship's boats to penetrate the reef and ascertain which, if any, of the islets would provide them with a haven.

The *Batavia*'s yawl, which was the smaller of the two boats that the big ship carried, had been launched while it was dark and now lay bobbing alongside in the surf. It was well suited to the task, and about seven in the morning the skipper and a handpicked crew pulled away to scout the archipelago. At nine o'clock they returned with encouraging news. They had visited several of the smaller coral islands, Jacobsz reported, and none seemed likely to be submerged by the tides.

Ariaen's discovery meant that there was a reasonable chance of saving the *Batavia*'s passengers and crew. But Pelsaert still faced something of a dilemma. The VOC, he knew, did not look kindly on servants who were unlucky or incompetent enough to lose its property. His duty to his employers was certainly to save the cargo first and worry about the lives of the passengers and crew only when the valuables were safe. But he doubted this was a realistic course of action. Even if he could keep control of the sailors, it seemed unlikely that the panicky soldiers and civilians on board would stand by while the boats ferried boxes of trade goods and chests packed full of silver to the islands. So the upper-merchant compromised. 'Because of the great Yammer that there was in the ship,' he duly noted, 'of Women, Children, Sick, and poor-hearted men, we decided to put most of the people on land first, and meanwhile to get ready on deck the money and most precious goods.'

It was the right decision. At 10 A.M., before the first boatloads of survivors could be got away, the relentless pounding of the surf finally put an end to the resistance of *Batavia*'s tortured hull. The ship burst open below the water line, and tons of foaming reef water began to pour into the hold. The breach was so vast that the caulkers and the carpenters had to flee before the swiftly rising flood. A good many of the supplies on board were lost, and it was only with considerable difficulty that a little food and water was salvaged from the stores.

The sight of bales of trade goods floating in the flooded hold was sufficient to persuade most of the passengers and crew to abandon ship, and the main deck was soon crowded with men and women jostling for positions along the sides. As was common at the time, there was no real order to the evacuation. The strongest forced their way into the boats, leaving women, children, and senior VOC officials behind. A dozen others leapt into the sea and attempted to swim to land. They all drowned in the surf.

Ariaen Jacobsz and his sailors worked all day, but, fully loaded, the *Batavia*'s two boats could hold no more than 60 people and the conditions were atrocious. Transferring frightened people from the pitching deck into a rolling, yawing boat was dangerous work that could not be hurried; a moment's inattention or the least miscalculation might hurl the fragile little craft against the ship, smashing it to pieces. And, once in the boat, the survivors had to be rowed the best part of a mile along the deep-water channel before they could be set ashore.

The boats' crews took them to the closest of the islands the skipper had scouted earlier in the day. It was tiny, a mere mushroom of coral rubble that measured only 175 yards from end to end and offered no real protection from the biting wind. During the afternoon, four more boatloads of survivors arrived. They did what they could to make themselves comfortable, but the islet was hard and flat and sterile, lacking not only food and water but even sand on which to lie and rest. There was no shelter. All in all, it left a good deal to be desired.

By nightfall, with the rescue operation hardly half-completed, some 180 people had been set on land. But parents had been separated from their offspring, husbands from their wives – and it had been so imperative to pack as many people as possible into the boats that the luckless survivors on the island found themselves with virtually no supplies. Jacobsz and his men had managed to land about 150 pints of poor drinking water, a dozen barrels of bone-dry bread and – at the insistence of the upper-merchant – a small casket of the most valuable trade goods, packed with precious stones, worked gold and jewelery that would have fetched 60,000 guilders* in the Indies. Such huge wealth was worthless on the reef; a few guilders' worth of sailcloth and blankets would have been of greater use.

At sunset, back on the *Batavia* again, Jacobsz motioned Pelsaert to one side and insisted that his place was on the island. 'It won't help at all that we save water and bread,' the skipper said, 'for everyone on land drinks as much as he can. To forbid this has no result unless you order otherwise.'

Twelve chests of VOC silver were still waiting on the main deck, but the merchant knew there was little more food or water to be had. He and Jacobsz jumped down into the yawl, intending to call at the little islet and introduce some form of rationing before returning to the *Batavia* for the money. But no sooner had they pulled away than a violent squall arose and the little boat had to run for safety inside the reef. Fierce winds whipped up the waves, and once again the stricken ship all but disappeared in a storm of surf and spray. It was evident there was no chance of boarding her again before dawn, and it was only with some difficulty the boat's crew contrived to fall back to the little island. They reached the survivors as they were settling down to an uncomfortable night. The conditions on the islet were appalling and, exhausted as they were, they slept only with difficulty, hard coral fingers in their backs.

On the *Batavia,* the plight of the other passengers and crew was equally unpleasant. About 120 people remained for the time being on board the sinking ship. For those on deck, the wind and rain brought with them the threat of exposure. Meanwhile, down below, the situation had deteriorated sharply in the absence of both the merchant and the skipper. Not every member of the crew had chosen to flee up to the main deck when the ship's hull burst. A good number – convinced, perhaps, that they were dead men

*The equivalent of £3 million at today's prices.

anyway – preferred to break into the gun-deck stores and drink themselves into oblivion among the casks of alcohol. One, Allert Janssen, a gunner from Assendelft in the North Quarter of Holland, made his way to the bottle room in the stern where the officers stored their personal supplies of wines and spirits. There he found his way barred by Lucas Gerritsz, the steward's mate. In normal circumstances, Janssen's very presence there, so close to the officers' quarters, would have been a flogging offence; now, though, it was different. The gunner drew a knife and slashed at Gerritsz's back, bawling: 'Out, cats and dogs – you have been masters here long enough, now I [will be master] for a while.' The steward ran for his life, leaving the bottle room unguarded, and soon several of Janssen's shipmates had joined him in sampling the fine wines and spirits within. Denied much alcohol for the better part of a year, these men quickly became dangerously drunk.

A second party of delinquents, led by a young VOC cadet named Lenert van Os and freed now from all fear of punishment, began to smash open the sea chests on the gun deck. They worked their way back along the ship, plundering as they went, until they reached the officers' quarters in the stern. No one tried to stop them and, emboldened by drink and desperation, they broke down the door of Pelsaert's quarters. A drunken young sailor named Cornelis Janssen, who was nicknamed 'Bean,' was among the first to enter. He reeked of alcohol and had festooned himself with a considerable array of knives. One blade had been thrust through the fabric of his hat, and several others protruded from the pleats of his breeches. Confronted with this piratical apparition, the remaining cabin servants fled, leaving the merchant's personal possessions to the mob. They rifled through the cabin and a Frisian seaman, Ryckert Woutersz, broke open Pelsaert's sea chest and scattered the contents all about in the search for valuables. Soon he came across the upper-merchant's personal collection of medallions. They were distributed among the rioters as booty.

Up on deck, the abandoned treasure chests of the VOC became an irresistible lure for anyone courageous or foolhardy enough to brave the shrieking wind and growling surf. An old soldier from the German town of Heidelburg named Jean Thirion proved bolder than the rest and chopped open one of the chests with a hatchet. Seeing what was happening, a handful of loyal sailors drove him off, and a carpenter was summoned to nail a length of plank over the breach. But by now discipline had all but broken down throughout the wreck. By morning the loyalists had themselves dispersed and a swarm of treasure seekers once again surrounded the damaged chest. They prised off the carpenter's plank and tipped the contents out on deck. Thousands of guilders, enough to make a man rich for several lifetimes, bounced across the planking, but such was the seriousness of the *Batavia*'s plight that even Thirion and his drunken friends saw little point in hoarding them. Instead they turned the coins into playthings, hurling great handfuls of currency at each other's heads in jest.

It was at about this time that Cornelis Janssen, still wearing his suit of knives, emerged from the Great Cabin with his share of the merchant's booty: a gold medallion set in agate. Walking to the side, he tucked the medal into his hat with other valuables and tossed it into the sea. 'There lies the rubbish,' shouted the inebriated Bean, 'even if it is worth so many thousands.'

❀

Back inside the coral crescent, where the roaring seas were calmed by their passage across the reef, rescue work got under way again an hour before dawn. The first priority was to move the majority of the survivors to a larger island. Filling both the boats with a total of 60 people, the sailors hauled up the deep-sea channel and around to the north side of a larger, womb-shaped island a mile from the *Batavia*. It was some 350 yards long and nearly as far across at its western end, but it tapered sharply to the southeast and for most of its length it was no more than 50 yards wide. Like the mushroom-shaped rock on which they had spent the night, it offered little in the way of shelter and no fresh water, but at least there was a small sandy beach where the boats could land, and room on the island for all the *Batavia*'s passengers and crew. By the afternoon about 180 men, women, and children had been transported there, together with a portion of their scant supplies of bread and water. Pelsaert, with 40 of the best seamen and a handful of favoured passengers, remained on the islet, where the skipper had taken care to retain almost all of the water and a good deal of the food.

Conditions outside the reef remained atrocious. With considerable daring, one more trip was made from the *Batavia* to land and a new group of survivors was brought to safety inside the coral, but after that the weather closed in once again and by afternoon the skipper did not dare to bring rescue boats alongside the ship. There were still 70 men on board, the majority of them much the worse for drink and the excesses of the night before, but sober enough by now to realise that the *Batavia* would soon break up under the constant pounding of the waves. For several hours Pelsaert kept the rescue boats hovering nearby, as much in the hope of recovering the money chests as of saving lives. He prayed for a break in the bad weather, but none came. At dusk the upper-merchant retreated back inside the shelter of the reef, calling to the men on deck that they should construct some rafts and save themselves.

By nightfall on the second day, therefore, the situation at the wreck site had deteriorated further. The survivors huddling within the reef had been split between two islands, and the rescue of another boatload of people from the ship meant there were now 60 more mouths to feed. But supplies were already running dangerously low. Despite their attempts at rationing, the water was all but gone. If more could not be found within a day or two, they would all die of thirst.

On the smaller islet, Pelsaert and Jacobsz debated what to do. The discovery that they had been wrecked in a coral archipelago had persuaded the skipper that they were probably somewhere in an all but unknown chain of islands that the Dutch called Houtman's Abrolhos* after Frederik de Houtman, the merchant who had first nearly run aground on them some 13 years before. The islands were completely unexplored, and it was uncertain whether any of them held fresh water. But they were known to lie several hundred miles to the east of the *Batavia*'s last estimated position, and a little less than 2,000 miles south of the Indies. If the ship was indeed in the Abrolhos, it might at least be possible for some of the survivors to reach Java in her boats.

The first imperative, however, was to find water. Pelsaert still wished to salvage the VOC's money chests from the wreck, but he suspected – probably quite correctly – that malcontents would seize the boats and conduct their own searches of the nearby islands if he failed to take decisive action quickly. He knew that to lose control of the yawl and the *Batavia*'s larger longboat would be disastrous, not only to his shaky authority over the now-scattered refugees from the wreck, but also to his own prospects of survival.

*'Abrolhos' is generally held to be a loan word from Portuguese, a corruption of the sailor's warning *'abri vossos olhos,'* or 'Open your eyes.' A similar archipelago off the coast of Brazil is known by the same name.

And supplies of water really were running short. So the upper-merchant authorised a search of the archipelago, beginning on the morning of 6 June. He also decided to transport one barrel of fresh water to the people on the larger island to the north.

Ariaen Jacobsz and his officers approved of the search for water, but grim realism left them aghast at Pelsaert's determination to succour those on the womb-shaped island, which – being within sight of the wrecked ship lying stranded on the reef – had by now been dubbed 'Batavia's Graveyard.' The 180 people on the island were stranded on a waterless lump of coral with neither a boat nor rafts upon which to escape; they had, the skipper reckoned, probably already consumed their supplies. The arrival of the upper-merchant with one small barrel of water would be of little comfort to them. They were much more likely to try to seize the boat.

Jacobsz told Francisco Pelsaert this, and he also warned the merchant that he could no longer expect the men to obey his every order. In situations such as this, those who had the skills to save themselves would do so – at the expense of others if need be. It was unrealistic to expect the rough-hewn sailors of the VOC to be exceptions to this rule, and they were unlikely to volunteer to help their comrades to the north if there was any chance the people there might damage one of the boats. 'They will keep you there, and you will regret it,' the skipper warned Pelsaert. 'Secondly, there is no-one who will sail with you.'

To the sailors' surprise, the upper-merchant persisted, and at length the high boatswain, Jan Evertsz, and six men were persuaded to take him to the larger island in the yawl. The sailors remained wary, though, and insisted that they would row away if Pelsaert went ashore and was held against his will. But it did not come to this; as they approached Batavia's Graveyard they saw such a crowd of people gathered on the beach that Evertsz grew apprehensive. When the merchant made as if to leap into the shallows with his barrel, the high boatswain hauled him back into the yawl, and the men rowed rapidly away, with the cries of those they left behind still ringing in their ears.

This unpleasant incident robbed Francisco Pelsaert of resolve. Next morning, rather than renewing his attempts to resupply the island, he accompanied some seamen who were going in the yawl to search for water elsewhere in the archipelago. This time they sailed several miles to the north, to two big islands the merchant had first noticed from the wreck. They dug for water in several places but discovered nothing more than a little brackish rain in hollows by the shore. For Pelsaert and for Jacobsz, their last real hope was gone. It now seemed certain there was no fresh water anywhere nearby. Moreover, the storms that had plagued them on the night of the wreck had blown themselves out and there was no prospect of more rain.

Next morning they began to build up their longboat's sides in preparation for a lengthy ocean voyage. While they were working, the *Batavia*'s yawl, which Pelsaert had sent over to the wreck, appeared on the horizon. Eleven men were on board, led by an officer named Gillis Fransz, but the longboat was a much more substantial craft than the little yawl and could hold 40 people in reasonable comfort. Fransz and his men were expert sailors, and when they asked to join the crew of the larger boat, their request was eagerly accepted.

Pelsaert and Jacobsz sailed four days after the *Batavia* had hit the reef, leaving nearly 200 frantic, thirsty people on Batavia's Graveyard, and another 70 stranded on the wreck. A braver commander, and a better leader of men, might have insisted that his place was with the bulk of the survivors. Pelsaert, by his own account, did wish to stay and help those whom he now left behind: 'It was better and more honest to die with them if we could not find water than to stay alive with deep grief of heart,' he wrote. But the sailors were determined to leave the archipelago, and in the end the upper-merchant chose to save himself. On the morning of 8 June he joined the sailors and the favoured passengers in the *Batavia*'s longboat. There were 48 of them, including two women and a babe in arms. Towing the yawl, they set sail and headed slowly north.

As he went, Francisco Pelsaert glanced back toward the crescent of white water that marked the reef, and the battered hulk that had once been his command. On board were several dozen of the worst cutthroats and drunkards who had sailed from Amsterdam, and one senior VOC official. He was the under-merchant – after Pelsaert, the most senior man on board. His name was Jeronimus Cornelisz.

CHAPTER I

The Heretic

'He was more evil than if he had been changed into a tiger animal.'
FRANCISCO PELSAERT

Jeronimus had never meant to go to sea. He was not a merchant by profession and had no family or interests in the East. He was, in fact, a man of education and refinement, who moved with ease among the upper classes of the United Provinces. At home in the Netherlands, his social standing had been higher than that of any other man or woman on board the *Batavia;* he had even outranked his superior on the ship, Francisco Pelsaert. Indeed, throughout his life – and he was 30 when he sailed for Java – the under-merchant would have had no reason to associate with what Dutchmen called the *grauw,* the rabble of criminals and paupers who occupied the lowest strata of society. Now, however, he had at least one thing in common with the thugs and sots who had made themselves at home on the wreck. He was a desperate man.

In the seventeenth century few people sailed to the East by choice. The Spiceries of the Indonesian archipelago were the source of unimaginable wealth, it was true. Yet the men who earned vast fortunes trading with the Indies were the astonishingly wealthy merchants who stayed at home in Amsterdam and Middelburg, Delft and Hoorn and Enkhuizen – not those who actually manned their ships and risked their own lives on the long sea voyage. For the ordinary traders and the sailors of the VOC, service with the Company did offer certain opportunities to profit from the spice trade. But it also exposed them to privation, disease, and early death. The life expectancy of a merchant newly arrived in the Indies was a mere three years, and of the million or so people who sailed with the VOC during the lifetime of the Company, fewer than one in three returned.

A small proportion of the million settled in the Indies and survived, but the climate and conditions accounted for most of the deaths at VOC's trading bases overseas. Lethal bouts of dysentery – 'the bloody flux' – were the principal scourge, but assorted plagues and fevers also took their toll. Some died in accidents at sea or in battle with the local people, and a good number perished at the hands of the Dutch authorities themselves, who ruled with considerable severity. A man in Jeronimus's position was, in short, much more likely to meet his doom in a place like Java than he was to make his fortune.

It is thus hardly surprising that throughout the history of the VOC the men who sailed aboard the East Indiamen were portrayed as the lowest of the low. In the popular perception, the Company was (in one contemporary's opinion) 'a great refuge for all spoilt brats, bankrupts, cashiers, brokers, tenants, bailiffs, informers and suchlike rakes'; its soldiers and sailors were violent, feckless and otherwise unemployable; and its merchants either disgraced debtors or plucked students who would risk anything for the chance to restore their failing fortunes.

Jeronimus Cornelisz was a merchant of this type: a man who had compelling reasons of his own for gambling his life on the lottery of an Indies voyage. When he left the United Provinces, he was almost bankrupt, a bereaved father – and also a dangerous and possibly wanted heretic. These misfortunes were entirely of his own making.

❀

Cornelisz came originally from Friesland, one of the most isolated and northerly of the United Provinces. It was a place apart, largely rural and with borders so well protected by a dense barrier of peat bogs, lakes, and marshes that only the most persistent travellers ventured in by road. The few who did, and made their way along the almost impassable mud tracks that led into the interior, found themselves riding through a land that was somehow not entirely Dutch.

The Frisian people certainly thought of themselves as different. They traced their ancestry back to Roman times and claimed descent from age-old tribes who had lived along the German border. Their cities were similarly ancient. Many Frisians disliked the Dutch and thought of them as interlopers, whose history hardly began before 1000 and who had usurped lands that had once been part of the semi-legendary Dark Age Frisian kingdom. Even in the 1620s, when the rise of Holland had long since reduced the province to a northern backwater and forced the inhabitants of its cities to work and trade with their richer cousins to the south, the majority of the population did not speak Dutch. The language of the countryside was Frisian, a tongue with certain similarities to English. Visitors from the southern provinces struggled to understand it.

Jeronimus Cornelisz was probably born into this environment in the year 1598. His family appears to have come from the area around the provincial capital, Leeuwarden, which was then a city of some 11,000 people; it is possible that their home was the smaller settlement of Bergum, five miles to the east, though the destruction of the relevant records makes it impossible to confirm this town as his birthplace. Cornelisz's father and mother were almost certainly well-off, and the province's surviving legal records suggest that they had connections with some significant local property owners. Beyond that, however, almost nothing is known of Jeronimus's early years. Even the names and occupations of his parents remain a mystery.

One thing is certain: Cornelisz would have attended school from the age of six. In the first years of the seventeenth century, the Dutch education system was by far the most advanced in Europe; all towns and most villages were provided with elementary schools, and the costs of schooling were subsidised by the state. In consequence, even the children of the lower classes received at least a general education, and foreign visitors to the country were frequently astonished to discover Dutch servants who could read.

These schools existed for a reason. The United Provinces had only recently converted to Protestantism, and the old Catholic religion was still practised by some Dutch families. The main purpose of the state primary schools was to produce new generations of Calvinists; consequently, the basic syllabus was confined to reading and Bible studies. Rival churches maintained establishments of their own, for the same reason. Although they were taught to read Scripture, not all pupils received instruction in writing, and parents who wished their children to learn such skills had to pay extra fees.

Arithmetic was considered too advanced to form part of an elementary education.

Many boys and most girls left school at the age of 8 or 10, but as the son of wealthy parents, Jeronimus may have continued his education at one of the famous Latin schools of the United Provinces. These schools, one of which was owned and run by each of the principal towns of the republic, took the male children straight from local schools at the age of 10 and gave them a thorough classical education. They taught Latin and Greek and offered boys a grounding in calligraphy, natural philosophy, and rhetoric as well. They were, however, much more than just places of learning, for the masters of the Latin schools prided themselves in turning out young humanists – men who looked beyond the stifling confines of contemporary religion to embrace the virtues and the values of ancient Rome. Thus, while the Dutch elementary school system existed to instill a rigid Calvinism into its pupils, boys who went on to graduate from the Latin schools were encouraged to abandon fixed patterns of devotion and think for themselves. The schools of Friesland and Groningen were particularly noted for their liberalism in this respect.

As a Frisian and, perhaps, the graduate of a northern Latin school, the young Cornelisz would have experienced an upbringing as far removed from the narrow strictures of orthodox Dutch Calvinism as was possible in the United Provinces. But he would also have been prepared for the highest callings in the Dutch Republic. A good number of the products of the Latin schools went on to become ministers or physicians. Others studied law or were trained as bureaucrats. The rest, who lacked either the scholastic aptitude or the wealth and social standing necessary to command a place at university, were generally apprenticed to one of the more gentlemanly professions.

For whatever reason, Jeronimus Cornelisz followed the latter path and began to train as an apothecary. In the early modern age, the medieval system of craft guilds remained strong throughout the United Provinces. Would-be blacksmiths and grocers, surgeons and tailors – all were required to find themselves a master and bind themselves to him for a period of between three and seven years. The master gave the student board and lodging and revealed to him the mysteries of his trade. In return, the student provided labour for the duration of his apprenticeship.

At the conclusion of the contracted period, the boy – by now a young man – was required to prepare one or more masterpieces, samples of work that, quite literally, demonstrated mastery of his chosen profession. These masterpieces were submitted for examination by officials of the relevant guild, and, if the apprentice was judged to have acquired a thorough knowledge of his trade, he was permitted to join the guild himself. This was a significant commitment. Membership of a guild brought with it certain obligations, and in particular the requirement to contribute regularly and liberally to guild funds. Many men who had successfully completed their apprenticeships never could afford to pay these fees and remained journeymen all their lives.

Jeronimus was probably apprenticed at some time between 1615 and 1620. His was a coveted position. In early modern Europe, qualified apothecaries had a monopoly on the preparation and supply of medicines and were therefore more or less assured a steady stream of customers. Their nostrums were complicated and expensive, and many grew rich supplying them. Gideon DeLaune, a French emigrant who had his dispensary at the English court, died leaving £100,000 and was more wealthy than the majority of the nobles whom he treated. Dutch apothecaries, while not quite so spectacularly rich, were generally well-off.

The number of illnesses requiring their attentions was endless. The major infectious diseases, endemic throughout the century, were plague – which proved fatal in somewhere between 60 percent and 80 percent of cases – leprosy, and typhus. Dysentery (which killed one in four of its victims), syphilis, tuberculosis, and typhoid were also commonplace. Those fortunate enough to escape the attentions of these killers often succumbed to virulent influenza – called 'the sweats' – smallpox, or malaria. Cancer was relatively scarce; few people lived long enough to develop it.

It is possible, even now, to determine with some precision just how common and how widespread these complaints were in the disease-ridden seventeenth century. There were, for example, no fewer than 123 saints in the Catholic heaven to whom those struck down by fever could pray for intercession, by far the largest number devoted to any particular affliction. A further 85 saints were kept busy with supplications from parents desperate for help with the wide variety of childhood diseases. Fifty-three more saints covered the panoply of plagues, and there were 23 whose sole concern was gout. Catholics even had a patron saint of haemorrhoids: St. Fiacre, an Irish priest who had lived a life of notorious mortification in the seventh century.

As an apprentice apothecary, the young Cornelisz would have spent at least three years learning to prepare the myriad potions, unguents, poultices, and clysters that were the stock-in-trade of the seventeenth-century pharmacist. The identity of his master is not certain, but there is at least a possibility that he was Gerrit Evertsz, an apothecary and corn-trader who ran a prosperous business in Leeuwarden from the early years of the century until his death some time after 1645. Evertsz was clearly someone with whom Cornelisz had a close relationship, since Jeronimus eventually asked him to take charge of his legal affairs in Friesland. If he was indeed the young man's master, Cornelisz had found himself an influential patron. Evertsz was one of the most prominent citizens of the Frisian capital, acting, in addition to his career in pharmacy, as curator of the city's orphans and an official receiver of bankrupts.

Apprentice apothecaries were not generally permitted to become masters before the age of 25, and this suggests that Jeronimus submitted his masterpieces – which would have been treatises on the proper treatment of some illness, or perhaps upon the preparation of a poison – in about 1623. Evidently they were good enough to impress his examiners and, as a newly qualified pharmacist, he now became a member of the trinity of physicians, apothecaries, and surgeons who made up the medical establishment of early modern Europe.

The physicians, who were university graduates, were by far the most haughty and prestigious of these three groups. They had laboured for years to master the medical theories of the time and reserved for themselves the sole right to write prescriptions and issue diagnoses. They were enormously grand and distant personalities, who charged huge fees, distinguished themselves from ordinary professionals by donning long gowns and mortarboards, and invariably wore gloves when seeing patients to ensure there could be no actual contact between them. Only the very wealthiest men could afford their services; even in the largest cities there were rarely more than a dozen physicians to every 50,000 people.

In the rare cases where some sort of physical intervention became necessary – and, given the contemporary ignorance of anaesthesia and antiseptics, this was always a last resort – a surgeon would be called. Surgeons ranked below both the physicians and the apothecaries in the trinity, and it was their duty to set bones, trepan skulls, lance boils, and deal with the more unpleasant and contagious ailments that were rife at the time. The treatment of venereal disease, done with solutions of mercury, was within the province of the surgeons. It also fell to them to treat the plague-stricken, since physicians generally shied away from the most virulent epidemics.

It was, however, far more common for a consultation with a physician to result in a referral to an apothecary. Contemporary medical opinion held that virtually all ailments could be traced to disturbances in the balance of the four humours that were thought to exist within the body, or mismanagement of the six 'non-naturals' that maintained good health or provoked disease. Apothecaries existed to prepare treatments designed to remedy such imbalances and manage the nonnaturals. If they did their job correctly, the full recovery of the patient was – at least in theory – guaranteed.

In the dingy recesses of an apothecary's shop lurked pots and pillboxes by the hundred – each containing one of the many hundreds of ingredients required to make the incredibly complex preparations of the day. Most drugs were concocted from parts of several different plants, always with an addition of animal products and sometimes with the admixture of metals. Roots and herbs were the principal ingredients, but apothecaries were also required to be familiar with considerably more exotic ingredients. Unicorn horn was greatly sought after. Excrement was widely prescribed – pigeon droppings were a cure for epilepsy, and horse manure was effective against pleurisy – and the sex organs of wild animals were held to be particularly efficacious. Dried wild boar penis, for example, was thought to reduce phlegm.

To modern eyes, at least, the most unusual ingredient in any apothecary's store was 'mummy,' ground human flesh taken (at least in theory) directly from plundered Egyptian tombs. It was a popular cure-all, supposedly effective against almost every ailment from headaches to bubonic plague. The best mummy had a 'resinous, harden'd, black shining surface,' an acrid taste, and a fragrant smell. When supplies from Egypt were hard to get, which they usually were, European bodies might be substituted, but it was important that the corpse from which the flesh was taken had not succumbed to disease. Although the very finest mummy was supposed to come from the remains of men suffocated in a

Saharan sandstorm, therefore, in practice the principal source was the bodies of executed criminals.

With one significant exception, the other ingredients an apothecary required were not so hard to find. Animal products could be had from butchers or specialist travelling salesmen. Pharmacists usually obtained the plants themselves, cultivating physic gardens or wandering the countryside in search of rare roots. The most important thing was that ingredients were fresh; almost every paste and potion had to be specially prepared on the day it was required, and the principal tool of the apothecary's trade was his mortar and pestle.

The one drug no apothecary prepared on his own behalf was theriac,* the main antidote to venoms of all sorts. It was used to treat snakebite and rabies and taken as a cure for poison, though it was most commonly prescribed to strengthen a patient who had been bled, sweated, and purged and whose condition was, nevertheless, deteriorating. Theriacs – there were several of them in existence – were particularly complex and potent medicines, and so difficult to make that only the senior apothecaries of the largest cities were trusted to prepare them. They contained up to 70 different ingredients and were unusual in that their single most important constituent was animal: viper's flesh. The best theriac came from Venice and was known as 'Venice treacle.' Venetian pharmacists bred their own vipers and mixed their theriac in bulk once each year. The concoction was exported by the Italian city-state throughout the rest of Europe, and no apothecary of the time would have been without it.

Nevertheless, medicines were not a Dutch apothecary's sole source of income. They were members of the St. Nicholas Guild, which included the grocers and spicers, and like them they had the right to sell fruit pies and ginger cakes. Many of the less reputable stocked beer, sometimes dispensing it surreptitiously and free of the heavy state taxes on alcohol. All of them made poisons, based on arsenic, which were used to control the extraordinary quantities of vermin that infested every town. This part of a pharmacist's work was strictly controlled by the local council, but, even so, it helped to give them a somewhat sinister reputation. When someone in a town died unexpectedly, there were often mutterings of potions brewed in dark back rooms. In their cluttered stores, the black-cloaked apothecaries merely smiled.

*The word derives from the Greek *theriake* and is the root of the English *treacle*.

Jeronimus Cornelisz set up shop in Haarlem, probably some time between 1624 and 1627. His reasons for settling in the province of Holland, rather than Friesland, remain unknown, but Haarlem was a much bigger and more cosmopolitan place than Bergum or Leeuwarden. It was the second city of the wealthiest and most important of the United Provinces and had a population of 40,000. It must have seemed a propitious place to establish a new business.

Haarlem was a typical Dutch town: raucous and bustling, but neat and tidy to a fault. It had sprung up a few miles inland from the coast, a little to the west of Amsterdam and just north of the dark and storm-swept inland sea known as the Haarlemmermeer. The whole city was girdled by a moat and a defensive wall, and the lazy waters of the River Spaarne, which flowed through Haarlem on its way to the sea, cut it into two unequal halves and brought in the ships that supplied many of its needs. Inside the walls the red-roofed houses were mostly made of brick, and all the major streets had been paved by the first years of the century. They were daily cleaned of rubbish and the ordure that still rained down from upstairs windows – a refinement quite unheard-of outside the Netherlands. All in all, Haarlem was a pleasant, busy place, less haphazard, less chaotic, and less dangerous than the great towns of England, Italy, and France.

The city had been built around eight main streets, all of which emerged into the Great Market that was the focal point of urban life. It was one of the largest marketplaces in the United Provinces and seethed with activity throughout the daylight hours. Its centre-piece was the Grote Kerk of St. Bavo, which was the largest and, some travellers reckoned, the most beautiful church in Holland, though it can hardly have been a peaceful place to worship. A large covered fish market, fully 60 yards long, had been tacked onto the north side of the church, while not 10 yards away, on the west side of the square, stood the substantial bulk of the New Meat-Hall, where during the week the contemplation of the devout would be disturbed by the unholy racket of cattle being slaughtered.

Not all the city was so grand. Away from the main thorough-fares there were warrens of little passageways and alleys where homes were smaller – just a room or two – and the inhabitants much poorer. A whole quarter of Haarlem was given over to cheap housing for the thousands of women who laboured in the bleacheries that had made the city famous, dyeing linen white in pits of buttermilk. There were other poorer areas nearby, packed full of Protestant immigrants fleeing the horrors of the Counter-Reformation. But, crowded as it was, Haarlem was a relatively wealthy place, and the people who lived along the streets leading to the Great Market were the wealthiest of all.

Cornelisz rented a house on one of these eight streets – the Grote Houtstraat, or Great Wood Street, which led from the market south through the city, over the moat, and into the wooded park that ran along the edge of the Haarlemmermeer. The young Frisian opened up a pharmacy on the ground floor and lived above the shop. He had a maidservant and a stuffed crocodile – which hung over the counter and was the principal symbol of the apothecary – and he was popular with his neighbours. He was also accepted by the city, becoming a full citizen, or *poorter,* of Haarlem at a time when such privileges were never granted lightly. This rank brought with it many privileges, including the right to vote.

Newcomer to Holland though he was, Jeronimus now seemed to be on the verge of great success. He had become a master of one of the most prestigious professions in the United Provinces. He was in business for himself, and his shop seemed ideally positioned to attract a clientele from among the citizens of one of the wealthiest towns in the Republic. In normal circumstances he could have looked forward to a life of prosperity, to the deference of his fellow citizens, perhaps even to a civic career and, eventually, a position on the town council. But the circumstances were far from normal. For Jeronimus Cornelisz, the future held nothing but disease, disgrace, and death.

The first blow fell in the winter of 1627. At some point in the middle 1620s, the apothecary had acquired a spouse. We know almost nothing of Belijtgen Jacobsdr, who appears in the town records as the 'lawful housewife' of Jeronimus Cornelisz, not even whether she was Frisian or Dutch. She was probably a number of years younger than her husband was and, like him, of a good family that was not quite in the uppermost strata of Netherlands society. It is not unlikely that she was herself an apothecary's daughter, since pharmacists tended to marry among themselves, and she certainly assisted her husband in his shop. If she was typical of the middle-class Dutch women of the day, Belijtgen would have been clever, somewhat educated, very capable, and not at all dominated by her husband. Foreign visitors generally lauded the women of the United Provinces as extremely pretty, contemporary tastes running to rosy-skinned and plump young wives and one Dutchman writing admiringly of girls who 'could fill a barrel with buttocks, and a tub with breasts.' Jeronimus's wife may have been all these things. But by December 1627 she was also seriously ill.

Some time in November, Belijtgen had given birth to a baby boy. The pregnancy had not gone well, and Belijtgen had been unable to leave her bed for several weeks before the birth. In her eighth month she had been so ill she had thought she was going to die and had even summoned a solicitor to her bedside to dictate a will that named Jeronimus as her 'universal heir.' But, in the end, she carried her baby for the full term and the boy was delivered safely. Several neighbors testified that he was a lusty child, free from blemishes and illness.

Belijtgen, on the other hand, suffered agonies after the birth. The midwife she had hired, an Amsterdam woman named Cathalijntgen van Wijmen, turned out to be uncouth, deranged, and dangerously incompetent. During her stay in Haarlem, Cathalijntgen danced and sang compulsively, confessed to suffering from 'torments inside her head,' and slept with an axe beside her bed. During Belijtgen's labor, she left part of the placenta in the new mother's womb. The decaying afterbirth became infected, and Cornelisz's wife contracted puerperal fever as a result.

This illness was a serious matter. In the seventeenth century, puerperal fever was frequently a lethal condition, and it made it impossible for Belijtgen to care for her son. Dutch infants of all classes were generally breast-fed by their mothers; it was universally agreed to be the best way to safeguard an infant's health, and wet nurses were seldom employed in the United Provinces unless the mother was physically incapable of producing milk. Belijtgen had no such difficulty; for a month or more before the birth, as was common at the time, her husband had paid an old woman named Maijcke van den Broecke to suckle his wife's breasts in order to stimulate the flow of milk.* But while she lay wracked with fever, Cornelisz's wife could not feed the child, and Jeronimus was forced to seek a nurse. His choice fell on a woman named Heyltgen Jansdr, who lived in an alleyway off the St. Jansstraat in the north quarter of Haarlem.

Cornelisz and his wife seem to have been notably poor judges

*Van den Broecke, who evidently took real pride in her work, later testified, before a solicitor that the resultant product tasted good.

of character. Their midwife had already proved to be a madwoman, and in Heyltgen Jansdr they had unearthed a similarly disreputable character. The least inquiry among her neighbors and acquaintances would have revealed her as a woman of hot temper and low morals, who was known to be unfaithful to her husband and who suffered from a mysterious and long-term illness. But, for whatever reason, the apothecary did not trouble to discover this.

It proved to be a fatal error. Within a few weeks of being placed with Heyltgen, the baby was extremely sick; within a few months he was dead. On 27 February 1628, eight months before he sailed on the *Batavia,* Jeronimus Cornelisz buried his infant son in the church of St. Anna, Haarlem.

The apothecary was devastated. The death of small children was commonplace at a time when half of all the children born within the Dutch Republic expired before they reached puberty. Yet there was nothing ordinary about the death of Jeronimus's child. The baby had not died of fever or convulsions, or any of the other diseases that usually accounted for infant mortality. He had died of syphilis.

The final agonies of Cornelisz's infant son would have been hard enough for his parents to bear. Babies who contract syphilis die bleeding from the mouth and anus and also suffer considerably from open sores and rashes, so much so that they are sometimes described as looking 'moth-eaten' at the moment of death. But for Jeronimus and Belijtgen the prospect of disgrace would have been as difficult to endure. Their families and neighbours were likely to assume that the boy had contracted the disease from his mother and that, in turn, implied that one or other of the parents had not been faithful. For a well-bred couple, living in a respectable part of town, this was a very serious concern. Their customers, meanwhile, would wonder if they might not catch the pox from their apothecary. For a fledgling business, this could be catastrophic.

It is very probable that Jeronimus's pharmacy was in financial difficulty even before the death of his son. The renewal of the Dutch war against Spain in 1621, which followed 12 good years of peace, had led to a sudden increase in military expenditure that put considerable strain on the resources of the Republic. In that year the Spaniards had added to the pressure by embargoing all trade with the United Provinces, blockading the coast, and all but ending Dutch trade with Spain, Portugal, and the Mediterranean. Spanish garrisons along the Rhine, Maas, Waal, and Scheldt halted river traffic between the Netherlands and Germany. The result was a severe economic depression in Holland, which lasted for much of the 1620s and proved to be the worst of the entire seventeenth century. Virtually all Dutch trade was affected by the slump, and even well-established businesses found it hard to stay afloat.

Cornelisz was far from well established. His pharmacy was still new, and he himself was young and freshly qualified. Many Haarlemmers must have preferred to do business with his older rivals even before the scandalous death of his son set tongues wagging in the Grote Houtstraat. Consequently, by the middle of 1628 Jeronimus was in serious financial difficulties. He had accumulated debts, which were mounting, and creditors, who had grown impatient. One man in particular, a merchant named Loth Vogel, was insisting that Cornelisz repay the money he owed. The apothecary lacked the necessary funds to do this. He therefore faced the looming prospect of bankruptcy, which – in the Dutch Republic in the seventeenth century – was a mortal sin.

Throughout the claustrophobic summer of 1628, the merchant Vogel pursued the apothecary while the apothecary pursued his wet nurse. Jeronimus knew by now that his only chance of restoring his damaged reputation – and, perhaps, of salvaging his business – lay in proving that his child had contracted syphilis from Heyltgen Jansdr. His actions that June, July, and August suggest a man preparing for a court case. Leaving Belijtgen to mind his failing business in the Grote Houtstraat, Cornelisz vanished into the maze of narrow alleyways off the St. Jansstraat, searching for those who knew the wet nurse. He listened to their stories and persuaded them to set down their misgivings about the woman in sworn statements.

Cornelisz found no fewer than nine of his own acquaintances to testify that Belijtgen was unmarked by syphilitic sores and ulcers, and six others, from north Haarlem, who confirmed that the wet nurse had been seriously ill for at least two years. It was alleged that Heyltgen had left the apothecary's son wailing and uncared for while she went out carousing of an evening; several of the nurse's neighbours remarked on the extraordinarily foul odour that hung over her bed whenever she fell ill; and one, Elsken Adamsdr, made a sworn statement in which she described how she had refused to change Heyltgen's sheets for fear of catching a disease. A number of the nurse's neighbours also testified that she was an unfaithful wife and had slept on several occasions with a local widower named Aert Dircxsz, whose nickname was 'Velvet Trousers' and who may himself have been syphilitic. Their evidence was hardly conclusive, but, taken together, the statements that Jeronimus collected were certainly enough to suggest that the boy's bereaved parents had right on their side.

Heyltgen Jansdr responded violently to Cornelisz's campaign. She publicly alleged that Belijtgen was so riddled with venereal disease that all her hair had fallen out and her scalp was festooned with ulcers. She twisted the scanty evidence she had collected in her own defence to make it appear stronger than it was. She even appeared again in the Grote Houtstraat, where she gathered a crowd outside Jeronimus's shop by cursing, beating her fists together, and screaming that Belijtgen was a whore, whose eyeballs she would rip out if she could.

Despite this ongoing personal horror, in the end it was not Heyltgen's lies but Loth Vogel and his demands for reparation that sealed Cornelisz's fate. Trade had continued to decline and the apothecary's financial situation had deteriorated further. On 25 September, Jeronimus appeared before his solicitor to transfer to Vogel the sum total of his worldly goods. It was not bankruptcy, but it might as well have been. Tables and chairs, sheets and blankets – even the pharmacist's marriage bed – were handed over in settlement of debts. With them went Cornelisz's pestle and mortar, his drugs and potions, and his stuffed crocodile.

The pharmacy on the Grote Houtstraat was closed; Jeronimus the apothecary was dead. But, no doubt quite unknown to Vogel, that was far from the end of the matter. Cornelisz the heretic was still very much alive.

❁

Jeronimus seems to have been brought up as an Anabaptist – a member of one of the smaller Protestant churches then established in the Netherlands. His home province, Friesland, had long been the religion's main stronghold in the Dutch Republic, and in 1600, when Cornelisz was still a child, as many as one in five of the population of Leeuwarden professed the faith.

The members of the Anabaptist church could easily be spotted on the streets of the Frisian capital, for even by the standards of the day they insisted upon sober dress, clothing themselves in black from head to foot and favouring baggy breeches and long jackets that had fallen out of fashion years before. Most Anabaptists were quiet, thrifty, conscientious, and hardworking, yet even in Leeuwarden their neighbors often viewed them with distaste and barely tolerated their religious views. Elsewhere in the republic they were sometimes actually persecuted.

Cornelisz's early faith thus assumes a certain significance, for the distrust that other Dutchmen felt when confronted by Anabaptism had strong roots in the history of the preceding century. The Anabaptists had not, in fact, always been model citizens. When Jeronimus's grandparents were young, their religion had been the scourge of northern Europe; militant members of the church had formed armies, captured cities, and been responsible for tens of thousands of deaths. This movement had eventually been crushed, but memories of its excesses persisted. In its pure form, Anabaptism was a fanatic's creed, and even in the last days of the century it still attracted agitators and iconoclasts.

The faith had first emerged during the 1520s, a period of unparalleled religious ferment that also saw the rise of the new Protestant religions of Martin Luther and John Calvin. Unlike Calvin – whose views came to dominate in Holland and who believed in predestination, the notion that the fate of every soul is fixed before birth – Anabaptists acknowledged the existence of free will and held that infant baptism was a worthless sham, for only a mature adult, they believed, could accept entry into the church of Christ. This doctrine was heresy to Catholics and Calvinists alike, but the early Anabaptists were dangerous for another reason. They were, without exception, fervent millenarians – convinced that the Second Coming would occur within a few months or years and determined to assist a vengeful Christ to reclaim his earthly kingdom, thus triggering the bloody occurrences prophesied in the Book of Revelation. To Anabaptists, those verses were no allegory. They were sure that Revelation described a literal series of events, which would begin with the construction of a new Jerusalem on earth, and end in an apocalypse that would consume all those who had not accepted the new faith.

The first Anabaptists firmly believed it fell to them to build this new Jerusalem, and their faith thus led them inexorably into conflict with the civil authorities of western Europe. Several bloody attempts were made to seize control of this city or that, and in 1534 thousands of members of the church streamed into the

Westphalian town of Münster, expelled all nonbelievers, and held the place for 16 months. The reprisals were appalling; when the Anabaptist 'kingdom' eventually fell, every defender capable of bearing arms was slaughtered, together with hundreds of women and children. A similar fate befell the members of another party, 40 strong, who stormed the town hall in Amsterdam in the hope of sparking a revolution there, while in Friesland – already a great stronghold of the faith – another group of 300 radicals was besieged within an old Cistercian abbey that its members had fortified and proclaimed their own Jerusalem. After the walls had been systematically levelled by artillery fire, the male survivors were hung or beheaded on the spot, and their women taken to the nearest river to be drowned.

Before the siege of Münster and the attempted seizure of Amsterdam, most Dutch cities had tolerated the presence of Anabaptist sects within their walls. Afterward, the new faith was fiercely persecuted everywhere. The Anabaptists had revealed themselves as dangerous revolutionaries who actively opposed the lay authorities wherever they encountered them and insisted that they owed no allegiance to any earthly lord. In Münster, they had gone so far as to overthrow the natural order, holding all property in common and dispensing food and possessions to each according to his need. Toward the end of the siege, indeed – when the men of the town were greatly outnumbered by the women – their leaders had even introduced a system of polygamy. The Anabaptists thus naturally attracted the radical, the violent, and the dispossessed, men who were fully prepared to achieve their aims by force. They were a genuine danger to the state.

Radical Anabaptism never recovered from the fall of Münster. Many of its leaders were killed or driven into exile, and their place was taken by men who were prepared to coexist with other Protestants and even Catholics. These pacifist Anabaptists could trace their roots back to the earliest days of the movement, and they had always existed side by side with the revolutionaries. Now, led by a Frisian preacher by the name of Menno Simmons, they came to predominate. The Mennonites opposed the use of force to achieve their aims and did not seek to overthrow the state. By the middle of the sixteenth century they had become so successful that Mennonism and Anabaptism had become synonymous, and persecution of the sect became gradually less severe. True, even in Leeuwarden the Mennonites were never granted real freedom of worship, and they were not allowed to proselytise or hold civic office. But by the time Jeronimus was born, the faith was no longer a barrier to success in most professions.

Nevertheless, revolutionary Anabaptism had not been altogether extinguished by the fall of Münster. A large group of surviving radicals flocked to the banner of a man named Jan van Batenburg, who saw nothing wrong in robbing and killing those who were not members of his sect. When Van Batenburg was captured and executed in 1538, the surviving Batenburgers turned themselves into a band of robbers and infested the Dutch border with the Holy Roman Empire for another dozen years. After that, the sect fragmented into several increasingly extreme and violent groups, the last of which persisted until 1580. In that year, the surviving radicals fled east and found their way to Friesland, where they concealed themselves among the local Mennonites and disappeared from view some 15 years before Jeronimus was born.

Cornelisz, we know, once claimed that he had never been baptised. The archives of Haarlem show that his wife, Belijtgen, was a Mennonite. Taken together, these two facts suggest that he was born to Anabaptist parents and remained a member of that church into early adulthood. But it is much less likely that he himself had faith in Menno Simmons's teachings. He married a Mennonite girl, and so he – and therefore his parents – probably did profess to be Mennonites themselves. But most Mennonites were baptised between the ages of 18 and 23, whereas Cornelisz reached the age of 30 without undergoing the ritual. This may indicate that he had become disillusioned with the church and left it altogether, but it could also be interpreted as a sign that he and his parents had picked up elements of the Batenburger's teachings. It is just possible that the apothecary's family may have been one of those that made its way to Friesland after the collapse of the last Anabaptist robber-bands, and quite likely that Cornelisz heard the radicals' beliefs discussed during his youth in the province. In time, he would demonstrate an apparent familiarity with their ideas concerning righteous killing and the communality of property and women. But this religious influence, which surely helped to shape his childhood, seems to have been tempered in adulthood. The reason for this is unclear, but if Jeronimus did attend a Latin school, he would have been exposed to humanism and the works of ancient philosophers and encouraged to think for himself.

By the time Cornelisz set off for Haarlem, then, other voices and other thoughts had probably begun to make their mark on him. And when he got there, he would quickly have discovered that his new home was far removed from the provincial narrowness of Bergum and Leeuwarden. Haarlem was a place where wealthy men pursued religious and philosophical inquiries largely free from the attentions of the Dutch Reformed Church. If one knew the right people, introductions could be arranged to certain circles where radical and even openly heretical ideas were freely discussed. Working on the Grote Houtstraat and dealing with some of the most influential people in the city, Jeronimus was in an excellent position to make such acquaintances. And it seems this is precisely what he did.

❁

The fencing club run by a certain Giraldo Thibault in Amsterdam was typical of the philosophical talking-shops that would have attracted Cornelisz. The club was located in a fashionable area of the town, and its habitués were mostly young, unmarried, very wealthy members of the city's ruling class. They generally came to Thibault daily, ostensibly in the hope of mastering his fashionable technique. But for many of the members the club's real attraction was that they could relax and mix informally with their peers, far from the ears of parents, wives, or ministers of the church. The salon was a fine place to meet interesting new friends. Thibault knew everyone worth knowing in the city, and his club was popular with artists, doctors, and professors as well as with the sons of wealthy burghers. One member of the fencing master's circle was Cornelis van Hogelande, who was professor of philosophy at the University of Leyden and also a leading alchemist. Thibault's brother-in-law Guillermo Bartolotti was the second-richest man in the Republic and had long been a major investor in the VOC. Another frequent visitor to the club was Johannes van der Beeck, one of the finest of Dutch painters; a sometime resident of Haarlem, he was better known by the Latin version of his name, 'Torrentius.'

Thibault himself was a good deal more than a mere swordsman. Many of his pupils revered him as a philosopher as well, and he and his friends are known to have discussed many of the topics that fascinated the humanists of the day. Talk in the salon ranged from alchemy and Greek philosophy to magic and mythology. The apparently unremarkable fencing club thus served as a conduit through which many new and revolutionary ideas found their way into the very heart of the Dutch Republic.

It is unlikely that Jeronimus himself was a pupil of Thibault's. He probably lacked the social standing required to gain entry to such an exclusive group. But he certainly had connections with some of the master swordsman's acquaintances, and, through them, he became familiar with some dangerous philosophies. These he seems to have absorbed and combined with the radical Anabaptist precepts he had picked up in his youth to create a strange, intensely personal creed – one that was not only explicitly heretical, but potentially murderous as well.

The man who linked Cornelisz to Giraldo Thibault's circle was Torrentius the painter. Jeronimus knew him in Haarlem, and though it is impossible to say with any certainty where or when they met, they did live in close proximity to each other, the apothecary in the Grote Houtstraat and the painter only 200 yards away in a house on the Zijlstraat. Cornelisz and Torrentius also had several acquaintances in common – Jacob Schoudt, whom Jeronimus used as his solicitor in his pursuit of Heyltgen Jansdr, had known the painter well for years, and Lenaert Lenaertsz, a well-respected local merchant, was very close to both of them. Apothecaries also sold many of the materials that artists needed for their work – white lead, gold leaf, turpentine – so it is possible that Torrentius acquired his supplies from Cornelisz. By the late 1620s the two men knew each other well enough for Jeronimus to be described as a disciple of the painter.

It was, without question, a potentially dangerous relationship for a newcomer to Haarlem to engage in, for Torrentius was a controversial figure throughout the Dutch Republic. He had been raised as a Catholic, even working for a while in Spain; and by 1615, back home in the United Provinces, he had acquired a reputation as a lively but dissolute companion who spent freely on fine clothing and roistering in the many taverns of the Dutch Republic. A bill that he and a group of friends ran up at the inn The Double-Crowned Rainbow, in Leyden, came to the staggering total of 485 guilders – more than 18 months' wages for a reasonably well-to-do artisan at that time. Part of this sum, at least, must have been incurred in paying for the services of women; the painter often claimed that adultery was not a sin and bragged that he had half the whores of Holland at his personal disposal.

In truth, many of the province's rich young men behaved in much this sort of way. But Torrentius was notoriously indiscreet, which made his activities unusually risky. Riotous living and consorting with prostitutes were severely frowned on by the church authorities and could easily attract the censure of otherwise well-disposed acquaintances. In Torrentius's case, plenty of shocked witnesses could testify to the artist's loose morals. His marriage, to a well-brought-up young girl named Cornelia van Camp, had been a disgrace; the couple quarrelled violently and when the union finally collapsed, Torrentius had gone to prison rather than pay for his wife's upkeep. The nudes and mythological scenes he painted also made him suspect, but it was the drunken conversations he indulged in, in the back rooms of taverns up and down the province, that particularly concerned his family and friends. On one occasion Torrentius and his company were heard to drink a toast to the devil. On another, in a Haarlem hostelry, they drank first to the Prince of Orange, next to Christ, and finally to the prince of darkness. A Leyden man named Hendrick van Swieten, who had been lodging in the same tavern, was reportedly so shocked he feared such blasphemy might cause the building to sink into the ground.

Deeply incriminating though it was, such evidence actually paled beside the tales that were told in Haarlem concerning Torrentius's apparently preternatural skill as an artist. The painter, it was popularly supposed, was actually a black magician who freely admitted that his masterpieces were not produced by human hands. Rather, it was claimed, he simply placed his paints on the floor next to a blank canvas and watched while supernatural music played and his paintings magically created themselves. Others whispered that Torrentius often went for walks alone in the woods south of Haarlem, where he was understood to converse with the devil. When he was seen purchasing black hens and roosters in the market, it was said he needed them as sacrifices to Beelzebub. Ghostly voices had been heard coming from his studio.

These accounts, and others, may well have been greatly exaggerated; Torrentius himself always claimed that many of his controversial comments had been meant as jokes. But, even so, there is little doubt that by the standards of the day, he was a heretic. Torrentius insisted, for example, that there was no such place as hell, arguing that it was ridiculous to suppose there was, since it was well known there was nothing beneath the ground but earth.

He told friends the scriptures were nothing but a collection of fables – a useful tool for keeping the population in check. He was overheard describing the Bible as 'the Book of Fools and Jesters.' He even mocked the suffering of Christ.

So far as Torrentius's critics were concerned, these views proved the painter was no Christian. Many believed he lived his life according to the precepts of Epicurus, the ancient Greek philosopher who wrote that true happiness is to be found in the pursuit of pleasure, and certainly his activities in Holland's taverns suggest an acquaintance with the Epicurean worldview. But for all this, Torrentius was not an atheist. He was, if anything, a Gnostic – a believer in the ancient heresy that God and Satan are equal in strength, and that the world is the creation of the devil. Like all Gnostics, the painter held that each man had a divine spark within him, which was suppressed by sin but could nevertheless be reanimated while he was still on Earth; indeed, he hinted to one correspondent that he himself had successfully completed this quasi-alchemical operation.

This was without question an intensely heretical philosophy. During the Middle Ages, thousands of people had gone to the stake for such beliefs, and even in the Dutch Republic of the 1620s, such views could be enough to earn a man a death sentence. Yet Torrentius apparently believed himself to be too well connected to run afoul of the church or the civic authorities. He openly discussed Gnostic philosophy with his friends.

Jeronimus Cornelisz came to share several of Torrentius's thoughts and may well have picked up a number of his views in discussion with the freethinking painter. Like Torrentius, the apothecary did not believe in the existence of hell. Like him, he saw merit in the Epicurean way of life. But Jeronimus went further than his friend in some respects, holding to philosophies that even Torrentius could not agree with. Where he came across such ideas remains a mystery; it may be that they, too, had been discussed at philosophical salons such as Thibault's fencing club, though the apothecary could also have heard them in his youth in Friesland. All that is certain is that they made even the Gnostic heresy seem harmless in comparison.

Cornelisz's central belief, it seems, was that his every action was directly inspired by God. 'All I do,' he explained to a handful of trusted acquaintances, 'God gave the same into my heart.' It followed that he himself lived his life in what amounted to a state of grace. This was an intensely liberating philosophy, and one that would have shocked any God-fearing Calvinist to the core. Taken literally, it implied that the apothecary was incapable of sin. If each idea, each action, was directly inspired by God, then no thought, no deed – not even murder – could truly be described as evil.

Twisted and simplistic though it might have seemed to any orthodox Christian, Jeronimus's strange philosophy had a long tradition. Its proper name is antinomianism, the idea that moral law is not binding on an individual who exists in a state of perfection. No other creed – not the Jewish faith, nor even the Muslim – held quite so much terror for the clergy of the Dutch Reformed Church, for no other philosophy was quite so dangerous to the established order.

The antinomian philosophy had existed in Europe since at least the early thirteenth century, when a group called the Amaurians began preaching it in Paris, mixed with the teachings of Epicurus. Similar beliefs cropped up again in Germany a century later, where a sect known as the Brethren of the Free Spirit emerged, eventually spreading throughout central Europe. On this occasion they persisted well into the sixteenth century.*

The Brethren divided humanity into two groups – the 'crude in spirit' and the 'subtle.' Those who failed to cultivate and ultimately release the divine potential that lay within them would always remain crude, but those who absorbed themselves in it could become living gods. As one historian of the movement explains:

'Every impulse was experienced as a divine command; now they could surround themselves with worldly possessions, now they could live in luxury – and now too they could lie and steal and fornicate without qualms of conscience, for since inwardly the soul was wholly absorbed into God, external acts were of no account ... The Free Spirit movement was, therefore, an affirmation of freedom so reckless and unqualified that it amounted to a total denial of every kind of restraint and limitation.'

Not every member of the sect exercised his licence to cheat and steal. The founders of the movement taught that perfect happiness was most likely to be found in quiet contemplation. But in truth

---

*The final flourishing of antinomianism actually occurred in Britain in the aftermath of the English Civil War, when a sect known as the Ranters espoused very similar ideas.

the Free Spirit was generally perceived, even among its adepts, as a movement of anarchy and self-exaltation. As such it was vigorously persecuted and never had a large number of adherents, even in its German heartland. From time to time the Catholic Church seems to have hoped that the sect had been stamped out altogether. But antinomianism was too potent a philosophy to be repressed for long. Although the Brethren of the Free Spirit vanished around 1400, their ideas found their way into the Low Countries under the guise of 'Spiritual Liberty.' A sect of this name was crushed in Antwerp around 1544, and the surviving Libertines fled from Flanders. Some of them turned up in Tournai and Strasbourg. Others vanished altogether. It seems at least possible that a few went north into what became the Dutch Republic.

Cornelisz, then, was apparently a Libertine – though not a very good one, for he ignored the more spiritual aspects of the faith in favour of the promise of complete freedom of action. In this he resembled Torrentius, his friend and teacher, and the two men might well have gone on enjoying their philosophical debates indefinitely had the painter not at last attracted the attention of the Dutch authorities around 1625. From then on, however, Torrentius found himself fighting for his freedom and his life. Labelled a heretic and hounded by both church and state, he became the first of Giraldo Thibault's circle to be persecuted for his beliefs. The thoughts and views of his acquaintances became of increasing interest to the authorities as well.

The seeds that led eventually to Torrentius's downfall were sown in the little German town of Kassel in the year 1614. It was there that a small group of German adepts produced an esoteric pamphlet that was not only to inspire generations of mystics but also to lead, at least indirectly, to Jeronimus's departure from Haarlem.

The pamphlet was an anonymous work of indeterminate origin purporting to be nothing less than the manifesto of a powerful secret society called the Order of the Rosy Cross. It was a potent call for a second reformation – a reformation, this time, of the sciences – which promised, in return, the dawning of a golden age. But what really excited those who read the work was its subtext – scraps of information about the mysterious Brethren of the Rosy Cross themselves.

The Order, said the pamphlet, had been established in the fif-teenth century by a man named Christian Rosenkreuz, who had spent many years travelling in the Middle East, collecting ancient wisdom and occult knowledge. The pamphlet stated that upon his return to Germany, Rosenkreuz created a brotherhood to ensure that his discoveries were put to use. There were eight Brethren of the Rosy Cross, and they moved from place to place, spreading secret knowledge, adopting the customs and the dress of the coun-tries where they lived, and living incognito. Each brother was a potent mystic in his own right, and each was tasked with recruiting a worthy replacement for himself as he grew old. Christian Rosenkreuz himself, the pamphlet continued, had lived to be 106. When he died, in 1484, the members of his order laid him to rest in an underground vault hidden somewhere within the borders of the Holy Roman Empire. The vault was then sealed for a period of 120 years, and its rediscovery by a member of the Order, in the first years of the seventeenth century, had heralded the dawning of a new age. The opening of the tomb was a signal for the Brothers of the Rosy Cross to step out of the shadows and make themselves at last generally known.

Two further Rosicrucian pamphlets appeared over the next two years, both of them anonymous and each making further revela-tions. It is not difficult to understand why they inspired the tremendous interest that they did. As well as promising the advent of a golden age, the manifestos hinted at the existence of a secret brotherhood that recruited most selectively and invited only the best and wisest to join its ranks. An invitation to join the Rosicrucians would thus be a supreme honour, and one that vainer readers dared hope might be extended to themselves. The fact that the Brethren of the Order appeared to travel incognito merely added to their dangerous allure. If no one knew just who they were or where they lived, it was at least possible that one or several dwelled nearby, and that they might be searching for converts.

Few people seem to have doubted that the pamphlets were the work of a genuine group of adepts; a number of prominent thinkers, including the French philosopher Descartes, devoted considerable efforts to searching for the Order. Several northern European states – among them the United Provinces – thus began to fear that they were faced with a genuine and dangerous new threat. Rumours that Rosicrucians had crossed the borders of the Dutch Republic reached several Calvinist ministers in 1624. In the following year, a secret agreement between French and Dutch Rosicrucians was purportedly discovered in a house in Haarlem. This threat – real or not – could not be tolerated, and in January 1624, the Court of Holland, which was the senior judicial body in the province, was ordered to investigate the Rosicrucian movement.

The task seemed impossible but, nevertheless, the Court did have some leads. Rumour and tittle-tattle suggested that the Rosicrucians of the Dutch Republic had their headquarters in Haarlem, where they assembled by night at a house in the prosperous Zijlstraat. Furthermore, the judges were informed, 'one Thorentius should be considered one of the most important members of the sect.' Armed with this name, the Court of Holland commenced an investigation that was to occupy it for the next four years.

'Thorentius' was not a hard man to identify, and the controversial painter was eventually seized in Haarlem in the summer of 1627, three years after the first testimonies against him had been recorded. In the interim, the civic authorities had discovered a good deal about Torrentius, his circle, and his penchant for drunken theological discussions in the taverns of the province. The artist was charged with heresy and with membership of the Rosicrucian order and interrogated on no fewer than five occasions. Torrentius freely admitted that he had jokingly claimed to possess magical powers, but he denied every serious charge that was laid against him. His interrogation continued from August to December without producing anything that would justify a trial.

By late autumn, the magistrates of Haarlem had grown weary of Torrentius's obduracy, and they applied to the Court of Holland for permission to resort to more violent methods. This was readily granted, and on Christmas Eve 1627 Torrentius was interrogated by a certain Master Gerrit, who was Haarlem's executioner and also its chief torturer. Heavy weights were tied to the painter's legs while four men hauled him into the air by ropes that had been attached to his wrists; he was left hanging in this way while more questions were put to him. Afterward he was stretched on the rack until his limbs were pulled from their sockets. A third torture damaged his jaw and left him temporarily unable to eat, and at one point, it appears, some attempt was actually made to shoot him. But the efforts of the torturers were to no avail. Through all this agony, Torrentius continued to deny he was a Rosicrucian. Supporters of the painter, who spoke to Master Gerrit in the tavern of the Gilded Half-Moon after the prisoner had been returned to his cell, were told he had impressed the executioner as an honest man. The only words Torrentius had spoken, Gerrit said, were, 'Oh my Lord, my God!'

In the absence of a confession, the burgomasters of Haarlem were forced to go to extraordinary lengths to obtain the verdict that they wanted. In January 1628, Torrentius was brought to court still crippled from his torture and tried on 31 charges *extra-ordinaris,'* a rare procedure that meant he was not allowed to mount a defence and could not appeal the verdict of the court. Instead, the judges heard a long parade of witnesses and statements damning him as an immoral heretic. In such circumstances, it was inevitable he would be found guilty, which he was after a truncated hearing. The prosecutor demanded that he be burned at the stake for his sins, but the aldermen of Haarlem baulked at this request. Instead, Torrentius was sentenced to 20 years in prison. This punishment began at once.

Undoubtedly the painter's silence, even under torture, saved him from a far worse fate and made it impossible for the magistrates to convict him of membership of the Rosicrucian order. The charge that he was a brother of the Rosy Cross, which had been the principal reason for his arrest, remained unproven. But Torrentius's resistance to the attentions of Master Gerrit had a further consequence. The authorities in Haarlem could not be certain how widely he had spread his heresies within the city, and though the evidence that they collected was sufficient for them to identify several dozen prominent members of his circle, they continued to suspect that others had escaped their grasp.

In his empty and abandoned store on the Grote Houtstraat, Jeronimus Cornelisz had reason to be thankful that his name had not cropped up during Torrentius's trial. But he knew there was no guarantee that some further investigation of the case would not occur and that any such action might easily compromise him. This fear, it seems, together with his bankruptcy, persuaded him that it might be best to leave the city.

The timing of Jeronimus's departure from his home certainly suggests that this was so. In the aftermath of Torrentius's trial, the burgomasters of Haarlem banished all the members of the painter's circle from the city. These suspected heretics were ordered out on 5 September 1628 and given a matter of weeks to settle their affairs. This period of grace coincides more or less exactly with the period that Cornelisz spent winding up his affairs and transferring what remained of his possessions to his creditor, Loth Vogel. At the end of the first week of October 1628 he appears to have fled from Haarlem. He went leaving his wife and his past life behind and took the road to Amsterdam, where the wharves and flophouses seethed with human flotsam just like him, all rootless and all headed for the East.

CHAPTER 2

Gentlemen XVII

'If this frothy nation have the trade of the Indies to themselves, their pride and insolencie will be intollerable.'

HENRY MIDDLETON

By rights, the town of Amsterdam should never have existed. Four hundred years before Jeronimus Cornelisz first passed through its gates, it had been little more than an obscure fishing village festering in the marshes at the southern limits of the Zuyder Zee. Its situation was undoubtedly unfavourable; the climate was appalling – cold and chill in winter, clammy, damp, and foggy for the remainder of the year – and access to the open sea was only possible via a maze of narrow channels, masked by sandbanks and so shallow that ships could not approach the harbour fully laden. There was, in short, little to suggest that Amsterdam would ever be a place of much significance. Yet by the beginning of the seventeenth century the village had overcome these natural disadvantages and become the richest city in the world.

This remarkable success was based on trade. As early as the fifteenth century, the Dutch had built one of the largest shipping industries in Europe, carrying bulk goods such as timber, tar, and salt from the Baltic to the North Sea and the Atlantic coast. The Hollanders were noted for their efficiency, low freight charges, and the sheer volume of their trade, which even then dwarfed that of their rivals. The men of Amsterdam were at the forefront of this business.

From around the year 1500, the old Dutch shipowners – who had made their profits solely as carriers – began to be supplanted by merchants who took advantage of the favourable geographical position of the Northern Netherlands to buy and sell goods on their own account. The seven provinces that would eventually form the Dutch Republic were ideally placed to profit from the growth of international trade, which at that time was centred in the ports of Italy and Spain. They were midway between Scandinavia and Iberia and at the confluence of seaways and river systems that linked the Atlantic coast with central Europe. Goods landed in Dutch ports could be sent quickly and cheaply to Germany and England, the Southern Netherlands and France.

The towns of Zeeland and the Zuyder Zee thus grew in wealth and population. For many years, however, the greatest fortunes continued to be made by merchants in the Southern Netherlands. The towns of Antwerp, Bruges, and Ghent were far bigger than Amsterdam and its great Zeeland rival Middelburg, and they had long been established as commercial centres for the trade in wool and cotton. Being large and wealthy places, they also attracted merchants specialising in luxury goods such as spice and sugar. Commodities of this sort were generally known as the 'rich trades' because they were so much more profitable than the bulk trades of the Dutch.

The merchants of the Southern Netherlands retained their dominant position until late in the sixteenth century. It was only in the 1570s that the people of the northern provinces at last began to overtake those of the south. One reason for this was the Dutch Revolt which broke out in 1572 and ran on against Spanish domination, until 1648. Before the war began, Amsterdam had been a town of 30,000 people – a good size for the time, but no more than a third the size of Antwerp and smaller, too, than Brussels, Ghent, and Bruges. By 1600, though, double that number lived within the city walls, and by 1628 the number of inhabitants had exploded to 110,000. Amsterdam was now larger than any of its southern rivals and, indeed, one of the four largest cities in Europe.

In an age when plague and pestilence visited the largest towns with grim regularity, and could carry off up to a fifth of the population within a year, such rapid growth could only be the result of mass immigration. Amsterdam became home to tens of thousands of new citizens during these years. A few, like Jeronimus Cornelisz himself, were from elsewhere in the Dutch Republic, but the majority were Protestant refugees from the Southern Netherlands, driven north by Spanish persecution and the war. Many of the refugees were merchants from the great cities of Flanders and Wallonia, who possessed both capital and experience. They helped to establish Amsterdam as a trading power in its own right. A new bank, a stock exchange, and all the other paraphernalia of a mercantile economy followed, and by 1620 the town had unquestionably become the greatest entrepôt in northern Europe. During the first third of the seventeenth century, this flood of cash and expertise made it easier to exploit fresh opportunities and open up new markets. The most important of these was the spice trade.

Why spice? Amsterdam, in truth, was built upon the taste of rotting meat. In 1600, when the science of food preservation was still in its infancy, most of the cuts sold by butchers or hung in larders throughout Europe were sour and decaying. The only things that masked the tang of decomposing flesh were spices such as pepper, which thus became the most-sought-after luxury goods of the day.

The great difficulty, so far as the merchants of Europe were concerned, was that spices came from far away. They were grown and harvested in a swath of southeast Asia stretching from India nearly to New Guinea, and though they had been known in Europe since Roman times, they had never been available in any quantity and could only be afforded by the rich. To get as far north as the Dutch Republic, they had to travel enormous distances. The annual harvest was first carried in small boats and on the backs of animals to the great trading ports of China, Indonesia, and the Coromandel Coast, where merchants from Asia, Persia, and Arabia paid good prices for it. From there the spice road headed west and north, eventually terminating in the Italian quarter of Constantinople. Venetian and Genoan skippers then carried the precious spices west, until at last they reached the markets of Italy, then France and Spain, and – finally – the cities of the United Provinces, where they were used to flavour roasts and stews, turned into medicines, and valued as preservatives. The whole voyage from Asian tree to European table took the best part of two years, and until the middle of the fifteenth century the merchants of the West had no real control over either the supply of spices or their price, which in the course of the long journey could increase a hundredfold.

It was only in 1498, when men from Portugal first rounded Africa and found their way to the Indian coast, that Europeans gained direct access to the markets of the East. For another century, the Portuguese and, to a lesser extent, the Spaniards explored the archipelagos that stretched from Sumatra to the

Philippines and produced the spice so greatly coveted at home. They kept their hard-won knowledge of the sea routes secret, reserving for themselves the lucrative new trade with the Indies. Profits from these ventures flowed into the coffers of the kings of Portugal and Spain.

By Jeronimus's day, however, fierce competition from the Netherlands and England had robbed Iberia of its monopoly. The Dutch and English East India Companies now controlled most of the markets of the East and shipped their wares home to London and the seaports of the United Provinces. Thousands of sacks of spices, to which were added tons of precious metals, porcelain, and cotton, were unloaded in the warehouses of these companies each year, and the wealth generated by their sale defied belief. The ships that thronged the busy roadsteads north of Amsterdam went halfway round the world to sail home full of spice; the closely guarded warehouses grouped along the wharves bulged with it; and the auction houses and the grocers' shops along the grander streets sold it, all at profits so enormous that men travelled to the town from all over Europe in the hope of sharing in them. The city had become a place where a man's readiness to chance a long voyage east was more important than his past, and where one or two successful speculations were all it took to restore a fortune. These were the qualities that attracted Jeronimus Cornelisz.

❁

Dutch interest in the Indies dated to the 1590s, when merchant immigrants from the south began to have an impact on the city's trade. During this decade herring, salt, and timber became less significant to Amsterdam than the more valuable commodities of the rich trades. Fleets were fitted out and dispatched north and west in search of all manner of luxury goods. Dutch merchants sailed to Muscovy to buy up furs, whale oil, and caviar, and to the Americas for sugar and silver. But it was clear, even at this early date, that the riches of the East would far surpass them all.

The Indies trade was at this time still in the hands of Portugal and Spain, whose domination of the Spiceries had been ratified a hundred years earlier by the so-called Treaty of Tordesillas. This agreement, sponsored by Pope Alexander VI, was signed in 1494, and under its terms Portugal and Spain agreed to split the world between them. The treaty assigned to Spain all undiscovered territories to the west of a line of longitude that ran from pole to pole a few hundred miles to the west of the Cape Verde Islands, and to Portugal all new lands to the east. In this way the Spaniards gained a formal title to the Americas and the Portuguese the right to exploit the Indies. Between them the two Iberian powers established a duopoly on trade with the West that did not always sit well with their own citizens; the great missionary St. Francis Xavier wrote of the Portuguese officials he encountered in the East: 'Their knowledge is restricted to conjugation of the verb *rapio,* to steal, in which they show an amazing capacity for inventing new tenses and participles.' Naturally enough, the Dutch and English – who coveted the Spice Islands for themselves – were even more unhappy with the arrangement.

Nevertheless, challenging Iberian domination of the East was no simple matter. Spain and Portugal had contrived to keep their knowledge of the Indies secret, and as late as 1590 neither the Dutch nor any other Western power had any real idea of the best way to reach the Spiceries, the precise location of the richest islands, or the disposition of the forces ranged against them. The information that the rivals of Spain and Portugal needed most – detailed sailing instructions for Far Eastern waters – was, moreover, the very thing most closely guarded by their enemies. In the days before the development of accurate maps and instruments, all seafaring nations went to great lengths to preserve the accumulated knowledge of their sailors, compiling decades of experiences to produce directions outlining all that was known about a given place or route. These instructions, which were known as rutters, were among the most jealously guarded possessions of the state. Iberian pilots and masters were under the strictest instructions to destroy their copies if threatened with shipwreck or capture, and they obeyed their orders so scrupulously that no sailing directions were ever found on board Spanish or Portuguese ships taken by privateers. More subtle efforts also failed; the Dutch sent spies to Lisbon to buy or steal copies of the rutters but with no success. Without an understanding of the information they contained, it was generally acknowledged that any expedition to the East would be a costly failure.

It was not until 1592 that a solution to this enduring problem presented itself in the shape of a young man named Jan Huyghen van Linschoten. Van Linschoten was originally from the herring port of Enkhuizen but had recently returned from a nine-year sojourn in the East, during which he had lived in Goa and spent two years in the Azores. He had learned fluent Portuguese and made the acquaintance not only of many influential men, but also of a number of humble navigators and ordinary sailors. In consequence, Van Linschoten was uniquely well informed not only about Portugal's possessions in the East, but also about the routes that her ships sailed and the Asian ports where they traded for their spices. This extensive store of knowledge was poured into three books published in Holland in 1595–6. It is no coincidence that the earliest Dutch expedition to the Indies sailed shortly after the first of these volumes was completed.

The rich merchants who had fitted out this fleet called themselves the *Compagnie de Verre* – the Long-Distance Company. They came from Amsterdam and were led by a rich and influential merchant by the name of Reinier Pauw, who (having made his fortune in Baltic timber) now wished to invest in Indies spice. Between them, Pauw and his merchant friends collected the staggering total of 290,000 guilders with which to fund an Indies fleet. This proved to be enough not only to equip four ships but also to supply them with a huge quantity of silver with which to purchase cargoes.

The expedition, known to the Dutch as the *Eerste Schipvaart,* or 'First Fleet,' was carefully planned over a period of more than three years and had the backing of the state itself. All four ships were heavily outfitted with guns supplied free of charge by a variety of Dutch cities, provided with the latest charts, and their pilots thoroughly schooled in navigation. Most important of all, shortly before they sailed in the spring of 1595, each skipper was given a hastily prepared rutter called the *Reysgeschrift.* It contained Jan van Linschoten's full sailing directions for the Indies.

The directors' only real mistake was to put the wrong men in command of the voyage. Several of the merchants given the responsibility of leading the expedition were temperamentally quite unsuited to the job. One, Gerrit van Beuningen – the upper-merchant of the fleet's flagship, *Amsterdam* – spent most of the voyage in chains, accused of the attempted murder of Cornelis de Houtman of the *Mauritius.* De Houtman in turn, was a hotheaded adventurer who had already served three years in a Portuguese prison for attempting to steal secret charts of eastern waters. Upon the first fleet's arrival at the Javanese port of Bantam, De Houtman was incensed to find the price of spices higher than he had expected; he responded by opening fire on the town with cannon. At the little fleet's next port of call, the Javanese boarded the *Amsterdam* and hacked a dozen members of the crew to death. Further down the coast, De Houtman's suspicions were aroused by the unprecedented friendliness shown him by the prince of Madura. He opened fire again, slaughtering the members of the welcome party. Finally, the upper-merchant's attempt to sail on to the clove-producing islands of the Moluccas was thwarted by a near mutiny among the crew. In the circumstances it was no surprise that when the surviving members of the *Eerste Schipvaart* returned to Amsterdam, after a voyage of more than two years, the value of the pepper in their holds was only just enough to defray the expenses of the expedition.

Reinier Pauw and his colleagues learned the lessons of the First Fleet well. Merging their Long-Distance Company with a rival concern organised by a group of merchants from the Southern Netherlands, they outfitted a second, larger fleet and dispatched it to the Indies in the spring of 1598. Within two years, the eight ships of the *Tweede Schipvaart* returned with their holds full of spice. Although the costs of this expedition were put at more than half a million guilders, the voyage yielded profits of 100 percent.

The profitability of the rich trades were thus demonstrated in decisive fashion. From now on the Amsterdam syndicate's biggest problem was deterring competition. Four rival Dutch fleets had set sail for the Indies in the same year as the *Tweede Schipvaart,* backed by merchants from the Southern Netherlands and Middelburg. In 1599 yet another consortium, the New Brabant Company, outfitted a fleet, and by 1601, no fewer than 14 Dutch fleets had sailed for the Indies and the United Provinces had overtaken Portugal as the leading trading nation in the East. But intense competition between the various Dutch syndicates drove up prices in the Indies – where the cost of spices doubled in the space of half a dozen years – while depressing profits back at home.

This situation could not be allowed to continue, and in 1602 representatives of the rival companies met to discuss the formation of a joint stock corporation that would merge their various interests into one vast company. The attractions of this proposition were obvious. The combined capital of such a company would give it substantial influence in the Indies; furthermore – by establishing control over the importation of spices to the Dutch Republic – the corporation could more or less fix prices as it wanted. The States-General, or parliament, of the United Provinces was in favour of creating a single company and was prepared to grant it a monopoly on all Dutch trade east of the Cape of Good Hope. The only real objections came from the merchants of Zeeland, who did not wish to be part of a concern dominated by the interests of Amsterdam.

It took five months of delicate negotiation to resolve the dispute, but – talks finally concluded – the various Dutch syndicates merged on 20 March 1602, forming the giant corporation known as the *Verenigde Oost-indische Compagnie*.* The overall management of the VOC was placed in the hands of 17 directors, the so-called *Heren Zeventien,* or Gentlemen XVII. This extremely influential group met two or three times each year, for up to one month at a time, and was responsible for the Company's commercial strategy. The VOC's six local chambers nevertheless retained considerable independence, each appointing a board of directors to govern its own affairs, building and equipping its own ships, and keeping the majority of its profits for itself.

The capital required to fund the chambers came from the merchants of the six towns themselves. There was little difficulty in attracting men anxious to put money in the rich trades; Amsterdam, which was by far the richest chamber, had more than a thousand individual investors, of whom almost 200 contributed in excess of 5,000 guilders apiece. Reinier Pauw, who had started it all, put up six times that amount, but, even so, the five largest contributions were all made by southern immigrants; the biggest investment was one of 85,000 guilders.

The new company was a success from the start. The first combined fleet sailed in 1602 and made an enormous profit. The VOC also enjoyed impressive success in fighting the Portuguese, who found themselves assailed by the substantial Dutch fleets that were arriving in the East. Even when they were themselves outnumbered, the Hollanders had the better ships and superior morale. By 1605 they had captured Ambon, Tidore, and Ternate – three of the most important Spice Islands, which between them produced almost all the world's supply of cloves. These victories confirmed the corporation as the most profitable, powerful, and important private business in the United Provinces: 'Jan Company,' the

---

*Commonly called the 'Dutch East India Company' by historians to distinguish it from its rival, the English East India Company.

people of the Dutch Republic took to calling it, in recognition of its primacy.*

❁

By 1615, with the continuing success of Jan Company apparently assured, Dutch traders in the East became increasingly confident and aggressive. The English trader Henry Middleton, who ran across the merchants of the VOC in Bantam, penned a vigorous protest at the escalating arrogance of 'this frothy nation.' He was not the only one to find the Hollanders' demeanor hard to stomach.

At home in the Netherlands, the Gentlemen XVII indulged in similar high-handedness. Although their victories had been won with guns supplied by the Dutch government, and though the Company's monopoly remained in the gift of the national parliament, the States-General, the directors of the VOC did not hesitate to assert their independence when the opportunity arose. 'The places and the strongholds captured,' they tartly told the States, 'should not be regarded as national conquests but as the property of private merchants, who were entitled to sell those places to whomsoever they wished, even if it was to the King of Spain.'

The leaders of the United Provinces, who depended on Jan Company to prosecute their war with Portugal and Spain in eastern waters, had no choice but to tolerate the Gentlemen's presumption. The same was not true of the English East India Company, whose fragile grip on the spice trade – painfully built up over several decades – was greatly weakened by Dutch aggression. 'These butterboxes,' another English merchant complained in 1618, 'are groanne so insolent that yf they be suffered but a whit longer, they will make a claime to the whole Indies, so that no man shall trade but themselves or by their leave.' He was right. Within a year the Dutch had all but cleared their rivals from the Indies; within three they had subdued the Banda Islands and seized the world's entire supply of nutmeg, the most sought-after spice of all. These actions, more than any others, guaranteed a lucrative future for Jan Company. By the middle of the 1620s, the Indies trade,

*The name 'Jan' is the Dutch equivalent of the English 'John' and was the most common Dutch male name of the time. The VOC's nickname thus reflected its status as the 'everyman' company of the United Provinces—one that affected every citizen's life for better or for worse.

which had been so fragmented and unprofitable only two decades earlier, had evolved into a well-organised monopoly. The six chambers of the VOC sat at the centre of a web of trade yielding unprecedented profits.

❈

All this wealth flowed directly into the coffers of the Company, and out again into the pockets of the company's principal investors – the great merchants of the Dutch Republic and, in particular, the directors of the six chambers themselves. The profits that were earned, and the dividends that were paid, were simply colossal. Returns of 1,000 percent or more were recorded on certain voyages, and dividends of 10, 20, or, in one case, even 100 percent were paid annually to the shareholders. The fortunes that the merchant princes of Amsterdam and Middelburg accumulated exceeded, in some cases, those of European royalty. The richest man in the Dutch Republic in the 1620s was Jacob Poppen, whose father Jan had been one of the earliest investors in the Indies trade. Jacob's total worth was put at 500,000 guilders – this at a time when it was possible to house and feed a family in Amsterdam on about 300 guilders a year.

Very little of the money ever found its way into the hands of the merchants and the sailors who actually risked their lives out in the East. Every VOC employee, from the upper-merchants down to the lowliest enlisted men, received only a modest salary and the guarantee of board and lodging for the duration of his employment. This arrangement was actually a good incentive for the poorer men who filled the lowest posts; it was unlikely that they would find much steady work in their hometowns. But it held little attraction for the merchants themselves, whose wages – it was commonly acknowledged – were scarcely large enough to live on, and who could expect no pension if they did survive long enough to retire. Since a good portion of the pay they did earn was retained by the VOC against their eventual return – partly as a precaution against desertion – and since staying too long in the East was tantamount to suicide, most sailed with the intention of making as much money as they could in as short a time as possible.

Among their number was the merchant Francisco Pelsaert, who – like so many of the Company's most valued men – had been born in Antwerp. Pelsaert was in many ways a typical servant of the VOC, although he came from a Catholic family and, since Jan Company hired only Protestants, had been forced to conceal his origins in order to secure his first appointment. For one thing, he had few family ties to keep him in the Netherlands – his father had died before he was five years old, and though his mother remained alive, she soon remarried and seems to have left the boy to be brought up by his grandfather. For another, though Pelsaert's relatives were wealthy, he himself had few resources; when his grandfather died, the old gentleman willed his estate to his wife and left nothing of significance to his ward.

Forced to seek a fortune of his own, Pelsaert – by now a man of 20 – secured an introduction to the Middelburg chamber of the VOC in the last months of the year 1615. The application was successful. Pelsaert was hired as an assistant – the lowest merchant rank, one that involved mostly humdrum clerical duties – at a salary of 24 guilders a month. Four months later he took ship for the East on board the *Wapen van Zeeland*.*

Nothing is known of Pelsaert's first three years in the Indies, but he must have been reasonably successful. He was promoted to the post of under-merchant around 1620 and dispatched to the Company's recently established base at Surat, on the northwest coast of India. There he was to help to open trading relations with the Mogul emperors – a dynasty so fabulously rich that their name has passed into the English language as a synonym for power and wealth. Within weeks of his arrival on the subcontinent, Pelsaert was dispatched to the imperial court at Agra to deal in cloths and indigo. His salary was increased to 55 guilders a month and, in 1624, to 80. By then the man from Antwerp had been promoted to the rank of upper-merchant and placed in command of the VOC's mission to the Mogul court.

This promotion was undoubtedly deserved, for Pelsaert had proved himself to be one of the Company's more vigorous and efficient servants. His principal achievements while at Agra were to secure control of the indigo trade (the rare blue dye was then an immensely sought-after commodity) and improve profits by switching the main trade in spices to Surat from the Coromandel Coast. But he also pressed the Gentlemen XVII to see India's rich potential as a trading base. The English East India Company was then still poorly placed on the subcontinent; had Pelsaert's

* *Weapon of Zeeland.*

recommendations been taken more seriously at home, the Dutch might have done more to challenge the steady rise of British influence in India.

Pelsaert's successes in the East, which soon attracted the favourable attention of the Gentlemen XVII, can be attributed to several factors. To begin with he was adept at languages, learning fluent Hindustani and picking up a working knowledge of Persian. He understood instinctively the need to impress his hosts by living ostentatiously and was careful to arrange for a constant stream of gifts – or bribes – to present to Indian officials. He also enjoyed the patronage and friendship of the principal Dutch merchant at Surat, the renowned Pieter van den Broecke, who like Pelsaert came originally from Antwerp.

In other respects, however, Pelsaert was far from typical of the VOC community in India. At a time when most Dutch merchants lived lives as far removed as possible from those of the native peoples of the East, he displayed a fascination for the everyday activities of ordinary Indians, whose harsh lives he described in unprecedented detail in reports sent to the Netherlands. The close relations he established with the Indian community also extended to a series of scandalous affairs with local women, which Pelsaert carried on with such reckless disregard that he eventually put at risk not only the future of his mission but even his own life.

Pelsaert's uncontrollable attraction to women was to be a feature of his entire career, but it was most evident during these early years in India. He was not alone in consorting freely with the women of the East; few European females went out to the Indies, most of those who did so died, and it was in any case generally believed that only the children of Eurasian couples stood any chance of survival in such unhealthy climates. But the majority of Dutchmen contented themselves with taking mistresses from among the servant classes, and abandoning them and their off- spring when the time came to go home to the Netherlands. Pelsaert enjoyed dallying with slave girls as much as did his col- leagues, but he was prepared to go much further than more prudent merchants believed wise. In the early 1620s, for example, he embarked on a dangerous affair with the wife of one of the most powerful nobles at the Mogul court in Agra, a relationship that developed so promisingly that he soon invited the married woman to his home. There the lady chanced upon a bottle of oil of cloves, a powerful stimulant normally served in tiny doses to dangerously ill men. Mistaking it for Spanish wine, she gulped down a substantial measure and promptly dropped dead at Pelsaert's feet. To escape retribution, the shocked merchant was forced to have the body buried secretly in the grounds of the Dutch settlement. He escaped detection, but though the Mogul potentate never did discover exactly what had happened to his wife, the scandal had at least one long-term repercussion for the VOC: for many years a local broker named Medari, who had somehow found out what had happened, used the knowledge to blackmail Jan Company into retaining his otherwise dispensable services.

Most of Pelsaert's fellow merchants disapproved of such sexual incontinence, but even they would have found his other great love – money – entirely comprehensible. Nor would they have been particularly shocked by the methods he employed to get it. Like most of his contemporaries, Francisco Pelsaert wished to taste the riches of the rich trades, and he had no intention of watching the Gentlemen XVII grow fat while he himself eked out a meagre salary.

The simplest way for Dutch merchants to make a fortune in the Indies was to deal in spices under the table, but this was not permitted. The VOC did allow its men to purchase minute quantities of cloves or pepper, but – jealous of its monopoly – the Company forbade more widespread private trade and rarely rewarded its employees' initiative. Even a man with 20 years' service, who did his best to serve the Company and brought home cargoes worth tens of thousands of guilders, could not expect a bonus as of right. The consequences were predictable. Underpaid and exposed to considerable temptation, the merchants of the VOC were thoroughly corrupt.

This fact was commonly acknowledged. 'There are no Ten Commandments south of the equator,' the common saying had it, and honest men were hard to come by in the East. Though personal belongings could be, and were, frequently searched to prevent the private importation of spice, fraudulent accounting was commonplace; it was a relatively simple matter to buy goods at a low price and claim they had cost much more, or to overvalue damaged stock. Nor were the merchants the only ones busily defrauding their employer. Many lesser servants of the VOC bribed fellow Dutchmen to overlook their private activities in the spice markets. Some traded in the name of Asian merchants, though this, too, was prohibited. 'There was no "esprit de corps" in the VOC,' one historian has noted. 'The Company as a body was avaricious, and its employees were often demoralised by its institutionalised greed... Every able-bodied man from the Councillor of the Indies down to the simple soldier considered it an absolute must to care for himself first.'

Jan Company, which was nothing if not a practical organisation, finally resigned itself to the practice of private trade, making only intermittent efforts to stamp it out. A merchant had to be exceptionally greedy or unlucky to be caught; most of those who were had been betrayed by jealous rivals. The most notorious example in Pelsaert's day was that of Huybert Visnich, who had run a VOC trading post in Persia. His salary was 160 guilders a month, but by the time he was denounced for fraud his private trade had amassed him a fortune estimated at no less than 200,000 guilders. Visnich fled to the Ottoman Empire, where he was eventually killed for his money in 1630. His former employers noted his death, with a certain satisfaction, as 'a well deserved punishment by God.' In truth, however, Visnich had simply taken better advantage of his opportunities than hundreds of other merchants who were equally corrupt.

Francisco Pelsaert was no exception to this rule. While at Agra, he used Company funds to set himself up as a moneylender, advancing cash to local indigo growers at an annual rate of 18 percent and pocketing the profits for himself. It was a risky business; he could hardly keep full records, for fear of an audit; the farmers who made up his clientele sometimes defaulted on their loans; and there was always the danger that a colleague would denounce him to the Company. But by initiating his successor in the deception when he himself returned to Surat, Pelsaert successfully evaded detection. By 1636, when his fraud at last came to light, the VOC had incurred sizable losses of almost 44,000 rupees.

❁

Word that there was money to be made in the service of Jan Company did not take long to spread through the United Provinces, and there can be little doubt that Jeronimus Cornelisz planned to recoup his lost fortune through just this sort of private trade. Whether or not the apothecary really had been compromised by involvement in the Torrentian scandal, his appearance in

Amsterdam in the autumn of 1628 clearly suggests that his chief concern was to restore his battered financial position. There were safer bolt-holes for religious dissidents than Amsterdam, most of them outside the borders of the United Provinces – but none that offered such a tempting combination of anonymity and opportunity.

The town that Jeronimus traversed was not yet fully formed. The horseshoe-shaped canals that still enclose the city centre had only just been built, running just inside to the walls, encircling the residential streets and the merchants' warehouses and leading north toward the crowded harbour. But even then their banks were lined with the thin, tall homes of Holland's leading citizens – the height of each building roughly denoting its owner's wealth and status – and the narrow streets so seethed with citizens hurrying to appointments that they were often clogged with carts and carriages. As early as 1617, the press of traffic in the city centre had grown so great that a one-way system had been introduced to ease congestion, but, even so, there was still noise and bustle everywhere. Amsterdam's merchants rose at 5:30 A.M., began work at seven, and laboured for an average of 12 or 14 hours a day. Their lives left them little time for strangers, and newcomers to the city often thought themselves invisible. The people of the city were so intent on making money that visitors passed unnoticed on the busy streets.

It is unlikely, then, that anyone noticed or talked to Jeronimus Cornelisz as he threaded his way through the crowded centre of the town and passed through the medieval city wall where it was pierced by the *Waag,* the old customs weigh-house. New fortifications, ordered when it was obvious the city was outgrowing its old boundaries, had been thrown up half a mile or so farther to the east, and the area between the walls had already become one of the commercial centres of Amsterdam. It was close to the harbour and had plenty of room for the construction of warehouses and wharves.

The town became much less cramped and crowded on the far side of the *Waag;* Cornelisz would easily have found what he was looking for. His destination was the East India House, which stood on the Kloveniersburgwal, a tree-lined canal that had once been the city moat, and close to one end of the Oude Hoogstraat, the old high street of Amsterdam. The House itself was an elegant, if not especially imposing, three-story brick rectangle completed in

1606 and built around a central courtyard. It was the main headquarters of the local chamber of the VOC.

Recruitment to Jan Company was a haphazard business. There were no tests and no exams; no references were required. Since only the desperate and the destitute applied, the VOC could not afford to be overly selective, and there were particular shortages of candidates from among the upper and the middle classes. So many merchants were required – most large ships required a staff of up to a dozen, generally an upper-merchant, an under-merchant, and 8 or 10 assistants, bookkeepers, and clerks – that the only explicit criteria were that a man should sign a five-year contract and that he should not be bankrupt, nor Catholic, nor 'infamous.' Even these rules were rarely enforced.

It is not clear whom Jeronimus visited in the East India House or how exactly he first established contact with the VOC. The web of friends and colleagues that Torrentius had built up throughout Holland included a certain Adriaan Block of Lisse, who had made his fortune in the East and possessed a good deal of influence within the Company. It is possible that he provided Cornelisz with an introduction to the directors of the Amsterdam chamber. It is equally possible that Jeronimus had made the acquaintance of someone with the necessary connections through his own family, or his wife's, or among the clientele of his failed business in Haarlem. Whatever the truth, it seems that the apothecary's age, his social status, and his knowledge of pharmacy – which at this time required detailed understanding of the properties of spice – were enough to convince the directors of the local chamber to overlook his recent and unfortunate disgrace. Cornelisz emerged onto the Kloveniersburgwal as a full-fledged employee of the VOC. He carried with him his commission as an under-merchant, and orders to sail for the Indies within a month.

Had Jeronimus continued to head east on leaving the East India House, he would have reached the Amsterdam waterfront at just the point where a narrow wooden bridge arched over to a little island known as Rapenburg. There, in two adjoining shipyards right under the city walls, the Amsterdam chamber of the Company was completing the East Indiaman that would transport him to the East. The yards, which were together called the Peperwerf, were still very new, but they were already the largest and the most efficient anywhere in Europe. By standardising the design and the components of their ships, the Gentlemen XVII had introduced many of the elements of what would now be recognised as mass production into their shipbuilding programme, cutting the time needed to turn out a large East Indiaman to as little as six months. This was staggeringly quick, but, even so, the vessels produced on the Peperwerf boasted a sophisticated design that made them far superior to the ships used by the English and the Portuguese. In Jeronimus's day Dutch East Indiamen were, in fact, the most complex machines yet built by man, and their advanced construction made them easier to load, cheaper to run, and able to carry much more cargo than their foreign counterparts.

There were several different sorts of ship, each designed for a specific task. The most expensive were East Indiamen of the *Batavia*'s class, which were called *retourschepen* ('return ships'). These vessels were specially designed to carry passengers as well as cargo and were built to survive long ocean voyages to and from the Indies. Next in importance was the *fluyt* – a cheap, flat-bottomed, round-sterned vessel with a high proportion of easily accessible cargo space – and, after that, the *jacht,* which was generally a light and handy craft built to carry no more than 50 tons of cargo.

Each type was built according to the Dutch 'shell-first' method, a revolutionary construction technique that called for a ship's external planking to be assembled and nailed together before the internal ribs and frames were added. As soon as this phase of the building work was finished, the half-finished East Indiaman would be floated and towed out to a 'cage' of wooden palisades 40 or 50 yards out in the waters of the River IJ, where she would be fitted out. The Peperwerf's slips were thus freed for work to begin on yet another vessel. In this way the VOC's yards completed 1,500 merchantmen in the seventeenth century alone.

The *Batavia* herself was no ordinary ship, but one of the greatest vessels of her day. The ship was named after the Javan town of Batavia, which was the capital of all the Dutch possessions in the Indies, and she displaced 1,200 tons and measured 160 feet from stem to stern – the very largest size permitted under Company regulations. She had four decks, three masts, and 30 guns, and her designer – the famous naval architect Jan Rijksen, still active and alert at the tremendous age of 66 – had given her not only a strong double hull (two three-inch thicknesses of oak, with a waterproof layer of tarred horsehair in between them) but an outer skin of deal or pine as well. This softwood sheathing protected the hull from attack by shipworm – the animals preferred burrowing from stem to stern through the soft planking to attacking the harder oak beneath – and as an added prophylactic her outer skin was studded with thick iron nails and coated with a noxious mix of resin, sulphur, oil, and lime. Finally, the sheathing itself was protected all along the waterline by the hides of several hundred roughly butchered cattle, which were tacked onto the pine. So long as the unladen *Batavia* rode high in the waters of the IJ, these skins gave the lower part of her hull the appearance of a mangy patchwork quilt. They would remain in place until they rotted and dropped off in the course of the vessel's maiden voyage.

Thankfully the cattle hides did not obscure *Batavia*'s brightly painted upperworks, which had been trimmed in green and gold, nor her richly decorated stern – an ostentatious refinement that the normally parsimonius Gentlemen XVII had authorised in an effort to overawe the peoples of the East. But all this attention to detail did not come cheap. As completed, and without supplies, *Batavia* would have cost the Company almost 100,000 guilders, a fortune at the time.

This considerable expense was necessary because – once built – the VOC flogged its ships until they were on the verge of falling apart. The stresses and strains that the *Batavia* would be exposed to in the course of a single passage to the Indies were enough to destroy a normal ship, and even with her triple hull a *retourschip* would rarely be expected to make more than half a dozen round trips to the East. Having served the Gentlemen XVII for some- where between 10 and 20 years, she would then be returned to the Zuyder Zee and broken up to provide timber for new housing. It is a testament to the immense profitability of the spice trade that by the time an East Indiaman had been turned back into lumber, the profit on her cargoes would have repaid her building costs several times over.

A *retourschip* of the *Batavia*'s size could load around 600 tons of supplies and trade goods when new (and newness made a differ- ence; after a year or two in service, when the hull became saturated with seawater, cargo capacity could fall by 20 percent). But the holds of an East Indiaman were only ever full when she sailed home so loaded down with spices that her gunports were some- times only two feet from the sea. There was virtually no demand for European goods in the Indies, and although merchantmen departing from the Netherlands did carry boxes of psalm books, hand grenades, cooking pots, and barrel hoops destined for the

Dutch garrisons of the East, the only bulky cargo shipped to Java was stone for the Company factories in the East. Each year the Dutch authorities in the Indies placed orders for further huge quantities of house bricks, which were sent out as ballast. Occasionally the *eysch* – the governor-general's annual order for supplies – included more exotic requests. This was the case in the autumn of 1628; down in the *Batavia*'s airless bilges, sweating workmen were already busy stowing an entire 25-foot-high prefabricated gateway, made up of 137 huge sandstone blocks weighing 37 tons in all, destined for Castle Batavia itself.

Fortunately for the Gentlemen XVII, there was one commodity that the people of the Spiceries were willing to trade for cloves and nutmeg. The local population might have little use for the Dutch linens and thick English cloth that were northern Europe's major exports at this time, but they did have an insatiable desire for bullion – preferably silver coin, which was the common currency of the East. *Retourschepen* therefore set out for the East carrying not trade goods but box after box of silver.

Gigantic sums of money – up to 250,000 guilders for each vessel, equivalent to about £12.5 million today – were supplied to the *retourschepen* in massive wooden chests. Each 500-pound case contained 8,000 coins, and the specie in a strongbox totalled about 20,000 guilders. This was enough to be a real temptation, and the risk of theft was such that the money chests were kept separate from the remainder of the cargo. The bullion was brought aboard no more than an hour or two before the crew weighed anchor and arrived under the watchful eye of no less than one of the Gentlemen XVII, who would demand an appropriate receipt signed by the skipper and the upper-merchant. Once aboard, the chests were stored not in the hold but in the Great Cabin in the stern, where only the most senior merchants had access to them. Then they were watched all the way to Java.

❁

By the last months of 1626, Francisco Pelsaert's existing three-year contract with the VOC was almost up. As one of the most experienced Company men in India, and the leader of a mission to Agra that had been a considerable success in commercial terms, the upper-merchant could normally have expected to be reemployed with a substantial increase in his monthly pay. On this occasion, however, there was no sign of a new contract, and when Pelsaert asked his superiors to resolve the matter, the VOC proved unexpectedly reticent.

The chief difficulty, it appears, concerned the Antwerp merchant's failings as a diplomat. One of the main goals of Pelsaert's mission had been to establish a Dutch presence at the Mogul court and secure favourable treatment for the VOC from the Emperor Jahangir.* This he had conspicuously failed to do. There were mitigating circumstances, it is true; in 1624 Jahangir had removed himself from Agra to Lahore, limiting Dutch access to the Mogul court. Nevertheless, Pieter van den Broecke, at Surat, soon concluded that the upper-merchant's diplomatic gifts were limited, and in 1625 he decided to send a second mission to Lahore. This embassy was led by a certain Hendrick Vapoer, who proved to have a real talent for dealing with the Mogul government. Vapoer's reward was Pelsaert's job in Agra.

Pelsaert was naturally incensed by this decision, more so when he learned that Vapoer would be paid twice what he had earned. But there was little he could do about it, and when his contract expired in March 1627 he returned overland to Surat. He arrived on the coast in May and there quarrelled with the generally easygoing Van den Broecke, whom he no doubt blamed for Vapoer's appointment. Van den Broecke did what he could to mend the damage, begging his old friend to stay in India, but Pelsaert was too proud to let that happen. He insisted on returning to the Netherlands instead.

Still smarting from his treatment at the hands of the VOC, the merchant took ship in Surat 10 days before Christmas. He was given a cabin in the old *Dordrecht,* sailing as a guest of the fleet president, *commandeur* Grijph. Pelsaert passed the time while he waited for the ship to sail in the company of Grijph; a fellow upper-merchant, Wollebrand Geleynssen de Jongh†; and the recently appointed skipper of the *Dordrecht.* The skipper's name was Ariaen Jacobsz.

The *Dordrecht* was Ariaen's first major command after a decade

---

*The name means 'World-grasper.'

†De Jongh was an old enemy of Pelsaert's, thanks to an incident in which the resident at Agra had paid a visit to his trading post carrying a Dutch flag before him, thus implying to the local Indians that he was the latter's superior, which he was not. De Jongh retaliated by charging that Pelsaert 'was considered by everyone to lie with every third word he said, and his mouth is rarely quiet.'

spent working in the inter-island trade. Jacobsz ought to have been anxious to make a good impression, but the heat and the humidity of Surat brought out the worst in him. For whatever reason, Pelsaert irritated the skipper – perhaps it was the upper-merchant's self-importance. Within days the two had fallen out to a dangerous degree.

The dispute that was to cause so much trouble on the *Batavia* had a most mundane beginning. Ten years in the draining climate of the Indies had given Jacobsz an unhealthy love of alcohol, and he refused to moderate his habits in the presence of three senior officers of the VOC. One night in Surat harbour the skipper became drunk and grievously insulted Pelsaert before the other merchants. Next day *commandeur* Grijph was forced to rebuke him, 'saying that that was not the manner to sail in peace to the Fatherland, and that he must behave himself differently.' Jacobsz blamed Pelsaert for this public dressing-down. Henceforth, as the skipper was later to explain, he always hated Pelsaert.

Grijph's presence prevented matters from going any further on the journey to the United Provinces, and Pelsaert arrived home in June 1628. The merchant spent July and August engaged in a successful campaign to win back the favour of the Gentlemen XVII. He had already composed two special reports – a chronicle and a *remonstrantie,* or dissertation, concerning trade in the subcontinent – in an effort to establish himself as an expert on Indian affairs; now he made a new suggestion for finding favour with the Mogul emperors. Jahangir, he pointed out, had never shown much interest in the gifts of Western emissaries. But he did seem to like jewels and silver.

Pelsaert's plan was to send large quantities of special silver plate to India. These goods, which he called 'toys,' would be carefully commissioned to suit the local tastes identified in his *remonstrantie* and could be relied upon to impress the Moguls with the power of the VOC. Items of silverware could be given as gifts, sold at the imperial court, or exchanged for spice. The toys would make a memorable impression and might also win favour and new trading privileges for the Dutch.

Impressed by Pelsaert's detailed knowledge of Indian affairs, the Gentlemen XVII agreed to commission plate to the upper-merchant's specifications. In doing so they took a considerable risk, for the final cost of the consignment of silver was almost 60,000 guilders. But so great was the VOC's new confidence in

Pelsaert that he now received not just a new and better contract, but instructions to accompany his toys back to India.

By late summer, then, Pelsaert found himself restored to favour. He would sail to Surat with his silver plate, the Gentlemen XVII decreed, travelling via the East Indies. The main autumn fleet was due to leave home waters late in October 1628 under the command of Jacques Specx of the *Hollandia* – a member of the Council of the Indies and one of the most senior and experienced traders in the VOC. It was expected to include several *retourschepen* of the largest kind, including the brand-new *Batavia*.

Though still being completed at the Peperwerf, *Batavia* already had a skipper. Ariaen Jacobsz's safe handling of the *Dordrecht* had so impressed the directors of Jan Company that they had chosen him, of all their sailors, to command the new ship on her maiden voyage. She had an under-merchant, too, in the untried, untested Jeronimus Cornelisz. All that she now required was an upper-merchant of ability and wide experience. One candidate seemed particularly suitable.

Francisco Pelsaert joined them just before they sailed.

CHAPTER 3

The Tavern of the Ocean

'Now and then persons of strange opinion come here.'
JACQUES SPECX

A great fleet was assembling near the island of Texel. Nearly a dozen huge East Indiamen lay at anchor in the Moscovian Roads while the sea around them swarmed with small boats full of sailors and barges packed with ballast for the holds. The *Batavia* was there, with several other large *retourschepen* moored close by – the *Dordrecht, 's Gravenhage,** *Nieuw Hoorn,* and *Hollandia.* A group of smaller vessels, *fluyten* and *jachten,* had anchored close inshore. The whole fleet was alive with preparations for the long voyage east.

It was now late October 1628. Autumn was the busiest time of year for the VOC; weather conditions in the Atlantic favoured a fast passage to the Indies for ships that left the Netherlands before Christmas, recruitment became easier as Holland's summer sailors became desperate for work, and ships reached the Indies at the perfect time to load fresh crops of spices. Before they could depart, however, each vessel had to take on board not only a cargo and a crew, but all the supplies required to sustain her for up to a year at sea. Into her 160-foot length the *Batavia* now had to pack 340 people with all their personal possessions, many tons of equipment, and material for the garrisons of the East.

Up from the barges came several thousand barrels of supplies, then sailors' sea chests by the hundred. Wood for the galley stove and ammunition for the guns was stowed below, and the deck was festooned with coils of rope and cable. Over the sides swarmed a

'The Hague of the Counts,' which is the Dutch name for The Hague.

multitude of ill-dressed sailors, whom Jan Evertsz and his men drove to work with curses and knotted lengths of rope. Next came the soldiers – a handful of young company cadets and noncommissioned officers leading a hundred undernourished men off to five years of garrison duty in the Indies – and finally, when the work of loading had been done, Jeronimus Cornelisz and the merchants of the VOC.

In all probability, the Frisian apothecary had never before stepped aboard a ship the size of the *Batavia*. Like most landsmen, his initial impressions of an East Indiaman were most likely wonder at her great size and alarm at the apparent frenzy up on deck. There are accounts, written by awestruck German soldiers, that testify to the remarkable impression a fully rigged *retourschip* made on those who came alongside her for the first time; 'true castles,' they were sometimes called, which seemed enormous when approached from sea level in a boat. Looking up as they came alongside, many merchants felt quite dwarfed by the sheer wooden walls that towered out of the water all around them and by the massive masts and yards soaring almost 200 feet into the air above their heads.

The chaos up on deck must have been even more disconcerting – the planking strewn with a disordered mass of gear, and ragged sailors rushing to and fro in response to orders the landsmen did not even understand. The constant motion of the anchored ship – which rolled incessantly in the choppy autumn sea – was very far from pleasant, but, dimly through their discomfort, Cornelisz and his colleagues would have been aware they were now committed to the voyage, and to whatever consequences might flow from it.

In the midst of all this bustle and confusion, the chief comfort to the novice tradesmen would undoubtedly have been the thought that they would not be expected to share quarters with the rabble milling around them. The most luxurious berths in the *Batavia*'s stern were always given over to the merchants of the VOC, and the area abaft the mainmast would become the exclusive preserve of the ship's officers, the merchants, and their servants. This arrangement at least ensured them some privacy and reduced the prospect of discomfort, since the ship pitched and yawed less violently by the stern. In the course of a nine-month voyage, such incidental mercies came to mean a lot.

The best quarters of all went to the most senior men aboard. Francisco Pelsaert and Ariaen Jacobsz shared the privilege of using what was known as the Great Cabin on the level of the upper deck. It was by far the largest room on the ship and easily the best lit, as it alone was fitted with lattice windows rather than portholes. Its centerpiece was a long table capable of seating 15 or 20 people, and it was here that Pelsaert and his clerks transacted their daily business while at sea and the senior officers and merchants ate their meals. The rest of the officers' quarters were located elsewhere in the stern. Jeronimus and half a dozen other distinguished passengers were shown to a warren of little cabins on the deck above, where the quarters were smaller and more spartan; the more junior officers and the Company clerks shared a large communal cabin just below the steersman's station. When it came to accommodation, the VOC had spared considerable expense. The private quarters were quite unheated, only marginally better ventilated than the rest of the ship, and less than the span of a woman's arms in breadth – but at least they offered the luxury of bunks instead of sleeping mats, sufficient room to put a writing desk and chair, and cabin boys to fetch and carry meals and empty chamber pots.

The allocation of these cabins was determined by rank and precedence. The best would have gone to Jeronimus, the undermerchant, who was after Pelsaert the most senior representative of Jan Company on board. Ariaen Jacobsz's second-in-command, the upper-steersman Claes Gerritsz, would have had another, and in normal circumstances the *Batavia*'s two under-steersmen (whose rank was roughly equivalent to a modern-day lieutenant's), the provost (who was responsible for discipline on board), and the most senior of the VOC assistants might also have expected cabins of their own.

On this voyage, however, the *Batavia* was carrying two high-ranking passengers whose presence upset the normal rules of precedence. One was a Calvinist *predikant,* or minister, named Gijsbert Bastiaensz, a citizen of the ancient town of Dordrecht who was sailing to the Indies with his wife, a maid, and seven children. The other was Lucretia Jansdochter, an unusually beautiful and highborn woman who came from Amsterdam and was travelling to join her husband in the East. Both would have been allocated cabins near Jeronimus's. In the close confines of the stern, the three of them could hardly help but become acquainted.

It is not difficult to guess whose company Cornelisz would have most enjoyed. Creesje (she was generally known by her diminutive) was not only youthful and attractive; she came from a family of merchants and thus commanded a social status equal to Jeronimus's own. Gijsbert Bastiaensz, on the other hand, was in many ways Cornelisz's opposite. He came from the most southern part of the province of Holland; he was 52 years old; and he was a strict, straightforward Calvinist with very little formal education. His scant surviving writings betray no hint of wit or intellectual curiosity; there was no room in his theology for the exotic speculations that the under-merchant entertained, and had Jeronimus dared to explain his true beliefs, the *predikant* would certainly have been scandalised by them. As it was, Cornelisz kept his own counsel on the subject and wisely chose to charm the preacher rather than confront him.

Gijsbert Bastiaensz was later to confess that he had entirely failed to recognise the undertows that lurked beneath Jeronimus's superficial decency. This failure was hardly surprising. The *predikant* was an honest and straightforward sort, of little intuition and less experience, whose horizons had until quite recently been limited to his calling and his church. Dordrecht was noted for its uncomplicated orthodoxy. A minister from such a town would hardly have encountered a creature quite like Cornelisz before.

Bastiaensz, it seems, was a typical example of the Indies *predikant*. Because the Reformed Church was quite devoid of missionary zeal – the doctrine of predestination implied there was little point in converting heathens – it was never easy to persuade ministers to serve in the east. The few who went were seldom members of the Calvinist elite. They were, rather, 'hedge-preachers': artisans whose religious views were frequently naive, and who, while preaching economy and restraint, were often in financial difficulties themselves.

The *predikant* of the *Batavia* was all these things and more. Gijsbert Bastiaensz was a member of the working classes of the Dutch Republic, who made a living with his hands and attended to church business when he could. But – like Jeronimus Cornelisz – he was a man on the verge of ruin, forced by the threat of bankruptcy to seek redemption in the east.

The minister's early life had been comfortable enough. His father, Bastiaen Gijsbrechtsz, had been a miller, and Gijsbert followed him into what appears to have been a well-established family business. In February 1604 he was married to Maria Schepens, the daughter of a Dordrecht wine merchant, and – as was common at the time – the couple produced a large family. There were eight children in all, four boys and four girls, and no fewer than seven survived infancy. The fact that so many of the children lived, and that their father was able to provide for them, suggests that – for the first two decades of the century at least – Bastiaensz controlled a profitable mill.

By the time that he was 30, the miller had become an elder of the Reformed Church of Dordrecht. Between 1607 and 1629, Gijsbert Bastiaensz served no fewer than five two-year terms on the town's church council, a proud record that suggests he was among the best-respected (and most strictly orthodox) churchmen in the town. Further proof of this contention can be found in the voluminous legal records of Dordrecht, where the *predikant* appears as an arbitrator, an executor, and a witness who stood surety in a number of legal cases. All of these were solemn duties assumed only by those whom the public trusted – men of unimpeachable integrity.

For all that, the mill that the *predikant* owned and ran for a quarter of a century was not a very grand one. He relied for his living on a *rosmolen* (a horse-powered mill) rather than one of the newer and more efficient windmills then becoming widespread in the Netherlands. During the severe depression of the 1620s, the owners of *rosmolens* often struggled to make a living, while millers who ground corn more quickly and more cheaply using windmills prospered. Gijsbert Bastiaensz was one of many who could not compete. Between 1618 – when he appears in the town records as a landowner with his own mill and 12 rented acres of grazing for his horses – and 1628, the *predikant*'s financial position disintegrated. At around the time that Jeronimus was transferring all his worldly goods to the merchant Vogel, Bastiaensz was signing his home and mill over to his own creditors.

His good name and his faith were of no help now, and there were no church livings to be had in Dordrecht. With eight mouths to feed, the *predikant* applied to be a preacher in the Indies. He was in Amsterdam by the second week of September, became an employee of the VOC at the beginning of the following month, and found himself on board *Batavia* a few weeks later. His wife and children, who had lived in Dordrecht all their lives, had been uprooted with him. The eldest boy was 22 years old and the youngest only 7; too young, no doubt, to understand how little chance there was the whole family would return alive.

In another cabin in the stern, Creesje Jans sat amid the handful of personal possessions she had been permitted to bring on board. She was 27 years old and had been married to a VOC under-merchant named Boudewijn van der Mijlen for nearly a decade, but her decision to join him in the Indies requires some explanation. Van der Mijlen had sailed for the East without her, apparently in 1625 or 1626, and it was most unusual for an under-merchant's wife to follow later and alone. In Lucretia Jans's case, however, the archives of her native Amsterdam provide a ready explanation for her presence on board the *Batavia*. Creesje was an orphan whose three infant children had all died, one by one. By 1628 she had no reason to stay in the United Provinces. Boudewijn, wherever he might be, was all that she had left.

Creesje had never known her father, a cloth merchant who died before she was born. When she was two years old, her mother Steffanie had remarried and her stepfather, a naval captain named Dirk Krijnen, had moved the family first to the Leliestraat, in a fashionable and wealthy quarter of Amsterdam, and eventually to the Herenstraat – then, as now, one of the more expensive and prestigious addresses in the city. Creesje's mother died in 1613, when her daughter was only 11 years old, and the girl became a ward of the Orphan's Court, while continuing, it seems, to live with her stepfather, her sister, Sara, and a stepsister, Weijntgen Dircx. Within a few years, however, Krijnen too was dead, a loss that may have helped to propel Lucretia into her early union with Boudewijn van der Mijlen.

The bride was 18 on her wedding day. According to the marriage register, Creesje's husband was a diamond polisher who lived in Amsterdam but came from the town of Woerden. The couple's three children – a boy named Hans and two girls, Lijsbet and Stefani – were born between 1622 and 1625, but none lived to reach the age of six. Such misfortune was exceptional, for even in the seventeenth century child mortality generally ran at no more than one infant in every two, and it is possible that the children may have succumbed to some epidemic. There is, however, no evidence of this; nor is much known of Boudewijn's business affairs. All that can be said is that he, too, most likely suffered badly in the recession of the 1620s. Certainly no successful diamond merchant would voluntarily join the VOC only to be sent, as Van der Mijlen was, to Arakan – a stinking, disease-ridden river port in Burma – to deal in slaves for the greater glory of Jan Company.

Boudewijn had received orders to sail for Arakan in the autumn of 1627, when he was living in Batavia, and it took so long – up to a year – for letters to travel from there to the Netherlands that Creesje was surely unaware her husband would not be in Java when she arrived. It seems equally improbable that her voyage was planned 12 months or more in advance, and that he knew she would be leaving the Republic. Most likely the last of Creesje's children died some time in 1628 and she, weighed down with grief, made the more or less impulsive decision to rejoin her husband, sending perhaps a letter in advance and settling her remaining affairs in time to secure a berth on the *Batavia*. She took with her no more than a few belongings and a lady's maid. Like Cornelisz and Bastiaensz, Creesje Jans had little reason to look back.

So much for the passengers in the stern. Like all East Indiamen, the *Batavia* was a segregated ship, in which the accommodation got more spartan as one moved toward the bow. Those of middling rank, particularly the 'idlers' (specialists such as the surgeons, sailmakers, carpenters, and cooks who were not expected to stand watch and work by night) lived down on the gun deck, though they too had the privilege of relatively spacious berths in the forecastle or the stern. The sailors and soldiers who made up more than two-thirds of the crew, on the other hand, were crammed into the space 'before the mast,' and it was a serious offence for any of them to appear aft unless their duties called them there.

This strict segregation served several purposes. It reinforced status and emphasised the divisions that existed on board between soldiers and sailors, officers and men. But it was also a practical measure. Seamen and troops were placed on separate decks because long experience had shown that they did not get along and would fight if they were billeted together. Ordinary seamen were to stay before the mast to minimise the ever-present threat of mutiny, and the entrance to the officers' quarters in the stern was fortified for the same reason.

The soldiers came off worst from these arrangements. Their quarters were two decks down on the orlop – what the Dutch called the 'cow-deck' – where the roof beams were so low it was impossible to stand upright, and which was so close to the water-line that it was equipped with neither vents nor portholes to provide a minimum of air and light. The orlop was actually part of the hold, and on return journeys it became a spice store. Uncomfortable though it was, it was not unknown for the troops to remain confined to this dark and airless deck for all but two 30-minute periods each day, when they were brought up under escort to taste fresh air and use the latrines.

The soldiers of the VOC were a particularly motley collection, misfits gathered more or less indiscriminately from all over northern Germany, the United Provinces, and France. A number came from Scotland, and there was even one Englishman – whose name appears as 'Jan Pinten' in the records of the voyage – among the soldiers on the *Batavia*. The troops were largely untrained, and at a time when local dialects and thick provincial accents were the norm, many found it difficult to understand each other, let alone the orders of their officers.

There is little evidence of any solidarity among soldiers of the VOC; thievery and casual violence were rife, and the only bonds that seem to have formed were friendships of convenience between men who hailed from the same town or district. Friends would keep an eye on each other's possessions, share food and water, and nurse each other if they fell sick. It was important to find a companion like this. Those who had no friend to turn to when they succumbed to illness might be left to die; *retourschepen* were fitted with sick bays in the bows, but officers and seamen received priority for treatment. A typical Dutch sailor, it was observed, 'shows more concern for the loss of a chicken in the coop than for the death of a whole regiment of soldiers.'

On the *Batavia* the majority of the troops were German. A number came from the North Sea ports of Bremen, Emden, and Hamburg, where the VOC maintained recruiting centres to gather up the dregs of the waterfront. Though some were decent men – it was not unknown for the younger sons of honourable but impoverished families to seek their fortunes in the Company's army – they were, on the whole, a potentially dangerous group of malcontents.

The soldiers were led by a Dutch corporal, Gabriel Jacobszoon, who had come on board with his wife. Jacobszoon was assisted by a *lansepesaat* (lance corporal) from Amsterdam called Jacop Pietersz, whose nicknames – he was variously known as *steenhouwer,* 'stone-cutter,' and *cosijn,* which means 'window-frame' – suggest a man with the considerable strength and bulk required to control the brutal men under his command. The Stone-Cutter and the corporal were in turn responsible to the young VOC cadets who were the only military officers on board, and who did not themselves share the discomforts of the orlop deck.

These youths were frequently junior members of old noble families whose lands, in the time-honoured tradition, were passed down from a father to his eldest son, leaving any other male children to make their own way in life. The crew of the *Batavia* included a dozen such cadets, at least four of whom – Coenraat van Huyssen, Lenert van Os, and the brothers Olivier and Gÿsbert van Welderen – appear to have had pretensions to nobility.

Van Huyssen is the only cadet of whom it is possible to say much. The *predikant* noticed him as a 'handsome young nobleman' who came from the province of Gelderland, and it would appear that he was a junior member of the Van Huyssen family that owned the manor of Den Werd, a fief near the German border in the county of Bergh. Over the years the Van Huyssens produced several members of the knighthood of the province, but their estate at Den Werd was small and not particularly productive. If Coenraat were indeed a scion of this family, it would not be surprising to find him seeking a living in the East. Perhaps he joined the Company's army with some friends; the Van Welderen brothers came from the provincial capital of Gelderland, Nijmegen, and it is not impossible that the three young nobles knew each other.

If the *Batavia*'s soldiers endured appalling hardships, conditions were only marginally better for the seamen on the gun deck. Their quarters stretched forward from the galley to the bows. Here there was headroom, and gunports offered light, but 180 unwashed men still lived together, crammed into less than 70 feet of deck that they shared with their sea chests, a dozen heavy guns, several miles of cable, and other assorted pieces of equipment. The gun deck was desperately cold in winter and unbearably hot and stuffy in the tropics. Hammocks, which had been introduced in the previous century, were still not widespread, and many sailors used sleeping pads instead, squeezed into whatever spaces they could find on deck. Worst of all, the gun deck was almost always wet, rendering even off-duty hours wretched for the many men who worked in heavy weather without an adequate change of clothes.

The very sight of an ordinary seaman was alarming to the genteel merchants in the stern, and it is not surprising that they were kept as far away from the passengers as possible. Dutch sailors in general stood apart by virtue of their shipboard dress –

loose shirts and trousers offered the necessary freedom of movement in an era of stockings and tight hose – and they had a reputation for being unusually rough and raw, even by the standards of the time. But those desperate or destitute enough to risk their lives on a voyage to the East had a particularly poor reputation, and ordinary merchant skippers and even the Dutch navy would not recruit men who had served the VOC.

'For sailors on board Indiamen,' one passenger observed, 'cursing, swearing, whoring, debauchery and murder are mere trifles; there is always something brewing among these fellows, and if the officers did not crack down on them so quickly with punishments, their own lives would certainly not be safe for a moment among that unruly rabble.' A *retourschip* sailor, wrote another, 'must be ruled with a rod of iron, like an untamed beast, otherwise he is capable of wantonly beating up anybody.'

Nevertheless, the seamen of the VOC did form a more or less cohesive group, united by the bonds of language and experience. Most were Dutch, unlike the soldiers, and all shared the unique dialect of the sea. The jobs they were expected to perform, from weighing anchor to making sail, required cooperation and encouraged mutual trust, and they were in general more disciplined and less disruptive than the troops.

The bulk of the mainmast, which ran right through the ship, marked the limit of the sailors' quarters. Here, halfway along the gun deck, there were two small rooms – one the surgeon's cabin and the other a galley lined with bricks and full of copper cauldrons. The galley was the only place on a wooden ship where an open fire was permitted, and in this tiny space the *Batavia*'s gang of cooks were required to prepare more than 1,000 meals a day. Then came a capstan and the pumps, and farther back again the quartermaster and the constable occupied two little cabins between the bread store and the armoury. Their quarters were directly below Pelsaert's Great Cabin, but for all those who lived down on the gun deck, the wooden beams that separated them from the more privileged inhabitants of the stern were much more than a purely physical barrier. They protected the merchants from the artisans and kept the officers safe from the men. On most East Indiamen, this was a necessary precaution. On the *Batavia,* it was to prove no protection at all.

The Gentlemen XVII had originally decreed that fleet president Specx would assume overall command of the winter fleet, a substantial convoy of 18 vessels. Francisco Pelsaert, in the *Batavia,* was to have sailed with them, his responsibilities extending no further than the ship under his command. Toward the end of the month, however, Specx was unexpectedly recalled to Amsterdam on business, and in view of the deteriorating weather the VOC took the unusual decision to split the fleet in two. Eleven ships would wait and sail with the president when he was ready. The other seven were to depart immediately under the command of the most experienced upper-merchant available.

Thus it was that Pelsaert found himself appointed *commandeur* of a whole flotilla of merchantmen: three *retourschepen* – the *Dordrecht* and *'s Gravenhage* as well as the *Batavia* – and three other vessels, the *Assendelft,* the *Sardam,* and the *Kleine David.* The final vessel in the squadron was the escort warship *Buren.* One ship, the *Kleine David,* was to sail to the Coromandel Coast of India to take on textiles, dyes, and pepper. The rest were bound for the Spice Islands – which, God willing, they might expect to reach in the summer of 1629.

Jeronimus Cornelisz and Creesje Jans probably had only the sketchiest ideas of the dangers they would face during such a voyage, but experienced merchants knew better than to underestimate the difficulties of the eastward passage. The distance from Texel to the Indies was almost 15,000 miles – more than halfway around the world. The voyage was the longest that any normal seventeenth-century ship would ever undertake, and conditions along much of the route were harsh. Most ships took eight months to reach Java, travelling at an average speed of two and a half miles per hour, and though one or two of the most fortunate reached their destination after only 130 days at sea, it was not unknown for East Indiamen to be blown off course and left becalmed for weeks or sometimes months at a time. The *Westfriesland* left the Netherlands in the early autumn of 1652 and eventually limped home two years later, having endured a succession of disasters and sailed no farther than the coast of Brazil. The *Zuytdorp,* which sailed in 1712, found herself becalmed off the coast of Africa and made the fatal decision to sail into the Gulf of Guinea in search of fresh water. Lack of wind trapped her there for five more months, and four-tenths of her crew died of fever and disease. The ship finally rounded the Cape of Good Hope nearly a year after leaving the United Provinces.

The Gentlemen XVII were roused to fury by the thought of such delays and even resented the need for all *retourschepen* to put into land at least once to rest and take on fresh supplies of food and water. In the early years of the VOC, ships had visited Madeira and the Cape Verde Islands, and sometimes St. Helena as well, but these calls could add several weeks to the voyage. By the 1620s most fleets outward bound called only at the Cape, about 150 days' sailing from the Dutch Republic. Most ships tarried there for about three weeks, long enough to nurse the sick, and restock, and the Cape became so useful that the VOC built a fort there in the middle of the century and settled colonists to provide fresh food for its ships. It was popular with the sailors, too, who took to calling it 'The Tavern of the Ocean' for the bounties that it promised them. To the directors of the VOC, however, the Cape was at best an unfortunate necessity, which slowed down the all-important flow of profit. They offered bonuses to merchants, skippers, and steersmen whose vessels made fast passages – 600 guilders for a voyage of only six months, 300 guilders for one of seven, and 150 for those who arrived in the Indies less than nine months after setting sail. Such measures seem to have had little effect. Some ships did make extraordinarily short passages; in 1621 the *Gouden Leeuw** completed the voyage from the Netherlands to the Indies in 127 days, and in 1639 the *Amsterdam* established a new record of just 119. But such speedy voyages were rare. The masters of most ships evidently preferred the comforts of the Cape to the lure of guilders in their pockets.

Francisco Pelsaert had never had to consider such necessities before. The additional responsibility that he now assumed was all the more daunting for being so unexpected. Still, even the most experienced fleet commanders had relatively little control over their ships; the vessels of a departing convoy could well spend weeks at anchor, waiting for good winds, and the order to sail – when it eventually came – could easily lead to chaos as unwieldy *retourschepen* manoeuvred in the tight confines of their roadsteads. Minor collisions were common and, though the ships all lit their huge stern lanterns to keep track of each other in the dark, it was rare for a convoy to stay together all the way from the Channel to the Indies.

Pelsaert's flotilla did not even leave the Zuyder Zee together.

Golden Lion.

The *Batavia* was left behind when the other six ships in the convoy sailed on 28 October 1628, and the *commandeur*'s new flagship did not finally get under way until the following day. The most likely explanation is that there was trouble in loading the *Batavia*'s cargo of silver and trade goods, but, whatever the reason, the *retourschip*'s passengers and crew soon had cause to regret the short delay.

On the first day at sea, the *Batavia* ran into an exceptionally violent storm while still off the Dutch coast. The crew was still green and untested, and before the ship could be got properly under control, she ran aground on the treacherous Walcheren sandbanks. Stuck fast and battered by the steep waves that built up quickly in the shallows, both passengers and crew had good reason to fear for their lives.

Storms were the greatest danger an East Indiaman could face, and stranding was one of the worst calamities that could befall her in a storm. Even in open seas, heavy waves could swamp a *retourschip,* or smash her sides, or make her roll until the masts dipped into the water and the sails filled with sea and carried the whole ship down. Aground, the waves could open up her seams, and if they were big enough to make the ballast shift, the weight of the guns, masts, and yards could tip her over, too.

The Walcheren Banks were a particularly deadly obstacle; though well within the home waters of the Dutch Republic, they claimed one ship in every five of the total lost by the VOC between Amsterdam and the Indies. The threat to the *Batavia* was considerable, and it took all Ariaen Jacobsz's skill as a seaman to get her off the banks without serious damage. The skipper not only bullied and encouraged his men to shorten sail and check the stowing of the ballast, but kept the ship intact until the storm had blown itself out. Then he floated the *Batavia* off on the tide. Careful checks revealed the hull was not too badly damaged and by morning on 30 October the ship was able to continue on her way.

Jacobsz steered west, heading for the Bay of Biscay and the Atlantic. At some point during the passage down the Channel, it appears, the *Batavia* came upon the battered survivors of the rest of Pelsaert's convoy. They had been savaged by the same storm that had nearly sunk their flagship, and the smallest of the *retourschepen, 's Gravenhage,* had been so badly damaged that she had been forced to run into the Dutch port of Middelburg for repairs that were to keep her there for about four months. The other six ships continued to steer west.

It was November now; the northern winter was drawing in, and the days were mostly short and cold and wet. For novice sailors such as Jeronimus Cornelisz, this was their first experience of the sea and it took time to get used to the constant motion of the ship, particularly in the stormy waters of the Bay. Surviving accounts written by voyagers to the East are full of the misery of these early days at sea, when seasickness was rife. Even the livestock on the main deck – carried to ensure a supply of fresh meat – suffered in this way. The pigs in particular were prone to bouts of *mal-de-mer*.

The shock of life at sea would have been considerable for Jeronimus and his companions. Within a week of sailing even basic cleanliness became a dreamed-of luxury for the passengers and crew of a *retourship*. There was no fresh water to spare for washing, and although one of the largest ships of her day, the *Batavia* was equipped with no more than four latrines. One pair was located on either side of the Great Cabin and reserved for the use of the people in the stern. The rest of the crew had to line up to use the remaining pair in the bows, which were nothing more than holes in the deck under the bowsprit. These heads were open to the elements and in full view of all those waiting in line. The only additional amenity was a long, dung-smeared rope that snaked through the hole in the latrine. The frayed end of the rope dangled in the sea and could be hauled up and used to wipe oneself clean.

This miserable existence was compounded in bad weather. All the gunports and the hatches had to be closed and battened down, and little fresh air penetrated below deck. The men stank of stale sweat and garlic (a popular cure-all at the time); everything was permanently damp, and it became too dangerous to venture to the latrines. Soldiers and sailors relieved themselves in corners or crouched over the ladders down to the hold,* and if the weather was bad enough for the pumps to be called into action, the urine and faeces that had been deposited below made an unwelcome reappearance. Rather than discharging into the sea, the *Batavia*'s pumps simply brought up filth and water from the bilges, 'fuming like hell and reeking like the devil' as one contemporary put it, and sent it cascading down the gun deck to slosh around sleeping seamen until it found its own way out through open ports and sluices. When the weather finally improved, the men would scrub

*When the stern of the *Batavia* was salvaged in the 1970s, archaeologists discovered large quantities of a black, phosphate-rich substance inside the hull. Analysis revealed the presence of gristle and cereal husks, suggesting the black mass was a layer of human faeces deposited in what had probably been the bilges.

the decks with vinegar and burn frankincense and charcoal down below in an attempt to clear the air, but for much of the passage the lower decks of the *Batavia* smelled like a cesspit. Those fortunate enough to travel in the stern were spared the worst of this unpleasantness, but every account of the journey east makes it plain that, during the first weeks at sea, even the most distinguished passengers endured discomforts they could scarcely have dreamed of back at home.

At length Pelsaert's convoy left the worst of the weather behind it and headed south. The winds became lighter as the ships entered the Horse Latitudes off the North African coast, and though there were occasional excitements – the first sight of dolphins, which often came to play around Dutch ships, and seaweed in the water, heralding the approach to the Canaries and the Cape Verde Islands – for the most part the voyage quickly became tedious. When the winds dropped there was relatively little for even the sailors to do, and for the soldiers, merchants, and passengers on board, day followed day with scarcely a break in the general routine.

In these circumstances, food quickly became a subject of consuming importance for the inhabitants of the *Batavia*. The passage of time was marked by the hot meals served three times a day: at eight in the morning, noon, and 6 P.M. These could be grand occasions; Pelsaert and Jacobsz ate in the Great Cabin, usually with the ship's senior officers and the most distinguished passengers as guests. Jeronimus Cornelisz and Lucretia Jans dined at the upper-merchant's table, along with Gijsbert Bastiaensz and his wife. Claes Gerritsz the upper-steersman would have been there, too, along with his deputies, the watch-keepers Jacob Jansz Hollert and Gillis Fransz – whose nickname, somewhat unnervingly, was 'Half-Awake.' Further down the table sat the provost, Pieter Jansz, and perhaps some of the junior merchants: young VOC assistants such as Pelsaert's favorite clerk, Salomon Deschamps of Amsterdam, who had been with him in India. But even these privileged people could not take an invitation to the merchant's table entirely for granted; there was another well-stocked table in the passenger accommodation at the stern to which they might occasionally be relegated and where the *predikant*'s children and the less-favoured merchants and officers ate. Here and in the Great Cabin there were napkins and tablecloths, pewter plates and tin spoons, cabin boys to bring the food and the steward to serve wine. The sailors and soldiers, on the other hand, dined where they slept, sitting on their sea chests and eating from wooden dishes with wooden spoons. There were no servants before the mast. Instead the men were grouped into messes of seven or eight, and one man from each mess acted as orderly to his shipmates in weekly rotation, fetching food from the galley in pails and washing the dishes afterward. The cook and his mates ate last of all, standing watch while the rest of the crew had their meals.

The quality of the food varied considerably. Officers ate better than the men and all on board enduring a progressively more unsavoury diet as the voyage progressed. Some effort was made to provide fresh food: as well as the live chickens, goats, and pigs carried in pens on the main deck, the topmost cabin in the stern – a low-roofed little hutch known as the *bovenhut* – served as a sort of greenhouse in which Jan Gerritsz, the ship's gardener, grew vegetables. On calm days fish were sometimes caught, but the tradition of the service dictated that no matter who reeled them in, the first landed each day went to the skipper, the next dozen or so to the merchants and the officers, and so on down the established lines of precedence. It was uncommon for much fresh food to reach the ordinary sailors and soldiers.

The men lived almost entirely on cask meat, pulses, and ship's biscuit, a sort of bone-dry bread often known as hard tack. Although it was possible, in the first half of the seventeenth century, to preserve some foods fairly well, the VOC was not renowned for the quality of its stores. On land, meat was cured by carefully rubbing it with salt (which drew out moisture), or hung for a while and then pickled by being repeatedly immersed in boiling brine or vinegar. Both processes killed bacteria and flavoured the meat and could produce surprisingly palatable results when done well. But such methods were costly and time consuming, and Jan Company baulked at the expense. For less money, its suppliers took freshly slaughtered pigs and cows and dunked whole sides of meat into seething cauldrons full of seawater without even draining off the blood, which seeped out later to sour the pickle. Meat preserved in this way was cheap but extremely salty. It needed to be soaked in fresh water before being cooked, but at sea it was generally boiled in brine, to preserve the limited supplies of drinking water on board, and emerged from the pot snow white with encrusted salt. Served, as it was, in an equally salty broth, it could burn the lips and induce a raging thirst.

Retourschepen also carried preserved fish, which was dried, not salted. The Vikings had crucified the cod they caught in their long-boats' rigging; Netherlanders impaled theirs and called them *stokvisch* after the Dutch word for the stick on which they threaded up to 30 split and gutted cod for air drying. The drying process produced bone-hard slabs of white fish that had to be softened up for cooking by being soaked, or beaten with mallets. Like salt pork and beef, stockfish was generally served in a stew with dried peas or beans. But fish was relatively difficult to preserve, and – at least according to the later records of the Royal Navy – it tended to go bad more quickly than preserved meats and was probably among the first stores to be consumed. The chances are that stockfish featured heavily in the meals served on the *Batavia* at this early stage in the voyage.

Even salt meat was difficult to store in the sort of conditions that confronted the little fleet as it neared the coast of West Africa under a tropical sun. In the absence of any form of refrigeration, conditions down in the hold quickly became unbearable. Ventilating the nether reaches of the ship was practically impossible, and the lowest decks became so stifling that it was not unknown for seamen sent into the storerooms to suffocate. Casks burst open in the heat, scattering their contents and providing food for the multitude of vermin that scurried and swarmed down below. When it rained and water seeped down into the stores, dried food rotted or became mouldy and infested, too.

Hard tack was the worst affected. This twice-baked bread contained no fats or moisture and would keep indefinitely in normal conditions, though it was so dry it cracked teeth and had to be dunked in stew to make it edible. Damp, it was easier to eat but became a perfect larder for the weevils that laid their eggs within and turned each piece into a honeycomb of tunnels and chambers full of larvae. Every sailor who made the passage to the Indies learned to tap his ration of bread against the sides of the ship before he ate it, to dislodge the insect life within. Any that remained were eaten anyway. Novice seamen learned to distinguish the flavours of the different species: weevils tasted bitter, cockroaches of sausage; maggots were unpleasantly spongy and cold to bite into.

On board ship, as on land, the officers and men not only ate differently but drank differently as well. Pelsaert and Cornelisz and the other senior officers were permitted to carry their own supplies of wine and spirits, in quantities proportionate to their rank; those who had reached the post of boatswain or above were also accorded double rations of the water and weak beer that was shipped for general use. The men were allowed spirits only to prevent disease, and their water and beer were prone to turn green with algae in the tropics. Water from the island of Texel was highly favoured by the VOC because its mineral content helped to keep marine growth at bay, but by the time the *Batavia* reached Africa her drinking water was slimy and stinking. It had even become heavily infested with tiny worms, which the sailors sieved with their teeth, and the daily three-pint ration was brought up from the hold 'about as hot as if it were boiling.'

Unfortunately for the people on board, the deterioration in the *Batavia*'s supplies of water and beer coincided with the onset of blazing weather, which caused both passengers and crew – many of them still dressed in the thick cloth suited to a northern winter – to sweat profusely and develop thirsts that were only heightened by the salty diet. Rationing was necessary to conserve the precious supply, however undrinkable it became. Almost every sailor, no matter how poor, possessed a cup in which to receive his ration; serving the men beer or water in a common jug inevitably led to violent disputes over who had received more than his fair share of liquid.

For all this, the men of the *Batavia* ate and drank well by the standards of the day. Their food was laden with sufficient calories to keep them working, and at a time when it was usual for peasants and artisans to eat meat no more than three or four times a month, a *retourschip*'s crew enjoyed it three or four times a week. Nicolaes de Graaf, a surgeon who made five voyages to the Indies between the years 1639 and 1687, observed that 'each mess gets every morning a full dish of hot groats, cooked with prunes and covered with butter or some other fat; at midday they get a dish of white peas and a dish of stockfish, with butter and mustard; save on Sundays and Thursdays when they get at midday a dish of grey peas and a dish of meat or bacon. Each man gets 4 lbs of bread (or usually biscuit) weekly, and a can of beer daily, as long as this lasts. They are also supplied with as much olive-oil, vinegar, butter, French and Spanish brandy, as they need to keep themselves reasonably healthy and fit.'

At the captain's table, there was no rationing. Pelsaert and Jacobsz, Cornelisz and Creesje ate meat or fish three times a day, and on special occasions 11- or 12-course feasts were served in the Great Cabin. It was a way to pass the time.

Boredom tested the patience of everyone on board during the long voyage south toward the Cape. In between meals, the passengers and crew passed the time with gossip and games. There was singing and sometimes the crew staged amateur theatricals. Gambling with dice was popular, though technically illegal, and draughts and tick-tack – a form of backgammon – were widely played. A few, chiefly among the officers, read for recreation, though most of the books available were the religious texts that the VOC, in a rare moment of piety, had determined to supply to all its ships. (Sir Francis Drake himself, on his voyage around the world, is known to have whiled away the hours by colouring in the pictures in his copy of Foxe's *Book of Martyrs.*) The handful of women on board knitted or wove lace; on some voyages, old records attest, they even took over in the galley on occasion, fed up with a diet of bread 'which lay like a stone in their stomachs.' The sailors enjoyed rougher sports. Fistfights were tolerated as an amusing diversion, and when they could the men played the 'execution game,' a contest involving forfeits that included being smeared with pitch and tar. This game was so dangerous that it could only be played with the express permission of the skipper.

Disputes flared rapidly amid the boredom and the heat. The fights that were not about the rations generally concerned the living space, or lack of it. With more than 330 people crammed into a ship only 160 feet long, privacy was almost impossible to come by. The men fought over space to lay their sleeping mats, and so disruptive was the problem of theft that stealing was punished almost as severely as murder. The temptation was great, however; most of the sailors and soldiers on board were almost destitute – they would hardly have been risking their lives in the Indies otherwise – and minor theft was a continual problem on every Dutch ship.

It was during this period of indolence and tedium that Jeronimus Cornelisz first revealed his heterodox views to the people of the *Batavia.* Talk in the Great Cabin in the stern turned quite frequently to matters of religion, and from time to time – far now from the grasp of the Reformed Church – the undermerchant enjoyed shocking the assembled company with his thoughts on some bit of doctrine. He was an unusually eloquent man and talked so persuasively that even his more inflammatory beliefs were somehow rendered almost palatable. Jacobsz and his officers, who seldom encountered educated men, found his smooth tongue almost hypnotic. The merchant was, in any case, careful not to stray too far into outright heresy. 'He often showed his wrong-headedness by Godless proposals,' the *predikant* recalled, much later on, 'but I did not know he was Godless to such an extent.'

In time, Cornelisz's practised charm seems to have made a great impression on the skipper, and somewhere off the coast of Africa the two men became friends. They had a number of interests in common, and the many hours the ship spent becalmed in the tropics provided them with ample opportunity to become better acquainted. It is safe to assume they touched on two subjects more than once: the fortunes to be made in the Spiceries, and the beauty of Lucretia Jans.

Creesje commanded the attention of many of the officers in the stern. With the exception of the provost's wife, who seems to have been considerably older, she was the only woman of any rank on board the *Batavia.* That alone would have been enough to engage the interest of men denied much female company for several months on end, but her remarkable beauty, which is attested to in the records of the voyage, undoubtedly enhanced this allure. There can be no question Cornelisz had noticed it. By the time the *Batavia* neared the West African coast, it would seem that the skipper and the *commandeur* – who both greatly enjoyed the company of women – were well aware of Creesje, too.

By the last days of December the ship had reached the southern limit of the Horse Latitudes,* which lay at 25 degrees north. By then, it would appear, the ship was short of either food or, more likely, drinking water, since Pelsaert made the decision to put in at Sierra Leone. Doing so was a violation of the VOC's sailing instructions which had, since 1616, designated the Cape of Good Hope as the sole permissible port of call on the voyage to Java. By putting in to port, Pelsaert made himself liable not only to a fine but to the condemnation of his employers. Moreover, even at this early date Sierra Leone – infested as it was with malaria and yellow fever – was so rotten with disease that it had earned a deserved reputation as a 'white man's grave.' To sail into port there was to

---

*So called because the region was prone to prolonged calms, resulting in water shortages that sometimes forced transport ships to force overboard the horses that they carried.

take a risk, and although it was not unheard-of for VOC ships to visit the African coast, those that called there generally did so as a last resort.

The first Westerners to visit Sierra Leone had been the Portuguese, who made contact with the local tribes as early as the fifteenth century. The people who lived along the coast were members of the Temne clan, which controlled much of the commerce with the interior. They lived on fish, supplementing their diet with rice, yams, and millet, and they traded food for swords, household utensils, and other metal goods when they could. By 1628 the Portuguese had also begun to purchase slaves in Sierra Leone.

Pelsaert had no need for slaves and was interested only in resupplying his ship, but, to general surprise, the *Batavia* did make one addition to her crew in the port. Rowing ashore to purchase supplies, Pelsaert's men noticed a single white face among the people waiting on the waterfront. It belonged to a 15-year-old boy from Amsterdam named Abraham Gerritsz, who had deserted from another Dutch East Indiaman, the *Leyden,* at the beginning of October and was by now just as anxious to leave the settlement. Pelsaert, who had been forced to transfer several of his own men to other ships in the flotilla at the beginning of the voyage, agreed to allow the boy to work his passage to the Indies on board the *Batavia.*

From Sierra Leone, the little fleet put back out into the Atlantic and headed south toward the equator. Here the winds grew less predictable again, and skippers were instructed to stay within the confines of what the Dutch called the *wagenspoor* – the 'cart-track,' two parallel lines crossing the ocean from northeast to southwest all the way from the Cape Verde Islands down to the equator. The *wagenspoor* was sketched in on VOC charts and marked the boundaries of the safest route. If a ship sailed east out of the cart-track, she risked becoming becalmed in the Gulf of Guinea. If she ventured too far west, she would rot in windless seas off the coast of Brazil.

Ariaen Jacobsz kept the convoy within the *wagenspoor* as it limped across the unpredictable doldrums around the equator. There was little wind and the weather was blisteringly hot now, so much so that it became all but impossible to sleep below and the crew sought the sanctuary of the deck at night. Planking warped in the heat, and the sun softened the tar that had been used to caulk gaps between the timbers, trapping animals that had been unwary enough to fall asleep along the cracks. Wax melted below decks, causing candles to ooze and run until they hardened into weird, squat shapes in the cooler evening air. The men wore only loin-cloths when they had to go below; passengers who had never experienced such unbearable temperatures wrote that the sun had 'dried the faeces within the body'; and in an era before the invention of effective balms and creams, everyone suffered agonies from sunburn. Cooling these burns in brine brought only temporary relief, and the salt in the water caused rashes that itched unbearably. The latter problem must have been exacerbated by the fact that, in the absence of fresh water, sailors traditionally washed their filthy clothes in urine.

❀

Down in the abandoned hold was the empire of the rats. Bloated rodents scurried between the supplies, gnawing their way into the casks of meat and nesting in the linen trade goods. Having learned that the wooden walls of barrels concealed huge quantities of food, they sometimes attacked the sides of the ships in error. Given time, rats could chew their way through the layers of oak planking in the hull, springing leaks that tested the pumps and kept the *Batavia*'s sweating gang of caulkers busy.

Nevertheless, the biggest irritants on the voyage were undoubt-edly the insects that swarmed through every crevice of the ship. Lice were a plague from which even the most senior of those on board were not immune. They lived and multiplied in clothing and could cause terrible epidemics of typhus. Many an East Indiaman lost a quarter or a third of her crew to the disease, and though the *Batavia* seems to have escaped its ravages, no doubt the lice would have infested every article of clothing on board the ship. Even Creesje and Cornelisz were required to join the other passengers and crew and delouse themselves each week on a special 'louse-deck' by the latrines in the bows. Determined hunting would have afforded them some relief, but as numerous contemporary letters and memoirs attest, such measures were only temporarily effective.

Nor were lice the only insects on board. Bedbugs lurked in the bunks and sleeping mats, and new ships such as the *Batavia* could be quickly overrun with cockroaches. The few days that Pelsaert's fleet spent at Sierra Leone would have been time enough to allow a few big African insects to find their way down below, where they would have multiplied with astonishing rapidity. The captain of one Danish East Indiaman was so maddened by the plague of scuttling vermin on board his ship that he offered his sailors a tot of brandy for every thousand cockroaches they killed. Within days, the crushed bodies of 38,250 insects had been presented for his inspection.

Tormented by the vermin and the heat, some Dutchmen were driven insane. By the late 1620s, the VOC had already become well acquainted with a variety of mental illnesses caused by the long passage east. Depression was not uncommon in the early weeks of any voyage, as those on board realised the magnitude of the ordeal they faced, and in some cases it was so severe that the victims refused to talk or even eat. Becalmed in the oppressive airs of the equator, others went mad as they waited long, excruciating days – sometimes weeks – for winds that never came. The archives of the East India Company contain many records of men who jumped overboard to end this suffering.

Even so, most voyagers enjoyed some good times, too. Surviving accounts tell of swimming in calm weather, skipping games and storytelling on sultry evenings. When the opportunity arose, there were wild celebrations of signal events such as the skipper's birthday. *Predikanten* such as Gijsbert Bastiaensz frowned on the unrestrained revelry that traditionally marked the crossing of the equator, but not even the VOC could ban the singing of bawdy sea shanties or the smoking of tobacco in long, thin Gouda pipes. The danger of fire being very great, however – in the years before the invention of matches, pipes were lit with red-hot coals fetched with tongs from a glowing brazier – smoking was permitted only before the mast, and then only during daylight hours.

It was not until March 1629 that, south of the doldrums at last, Pelsaert's fleet picked up the northeast trade winds that took the ships on toward the coast of South America, and then the Brazil current, which swept east to the Cape of Good Hope. But now, just as the voyage was becoming bearable again, debilitating illness struck.

The little convoy had entered the scurvy belt, an area of the South Atlantic that stretched from the Tropic of Capricorn all the way to the Cape. In the 1620s (and for another 200 years), scurvy was a menace on every lengthy ocean voyage, generally manifesting itself three to four months after a ship had left port. The first cases usually occurred among the most malnourished members of the crew, and it was only when a vessel was becalmed and drifted slowly across the ocean for months on end that the officers suffered with the men, but the symptoms of the disease were unique and all too familiar to veterans of the Indies trade such as Jacobsz and Pelsaert. They included painful and swollen legs, foetid breath, and spongy, bleeding gums. After a while, the victim's mouth became so swollen and rotten with gangrene that his teeth would fall out one by one. Eventually – after about a month of suffering – he would die an agonising death.

Cases of scurvy occurred on almost every voyage to the Indies; a *retourschip* usually lost 20 or 30 men to the disease, generally between the equator and the Cape. Sometimes the death toll was far worse. On the *Eerste Schipvaart* of 1595, more than half the men in the fleet were dead of scurvy by the time the ships reached Madagascar. When the handful of survivors finally reached Texel two years later, there were not enough fit men left on board one of the ships to lower her anchors.

Little progress had been made in treating the disease by the time the *Batavia* sailed three decades later. Scurvy is caused by a deficiency of vitamin C, which is found in fresh food and particularly in fruit and fruit juice – supplies of which had usually run out by the time a ship reached the equator. But this fact was unknown in 1628, and doctors differed as to what caused the illness and how it should be treated. Foul air below decks was often blamed for the disease, as was a surfeit of salt meat. Wine was a popular, if ineffective, remedy. Perhaps surprisingly, the vitamin-rich juices of lemons and limes – which were to be recognised, late in the next century, as a preventative and cure – were already known to be effective in combating scurvy, although no one fully understood why. They were prescribed as a remedy by a number of naval surgeons, and quantities were carried aboard some ships, particularly those of the rival English East India Company. But this cure was only one among many tried by the VOC, and its unique efficacy was not recognised in the seventeenth century. In consequence the *Batavia* lost nearly a dozen seamen to scurvy on the passage between Sierra Leone and the Cape.

The dead men were buried at sea. There was not enough wood for coffins, so the deceased were sewn up inside a spare piece of sailcloth and, after a short burial service, tipped into the sea. A dead sailor's mess-mates would try to make sure that his body was well weighted with sand or lead, in the hope that it would sink too quickly for the sharks that were by now a common sight around the *Batavia* to tear it apart.

Even in the seventeenth century, sharks enjoyed an evil reputation for ferocity, and Dutch sailors sometimes told stories of fish that had been caught and cut open to reveal the severed legs or arms of recently deceased shipmates in their bellies. Seamen viewed all sharks as man-eaters and would go to considerable trouble to hook them on their lines. Sometimes a captured fish would be killed and put to good use on board – the rough, sandpapery skin was used to sharpen knives, heart and liver became ingredients for the surgeon's nostrums, and the brains were turned into a special paste that was thought to ease the agony of childbirth. But on other occasions, the men of a *retourschip* would exact revenge for all the sailors who had died between the jaws of a shark. It was considered fine sport to torture a captured monster by gouging out its eyes and cutting off its fins. Then an empty barrel would be tied to the mutilated animal's tail and the shark would be returned to the Atlantic. Unable to see or swim or dive, the wounded fish would thrash wildly in gouts of its own blood, endlessly circling and smashing into the sides of the ship until it either died of exhaustion or was eaten by its fellow predators.

Cruel sports such as this were among the few permitted outlets for the baser instincts of the men. Violence and disputes were severely punished, and the total lack of privacy made any form of sexual activity all but impossible for those who lived before the mast. On the great majority of East Indiamen this problem was exacerbated by the fact that there were no more than a handful of women on board – and most of those were either married or prepubescent. A few of the men (though not, it seems, too many) were active sodomites, but the penalties for being caught engaging in a homosexual relationship were draconian; if the *commandeur* decreed it, the lovers could be sewn, together, into a sailcloth shroud and thrown alive into the ocean. The great majority of such affairs were thus conducted not among the men of the lower deck but between officers and common sailors, since the officers alone had access to private cabins and the status to coerce their partners (some of whom, at least, were unwilling) into silence.

The *Batavia,* however, carried an unusual number of female passengers. There were at least 22 women on the ship, and although most were married and were travelling to the Indies with their husbands, a few were to all intents and purposes unattached. This was a little peculiar, as the VOC had already learned from bitter experience that to allow unmarried women to sail alongside several hundred young men – all tight-packed together with little to occupy them for anything up to nine months – inevitably led to trouble.

As early as 1610 the Company's first attempts to procure wives for its lonely merchants in the Indies had ended in humiliation when Governor-General Pieter Both was dispatched to Java with 36 'spinsters' who turned out to be prostitutes. A few years later Both's successor, Jan Coen, abandoned the attempts he had been making to purchase slave girls in the East and had the orphanages of the Netherlands scoured for young Dutch women instead. 'You, Sirs,' Coen lectured the Gentlemen XVII in his uniquely blunt style, 'would only send us the scum of the land, [and] people here will sell us none but scum either … Send us young girls, and we shall hope that things will go better.' These 'company daughters' were packed off to the *Batavia* and provided with food and clothing on the voyage east on the understanding that they would marry when they got there. Most were between 12 and 20 and sailed with only a single chaperone to look after groups of up to several dozen girls. Unsurprisingly, even the plainest of the 'daughters' attracted the unwelcome attentions of the crew long before the coast of Java appeared over the horizon.

By 1628 Jan Company had learned from these mistakes. It was now rare for any women, other than the wives and daughters of its most senior merchants, to be granted permission to sail out to the Indies. But for some reason the VOC's proscriptions appear to have been flouted on the *Batavia*. It is probable that some of the women who found their way on board, including a group of half a dozen sailors' wives, were actually stowaways. Certainly councillor Jacques Specx, who commanded the larger half of that year's Christmas fleet, uncovered a host of whores and common-law spouses on the ships in his flotilla, writing home from the Bay of Biscay: 'We want for nothing save honest maids and housewives in place of the filthy strumpets and street wailers who have been found (may God amend it) in all the ships. They are so numerous and so awful that I am ashamed to say any more about it.' Pelsaert appears to have checked his ships less scrupulously than Specx. Any stowaways on the *Batavia* managed to remain hidden until it was too late to send them back.

Among the unchaperoned women on Pelsaert's ship were the alluring Lucretia Jans and Zwaantie Hendricx, her travelling companion and maid. They made an unlikely couple: Creesje patrician and aloof, her servant Zwaantie earthy and available. Whether Zwaantie had been Lucretia's maid in Amsterdam is not known; it has been suggested that she was hired – and hired in haste – solely to accompany Creesje on the voyage east. The contention is unprovable, but it fits the facts, for these two women were uneasy companions, and the ill feeling that sprang up between them was to be the cause of considerable trouble on board the *Batavia*.

The problems began shortly after the ship sailed from Sierra Leone. During the crossing of the North Atlantic, Ariaen Jacobsz had become infatuated with Creesje Jans. The skipper, who had left a wife at home in Durgerdam, somehow persuaded himself that he could attract Lucretia, who was not only married, but several degrees his superior in social status. He quickly learned otherwise. Creesje rejected his initial advances, but apparently she did so gently, for they remained for a while on friendly terms. But as the *Batavia* set course for the *wagenspoor,* and Creesje continued to resist, her relationship with Jacobsz began to deteriorate.

Jeronimus saw what Pelsaert and the rest had missed. As the *Batavia* left the African coast in her wake, he tackled Ariaen in private. 'I chided him,' the under-merchant later recalled, 'and asked what he intended with that woman. The skipper answered that because she was fair, he desired to tempt her to his will, and to make her willing with gold or other means.'

Jacobsz's bribes appear to have been as unwelcome to Creesje as his earlier advances, and this time she must have told him so in blunter terms. Abruptly the skipper broke off the pursuit. But long before the ship approached the Cape, the irrepressible Ariaen had picked up another scent. This time the object of his affections was Zwaantie, and this time he was successful.

It never was explained whether the *Batavia*'s skipper seduced the maid because he desired her or simply to spite her mistress. Whatever the reason, the burgeoning relationship between Ariaen and Zwaantie placed Lucretia in a delicate position. It was impossible to keep secrets on board ship, and Jacobsz's scandalous dalliance with the maid was soon a public humiliation for Creesje; but she could hardly avoid the skipper all the way to the Indies, and while they remained at sea he could make her life less than pleasant if he chose. Furthermore, it was unthinkable for a woman of her station to travel without a servant, but there was no obvious replacement for Zwaantie on board the *Batavia*. Creesje had little choice but to make the best of the situation.

As for Jacobsz and his mistress, they seem to have been united not only in their dislike of Lucretia – the skipper smarting from rejection, the maid from the real or imagined slights of her employer – but by their lustful natures. Ariaen was 'crazed anew' by his passion for the servant girl, while Zwaantie, so the cook's gossipy wife confided to Jeronimus as they approached the Cape, 'was a whore' who denied her lover nothing. If the under-merchant desired proof of this allegation, it soon presented itself. Repairing to the officers' privy in the stern one day, he opened the door to find the skipper already there, making love to Zwaantie in the awkward confines of the closet.

So the *Batavia* and her consorts neared the Cape of Good Hope. As Jan Huygen van Linschoten had predicted in his *Reysgeschrift*, the first indication that they were approaching land was the sight of Cape gannets – white birds with black-tipped wings that the Dutch called 'velvet sleeves' – wheeling and calling around the convoy while it was still well out to sea. A day or two later, the sailors began to notice mats of broken, trumpet-stemmed reeds floating in the water and then the bones of dead cuttlefish bobbing on the waves. These were sure signs that the *Batavia* was within 30 miles of land.

They dropped anchor under Table Mountain on 14 April 1629, having been nearly six months at sea. The Cape was quite unlike the coast at Sierra Leone. It was delightful country, green and teeming with life. Since its discovery by Batholomeu Diaz in 1488, the Tavern of the Ocean had become a port of refuge for almost every European vessel heading east. English and Dutch, French, Portuguese and Danes all came to barter for supplies with the Hottentots who farmed cattle in the hinterland.

Ships heading for the Coromandel Coast rarely put in at the Cape, but on board the *Batavia* and the *Sardam*, the *Dordrecht*, the *Assendelft*, and the little warship *Buren*, men readied the ships' boats and carried the scurvy-ridden and the sick ashore. Landing parties set up sailcloth tents for them along the edge of the beach. Other seamen hunted sea lions and penguins along the beach, or fished and gathered mussels from the rocks while they waited for the Hottentots' arrival.

It was Pelsaert's duty to negotiate for supplies of food. The natives of the Cape had grown used to dealing with visitors from Europe. A mutually beneficial trade had sprung up, for the Hottentots had oxen and sheep to sell, and the sailors iron hoops and copper plates that could be fashioned into ornaments and spears. The rate of exchange seemed laughably advantageous to the Dutch, who on one occasion bartered a copper bracelet for a sheep, and on another received 'three oxen and five sheep for a crooked knife, a shovel, a short iron bolt, with a knife and some scraps of iron, worth altogether perhaps four guilders in Holland.' But metal was hard to come by at the Cape, and for their part the Hottentots seemed content that it was they who had the better of the deals.

Neither party really understood the other. The Dutch thought the inhabitants of the Cape primitive and ugly, and their journals contain numerous disparaging comments concerning the near nakedness of the Hottentots and the foul smell of the animal fat they rubbed into their bodies to insulate against the cold. The Africans found the Dutch greedy and violent, and in the early years of the seventeenth century men on both sides died as a result of this mutual mistrust.

Pelsaert's greatest problem was communication. Europeans could not understand a word of the extraordinary language of the bushmen, who talked by clicking their tongues – 'their speech is just as if one heard a number of angry turkeys, little else but clucking and whistling,' one baffled merchant wrote – and when the Hottentots eventually appeared the *commandeur* had to rely on mimicry and mime to make his wishes known. Indeed, everything about the Cape 'savages' seemed alien to the Dutch, and they were utterly repulsed by the Hottentot diet. The locals liked their meat uncooked, and their greatest delicacy, the Dutch observed, was the intestines of an ox, which they 'ate quite raw after shaking out most of the dung.'

It took Pelsaert some time to secure the necessary supplies, and his absences ashore had consequences he could hardly have predicted. While Pelsaert was inland bartering for sheep, Ariaen Jacobsz took a boat and embarked on an illicit pleasure trip around the bay in the company of Zwaantie and his friend Jeronimus Cornelisz. Afterward the little group rowed from ship to ship in the southern dusk, enjoying the hospitality of the other vessels in the fleet until Jacobsz became thoroughly inebriated. The skipper's behaviour deteriorated rapidly, and he began to lash out with his fists and tongue. By the time the *commandeur* returned to the *Batavia,* several complaints had already been lodged against him.

The episode reflected badly on Pelsaert and his flagship and greatly worried the *commandeur.* 'They went ashore without my knowledge when I had gone in search of beasts,' he recorded in his journal, 'until the evening, when they sailed to the *Assendelft* where Ariaen behaved himself very pugnaciously, and at night time went to the ship *Buren,* where he behaved himself worse.' Jacobsz, the *commandeur* concluded, had been 'very beastly with words as well as deeds.'

The skipper's behaviour was a serious problem for Pelsaert. The drunkenness and violence were bad enough, but the fact that Jacobsz had taken a boat without the *commandeur*'s permission was worse. It was clear that the skipper would have to be disciplined if the *commandeur* was not to lose face, and early the next morning Pelsaert called Jacobsz into the Great Cabin and 'chided him over his arrogance and the deeds committed by him, saying that if he did not refrain from his unheard-of behavior, [I] would take a hand; with more other good admonishments.' This dressing-down, like Ariaen's antics with Zwaantie, could not be kept secret for long, and it was soon the talk of the *Batavia.* The skipper had been humiliated, and his old antagonism for Francisco Pelsaert was rekindled.

Jacobsz smouldered while his men slaughtered cattle on the beach and packed the fresh meat into empty barrels. Down below, the carpenters and caulkers finished their repairs and made things ready for the voyage across the Southern Ocean. They were ready to weigh anchor by 22 April, having spent only eight days at the Tavern of the Ocean – less than half the typical duration of a visit to the Cape.

The *Batavia* that sailed from Table Bay was not the ship that had left Amsterdam the previous October. Ten of her men were dead and now she creaked with fatigue and crawled with vermin. She was full of tired and squabbling passengers. But in this the *Batavia* was no different from the majority of East Indiamen that sought shelter at the Cape and could count herself more fortunate than many. What made Pelsaert's flagship unique was not that there was unrest, but the exalted rank of those embroiled in the dispute. So long as the *commandeur* and the skipper of a *retourschip* acted together, rivalries and sexual jealousy among the crew could be dealt with easily enough. But once the two most senior men on board took issue with each other, there was no one to restrain them or their growing enmity.

Up on the quarterdeck, Jeronimus stood with his friend the skipper as Jacobsz nursed his wounded pride. 'By God,' muttered the old sailor, glancing at the other vessels in the fleet, 'if those ships were not lying there, I would treat that miserly dog so that he could not come out of his cabin for fourteen days. And I would quickly make myself master of the ship.'

This was dangerous talk. What the skipper threatened was mutiny, and if Pelsaert had heard what was being said he would have been within his rights to have Jacobsz thrown overboard or shot. But Jeronimus neither demurred nor went to tell the *commandeur*.

The two men stood in silence for a while, and the skipper's words hung in the autumn air as Cornelisz considered them. At length the under-merchant spoke.

'And how would you manage that?' he asked.

CHAPTER 4

Terra Australis Incognita

'I am for the devil.'

ARIAEN JACOBSZ

Slowly, over several days, the bones of a plot emerged. Hunched together at the rail as the *Batavia* ploughed through the rough waters east of the Cape, the skipper and the under-merchant planned a mutiny that would give them control of the ship. They spoke of ways of subduing the majority of the crew, and the necessity of murdering those who would not join them. They lingered in pleasurable debate as to Pelsaert's fate and thought of turning pirate and preying on the commerce of the Indian Ocean. They dreamed of a comfortable retirement in some Spanish port, far beyond the reach of the VOC. Above all, they talked because they needed one another.

It seems to have been Cornelisz who turned the skipper from a mere malcontent into a mutineer. Ariaen Jacobsz was no longer young. Two decades at sea – and several debilitating voyages to the East – had made the skipper tough, but the years had drained him of his vigour. The six-month journey to the Cape had exhausted him. Though it was common for the skippers of East Indiamen to find their supercargoes an irritant, Jacobsz was no longer sure he had the energy to turn his mutinous thoughts into deeds. Much as his hatred of Pelsaert gnawed him, left to himself he would probably have grunted and chafed without ever taking action. Months later, Cornelisz would recall that as they stood together at the stern, he heard his friend repeat a single sentence over and over again: 'If I were younger,' Jacobsz had muttered, 'I would do something else.' But with his friend the under-merchant beside him, Ariaen felt emboldened. The very fact that Jeronimus could stand with him on the quarterdeck, coolly discussing the prospect of violence, was a spur in itself.

In his journal, Pelsaert eventually came to realise this. 'Jeronimus Cornelissen,' he mused,

> 'having made himself a great friend and highly familiar with the skipper, moulded their similar intelligence and feelings into one, the skipper being innate with prideful conceit and Ambition, so that he could not endure the authority of any over him. Moreover, he was mocking and contemptuous of all people. Further, he was inexperienced or inept in getting on with people, in so far as it did not concern sea-faring. But Jeronimus, on the contrary, was well-spoken and usually knew how to polish the Truth of his lying words; he was far more sly and skilled in getting on with people … So that Jeronimus was the tongue of the skipper and served as pedagogue to insinuate into him what he should answer if I wanted to speak to or admonish him.'

As for Cornelisz, he cared little what befell Francisco Pelsaert. He encouraged the skipper's fantasies simply because he knew he could not seize the *Batavia* by himself. To do that he would need sailors, whose loyalty he did not command, and the ability to navigate, which only Ariaen and his steersmen possessed. Granted the men and the skills he needed, however, Jeronimus scented a prize greater than mere revenge. As he well knew, the lumbering *Batavia* contained riches greater than any he could dream of earning in the East.

Cornelisz had motives of his own for mutiny. As the owner of a failed business, with an abandoned wife and a dead child, he had no particular desire to see the United Provinces again. As a near-bankrupt seeking his fortune in the Indies, he was engaged in an enterprise that left him not much more than a 50/50 chance of coming back alive even if he was successful. And as a VOC officer with ready access to the Great Cabin in the stern, he had seen the dozen chests of money there and knew they contained a fortune that would allow anyone who seized it to spend what was left of his life in consummate luxury. Furthermore, as someone of decidedly heretical beliefs, the under-merchant simply did not experience the pangs of guilt and conscience that a pious Dutchman might have felt in plotting rebellion and murder.

In this, as in so much else, Jeronimus Cornelisz was unique; it was unheard-of for an officer of the VOC to mutiny. Skippers, too, were generally loyal. But Jeronimus and Ariaen began to look for confederates among the crew confident they would find men enough to follow them. The soldiers and sailors of the Dutch East India Company were always ready to revolt.

Harsh treatment, poor wages, and the terrible conditions on the voyage to Java frequently combined to produce outbreaks of trouble on board VOC ships, although the unrest generally fell well short of the sort of bloody uprising Cornelisz and Jacobsz had begun to contemplate. Most mutinies were little more than shipboard protests, which flared up rapidly and were over quickly. They were led by ordinary seamen – the ringleaders were almost always foreigners, not Dutchmen – and usually took the form of a complaint against conditions on board, or concerns about the seaworthiness of a tired old ship. They rarely involved much violence and might more accurately be described as a form of strike.* Such mutinies were generally settled by concessions – perhaps by increasing rations or an agreement to restrain excesses in discipline. Once the officers had recovered control of the ship, it was normal to treat the majority of the rebels relatively leniently. One or two ringleaders would almost certainly be executed, if they could be identified, but most of those involved could at least hope to escape with their lives.

Full-fledged mutinies, led by a relatively small group of men who had actively conspired to take over a ship, were extremely rare. They required careful planning, access to weapons – which were generally kept under lock and key in the ship's armoury in the stern – and the cooperation (whether it was given willingly or not) of an officer who knew how to sail the ship. Even if all these conditions were met, such rebellions were highly risky and invariably entailed serious consequences for those concerned. Either the mutiny would be put down, in which case anyone actively involved would be condemned to death, or it would succeed. In the latter case, the mutineers almost always felt compelled to murder most of the officers and many of the men. They knew these actions could never be forgiven and that the agents of Jan Company would pursue them for the rest of their lives.

*Indeed the word *strike* itself has nautical origins; it refers to the striking of a vessel's sails, which was usually the first thing rebellious sailors did to assert their control over the ship.

Jacobsz and Cornelisz must have realised this, but they also knew that such things did occur. Half a dozen major mutinies had broken out in the fleets of the VOC between 1602 and 1628, most recently in 1621 on a ship called the *Witte Beer** and most seriously in 1615 on board the *Meeuwtje* and the *Grote Maen*.† The latter ships were part of a fleet sent to explore a westward route to the Indies via Cape Horn. While they were still in the Atlantic, 14 men on the *Meeuwtje,* led by a sailor and a carpenter, conspired to seize the ship, but word of the plot reached the ears of the officers, and the two ringleaders were hung. The other dozen men were spared because they had expressed remorse, and rather than being punished they were simply dispersed among the other vessels of the fleet. Three months later there was a second mutiny on board the *Meeuwtje*. The ringleaders of this affair were pitched overboard and left to drown, but again the bulk of the mutineers were spared. This leniency on the part of the vessel's upper-merchant proved to be a serious mistake. Soon a storm sprang up and the *Meeuwtje* disappeared. In time the VOC established that a third mutiny had occurred. This one had been successful. The ship had been sailed to La Rochelle and handed over to the French; only one of the mutineers, a man who made the mistake of venturing back onto Dutch soil, was ever caught and punished.

The example of the *Meeuwtje* may have suggested to Jacobsz and Cornelisz that it was possible to seize an East Indiaman and escape unscathed. But the skipper and the under-merchant must also have realised that the lessons of the mutinies had been well learned by their masters in the Netherlands. Leniency was no longer tolerated. Henceforth all captured mutineers would be put to death immediately, or punished so severely that they wished for it.

Discipline on board a *retourschip* was brutal at the best of times. The frugal Dutch might punish minor crimes such as blasphemy and drunkenness with a system of fines, but physical violence, or the threat of it, earned violent retribution. At the slightest hint of insolence to an officer, a malefactor could be manacled hand and foot and thrown into 'hell' – a tiny cell in the forepart of the gun deck where the wind whistled maddeningly through the slats. This prison was so small that it was impossible either to stand or to lie down, but men could be left to rot there for weeks at a time. Fighting with knives, a common activity that the Dutch called

White Bear.
†The *Little Seagull* and the *Great Moon*.

snicker-snee, was an even worse offence. Article XCI of the VOC regulations was explicit on this point. 'Anyone pulling a knife in anger,' it ordained, 'shall be nailed to the mast with a knife through his hand, and shall remain standing until he pulls his hand off.' In practice this meant that the condemned man was led to the mast with his weaker hand strapped behind his back. His working hand was then impaled to the mast, and the victim had to choose between tearing it in half by pulling sharply downward, or easing the hand slowly and agonisingly from side to side until the wound was so big it was possible to pass the haft of the knife right through it. Whichever method he chose, he would likely never work at sea again.

In these circumstances, it is not surprising that after 1615 the most common sentence for a rank-and-file mutineer was 200 lashes, enough to reduce a man's back to pulp, kill many who endured it, and scar the rest for life. In Dutch service, mutineers were doused with seawater before their lashes were inflicted. This refinement ensured that salt was driven into the wounds, which acted as a crude antiseptic but redoubled the agony of the punishment. More serious cases were dealt with by dropping the mutineer from the yardarm or keelhauling him.

The former sentence involved pinioning a man's hands behind his back and tying a long, stout rope around his wrists. Lead weights were secured to his feet and he was then dropped 40 or 50 feet toward the sea, falling until the rope went taut. The sudden deceleration inevitably dislocated the mutineer's shoulders, and his wrists and arms were often shattered, too. The man was then twice hauled back up to be dropped again, a punishment that in his broken state was even more painful than the fall itself. Having been dropped three times, the mutineer would then usually be lashed as well.

Keelhauling, which was a Dutch invention, was generally regarded as an even more severe punishment. Sentence was carried out by tying a man's arms together above his head and binding his legs. He was given a sponge to bite down on, and a long rope was then passed under the keel of the moving ship and the ends secured to the sailor's limbs so he could be pulled from one side of the vessel to the other. When the idea was first conceived, keelhauling almost always resulted in the death of the condemned man, who would either be cut to pieces by the barnacles covering the bottom of the ship or decapitated as he smashed into the hull.

The ingenious Dutch found a solution to this problem, and soon each VOC ship was supplied with a special full-body harness, made of lead and leather, into which a man could be strapped. The harness was equipped with a flag on a long pole. By adjusting the length of the ropes until the flag was a certain height above the water, it was possible to ensure that the mutineer was dragged under the keel rather than across it, and the lead harness protected him from any incidental contact. Keelhauling, too, was generally repeated three times before the punishment was completed. Nevertheless, in an era in which only one man in seven could swim, it was such a terrifying ordeal that the full sentence was often not completed for fear that the victim would drown.

Soldiers and sailors desperate enough to risk such punishments would hardly baulk at killing the officers who would inflict them, and the men whom Cornelisz and Jacobsz recruited to their plot were undoubtedly a rough lot. Significantly, however, they also included a number of senior officers and experienced soldiers and sailors of the sort required to run the *Batavia* successfully.

A good deal of care would still have been required. Rumours travelled swiftly below decks, and the slightest word to the upper-merchant might have proved fatal. But on a *retourschip* crewed by the dregs of the Amsterdam waterfront they were always malcontents and, between them, the skipper and the under-merchant knew of several men who could be tempted by the lure of easy money and spurred by hatred for the VOC. The first man Ariaen approached appears to have been the bos'n's mate, who was a cousin of the skipper and presumably a man in whom Jacobsz had full confidence. The most important addition to the ranks of the mutineers, however, was unquestionably the bos'n himself.

Jan Evertsz, the *Batavia*'s high boatswain and thus the most senior officer – after Jacobsz and the three steersmen – on the ship, came from Monnickendam, a small fishing port on the coast north of Amsterdam with a reputation for producing a particularly brutal sort of sailor.* He was probably still in his twenties, and it was his job to implement the orders of the skipper, with whom he necessarily had a close relationship. Like other high boatswains, Evertsz most likely stood watches while at sea and would have been on his way to becoming a skipper himself. 'As the master is to

---

*So freely did the townsmen engage in vicious tavern brawls that in seventeenth-century Holland the act of smashing a glass of beer over an opponent's head was known as a 'Monnickendam Kiss.'

be abaft the mast,' one contemporary authority explained, 'so the boatswain, and all the common sailors, are to be afore the mast … The boatswain is to see the shrouds and other ropes set taut, the deep sea line and plummet [lead] in readiness against their coming into soundings. In a fight he must see the flag and pendants put forth, and call up every man to his labour and his office. And to conclude, his and his mate's work is never at an end, for it is impossible to repeat all the offices that are put upon them.'

The high boatswain's tasks thus required him to be a first-rate seaman. With few exceptions, boatswains were men of long experience who had been promoted from the ranks, and their rough manners and coarse humour made them uncomfortable companions for the passengers in the stern. As the man charged with keeping order among the crew, Evertsz must have been brutal and decisive. As the man in day-to-day command of the ship's 180 sailors, he was also well placed to pick out trouble makers. He was the ideal recruit to the mutineers' cause.

It seems to have been the skipper who sounded out Evertsz, and Evertsz who found other mutineers to join them. Among their number were Allert Janssen, of Assendelft – a companion of Jacobsz's who had already killed one man in the Dutch Republic – and Ryckert Woutersz, a loudmouthed gunner from Harlingen. Sensibly, the skipper and the high boatswain kept the names of these recruits to themselves, and even the other mutineers did not know exactly who was implicated in the plot. It is thus difficult to ascertain how many sailors were involved. There may have been as few as half a dozen of them at first.

One of the most unusual features of the plot on Pelsaert's ship was the way in which its tentacles extended into every part of the vessel. Most mutinies were the work of a small, tight-knit group of sailors, but the rebellion planned on the *Batavia* encompassed merchants, cadets, and soldiers, too. It is possible to discern the devious hand of the under-merchant in this unprecedented development. Jeronimus was an articulate man possessed of great powers of persuasion. Those he so charmed came in the end to see him as a 'seducer of men,' and he would certainly have had a good deal of influence among the VOC assistants on the ship. Given the traditional antipathy between the soldiers and the sailors of Jan Company, it was possibly his job to sound out the men down on the orlop, too.

Coenraat van Huyssen, the army cadet from Gelderland, may

have been Cornelisz's chosen instrument. Impetuous, hotheaded, with a lust for violence, Van Huyssen and his compatriot Gÿsbert van Welderen were in the vanguard of the mutineers' party from the beginning. The young *jonkers** soon took to sleeping with their weapons in their hammocks, and Van Huyssen boasted to the others that he would be 'amongst the first who jumped with a sword into the Cabin, in order to throw the *commandeur* overboard.' Perhaps through him, the mutineers soon made the acquaintance of 'Stone-Cutter' Pietersz, the lance corporal from Amsterdam whose influence over the troops on board was roughly equivalent to the sway that Evertsz held over the sailors. Like the high boatswain, Pietersz was an important addition to the ranks of the mutineers. His role was probably to suggest the names of soldiers he could trust and to identify those whose loyalty to the Company was such that they would have to be disposed of when the mutiny was done.

Between them, the under-merchant, the high boatswain, and the corporal formed a uniquely dangerous triumvirate. With the skipper at their side, their influence extended to every corner of the ship, and the power they wielded was such that – even had word of the mutiny got out – the bravest man on board would have hesitated to denounce them to the *commandeur*. Together, they had every prospect of success.

To seize the ship, the *Batavia*'s rebels first had to separate their vessel from her consorts, and thus from all possibility of aid. This was the principal lesson of the repeated mutinies on board the *Meeuwtje,* which had only finally succeeded when the ship had become detached from her fleet. In the *Batavia*'s case it was easily accomplished; soon after the convoy left Table Bay, Jacobsz took advantage of the variable winds south of the Cape to drift slowly away from the other ships in the convoy. It was all too common, in the days when the VOC sent ships of wildly differing quality to the East, for the vessels of a fleet to become detached from one another in this way, and even though the *Batavia* had kept company with the little warship *Buren,* the old *Dordrecht,* the *Assendelft,* and *Sardam* all the way from Holland, no one seems to have suspected anything was wrong.

Next, and far more problematically, the under-merchant and the skipper had to recruit a large enough body of men to enable

*A member of the Dutch nobility.

them to take control of the *Batavia*. On the *Meeuwtje,* which was a smaller vessel, a core of 13 rebellious sailors had been identified, but, given the eventual disappearance of the vessel, others must have remained undetected. On other East Indiamen, groups of up to 60 malcontents conspired to seize their ships. In their first month back at sea, Jacobsz and Cornelisz persuaded somewhere between 8 and 18 men to join them. Ranged against 300 neutrals and company loyalists, this was nowhere near enough to guarantee success. Further action was required.

❀

While the skipper and the under-merchant pondered what to do, and the *Batavia* nosed her way southward into the freezing waters of the Southern Ocean, Pelsaert himself offered an apparent solution to their problem. A day or two after they had sailed from the Cape, the *commandeur* fell dangerously ill.

The nature of Francisco Pelsaert's malady is nowhere specified, but it kept him in his bunk for weeks and came so close to killing him that his recovery was not expected. His illness appears to have been a fever of some sort, possibly malaria contracted during his time in India. Had the upper-merchant succumbed, Cornelisz and Jacobsz could have taken control of the ship by right, without the need for mutiny. So – unknown to all but a handful of the passengers and crew – throughout late April and early May 1629 the fate of the ship lay in the hands of one of the most important of all the members of the *Batavia*'s crew. He was named Frans Jansz and he came from the old North Quarter port of Hoorn.

Jansz was the *Batavia*'s surgeon. His practice was conducted from the tiny dispensary on the gun deck, which was scarcely more than five feet square, and his only tools were a set of surgeon's saws, a small apothecary's chest, and – because all seventeenth-century surgeons doubled as barbers – a handful of razors and some bowls. With these scant resources, and the assistance of an under-barber, Aris Jansz, he was responsible for the health of all 320 people on the ship.

Of all the officers on board *Batavia*, Frans Jansz was probably the most popular among the passengers and crew. In the course of a typical journey from the Netherlands to Java, almost 1 in 10 of a *retourschip*'s crew would die, and a much larger number would fall ill and require treatment. If the proportion of the sick and the dead exceeded certain ratios, the ship would become unmanageable and might be lost together with her crew. Jansz, then, was the chief hope not only of Francisco Pelsaert, but of all those on the *Batavia* who wished to reach the Indies without undue drama.

It is not possible to say whether or not the *Batavia*'s surgeon was worthy of the trust that the ship's crew placed in him, but the likelihood is that he was not. The Gentlemen XVII always experienced great difficulty in attracting competent medical men. The dangers of the journey east were such that no successful physicians or apothecaries could possibly be induced to go to Java. Even reputable barber-surgeons were hard to come by. Unlike merchants, surgeons had relatively few opportunities to profit in the East, and since they endured similar risks, the standard of those who could be lured to serve at sea was often very low.

On a good many East Indiamen, indeed, the problem of obtaining decent treatment was exacerbated by the dangers of the job. Shut up in their dispensaries below decks and constantly exposed to sick and dying men, the mortality rate among sea surgeons was far higher than it was among surgeons on land. Though most *retourschepen* did carry at least two barbers, it was far from uncommon for both men to expire in the course of a voyage, and if that happened, an untutored sailor would be pressed into service as a make-do surgeon. Men who found themselves in such a situation had no idea how to bleed a patient or amputate a shattered limb. They were simply expected to get on with it.

On ships such as the *Batavia* where the barbers did survive, the quality of care could occasionally be good. Seventeenth-century surgeons had one inestimable advantage over the physicians and the apothecaries who were their nominal superiors: they were practical men, and learned their trade from experience.* Freed from reliance on the false principles of the physicians, surgeons were generally effective in setting broken bones and treating the normal run of shipboard injuries. Some were undeniably conscientious men, who did all they could for the sailors in their care, and a few had passed special 'Sea Exams' that qualified them to deal with the full range of shipboard injuries – 'fractures, dislocations, shot-wounds, concussions, burns, gangrenes, etc.'

*At this time the Dutch surgeon's guild possessed the right to dissect one executed criminal annually for the instruction of its members, so that—as its charter put it—'they would not cut veins instead of nerves, or nerves instead of veins, and would not work as the blind work in wood.'

Jan Loxe, a sea surgeon who sailed later in the seventeenth century, left notes that indicate the unpleasant nature and likely extent of Jansz's work. 'First thing in the morning,' he wrote in his journal,

'we must prepare the medicines that have to be taken internally and give each patient his dose. Next, we must scarify, clean and dress the filthy, stinking wounds, and bandage them and the ulcerations. Then we must bandage the stiff and benumbed limbs of the scorbutic patients. At midday we must fetch and dish out the food for sometimes 40, 50, or even 60 people, and the same again in the evening; and what is more, we are kept up half the night as well in attending to patients who suffer a relapse, and so forth.'

Stamina, then, was one requirement for a surgeon. Another was great strength – enough to hold down a conscious, screaming man while amputating a shattered limb without the benefit of anaesthetic. But Jansz, and sea surgeons like him, were also required to have a working knowledge of Cornelisz's art, and it was to the apothecary's chest, packed by the Gentlemen XVII's own pharmacist in Amsterdam, that Frans Jansz would have turned in order to treat Pelsaert.

A typical sea surgeon's apothecary's chest opened to reveal three drawers, each minutely subdivided into small rectangular compartments and packed with the products of the contemporary pharmacy: approximately 200 different preparations in all. In treating Pelsaert, Jansz may well have turned to theriac, which was often administered to patients suffering from malaria two hours before a paroxysm was anticipated in order to strengthen them for the coming ordeal. Mithridatium – a 2,000-year-old antidote, originally from Persia, which was supposed to neutralise venom and cure almost any disease – was another well-known treatment. Elsewhere in the chest other drawers contained 'Egyptian ointment,' a sterilising balm made from alum, copper, and mercury; the sovereign remedy of mummy; and a variety of oils and syrups fortified with fruits and spices, as well as cinnamon water, camphor, aloes, myrrh, and extract of rhubarb.* As a contemporary English book, *The Surgeon's Mate,* explained, the

---

*Strong taste was frequently thought to be a guarantee of potency at this time.

provision of so many medicines was hardly excessive, 'for although there may seeme many particulars, yet there wanteth at the least forty more.'

For 20 long days, the surgeon dosed and purged the *commandeur*, trying a variety of treatments in an attempt to cure his illness. And as the *Batavia* surged onward through the boiling waters of the Roaring Forties at the bottom of the world, the upper-merchant's fever slowly ebbed away. Whether his recovery was attributable to Jansz's ministrations or, more likely, to a robust constitution, it is impossible to say. Whatever the reason, three weeks after he had taken to his bunk, and to the consternation of the mutineers, Francisco Pelsaert reappeared on deck.

❉

Ariaen Jacobsz had been enjoying himself in the upper-merchant's absence. For almost a month he had been the undisputed master of the ship, and his self-confidence had increased proportionately. He had faced down those who sneered at his dalliance with the servant Zwaantie Hendricx, and publicly acknowledged the girl as his companion. Indeed, so enamoured was he of her blowsy favours that he vowed (as Pelsaert later heard) 'without taking any thought of his honour or the reputation of his office, that if anyone made even a sour face to the foresaid Zwaantie, he would not leave it unrevenged.'

Jacobsz made a powerful protector, and it is not surprising Zwaantie 'readily accepted the caresses of the skipper with great willingness and refused him nothing, whatsoever he desired.' Nevertheless, Ariaen remained either unable or unwilling to commit himself fully to her; south of the Cape, when their frequent couplings led Hendricx to suspect she had conceived, the skipper shied away and asked her to spend an evening with his friend Allert Janssen. He got the pair of them drunk and left Zwaantie alone with Janssen, 'who has done his will with her, because [Jacobsz] thought that she was pregnant and that she should wed Allert.'

The serving girl seems not to have minded this, and the skipper soon missed having her in his bed when it transpired the pregnancy was a false alarm. Within days they were together once again. But something must have changed in their relationship, for Ariaen now took to making dangerous promises to Zwaantie. Convinced

Pelsaert was as good as dead, the records of the voyage relate, 'he took from her the name and yoke of servant, and promised that she should see the destruction of her Mistress and others, and that he wanted to make her a great Lady.' Pelsaert's recovery was thus a setback for the skipper and for Zwaantie. In consequence, Jacobsz resigned himself to action, shrugging: 'I am still for the Devil; if I go to the Indies then I have come to shame in any case.'

It was now 13 May, and so confident had Jeronimus been that the *commandeur* would die that for the best part of a month he and Ariaen had not bothered to seek out further mutineers among the crew. Pelsaert's unexpected recovery forced a rapid reassessment of their plans. If they were to be successful now, Cornelisz and Jacobsz needed to more than double the number of men they could rely on when the moment came to mutiny. Apparently, the two malcontents had already approached their own most trusted acquaintances, and those of Jan Evertsz and Jacop Pietersz, too. To sound out others, in whom they had less confidence, would be to take a considerable risk. A better way of proceeding, they now decided, would be to rouse the whole crew against the *commandeur*.

They selected as their instrument the unattainable Lucretia Jans. She was, they knew, as desired by Pelsaert as she had been by the skipper. By arranging for her to be attacked by masked members of the crew, they expected to provoke the upper-merchant into punitive retaliation; and by concealing the identity of her assailants, they hoped that any measures that were taken would be manifestly unfair to the majority of the men on board. Thus, they thought, a larger number of the crew could be persuaded to support their mutiny.

'The skipper and Jeronimus,' Pelsaert later recorded in his journal,

'in the presence and with the knowledge of Zwaantie, decided after long debates and discourses, what dishonour they could do the foresaid Lady, which would be most shameful to her and would be supposed the worst by the *commandeur*. In order therefore that confusion might be sought through her and through the punishment of those who took a hand in it, Jeronimus proposed that she should be given a cut over both cheeks with a knife, which could be done by one person, and few would perceive that they had been the instigators of it. The skipper was of another mind, that it would be better that many should have a hand in it,

then the *commandeur* could not punish the many, or there would
be a big outcry, and if the *commandeur* should let it go unnoticed,
then there was time enough to give her cuts on the cheeks.'

This strange plot, which is unique in all the annals of the sea, was
hurriedly conceived within a day of Pelsaert's emergence from his
cabin. It must have owed a good deal to Jacobsz's desire to
revenge himself upon the woman who had spurned him off the
coast of Africa. The skipper's hand, and Zwaantie's too, can certainly be discerned in the selection of Jan Evertsz as the man to
assault Creesje, and also in the bizarre and humiliating way in
which the high boatswain carried out his task.

The plotters decided to seize Lucretia as she left the merchant's
table to return to her own cabin on the evening of 14 May. It
would be pitch-dark by then, and many of the crew would already
be asleep. Swiftly, Evertsz set about recruiting men willing to take
part in the assault. Some, and perhaps all, of the group that he
approached were established mutineers. There were eight of them
in all, including Allert Janssen and Ryckert Woutersz, all lounging
on the *Batavia*'s foredeck in the early afternoon. The most senior
was the quartermaster, Harman Nannings. The youngest was
Cornelis Janssen, the 18-year-old Haarlem sailor known to all as
'Bean'; though still little more than a boy, his 'innate and
incankered corruptness' made it natural for Evertsz to think of
him. All but one of the others were gunners, and thus probably
friends of Woutersz and Allert Janssen. 'Men,' Evertsz told them,
'there is an assault on our hands. Will you help to give the prince a
pleasant outing?'*

There was a good deal of enthusiasm for the 'trick' that was to
be played on Creesje. Only one member of the group, an Alkmaar
man named Cornelis Dircxsz, declined to have anything to do with
the idea, and he did nothing to prevent the attack. Plainly, Evertsz
felt sure that none of his sailors would dare betray him. His
confidence was not misplaced.

With the high boatswain at their head they were eight strong,
and much more than a match for one young woman taken by surprise. It was already late when Creesje left the Great Cabin after
dinner. She stood silhouetted for a moment against the lanterns
that swayed back and forth over the table, and they could see that

---

*A contemporary Dutch phrase meaning 'to have a right royal time.'

it was her as the door swung shut. There was a momentary rustle in the darkness; she gasped and started, then she was being forced onto the deck. Hostile eyes glinted from behind cloaks drawn tightly over faces. As she sprawled on her back, uncomprehending, helpless, they seized her by the legs and dragged her across the deck into an unfrequented corner of the gallery. She felt her skirts lifted, and rough hands groping underneath. Other fingers spread a sticky, stinking mess across her face. There were no cuts; she did not scream; the assault lasted only seconds and then she was alone and huddled, shaking, against the rail. Her dress was filthy, and her face and legs and genitals had been thickly smeared with tar and dung.

Word of the attack on Creesje Jans spread rapidly throughout the ship. It was by far the most sensational event that had occurred since their stranding on the Walcheren Banks and must have been the principal topic of conversation on board for many days. The *commandeur* himself, as Jacobsz and Cornelisz had anticipated, took the news 'very violently and to the highest degree.' Pelsaert was no policeman, but he investigated the assault as thoroughly as he was able, and Evertsz was soon back at work, spreading rumors:

> 'This had been the true aim which they thought to have brought off: to let it be spread by the High Boatswain that the people would be punished or brought to grief for the sake of Women or Whores, which the skipper would never permit to happen, so long as he lived.'

Yet to the chagrin of the conspirators, Pelsaert actually took no action that might render him disagreeable to the crew.

The upper-merchant's restraint can only have one explanation. It was quickly evident that while Creesje herself had no idea who the majority of her assailants might have been, she had recognised Jan Evertsz, and unsupported though her testimony was, Pelsaert could have had the high boatswain arrested and punished on this evidence alone. He failed to do so, partly because he was still ill, but also because he had at last begun to glimpse the nature of the forces ranged against him. The merchant 'especially suspected,' the *Batavia*'s journal observed, 'from many Circumstances of which he had become aware during his illness, that the skipper had been the Author of it.' If so, he no doubt also recognised the risk he himself might run by ordering the arrest of both Evertsz and Ariaen Jacobsz – two of his highest-ranking sailors.

The skipper remained sanguine, unaware that he himself was now suspected. He was certain that the *commandeur* was merely biding his time. Once the *Batavia* neared Java – and the support of the Dutch authorities there – Pelsaert would surely act, arresting suspects and clapping them in chains. This development could still be the signal for a mutiny.

By now, the plot was fairly well developed. Led by Jacobsz, a small group of dependable men would rise up in the small hours of the morning, when the great majority of those on board were asleep. They would batter their way into the *commandeur*'s cabin, seize Pelsaert and toss him into the sea, while the main body of mutineers broke out their concealed weapons and nailed down the hatches to the orlop deck to prevent the soldiers intervening. Once it became clear that the rebels had control of the *Batavia,* fear and greed would make it a simple matter to recruit the 120 or so sailors and gunners needed to run the ship. In the absence of any spare boats, or a convenient island on which to maroon them, the rest of those on board – 200 or so loyal officers, useless passengers, and unwanted men – would have to follow the *commandeur* over the side.

The remainder of the plot was equally straightforward. With a powerful new ship at their disposal, the mutineers would turn to piracy. Putting in to Mauritius or Madagascar for supplies, they would prey on the rich commerce of the Indian Ocean for a year or two, until they had accumulated sufficient loot to make every man on board wealthy. When that had been achieved, they would settle down to enjoy their money well out of the reach of the VOC.

So the skipper and the under-merchant sat back and waited for Pelsaert's reprisals. The *commandeur* would act, Ariaen predicted, when *Batavia* sighted the Australian coast.

For the men of the *retourschip,* the great red continent was little more than a void on the charts they carried. 'Terra Australis Incognita,' they called it: 'the unknown South-Land.' Even in 1629, its very existence was based more on supposition than on fact. Early geographers, such as the Greco-Egyptian Ptolemy, writing in A.D. 140, had imagined a world divided into four gigantic continents. Europe, and what was known of Africa and Asia, was believed to occupy the northeast portion of the globe. This massive land mass seemed to require a counterbalance. From the earliest days, therefore, world maps showed a giant continent south of the equator, girdling the Earth and in many cases joining South America and Africa to China.

As the Portuguese and Spaniards pressed southward in the fifteenth and sixteenth centuries, it gradually became apparent that the South-Land could not be as big as had been supposed. Ships rounded the Cape of Good Hope and Cape Horn without sighting it and sailed northwest across the Pacific and east through the Indian Ocean without finding any trace of the mysterious continent. By the time the VOC was founded, almost the only place left to look was the great blank that still lay south of the Indies and west of the Americas.

Contemporary globes and maps continued to indicate the presence of Terra Australis in this area. Over the years, elements of fantasy had crept into descriptions of the South-Land, and in the sixteenth century faulty interpretation of the works of Marco Polo led to the addition of three imaginary provinces to maps of the southern continent. The most important of the three was Beach, which appeared on many charts with the alluring label *provincia aurifera,* 'gold-bearing land'; sailors often referred to the whole South-Land by this name. The other imaginary provinces were Maletur (*scatens aromatibus,* a region overflowing with spices) and Lucach, which was said as late as 1601 to have received an embassy from Java. The existence of these provinces was an article of faith for most Europeans; in 1545 the Spaniards had actually appointed a governor of the nonexistent Beach – a certain Pedro Sancho de la Hoz, who was one of the conquistadors of Chile. Even the more pragmatic Dutch did not entirely disbelieve, for their ships had occasionally stumbled unexpectedly across a coast that they believed must be part of Terra Australis.

In the first years of the VOC, the Company's sailors had largely kept to the sea lanes established by the Portuguese. From the Cape of Good Hope, these ran north along the African coast to Madagascar, and then northeast across the Indian Ocean to the Indies. There were, however, significant problems with this route. The heat was frequently unbearable, the Portuguese unfriendly, and there were numerous shoals and shallows to negotiate along the way. Furthermore, once north of the Cape, contrary winds and currents made the voyage extremely slow; journeys of up to 16 months were not uncommon. Frequent cyclones also occurred, which caused the loss of many ships. The Dutch persisted with the Portuguese route, unsatisfactory as it clearly was, only because they knew of no alternative.

Then, in 1610, a senior VOC official named Henrik Brouwer discovered an alternate passage far to the south of the established sea lanes. Heading south rather than north from the Cape of Good Hope until he reached the northern limits of the Roaring Forties, he found a belt of strong, consistent westerlies that hurried his ships toward the Indies. When Brouwer estimated that he had reached the longitude of the Sunda Strait, which divides Java and Sumatra, he had his ships turn north and reached the port of Bantam only five months and 24 days after leaving the United Provinces. He had cut about 2,000 miles from the journey, out-flanked the Portuguese, more than halved the time taken to com-plete the outward voyage, and arrived in Java with a healthy crew to boot.

The Gentlemen XVII were suitably impressed. Faster voyages meant increased profits, and from 1616 all Dutch ships were enjoined to follow the 'fairway' Brouwer had discovered. So long as the VOC's skippers kept an accurate reckoning of their position, it was undoubtedly a far superior route. But the strong winds and fast currents of the Southern Ocean made it all too easy to under-estimate how far east a ship had sailed. When this occurred, the vessel would miss the turn to the north and find herself sailing dangerously close to the barren coast of Western Australia.

There were several near disasters. In 1616 the East Indiaman *Eendracht** unexpectedly encountered the South-Land after an unusually fast passage from the Cape, and sailed north along the coast for a few hundred miles. The charts her officers drew were incorporated into the VOC's rutters, which henceforth indicated the existence of a small portion of the Australian shore, called Eendrachtsland; but it was by no means certain at the time whether this new coast was the South-Land or some smaller island. In any case, communication with Europe was so slow that news of the discovery took a long time to reach the ears of many skippers and when, two years later, another ship – the *Zeewolf*† – chanced on what was almost certainly the North West Cape, her skipper

* *Concord.*
† *Seawolf.*

was considerably alarmed 'as we have never heard of this discovery, and the chart shows nothing but open ocean at this place.'

The *Eendracht* and the *Zeewolf* were fortunate to come on the coast in daylight and light weather. A clumsy, square-rigged East Indiaman encountering land by night or with a strong wind at her back could easily find herself ashore long before she could turn away. Only a few months before the *Batavia* arrived in Australian waters, another Dutch ship, *Vianen*,* had actually run aground on a sandbank off the northwest coast, and her skipper had to jettison a valuable cargo of copper and pepper to float her off.

In such circumstances, it was perhaps inevitable that a ship would come to grief somewhere on the Australian coast sooner rather than later. In the event, the English East India Company – which in 1621 ordered its ships to follow the new Dutch route without really understanding its dangers or having access to even the fragmentary charts that the VOC possessed – was the first to lose a vessel. The ship in question was the East Indiaman *Tryall*, which sailed from Plymouth under the command of one John Brookes and struck an undiscovered shoal somewhere off the North West Cape shortly before midnight on 25 May 1623.

It might almost have been a dress rehearsal for the loss of the *Batavia*. As the *Tryall* filled with water, Brookes took the sounding lead and found less than 20 feet of water under the stern. Realising that his ship could not be saved, he spent the next two hours loading as many of his employer's 'spangles' as he could into a skiff. At four in the morning, 'like a Judas running,' in the words of his own first mate, Thomas Bright, the captain of the *Tryall* 'lowered himself privately into the boat with only nine men and his boy, and stood for the Straits of Sunda that instant without care.' He was only just in time to save himself. Half an hour later, the ship broke up under the pounding of the surf, and although Bright managed to launch the longboat and save another 36 members of the crew, almost a hundred sailors were left to drown.

Brookes and Bright separately succeeded in reaching Java, where the first mate wrote a disgusted letter accusing his captain of stealing Company property and abandoning his men. For his part, Brookes composed a comprehensively mendacious report, claiming to have followed the established Dutch route to the Indies when he had in fact been sailing several hundred miles to the east

*She was named after a lordship in the southern part of the United Provinces.

of the accepted sea lanes. His error not only led directly to the loss of his ship; it also provided an early warning of the unknown dangers of the South-Land coast that Jan Company would have done well to heed.

The extreme difficulty that both the VOC and the English East India Company had in determining the position of their ships had its root in the most intractable navigational problem of the day: the impossibility of finding longitude at sea. Latitude, the measure of a ship's distance from the equator, can easily be determined by measuring the angle that the sun makes with the horizon at its zenith. Calculating longitude is much more difficult. The prime meridian is a purely artificial creation in any case – in the 1620s the Dutch measured longitude west and east from the tallest peak on Tenerife – but, wherever it is said to lie, the sun passes directly overhead once each 24 hours on its way to lighting the whole 360 degrees of the globe in the course of a single day. In one hour, therefore, it traverses 15 degrees of longitude, and it follows that a ship's position can be determined by comparing the time in a known location (such as a home port) with the local time at sea. This feat became possible only with the invention of dependable chronometers in the second half of the eighteenth century. In 1629, Ariaen Jacobsz and his men tracked the passage of time with hourglasses, which were not remotely accurate enough for navigation.

Unable to determine their longitude precisely, Dutch sailors resorted to dead reckoning. They calculated their position from the colour of the water, the appearance of seaweed, and birds circling overhead. Far out to sea, the only way of plotting progress on a chart was to estimate the distance run since the last landfall. The Dutch did this with a ship's log – which in the seventeenth century meant tossing what was literally a chip of wood into the sea from the bows and timing it as it bobbed between two notches on the gunwale. From this they calculated their speed, and thus their approximate position.

The log was hardly a precision tool; the only way to time its progress along the side was to use a 30-second hourglass or a human pulse, and in any case it could not indicate the prevailing currents. Plotting a ship's position correctly was thus all but impossible. Errors of 500 miles or more were commonplace, and it is in retrospect surprising that Dutch navigators did not find themselves cast up on the Australian coast more often than they did.

As they neared the end of their long journey, then, Jacobsz and his steersmen were trusting in dead reckoning and intuition to keep the *Batavia* clear of the South-Land's shores. The charts available on the ship were of at best limited use to them; the most up-to-date available, drawn in the summer of 1628, showed only broken fragments of the coast and the scattering of islands that the Dutch had occasionally encountered up to 60 miles off shore. Probably the skipper hardly bothered to consult them; in the early days of June he still believed he would not sight Terra Australis for another week or so.

In fact, a deadly obstacle now lay in the *Batavia*'s path. In 1619 the upper-merchant Frederick de Houtman – the brother of the man who had led the *Eerste Schipvaart* east in 1595 – had stumbled on and lent his name to Houtman's Abrolhos, the low-lying chain of reefs and islands that formed the principal obstacle to Dutch ships heading north along the Australian coast. He had been sailing from the Cape to Java in the East Indiaman *Dordrecht* (the same ship, groaning with age, was now a part of Pelsaert's fleet) when he unexpectedly 'came upon the south-land Beach' only six weeks out of Table Bay. Veering west and out to sea, the *Dordrecht* sailed north for 10 more days until De Houtman chanced on the islands of the Abrolhos where his charts indicated there should be only open sea. The surrounding reefs were plainly dangerous, and he did not survey them, merely sketching in their presence on his charts. The same islands were sighted by the *Tortelduif** in 1624, but the skipper of that ship told few men what he had seen.

No other *retourschip* chanced on the Abrolhos before 1629, so Ariaen Jacobsz would have known nothing but the fact of their existence. No maps existed to tell him there were three groups of islands, stretched out south to north. No rutter recorded that even the largest of them was so low that the archipelago could not be seen from any distance, nor that it sprawled across almost a full degree of latitude, directly in the path of the *Batavia*. No instinct told Jacobsz that he should shorten sail by night and proceed cautiously by day.

When the ship struck, she therefore did so at full speed.

* *Turtledove.*

CHAPTER 5

The Tiger

'Everything that has been done is not my fault.'
JERONIMUS CORNELISZ

It was as though they had been cast up on the edges of the world.

Even today, on sullen afternoons, the islands of the Abrolhos are monochrome and listless – so drab they seem to suck the colour from the sky. It is as if the archipelago lies somewhere at the bottom of the ocean, and the steel-tinged light suffusing it has filtered through a hundred feet of water. Deprived of sun, the sparse vegetation turns the colour of old parchment; the clouds are dull and specked with quartz; even the sea is grey. The only thing alive there is the wind.

The gales blow endlessly throughout the southern winter, tearing up from the Roaring Forties and billowing so hard that they bend the low scrub double. Wind cracks and rattles canvas and whistles in the gaps between the coral. From May until July, the islands are swept repeatedly by storms, which rage for up to 10 days at a time, pile up surf against the reefs, and smash anything in their path, sending spray 30 or 40 feet into the air. The winds can rise to hurricane force – as much as 80 miles per hour, enough to ground the islands' seabirds and knock the breath from any man who walks into them. They are made unbearable by the fact that there is virtually no shelter anywhere in the Abrolhos. On Batavia's Graveyard, only a slight depression on the northeast shore affords any protection from this elemental fury.

The climate in the islands, which can be stifling in summer, is generally mild throughout the winter, which is the rainy season. The monthly rainfall from June until August is roughly four inches, but from September this figure drops to less than half an inch a month. Even when it rains, moreover, the water hardly ever pools on the ground in the Abrolhos. It trickles through the coral and back into the sea, leaving all but a handful of the 200 islets in the group quite dry and lifeless.

Batavia's Graveyard, which lies in the northernmost part of the archipelago, is like this. It is a barren strip of coral rubble, 500 yards long, less than 300 yards across, and roughly triangular in shape. Its widest part stretches almost north to south along the edge of the deep-water passage discovered by Ariaen Jacobsz on the morning of the wreck; from there, the island tapers rapidly and almost to a point as it runs southeast. It is low and flat and featureless and can be crossed from side to side in less than 3 minutes, or circumnavigated in a little under 20. There are no hills, no trees, no caves, and little undergrowth; the highest point is only six feet above sea level; and though there are two small beaches on the western side, and some sand has found its way inland, this soil is nowhere more than two feet deep. Most of the ground is nothing more than shingle, slick in places with deposits of guano and treacherous to walk on. Although it is home to thousands of seabirds and several colonies of sea lions, Batavia's Graveyard has no pools or wells, and thus no native land animals. It is dead, desolate, and utterly unwelcoming.

When the first of the *Batavia*'s men came ashore in the archipelago, they found no sign of any human habitation. The Abrolhos were too far from the Australian coast, almost 50 miles, to have been visited by Aborigines; nor had any Europeans landed there prior to 1629. Nevertheless, nearly 300 of the 322 people who were on board the *retourschip* when she ran aground had survived the stranding of the ship – a remarkably high proportion in the circumstances – and by the evening of 5 June, the ragged beginnings of a settlement had been established in the islands.

By now it was nearly two days since their ship had run onto the reef, but the survivors were still split into three groups. The majority, about 180 men, women, and children, had been put ashore on Batavia's Graveyard. A further 70 men, including Jeronimus Cornelisz, remained stranded on the wreck, and the skipper had based 50 sailors and both the boats on his little islet close to the wreck. Ariaen's party included not only Pelsaert but all of the *Batavia*'s senior officers. Between them, they controlled most of the food and water and all of the charts and navigational instruments that had been salvaged from the ship.

These dispositions were no accident. Jacobsz had displayed a good deal of bravery in the aftermath of the wreck, risking his life repeatedly to save the people on the ship. But he also understood with perfect clarity that none of them would ever see the Netherlands again if the boats could not reach Java to fetch help. He and his officers had the skills to sail them there; the people on Batavia's Graveyard did not. In his own mind, therefore, Ariaen felt justified in doing what he could to improve his own chances of survival.

The survivors on Batavia's Graveyard thus found themselves with neither leadership nor adequate supplies. The great majority – at least 100 – were common soldiers and sailors of the VOC, and another score were either petty officers or idlers such as coopers, carpenters, and smiths. Creesje Jans was there, with about 20 other women, almost all of whom were wives of members of the crew; and of the remaining 50, more than half were youths and children. Most of these were cabin boys aged 14 or 15, but several were even younger than that, and one or two were babes in arms who had actually been born on board the *Batavia*. Fewer than two dozen members of the group were officers, and, of these, seven were inexperienced VOC assistants who would have been only in their early twenties, and 11 merely Company cadets.

All this left at best half a dozen men to control and lead more than 170 frightened, cold, and hungry people, perhaps a quarter of whom were foreigners with an imperfect grasp of Dutch. To make matters worse, this tiny handful of officers could no longer rely on fear of the VOC to back up their orders. Authority was now a matter of persuasion, compromise, and cooperation – something none of them would have experienced before.

The calibre of the men on the island left a great deal to be desired. The only officer of any rank was Frans Jansz, the surgeon, whose popularity among the crew was no substitute for his inexperience of command. Nevertheless, in the first few days after the wreck, it would appear to have been Jansz who began to organise the survivors and who set about establishing a council to lead them, as was required by the customs of the VOC.

Jan Company was run by councils and committees. The Gentlemen XVII controlled the business as a whole, and each chamber had its own board of directors. In Java, even the governor-general worked through the Council of the Indies, and the highest authority in any VOC flotilla was not the fleet president, acting alone, but the *Brede Raad,* or Broad Council. While the ships were at sea, every upper-merchant and skipper in the squadron was entitled to a seat on this council, which dealt not only with any questions of broad strategy but also with criminal offences. Because it was commonplace for the vessels of a fleet to become separated on their way out to the Indies, however, each *retourschip* also had its own ship's council, with a normal membership of five. This council would typically consist of the skipper and the upper-merchant together with the vessel's under-merchant, upper-steersman, and high boatswain, but the *raad* that was now set up on Batavia's Graveyard was, necessarily, very different.

In all likelihood, the surgeon's main supports would have been the *predikant* and the one real figure of authority on the island – the provost, Pieter Jansz. It had been the latter's task to administer discipline on board ship, although his authority derived largely from the skipper and he actually ranked somewhere below the cooper and the carpenter in the *Batavia*'s hierarchy. It might be conjectured that the remaining members of the council would have been a petty officer, representing the sailors on Batavia's Graveyard, and Salomon Deschamps, Pelsaert's clerk, who was the most senior VOC employee actually on the island. This group would probably have turned to Gabriel Jacobszoon, the corporal of the 70 or more soldiers in the survivors' party, for assistance; his men were a natural counterbalance to the sailors on the island. But even with the corporal's support, the council lacked natural authority and probably struggled to keep order in the face of any real opposition from the men.

The need for such a body had been starkly demonstrated during the first day on Batavia's Graveyard. At first the survivors' chief emotions must have been relief, curiosity about their new environment, and considerable uncertainty as to what they should do next; but it would have taken only a short time to explore the island, and by the afternoon of 5 June the first pangs of hunger and thirst had unquestionably driven at least a few people to take what they needed from their limited supplies.

In some respects this was a natural reaction; the survivors knew that there was more food and water on the wreck and did not realise that foul weather, and the rioting soldiers and sailors still on board, had prevented Pelsaert and Jacobsz from salvaging more barrels from the stores. Nevertheless, once it became clear that some people were helping themselves to the barrels on the island, others would have hurried to secure a fair share for themselves. Already the once-disorganised mass of people on the island had begun to coalesce into small groups, half a dozen to a dozen strong, bound by some sort of common tie – soldiers, sailors, families, men who came from the same town, and others who had messed together on the ship. Emboldened by their numbers, these groups, it would appear, demanded what they wanted from the stockpile. A good deal of the food and most, if not all, the water, was thus consumed within 24 hours of the survivors' arrival on Batavia's Graveyard.

By evening on the third day, 6 June, the people on the island had begun to realise their mistake. There had been no more rain; a thorough search of the whole island had revealed no wells; and Pelsaert's one attempt to bring more water had failed in circumstances that suggested there would be no others. The survivors were already suffering from thirst but, without boats, they had no means of leaving Batavia's Graveyard to search for water. All 180 of them were trapped on an arid prison – one that, without another rainstorm, would quickly kill them.

As the drought continued into a fourth day, and then a fifth, the survivors' agonies became intense. Without water, their bodies swiftly became dehydrated; after a day or so, saliva thickened into an unpleasant paste, and soon after that their mouths ceased to produce it altogether. Thereafter the symptoms only became worse: tongues hardened and swelled; eyelids cracked; the eyes themselves wept tears of blood. Throats became so dry that even breathing seemed difficult.

Ten of the people on the island died. The old and young would have been the first to weaken, but after four or five days without water all of the survivors would have been affected to a considerable degree. They clung to life by adopting the strategies that shipwrecked men and castaways have always turned to. Most, from the *predikant* down, drank their own urine; a few threw aside their caution and gulped seawater; a third group chewed incessantly on lead pellets in the vain hope that they could generate enough saliva to afford at least some relief. It is very likely, though the sources do not mention it, that they also killed seabirds and sea lions in order to drink their blood.

None of these methods of relieving thirst are particularly effective. Drinking one's 'own water,' as Gijsbert Bastiaensz put it, would have helped the survivors to reduce the risk of dehydration, but urine contains so many salts that it is worse than useless for quenching thirst. So too is seawater, and though it can be safely drunk in small quantities, one and a half pints – which contains the equivalent of an adult male's daily requirement of salt – is the most that should be consumed in a single day. But the *Batavia*'s survivors had no way of knowing this. So potent is the folklore on the subject, which insists that drinking seawater leads invariably to madness, that they, like most shipwrecked sailors, no doubt refused it until they were already so dehydrated that it would have done them much more harm than good.

After three or four days without water, sheer desperation forced the people on the island to try to get fresh supplies from the wreck. There was not yet enough driftwood to build a raft, but the *predikant*'s servant-girl, whose name was Wybrecht Claasen, was a strong swimmer, and she volunteered to try to reach the ship without one. The *Batavia* was almost a mile away, but it was possible to wade across at least part of the shallows, and after two attempts the girl contrived to reach the reef. She hauled herself onto a rock within hailing distance of the ship, calling for a rope, and the people on the wreck hurled over a line. Claasen tied the rope around her waist and was hauled on board through the breakers – 'not without great danger to her life,' as one of those watching from the island observed.

Remarkably, the maid did manage to return safely to Batavia's Graveyard. It does not seem possible that she brought much water with her, but even a small amount would have helped to revive them and, in any case, her exploit was important from a purely moral point of view. It was the first real triumph the survivors had enjoyed since they had reached the island, and an important sign that they could take matters into their own hands, rather than waiting passively for death. In that respect, at least, the worst of their ordeal was now over.

Nevertheless, many more of the *Batavia*'s passengers and crew would have died of thirst within another day or so had it not been for a squall that mercifully struck the island on the sixth day, 9 June. In no more than an hour or two, the survivors collected so much fresh water in pieces of sailcloth spread out on the coral that they more than replenished their supplies. The rain continued through the night, and though it never fell more than intermittently thereafter, from then on there was always just enough to provide a modest ration for them all.

The position of the people on the wreck could not have been more different. The 70 men stranded on the *Batavia* had plenty to eat and drink; indeed the free access they now enjoyed to the private quarters in the stern, where the officers had kept their personal supplies, meant that most were better fed and watered than they had been for years. On the other hand, the ship herself was partly filled with water and, under the constant assault of the surf, she was rapidly disintegrating.

The *Batavia* held together for nine days, until, on 12 June, the breakers finally destroyed her. Long before that, however, it had become difficult to find a place on board that was still safe and dry, and the survivors' discomfort was only increased by the certainty that when she did break up they would all be tipped into the booming surf. The majority of those left on board – Jeronimus Cornelisz among them – could not swim; these men must have taken Ariaen Jacobsz's advice and built crude rafts or piled loose planks and empty barrels on the deck to be certain that they would have something to hang onto when the moment came.

Even the stronger swimmers could hardly have been confident of reaching shore. They had watched while the men who had jumped overboard on the night of the wreck were smashed against the coral and drowned, and knew that it took luck to get across the reef alive. So for a week they sat and waited for the ship to disappear beneath them, and while they waited, most of them drank. They were, one of their number later recalled, 'left in such a desolate state.'

The destruction of the *Batavia,* when it finally occurred, happened so rapidly that the men on board were taken by surprise. Battered to the point of disintegration by the surf, the ship's port side burst open and 'the wrecking went on so quickly and easily that it was like a miracle.' As the waves rushed in, anyone caught down below must have drowned almost immediately. Even the men on deck hardly had time to reach their life preservers before they found themselves afloat. For most the end was quick; the breakers held them under or knocked them senseless on the coral so that they drowned. The lucky ones were swept right over the reef into the calmer waters beyond, but only 20 of the 70 men on board managed to float or swim ashore.

Jeronimus Cornelisz was not among them. When the *Batavia*'s upperworks disintegrated, his fear of drowning had prompted him to climb, apparently alone, along the *retourschip*'s bowsprit. The forward section of the ship had then broken away, with him still in it, and somehow drifted safely to the shallows. The under-merchant stayed there, clinging to his spar, for two more days, until the bowsprit fell apart beneath him. Then he floated to the island in a mass of driftwood, the last man to escape *Batavia* alive.

❉

Jeronimus staggered ashore on Batavia's Graveyard cold, wet, and utterly exhausted. He had been 11 days on the wreck, the last two of them alone, exposed to biting southeast winds and in terror for his life. Now he was jelly-limbed and spent, in desperate need of hot food and a place to rest.

The people of the island ran to meet him on the beach and half-helped, half-carried him into their camp, where he was gratified to find that he was treated with great deference and respect. Frans Jansz and his councillors came to greet him, and he was pressed to take dry clothing and something to eat. Then, when he had filled his stomach, he was urged to rest.

Cornelisz slept for hours in a borrowed bed and awakened to the sound of many voices. The campsite in the northeast quarter of the island had by now grown to quite a size, and it was alive with activity. The first crude tents had already been erected from spars and scraps of canvas cast up on the coral, and small groups of sur-vivors were busy hunting birds or spreading strips of sailcloth to catch rain. Others scavenged washed-up bits of planking from the ship for fires.

The destruction of the *Batavia* had substantially increased this bounty. The survivors' coral islet lay directly in the path of the winds blowing from the wreck site, and large quantities of drift-wood now appeared, along with barrels from the stores. Over the next few days, 500 gallons of water and 550 gallons of French and Spanish wine were washed ashore, together with some vinegar and other victuals. The barrels were manhandled up the beach and left, under guard, in a central store; the spars and planks were gathered by the carpenters, who set to work to turn them into skiffs and rafts.

The appearance of these additional supplies was welcome, but one look at the meagre contents of the store tent convinced

Jeronimus that Batavia's Graveyard would not support a large population for too long. With the arrival of the survivors from the wreck, the number of people on the island had grown to 208 men, women, and children. Even living on half rations, they would consume nearly three tons of meat and 1,250 gallons of water a month, enough to empty the stores in a few days. To make matters worse, the natural resources of the cay were already almost exhausted. During their first week on the island, the survivors had killed and eaten hundreds of birds, and so many sea lions that the colonies that had once crowded the beaches were all but gone, slaughtered for their meat. The rains were still intermittent and could hardly be relied on, and while they waited for the rafts to be completed there was still no way of leaving the island. Their position was precarious in the extreme.

It was for this reason, more than any other, that Cornelisz was welcomed when he came ashore. It was now the middle of June, and the people of Batavia's Graveyard had seen nothing of Francisco Pelsaert for well over a week. For a few days Frans Jansz and his councillors had dared to hope that their *commandeur* would return with barrels full of water, but by now it had become only too clear that Pelsaert had left the Abrolhos and was unlikely to return. With the upper-merchant gone, Jeronimus, his deputy, was the natural leader of the *Batavia* survivors. It was no surprise that the surgeon turned to Cornelisz for help.

Within a day or two the under-merchant was elected to the *raad*. As the senior VOC official in the archipelago, he was entitled to a seat on the ship's council, and his education and quick wit made him so much more articulate than his fellow councillors that they deferred to him, at least at first. The scant surviving evidence suggests that Cornelisz quickly came to dominate the group.

Jeronimus enjoyed his new position of authority, and his willingness to join the *raad* is easily explained. On the *Batavia,* he had possessed no real power, but on Batavia's Graveyard he was listened to attentively, and the orders that he gave were scrupulously obeyed. He had the luxury of a large tent to himself, and the *commandeur*'s own clothes – which had been salvaged from the wreck – were placed at his disposal. The under-merchant thus acquired by right the very things he had once planned to seize by mutiny. In his private quarters, surrounded by his requisitioned finery, Cornelisz became a man of consequence at last – the ruler, in effect, of his own small island kingdom.

Assured of the respect and deference he craved, Jeronimus threw himself into the business of survival. For a few days he was everywhere, striding about in Pelsaert's sumptuous clothing, issuing an endless stream of orders and working energetically to improve the camp. He sent out hunting parties, supervised the erection of more tents, and oversaw the completion of the boats. The *Batavia* survivors were grateful for his efforts. 'This merchant,' wrote Gijsbert Bastiaensz, 'in the beginning behaved himself very well.'

In truth, however, Cornelisz soon tired of his exertions. He might adore the rigmarole of leadership, but he had no time for the responsibilities that it entailed. The work was hard, the detail bored him; and though he had enjoyed his welcome as a saviour, he remained utterly self-centred. The fact was that the under-merchant did not care whether the people he was protecting lived or died. On the *Batavia,* where his shipmates had stood in the way of his plans for mutiny, he had been willing to kill them all to seize the ship. On Batavia's Graveyard, the same men had become mere mouths to feed, and he was still prepared to see them dead if he thought that it would benefit himself.

By the beginning of the latter half of June, moreover, Jeronimus's inherent ruthlessness had been buttressed by a sobering discovery: rumours of his planned mutiny were circulating on the island. The man who had unveiled the plot was Ryckert Woutersz, one of Jacobsz's recruits, who had taken considerable risks on the *retourschip* at the skipper's behest, 'sleeping for some days with a sword under his head' while he waited for the call to action. Outraged to discover that Ariaen had fled the archipelago without him, Woutersz determined to betray his master, 'telling in public what They had intended to do, [and] complaining very much about the skipper.' For some reason the man's initial allegations had been more or less ignored; perhaps the other survivors were too much racked by thirst to care about his stories, or they simply did not believe him. Now that the situation on the island had improved, however, fresh whispers had begun to sweep the camp. Jeronimus's name, it seems, had not been mentioned; Woutersz may not even have known of the under-merchant's involvement. But Cornelisz guessed that it might yet emerge. It was not the sort of matter he could afford to ignore.

Alone in his tent, Cornelisz took stock of his position with cold-eyed detachment. To begin with, he had to assume that Pelsaert and the skipper were by now on their way to the Dutch settlements on Java. Ariaen, he hoped, might yet find some opportunity to murder the *commandeur*, tip his body overboard, and change course to some other European port – possibly Portuguese Malacca. In that case the *Batavia* survivors would perhaps be rescued by foreigners and the revelation of the mutiny would cease to matter.

Nevertheless, as Jeronimus knew, there was every chance that Jacobsz and Jan Evertsz would get no opportunity to dispose of Pelsaert. In that case, much would depend on the skipper's skill. The chances of an open, overloaded boat completing such a lengthy ocean voyage were poor, but Ariaen was a first-rate seaman and it was at least possible that he would reach the Indies. If he did, the Company would certainly dispatch a rescue ship, most probably a *jacht*, to recover its money chests and pick up any survivors. Provided that Jeronimus could stay alive long enough for the *jacht* to reach them – perhaps another month or two – he might yet find himself stepping ashore in Java.

In most circumstances, that too would be a welcome outcome, but Ryckert Woutersz's allegations were a problem. Jeronimus was, he knew, immune to normal criticism in the Abrolhos; the *Batavia*'s men had no wish to risk angering the leader of the *raad* by taking issue with him. But his power was not absolute, and while the other members of the council could band together to outvote him, any suggestion that he had planned to mutiny would be catastrophic. Such a thing could not be laughed off or forgotten, and if there ever was a full investigation of the matter, Cornelisz's actions on the *retourschip* might prove to be his death sentence. The Dutch authorities would be bound to take the allegations seriously, and they would not hesitate to torture any suspects who fell into their hands. There was every likelihood that the truth would be uncovered in this way, and the ringleaders, including Jeronimus, exposed and executed. No matter what else might occur, therefore, Cornelisz himself could not risk going to the Indies.

What, then, was he to do if a Dutch rescue ship arrived? To a man as ruthless as Cornelisz, the answer appeared obvious. A *jacht* might carry a crew of no more than 20 or 30 sailors, so few they could be overwhelmed in a well-planned attack. Given the support of enough determined men, he could make himself the master of a rescue ship. There would be no need then to go to Java. Instead he could pursue the plan he had conceived in the Southern Ocean: turn pirate, make a fortune, and retire to some foreign port to enjoy the fruits of his endeavour.

Even if there turned out to be no rescue and no voyage, Cornelisz could see advantages to freeing himself from the restraints he laboured under in the Abrolhos. As things stood, there were distinct limits to his power and authority. His suggestions might always be respected, and his orders generally obeyed, but there were still four other councillors on the *raad,* and he could be out-voted. The matter was made more serious by the fact that Jeronimus's colleagues did not share his views on the need to hoard their limited supplies. Frans Jansz and the other councillors, the under-merchant had begun to think, would kill them all with their ridiculous insistence on eking out a ration to every man, woman, and child on the island. That was something he could not allow to happen.

Sometime during the third week of the month, therefore, Jeronimus made up his mind to instigate the mutiny that he had planned on the *Batavia.* The circumstances were, of course, now very different. There was no longer any ship to seize; the under-merchant's closest ally, Ariaen Jacobsz, had deserted him; and – most importantly – it would no longer be nearly such an easy matter to control the majority of loyalists in the crew. But Cornelisz's goals had hardly changed. Jeronimus sought wealth, power, comfort, and security, and he was prepared to go to any lengths to secure himself these luxuries.

It took the under-merchant perhaps a week to recruit the men he needed to seize power on the island. Exactly how he managed this was never revealed in any detail. The survivors' situation – stranded, short of food and water, and apparently abandoned by the VOC – no doubt made his task easier than it would otherwise have been, and the fact that up to a dozen of the sailors and soldiers who had been ready to mutiny on the *retourschip* had found themselves trapped on Batavia's Graveyard was a significant advantage. But he also had his own abilities to call on – a quick, if perverse, mind and a pathologically charming tongue.

The Jeronimus of Pelsaert's journals remains at best a half-drawn figure: ruthless and deadly, certainly, yet also someone whose real personality has always been obscured by layer upon layer of lies and special pleading. But he was, it seems, a truly charismatic figure – able to persuade a varied group of men that their interests were identical to his – and his talk of the wealth and luxury that might yet lie within their grasp certainly made enticing listening for men trapped in the grey surrounds of Houtman's Abrolhos. Cornelisz was obviously and genuinely clever, and so vital that he stood out among the failures, novices, and second-raters who peopled the *Batavia*'s stern. He was also self-assured and eloquent in a way that awed men who were neither. The rabble of the gun deck and the educated assistants of the stern alike seem to have found him irresistible. Long before the end of June he had gathered about two dozen followers around him and felt ready to put his plans into action.

Most of Jeronimus's men had been with him on the *Batavia*. The most valuable of them were a handful of army cadets, men such as Coenraat van Huyssen and Gÿsbert van Welderen who had sailed for Java in the comparative luxury of the stern and discovered they had little taste for life on Batavia's Graveyard. They were young – no more than 21 – and inexperienced, and so were unlikely to dispute the under-merchant's leadership. And since they knew how to handle weapons, the common people on the ship instinctively deferred to them. Several soldiers, led by lance corporal Jacop Pietersz, had also been part of the conspiracy on the *retourschip*. The best of these were German mercenaries, who were also mostly strong and young; Jan Hendricxsz, from Bremen, was 24, and Mattys Beer, of Munsterbergh, was no more than 21. These men, along with several of their comrades, may well have seen action in the Thirty Years' War,* gaining invaluable military experience along the way. The third and smallest group of mutineers consisted of a few men from the gun deck, mostly sailors whom Jacobsz had recruited but had been unable to take with him on the longboat. The skipper's good friend Allert Janssen, who had been among the party that assaulted Creesje Jans, was the leading member of this group.

The *Batavia* mutineers had concealed their true numbers so effectively that it is now impossible to say with any certainty which of the other members of the under-merchant's gang had been

---

*This brutal internecine conflict had raged throughout the Holy Roman Empire since 1618. It was notable not merely for its battles, but for the unusually appalling treatment meted out to the civilians on either side. The slaughter of women, children, and other noncombatants was commonplace throughout the war. It is not impossible that men such as Hendricxsz, Beer, and the other German mercenaries who joined Cornelisz may have been hardened by participation in such massacres.

recruited on the ship. It seems likely that Rutger Fredricx, a 23-year-old idler from Groningen, was among the first men to be approached – he was the *Batavia*'s locksmith, and his skills would have been invaluable to mutineers who needed to imprison or restrain up to 200 of their colleagues. One or two of the VOC assistants were also aware of the conspiracy, and since they must have worked closely with Jeronimus on board the *retourschip* it may be that they, too, were among the earlier recruits. The remainder of the under-merchant's followers appear to have been approached after the *Batavia* was wrecked. They would probably have been recruited from among the friends of the existing mutineers, or those who complained most bitterly about the discomforts of island life.

One of the assistants was of particular importance to Jeronimus. His name was David Zevanck, and he came from a rural area a little to the north of Amsterdam. Zevanck, like the others, was still young, and there are indications that he came from a good family, one that owned property and had some pretensions to gentility. How he had come to sail with the *Batavia* remains unknown. As one of the ship's clerks, he must have been an educated man, but there was also a hard edge to his character. He was physically strong and handy with a sword, and of all the people on the ship, he was perhaps the closest to Cornelisz in ambition, ruthlessness, and character. Now he became the under-merchant's principal lieutenant, organising the men for him and ensuring that his orders were obeyed.

Beginning in the third week of June, Cornelisz began to plot rebellion, 'acting very subtly and gradually, so that in the first 20 days it could not be perceived.' The under-merchant detached his followers from the other survivors, billeting them in two tents together with their weapons, and he collected all the other swords and muskets on the island into a central store that he alone controlled. Next, he prevented the ship's carpenters from putting into action a plan to build their own small rescue vessel from the wreckage of the *retourschip,* and he began to look for ways of reducing the number of people on Batavia's Graveyard. The latter was a necessary precaution, he and Zevanck agreed – both to conserve the limited supplies and to reduce the risk that their conspiracy might be uncovered. As things stood, the mutineers were still outnumbered about six to one by the other men on the island. The intention was to reduce the disparity by half.

The under-merchant's solution to this problem was simple but effective. He sent his followers to explore the islands, using the first of the little skiffs that the carpenters had built from fragments of driftwood. Their purpose was not so much to find freshwater wells and new colonies of sea lions – which was what the people of Batavia's Graveyard were told – as to provide the under-merchant with detailed information about conditions elsewhere in the archipelago. From Cornelisz's point of view, it made little difference whether his men located additional supplies or not. What he needed was merely an excuse to send parties of survivors to the other islands in the group.

Within a day or two, the mutineers returned, reporting to Jeronimus that they had found nothing of any value in the Abrolhos. Like Pelsaert and his sailors, the under-merchant's men had searched the two large islands to the north without finding any sign of water. They had also visited a pair of smaller islets, one less than half a mile away on the western side of the deep-water channel that ran along one side of Batavia's Graveyard, and the other a little farther to the south. The closer of the islets was a long, thin, sandy spit that ran north to south for nearly a mile and was crowned with a narrow ridge covered in coarse grass and low vegetation; it was home to large flocks of birds and hundreds of sea lions – so many that the boats' crews took to calling it Seals' Island – but the few pools discovered at its southern tip were brackish and undrinkable. The other, which was the islet where Ariaen Jacobsz had set up his temporary camp, was just as desolate. The mutineers found nothing there but a few empty biscuit barrels, and the cay itself, which they named Traitors' Island in bitter remembrance of the men who had abandoned them, was a mere pancake of loose coral. Its one resource was driftwood, which littered the entire southern shore.

Neither of these islands could possibly support more than a handful of people for any length of time, but the under-merchant did not care. 'He said that the number who were [on Batavia's Graveyard] together, about 200, must be reduced to a very few,' Gijsbert Bastiaensz recalled, and Cornelisz glibly announced that his men had made important discoveries. 'Those people coming back again had got enough information that there was not any consolation there for any Human Beings,' remarked the *predikant*, 'but the Merchant ordered them to say that there was water and good food for the people; whereupon some others were ordered to go, and others went of their own accord to know truthfully if there was Water.'

One group of about 40 men, women, and children were taken to Seals' Island. They were provided with a few barrels of water and promised that fresh supplies would be ferried to them whenever they were needed. A smaller party, 15 strong and commanded by the provost, Pieter Jansz, travelled to Traitors' Island. They took with them all the tools they needed to make rafts on the islet. Jeronimus had promised them that they could make their way to the larger islands to the north as soon as the boats were ready.

Shortly afterward, towards the end of the third week of June, it was announced that the 'High Land' to the north was also to be colonised. These two large islands had now been searched for water twice without success – by Pelsaert on 6 June and by Zevanck and his men a fortnight later – but the survivors on Batavia's Graveyard did not know this, so there were no protests when a third detachment, 20 strong, was sent to hunt for hidden wells. Almost all of the members of this party were troops who had remained loyal to the Company; they included 'some of the boldest soldiers,' the *predikant* believed. Jeronimus saw to it that they were only lightly equipped and ensured that they were issued neither weapons nor a boat. The men were told to light signal fires when – or if – they found fresh water and were promised that they would be picked up when the fires were seen. In fact, Cornelisz had no intention of returning for them and hoped that they might die of thirst.

The group sent to the High Land included two young cadets, Otto Smit and Allert Jansz, but its real leader seems to have been a private from the small town of Winschoten in Groningen whose name was Wiebbe Hayes. Nothing at all is known about Hayes's background, age, or military experience, but we know that the under-merchant had picked him out from among the 70 or more private soldiers on the *Batavia,* which implies that he possessed a certain presence. Unknown to Jeronimus, however, Hayes was also a man of considerable ability, and his character and sense of purpose seem to have been unusual for a private soldier of this time. It appears unlikely that he was a member of the *grauw,* the impecunious and uneducated rabble who had peopled the lower decks of the *Batavia,* and possibly he, like Coenraat van Huyssen and David Zevanck, came from a comfortable background and had somehow fallen on hard times. It was not entirely unknown for the children of respectable but impoverished parents to enlist with the VOC as ordinary soldiers, but if Hayes did come from such a family, he plainly had even less money and influence than men who could at least secure themselves commissions as cadets.

In any event, Wiebbe was able to keep his men alive on the High Land for almost three weeks. The soldiers soon discovered – as had Pelsaert and Zevanck before them – that there were apparently no wells on the smaller and more easterly of the two islands, but they did find small puddles of rainwater among the coral, and these sustained them while they completed their exploration. After several days, they moved west onto the larger cay, waiting for low tide and stumbling across the mile of mudflats that separated the islands to begin the search again. There they found abundant wildlife but no water, and once again they had to scour the ground for little pools of rain. Again, they found just enough to keep them alive. They continued this precarious existence for 20 days, searching endlessly for wells, hunting for food, and keeping watch for rafts from Batavia's Graveyard that never came.

❀

The first part of Jeronimus's plan was now complete. The dispatch of landing parties to the four outlying islands had reduced the population of Batavia's Graveyard by one-third, to somewhere between 130 and 140 people, and nearly four dozen able-bodied men and two dozen boys had been lured onto other cays where they posed no threat and would most likely die. Cornelisz and his followers were still outnumbered by the loyalists among the crew, but the under-merchant guessed that few of the 90 other adult males still with him on Batavia's Graveyard had much stomach for a fight. He now guessed he could survive until a rescue ship arrived. The trick would be to seize it when it came.

The notion of capturing a *jacht* was certainly enticing, but Jeronimus knew that it would be no easy task. A frontal assault was out of the question; even the smallest VOC craft had cannon, boarding pikes, and muskets enough to fend off an attack. Nor was it likely to be possible to surprise and seize a ship at anchor in the archipelago, since the attackers' boats would be seen approaching from a distance.

A better way, the under-merchant thought, might be to lure the *jacht*'s crew onto land. If a boatload of sailors from a rescue ship were to come ashore on Batavia's Graveyard, they would be out-numbered by Cornelisz's men. And if the mutineers could cut the landing party's throats, they would probably leave themselves no more than 20 men to deal with on the ship.

Jeronimus, we know, believed that this idea had merit. But he also saw at once that it could not succeed while there were so many people on the island. For one thing, the supplies of food were still so low that they might all starve before a rescue ship arrived. For another, most of the *Batavia* survivors were still loyal to the VOC; there was every chance that they would try to warn their rescuers of the danger they were in. Once again, the solution to the problem struck the under-merchant as self-evident. The people in his way would have to die.

Most leaders would have baulked at the idea of slaughtering 120 of their own men, women, and children, but Cornelisz regarded the prospect with his customary detachment. He was the leader of the ship's council and thus invested with the power of the VOC. In his warped view those who opposed him, or were likely to, were mutineers themselves. As for the remainder of the survivors, those on the other islands, perhaps he simply believed that they would soon be dead, and never bothered to consider what might happen if they lived.

❁

The killing began in the first week of July.

Jeronimus had waited several days for the opportunity to spring his mutiny. He wanted, first of all, to snuff out dissent, and since the members of the *raad* were the most likely source of opposition, that meant finding a pretext to dissolve the existing council. The chance to do this arose when the under-merchant was informed that a soldier named Abraham Hendricx had been caught tapping one of the barrels in the stores. Under interrogation, Hendricx confessed to having crept into the store tent several times before, and to sharing his bounty with one of the *retourschip*'s gunners. In the survivors' straitened circumstances, the theft was punishable by death. The gunner's culpability was, however, harder to establish, and there seemed to be a good chance that the *raad* would spare his life. Jeronimus, it seems, decided to exploit this fact by demanding that both the guilty men be executed, fully expecting to be met with opposition.

'On 4 July, when Abraham Hendricx, from Delft, had tapped a Wine barrel several times and drank himself drunk – and had also given up some to a gunner, Ariaen Ariaensz, so that he also became drunk – Jeronimus proposed to his council, which he had called together, that they were worthy of death without grace or delay, and must be drowned forthwith.

'The council consented insofar as it concerned Abraham Hendricx, because he had tapped the barrel, but insofar as it concerned the other, Ariaen Ariaensz, they made difficulties and would not vote to sentence him to Death. Whereupon Jeronimus burst out, and said, "How can you not let this happen? Nevertheless, you will soon have to resolve on something quite else." At which words each one became afraid, and could not understand what he meant by that.'

Precisely what Cornelisz intended became clear enough next day, 5 July, when the under-merchant suddenly dissolved the *raad* and removed all the other councillors from their posts. This extreme, but not illegal, move allowed him to 'choose for his new council such persons as accorded with his desires, to wit, Coenraat van Huyssen, cadet; David Zevanck, assistant; and Jacop Pietersz Cosijn, lance corporal.'

With this council of mutineers in place, Cornelisz at last felt secure. Zevanck and the others could be relied on to follow his instructions, and the other people on the island were unlikely to take issue with their edicts, so long as they were dressed up with a veneer of legality.

The under-merchant proved this point immediately by executing Hendricx* and accusing two carpenters named Egbert Roeloffsz and Warnar Dircx of plotting to make off in one of the little homemade yawls. The latter charge seems to have been based on nothing more than island gossip, but the new *raad* had no compunction in passing death sentences on both men and, significantly, there was no sign of dissent among the rank-and-file survivors. Roeloffsz and Dircx were killed later the same day by two of Jeronimus's men, Daniel Cornelissen and Hans Frederick, both cadets. 'Daniel,' the *Batavia* journals relate, 'has pierced the foresaid Warnar with a sword; of which he boasted later, saying that it went through him as easily as butter ... [and Hans Frederick] has let

---

*The indications are that Ariaen Ariaensz somehow escaped and contrived to make his way to Wiebbe Hayes's Island.

himself be used very willingly [and] has also given two or three hacks to Warnar.'

Cornelisz thus contrived to rid himself of not one but three possible opponents within a day of seizing control of the ship's council. He was, however, perfectly aware of the overriding need for caution in the methods he employed. He and his men were still heavily outnumbered, and it was important to proceed so that the people of the island did not suspect that their numbers were being systematically reduced. Some better way had to be found of disposing of the strongest loyalists covertly, so that even their friends did not realise they had gone.

Batavia's Graveyard itself was useless for such purposes. It was so small that a missing man would soon attract attention, and so barren that a body would be difficult to hide. Cornelisz's solution was simple but effective. He announced that he was sending reinforcements to assist Wiebbe Hayes in the search for water. Several small parties – three or four people at a time – were to leave for the High Land in the coming week. These men, it was made clear, were likely to be gone some time. They were to remain with the soldiers until water had been found.

The *Batavia* survivors saw nothing unusual in such a plan. Jeronimus had made no secret of his desire to reduce the numbers on Batavia's Graveyard, and it was obvious, from the absence of signals, that Hayes and his men had been unable to find water; they would no doubt welcome some assistance. Since there were no rafts to spare, it also made sense for the reinforcements to be rowed north by boatmen who would – of course – return alone. Only the under-merchant knew that the oarsmen would be chosen from the ranks of the most determined mutineers.

Cornelisz's scheme was put into action immediately. The first party of reinforcements consisted of two soldiers and two sailors, who were to be rowed to the High Land by Zevanck and six of his strongest men. Four of the mutineers were Company cadets, and they were reinforced by Fredricx, the locksmith, and a soldier, Mattys Beer. Cornelisz's followers thus outnumbered their intended victims by almost two to one.

The little group set off on a raft from Batavia's Graveyard, rowing along the deep-water channel until the island had almost vanished in the distance. As soon they were well away from any help, the unsuspecting loyalists were set upon and taken by surprise. Their hands and feet were tightly bound and three of them were tipped overboard to drown. The fourth, a Company cadet called Andries Liebent, begged for his life and he was spared on condition that he pledged his loyalty to the mutineers. No one on Batavia's Graveyard seems to have thought it odd that Liebent had returned, and the trap was judged to have worked so well that it was used again only two days later, when Hans Radder, a cadet, and the *Batavia*'s upper-trumpeter, Jacop Groenwald, were killed. These men were enemies of Mattys Beer, who had maliciously denounced them to Jeronimus as 'cacklers.' The pair were trussed up by Zevanck and his friends and held under the water while they drowned. Again, however, Zevanck spared an intended victim. This man was an assistant from Middelburg by the name of Andries de Vries, who was only in his early twenties and begged loudly for mercy. 'Having been bound, he was set free and his life was spared for the time being,' the *Batavia*'s journals note. But De Vries, like Liebent, had to pay a price to save his life: he was sworn to serve Jeronimus and to do as he was told.

Thus far, Cornelisz's schemes had all succeeded admirably. The under-merchant had quietly recruited at least a score of determined men to do his bidding. He had successfully reduced the numbers on Batavia's Graveyard, limiting the demand on his supplies and dividing his potential enemies into four separate camps, none of which had any contact with the others. He had silenced dissent by dissolving Frans Jansz's *raad* and made his principal lieutenants councillors in its stead. Then he had begun to murder the *Batavia* survivors – the very people he was sworn to protect. By the end of the first week of July, he had killed eight of them, five covertly and three publicly, as thieves, and there seemed to be no reason why he could not deal with the remainder in the same manner, at least until the ranks of loyalists on the island had been so thinned that it would hardly matter if he revealed himself. As for the 14 men with Pieter Jansz, the 20 who had gone with Hayes, and the 45 whom he had ferried to Seals' Island, they posed no immediate threat and could safely be ignored.

Hayes's party was, it seems, the only one to cause Jeronimus concern. The survivors who had gone to Seals' and Traitors' Islands were mixed groups of men, women, and children, unlikely to put up much of a fight, but the men on the High Land were all soldiers – tough, self-reliant, and capable of making trouble. It was perhaps for this reason that the under-merchant had sent Wiebbe's party as far away from Batavia's Graveyard as he could and left the men without a boat on islands where he knew that they would struggle to survive. As days and then weeks passed without signals from the High Land, Cornelisz may have assumed that his enemies had died of thirst. That would have been to his advantage, but his plans did not depend on it. He was content to leave Hayes where he was for the time being – so long as he did not find any water.

In any normal circumstances, the discovery of wells on the High Land would have come as a huge relief to the survivors of a wreck. Jeronimus's scheme for the capture of a rescue ship, however, depended on dividing the *Batavia*'s people into different camps, which he could deal with one by one. If water were found, however, the survivors would expect Cornelisz to gather all four of his parties at the wells, with the inevitable result that the mutineers would once again find themselves in a small minority. This was something that the under-merchant could not allow to happen.

The discovery of several cisterns on the High Land, which occurred on 9 July, thus threw his schemes into utter disarray. The under-merchant watched in disbelief as first one beacon, then a second, then a third, flared into life along the shoreline of Hayes's islands. These signal fires confirmed that Wiebbe was still alive, 20 days after he and his men first went ashore, and informed the people of Batavia's Graveyard that the longed-for water had been found. They were also the agreed sign that rafts should be sent to pick up the landing party.

For the first time since he had come ashore, Cornelisz found himself in a quandary. The signals could not be concealed – the beacons were clearly visible from the survivors' camp – and yet they had to be ignored. Jeronimus had no intention of permitting Hayes and his troops to leave the High Land, but by refusing to send rafts to rescue them, he and his councillors gave the men and women of Batavia's Graveyard the first clear indication that the councillors of the *raad* did not have their best interests at heart. Wiebbe, too, would doubtless realise that something was wrong, and it would no longer be easy to surprise him. To make matters worse, the soldiers could now survive indefinitely on their island, while Cornelisz and his men remained dependent on the intermittent rains for their own supplies of water. Hayes's fires were thus not merely signs but portents – an indication that Jeronimus's plot was beginning to unravel.

Almost as soon as the signal beacons were lit, indeed, Cornelisz noticed a flurry of activity on Traitors' Island. He and his followers could see the people there struggling to launch two small, hand-made boats from the north side of their coral cay. Pieter Jansz was the first man aboard, and he was followed by his wife and child. Then came a German soldier, Claes Harmanszoon of Magdeburg, whose wife was also with him, and a woman named Claudine Patoys, who took a child with her. The other members of the party were all men: a mixed group of soldiers and sailors, almost all Dutch. They picked up rough paddles carved from driftwood and began to propel their rafts through the shallows, heading north.

Cornelisz knew at once where they were going. He had lured the provost and his men onto their barren islet with the assurance that they could sail on to the High Land when the soldiers there found water. It had been an empty promise, of course, but evidently Jansz had been watching out for signal fires, looking for any opportunity to leave his miserable base, and now he was making for Hayes's Island. The prospect of reinforcements reaching the soldiers on the High Land infuriated the under-merchant. While Jansz's rafts were still some way off, he summoned the members of his council for a hasty consultation. Together, they decided to attack.

Traitors' Island was only half a mile away, and there was little time to waste. Zevanck and Van Huyssen ran to gather their famil-iar accomplices – Gÿsbert van Welderen, Jan Hendricxsz, and Lenert van Os – and hurried to the beach where they kept their boats. Two other members of Jeronimus's gang came with them – they were Lucas Gellisz, a young cadet from The Hague, and Cornelis Pietersz, a common soldier from Utrecht – but this, it seems, was as many as their fastest yawl could carry. The seven men seized oars and steered southwest to intercept the rafts.

Pieter Jansz must have been alarmed to see the mutineers. The provost may well have guessed that Zevanck and his friends intended violence, for the murders of Hans Radder and Jacop Groenwald had taken place within sight of Traitors' Island, but he soon realised that he could not evade the yawl. His clumsy rafts were so much slower than the neat rowing boat the *Batavia*'s car-penters had built that Zevanck and his men had little difficulty in catching him.

The rafts were in the middle of a stretch of deep water when the mutineers caught up with them. As the yawl came within hailing distance, Zevanck raised his voice and called out to Jansz, demanding to know where he and his companions were going. Then he ordered the provost to change his course and make for Batavia's Graveyard instead.

While this was happening, the mutineers' yawl had swung alongside the provost's raft, and Gellisz, Pietersz, Hendricxsz, and Van Os swarmed from one to the other, armed and full of menace. Three or four of Jansz's men attempted to escape by hurling themselves into the sea, where they quickly drowned. The rest offered little resistance, and in less than a minute Zevanck's men had relieved the provost of his command. Soon both the rafts were heading for the under-merchant's island.

Jansz must by now have become seriously concerned for the safety of his family, but there was little he could do to protect them. He and his men watched uneasily as Zevanck jumped into the shallows and ran up the beach to where Jeronimus was standing by the entrance to his tent. The two men consulted for a moment, then Zevanck turned and hastened back toward the rafts. '*Slaet doodt!*' he was shouting. 'Kill!'

Lucas Gellisz had got into the water and was holding the rafts steady. Hendricxsz, Pietersz, and Van Os were still on board. Quickly, the three men drew their swords and cut down the provost and his child. Two, perhaps three, of the remaining men were also killed, as was Claudine Patoys's child, but for once the mutineers had found themselves outnumbered, and four of Jansz's party threw themselves over the side into water that came up to their waists. Two of them were sailors – friends named Pauwels Barentsz and Bessel Jansz, who both came from the little port of Harderwijk in Gelderland. The other pair were soldiers, Claes Harmanszoon and Nicolaas Winckelhaack. These men had apparently not realised that Cornelisz himself had ordered the attack, for they staggered out of the sea loudly imploring the under-merchant for protection. Jeronimus gazed down as the four men sprawled at his feet, soaked and breathless, panicked, desperate. 'Give them no quarter,' he declared.

Jan Hendricxsz had come running up the beach behind the men, his sword still in his hand. Now he lunged at Pauwels Barentsz, carving a great wound in his side. Barentsz fell backward onto the sand as Andries Jonas – another of Cornelisz's followers and, at 40, the oldest of the mutineers – loomed over him and thrust a pike right through his throat, turning the sailor's screams to blood-flecked gasps and pinning him down while he died. Hendricxsz, meanwhile, slashed at Winckelhaack, killing him immediately, after which he wounded Bessel Jansz. Rutger Fredricx came to join him, 'striking the mentioned Bessel with his sword until he was dead'; then the locksmith, alone, slew Harmanszoon as he fled back through the shallows. That left only the three women on the rafts. Zevanck, Van Huyssen, and Van Welderen bundled them into the yawl and sculled out into the channel, where the water was more than 100 feet deep. They then pushed Jansz's wife, and Harmanszoon's, and Claudine Patoys into the sea where – weighed down by their wet skirts – they drowned.

The massacre of the provost's party, which took place in full view of the 130 survivors on Batavia's Graveyard, brought the under-merchant's plot into the open for the first time. For three weeks or more, the people of the island had accepted Cornelisz as their leader without question; now they saw him as he really was. Jeronimus may well have tried to justify his actions; it is possible he argued that Pieter Jansz had been a traitor to the Company for fleeing to the High Land in defiance of the orders of the council. But, if so, it did him little good. Even the most trusting of the *retourschip*'s crew understood that the killings they had witnessed were nothing less than cold-blooded murder – and mutiny against the authority of Jan Company. And although the VOC loyalists still outnumbered the under-merchant's gang by about four to one, they were powerless to stop them. Cornelisz controlled all the weapons on the island, and only his followers had access to the swords, daggers, and axes in the stores. The island was so small and barren that there was nowhere to hide, and the boats were always guarded. Moreover, by a bitter irony, Jeronimus himself was now the living embodiment of the Gentlemen XVII in the Abrolhos. As the leader of the *raad,* he claimed the allegiance of all of the survivors. Any attempt to oppose him – even the least dissent – might itself be classed as mutiny against the VOC. Those who had watched as Pieter Jansz was hacked to pieces now understood that such actions would be punished with the utmost severity.

It was, then, hardly a surprise that at least another dozen men declared for Cornelisz over the next few days. Most appear to have joined the under-merchant in the hope of saving their own lives; a few were no doubt attracted by the prospect of better rations and freer access to the boats and stores. The majority of these opportunists were idlers or soldiers from the orlop deck, but at least one was an officer – an assistant from North Holland named Isbrant Isbrantsz. Frans Jansz, too, now that he had seen what Jeronimus was capable of, threw in his lot with the mutineers.

As it transpired, the new recruits played only minor roles in events on the Abrolhos, although they would sometimes be required to join the others in a show of force. Jeronimus, it seems, never really trusted them and frequently demanded some demonstration of their loyalty. For their part, the camp followers feared Cornelisz almost as much as did the other people on the island.

🐞

The first mutineer to be tested by the under-merchant was a German soldier named Hans Hardens. He came from Ditmarschen, a province close to Denmark's border with the Holy Roman Empire. Having taken service with the VOC for a five-year term, Hardens had boarded the *Batavia* with his wife, Anneken, and his six-year-old daughter, Hilletgie. All three of them had survived the voyage and the wreck and found themselves together on Batavia's Graveyard.

Hardens, so far as one can tell, had played no part in the conspiracy on board the ship, but he had gravitated towards Cornelisz's circle in the month after the wreck, apparently in the hope of feeding and protecting his wife and daughter. In time he became one of the more active mutineers, though he was hardly the most violent. Nevertheless, there was something about him that gave Jeronimus pause. The soldier may have been too slow to obey an order, too free with his opinions, or perhaps too friendly with Frans Jansz. So Cornelisz invited Hardens and his wife into his tent and – while they ate and drank together – sent Jan Hendricxsz to strangle their little girl.

Hilletgie Hardens was the first child to be killed on Batavia's Graveyard, but if her death was intended to test Hans Hardens's loyalty, Jeronimus must have been satisfied with the result. No matter what his private grief, Hardens knew he had no choice but to stick to his allegiance to the mutineers, especially if he was to have any hope of protecting his wife. Three days after his daughter's murder, Hardens swore an oath of fealty to his comrades: a solemn vow, a 'written unbreakable agreement, the greatest oath that anyone can take, to be faithful in everything.'

The brutal killing of the little girl perhaps affected the *Batavia* survivors more than any of the other early murders. Most of the other victims had at least been tried by the ship's council, while Pieter Jansz and his men had arguably been guilty of disobeying Zevanck's orders. Awful though their deaths had been, there had at least been some sort of explanation for them. Hilletgie's murder seemed senseless in comparison, for not even Cornelisz argued she had been guilty of a crime. Her death thus marked a significant deterioration of conditions in the archipelago. From then on, none of the *retourschip*'s passengers and crew could be certain they were safe. Showing loyalty to the under-merchant, obeying orders and working hard were no longer any guarantee of Jeronimus's favour. He and his followers had begun to murder indiscriminately.

Matters were very different for the members of the under-merchant's gang, who now felt a sense of liberation. The first days of the mutiny cannot have been easy for David Zevanck and his friends. Their work was difficult and dangerous, and the risk of discovery was real. By the middle of July, however, the assistant and his friends had gained considerably in confidence, parading openly about the island, fully armed, and taking what they wanted for themselves. 'The whole day long it was their catch-call, "Who wants to be boxed on the ear?"' remembered Gijsbert Bastiaensz.

'So we all of us together expected to be murdered at any moment, and we besought God continuously for merciful relief...O cruelty! O atrocity of atrocities! They proved themselves to be nothing more than highwaymen. Murderers who are on the roads often take their belongings from People, but they sometimes leave them their lives; but these have taken both, goods and blood.'

Among their many privileges, Cornelisz's most trusted men enjoyed better rations than the other *Batavia* survivors, eating cask meat instead of sea lion and bird, and drinking wines and spirits rather than rainwater. They had better clothes and larger tents, and their access to the boats gave them a freedom of movement that was denied to the loyalists. Significantly, the mutineers also experienced – for the first time in their lives – complete freedom from the constraints that had previously governed them. In the United Provinces they had generally been men of little significance and few resources, who struggled to make a living and were subject to the rule of law. In the Abrolhos they had status and wielded power over men and women who were their nominal superiors. They felt, moreover, little fear of retribution. Cornelisz's position in the archipelago appeared to be unchallengeable, and the prospect of arrest and punishment remote.

Jeronimus had perhaps derived some satisfaction from crushing Hardens, for he next turned his attention to Andries de Vries. The young Zeelander was lucky to be alive, having escaped death by drowning at the beginning of the month, but he had yet to demonstrate his loyalty to the men who had spared his life. On 10 July Jeronimus gave De Vries that opportunity. He was told to prove his worthiness by killing on the under-merchant's orders.

The chosen victims were people in the sick tent. There were 11 of them in all – useless mouths, Cornelisz observed, who were so weakened by scurvy and fever that they would offer no resistance. De Vries crept into their tent by night and cut their throats, one by one, while Zevanck, Van Huyssen, and Van Welderen stood over him to make quite sure he carried out his task. Three days later the assistant was compelled to return and slaughter another four or five men who had taken sick in the interim.

From then on, to fall ill on Batavia's Graveyard was to receive a death sentence. First Jan Hendricxsz and Allert Janssen slit the throat of Jan Pinten, the island's only English soldier, while he lay in bed; then a sick cabin boy went the same way. A few days later, De Vries and Janssen conspired to end the life of Hendrick Claasz, a carpenter. These killings also took place by night. The only invalids to be spared were friends of the mutineers: Hans Frederick, who had already helped to kill one man and may have been one of Hendricxsz's associates, and Olivier van Welderen, who was Gÿsbert's elder brother.

Having disposed of the sick, Jeronimus turned his attention back to the stronger survivors. On the evening of 12 July the under-merchant sent his favourite killer, Hendricxsz, out to rid him of Passchier van den Ende, a gunner, and Jacop Hendricxen Drayer,* who was a carpenter. These men were to be confronted by the old allegation that they had stolen something from the stores.

*The word *draijer* means 'turner' and thus denotes Hendricxen's profession.

It was, it seems, a typically blustery Abrolhos night, for the shrieking of the wind and the snap and crack of canvas walls masked the sound of Hendricxsz's approach. Van den Ende and Drayer only realised he was there when the flaps of their tent were suddenly thrown back and the German soldier emerged from the darkness like a vengeful angel, flanked by Zevanck, Van Os, and Lucas Gellisz.

The sailors realised at once that their lives were forfeit:

'[Jan] went into their tent and asked Passchier if he had any goods hidden there ... He answered weepingly, "No," and begged that he might be allowed to say his prayers, because he thought that it would cost him his life. But Zevanck said, "Get on with it." Thus Jan Hendricxsz threw him to the ground and cut his throat.

'The other one, Jacop Hendricxen Drayer, begged bitterly for his life, whereupon Zevanck and the others went to Jeronimus and said that Jacop was a good carpenter and should he not be spared. But Jeronimus answered, "Not at all, he is only a turner and furthermore he is half-lame. He must also go. He might become a babbler now or later."'

With that, the murderers returned to Drayer's tent. Remarkably, the hapless turner was still there, waiting for them. Perhaps his injured leg made it useless for him to attempt to flee; perhaps he genuinely hoped for mercy. If so, one glance into Hendricxsz's blank eyes would have informed him of his error.

Disposing of a crippled man should not have taken long, but for all his disability, Drayer proved almost impossible to kill. Hendricxsz pushed him to the ground, and Van Os sat astride the turner's hips while his friend stabbed him repeatedly in the chest. The dancing flame of Zevanck's lantern set a shadow play of murder flickering against the canvas walls, but even with the benefit of light the German could not find Jacop's heart. First one knife hit a rib and snapped in two, then a second broke uselessly in half. Hendricxsz seized another pair of daggers and drove them deep into his victim's neck, but anger had made him careless and his thrusts missed Drayer's windpipe, arteries, and veins. The two knives sliced through muscle and struck bone; their blades splintered on the turner's spinal column and the mutineer found himself holding another pair of useless hafts. Jacop was still alive, and Hendricxsz, breathing heavily, had to thrust slippery fingers into the spreading pool of blood beneath the body, fumbling for a sliver of broken knife with which to slit his victim's throat.

❋

For Jeronimus's mutineers, the glut of killings in the first half of July substantially improved conditions on Batavia's Graveyard. By the 14th of the month, they had disposed of almost 50 men, women, and children, almost a third of whom had been too ill to put up any sort of fight. These deaths had reduced the population of Batavia's Graveyard to about 90 people, of whom almost half were either active mutineers or hangers-on who had pledged loyalty to Cornelisz in the hope of saving their own lives.

By now, the mutineers' chief enemy was boredom. The *Batavia* journals tell us almost nothing about how they passed the time from day to day. Some were set to catching fish and birds; others, evidently, must have mounted guard, watching the campsite and the boats. We know they sometimes fashioned makeshift weapons such as morning stars – lethal clubs manufactured from strips of lead that had been bent in half, studded with long iron nails and threaded through with a short length of rope so that they could be swung at the heads of future victims – and that Jeronimus occasionally invited a few men to his tent. There, amid overflowing bales of trade goods and company stores purloined from the wreck, the under-merchant plied his followers with wine and showed off their most prized possession – Pelsaert's case of valuables, which had been landed on Traitors' Island and abandoned there when the *commandeur* left in the overloaded longboat.

Inside the case were four bags of jewels, worth nearly 60,000 guilders, which the merchant would allow his men to run through their fingers, and a large agate cameo, almost a foot from end to end, which Pelsaert was taking to India at the request of an Amsterdam jeweler called Gaspar Boudaen. The cameo had been carved in the Eastern Roman Empire early in the fourth century, possibly on the orders of Constantine the Great; it depicted a classical scene, and the *commandeur* believed that it would find favour at the Mogul court. Boudaen had mounted it within a golden frame studded with precious stones, creating a piece so rare and valuable that even the Gentlemen XVII had not been permitted to inspect it before it was loaded onto the *Batavia*. Pelsaert had anticipated selling the jewel at a profit of perhaps 50 percent; the VOC was to receive more than a quarter of its value as commission, but in all likelihood the *commandeur* had also arranged to keep a portion of the sale price for himself. The cameo had thus been central to his hopes of earning a fortune trading luxuries and 'toys' with the Great Mogul, and now it assumed an equally important place in Jeronimus's plans.

While he watched his men caress the agate, the under-merchant spoke seductively of the wealth that they could earn from piracy. The mutineers were captivated by the stories that their leader spun. They were, said Andries Jonas, later, willing to do Cornelisz's bidding, 'for they were led into thinking that they would all be rich for life.'

While the under-merchant's men lay back and dreamed of wealth and luxury, life for the remaining loyalists became a waking nightmare. They all existed in a constant state of fear. Trapped on a tiny island with a group of ruthless murderers, there was little they could do to save themselves. They were thousands of miles from everything they knew and just as far from help. They were unarmed, with nowhere to hide and no way to escape. Life on Batavia's Graveyard thus became a matter of waiting for one's turn to die.

The apparently arbitrary nature of the killings only made things worse, for it was impossible to know who would be the mutineers' next victim. The under-merchant's followers had grown accustomed to murder and needed little excuse, or none, to kill again. Standing out in any way – being too loud or too quiet, or failing in some task – could only hasten the inevitable moment when Zevanck or Jan Hendricxsz would appear, ready with some trumped-up charge and brandishing a sword.

Days in the Abrolhos were bad enough – but the nights were worse. Most of the murders took place after dark, when the islands seem to bulge with wind and even the endless thunder of the surf is drowned out by the calls of terns and mutton birds,* whose endless keening sounds exactly like the screams of human babies. By mid-July the moon had waned, so that the only illumination came from stars pulsing feebly from behind the scudding clouds, and the survivors had grown wary of approaching lights. Once the bobbing firefly of a watchman's lantern, threading its way through the little settlement, had been a symbol of security. Now it could,

---

*A species of petrel, common throughout Western Australia.

and often did, mean death. Lying in their makeshift beds, shifting uneasily on the tilting plates of fan coral that littered the ground, the loyalists caught their breath whenever lamps approached. They waited for the sickly yellow glow to pass their tents and leave them alive, knowing all the while that one day it would not.

※

In the mornings, when Jeronimus arose, he could look west across the half-mile of deep water that separated him from Seals' Island and see the figures of the men and women he had landed there moving about their own camp, almost opposite his own. He had left them unmolested for the best part of a month, while never doubting they should go the way of Pieter Jansz's men eventually. By the middle of July, with the provost and the sick safely out of the way, he felt ready to attack.

There were still 45 survivors on the cay. Without supplies from Batavia's Graveyard they would have struggled to find sufficient food and water to feed themselves, and many of them must have been ill and exhausted. Their leaders – Cornelis Jansz, a young assistant from Amsterdam, and Gabriel Jacobszoon, the corporal – had no more than 10 or 12 men under their command. The other members of the party were either boys (perhaps two dozen of them) or women with young children.

It is not clear how much these people knew of Cornelisz's activities, but the murders of 9 July would have been clearly visible to anyone watching from the other side of the deep-water channel, and if Jansz and Jacobszoon really had no contact with the small boats that now ventured out to fish, they must have wondered why. It seems that the assistant and the corporal at least guessed what Jeronimus was planning, for they, like the provost's men, had begun to construct rafts. Three or four were being assembled on the west side of their island, out of sight of Batavia's Graveyard. The boats were just about complete when, on 15 July, the under-merchant's men appeared, paddling a yawl across the channel separating the islands, heading directly for their campsite.

Jeronimus, who was growing rapidly in confidence, had sent no more than seven of his men to tackle the people of Seals' Island. Zevanck and Van Huyssen were to lead the attack; with them went Jan Hendricxsz, Lenert van Os, Cornelis Pietersz, and a Swiss cadet called Hans Jacob Heijlweck. The last member of the party was the surgeon, Jansz, who had thus far played no part in any killings. It seems likely that Jeronimus ordered him to go, and that Jansz felt it wise to demonstrate his loyalty by obeying.

Cornelisz had issued precise instructions – 'Kill most of the people,' he had said, 'children as well as some men, and leave alive for the time being only the women who are there' – and for once Zevanck showed no interest in creating any pretext for his crimes. This time there were no accusations of treachery, no mention of any stolen goods. The mutineers had been issued with swords, daggers, and morning stars. They landed, drew their weapons, and attacked.

Van Os was among the first to leap ashore. 'Lenert, immediately after he arrived, has stabbed one boy right through the body, and another through his buttock, and also Jacop de Vos, tailor, right through his side,' one account of this episode explains, 'and as soon as they have come there Jan Hendricxsz has stabbed to death five cabin boys and two men.' The other mutineers split up, chasing and cutting down their unarmed opponents throughout the camp. Some of the men, including the corporal, had wives and families to protect, and they were probably among the first to die. The rest made for the rafts or hid. Eight men, including Cornelis Jansz, reached the boats and managed to escape, eventually finding their way to the High Land to the north. Several of the surviving cabin boys hid themselves among bushes in the middle of the island. The rest took to their heels and ran, heading north along the mile-long cay so nimbly that the murderers could not keep up.

Zevanck tackled this problem with his usual brutality. The mutineers had captured one of the cabin servants during their initial assault – he was Abraham Gerritsz of Amsterdam, the young deserter whom Pelsaert had rescued from Sierra Leone. Now he was dragged in front of the assistant. 'Boy,' Zevanck explained, 'you must help lustily to kill, or be in a fix yourself.' Gerritsz proved 'very willing' to comply, though he perhaps obeyed more out of fear than real blood lust; in any case, he soon managed to catch another child of about his age, 15. The fleeing youth was wrestled to the ground, and, after a short struggle, Gerritsz pinned him down and killed him with a knife. The remainder of the boys – 15 in all – could not be found, and eventually the mutineers gave up the search and turned their attention back to the camp.

The initial attack had left at least four men and six boys dead. Half a dozen more were badly wounded and now lay sprawled on the coral, no longer able to defend themselves. Zevanck and his friends dragged these men into the sea and held their heads under the water until they drowned. Four pregnant women – one of them Laurentia Thomas, the corporal's wife – were found among the tents but spared in compliance with Jeronimus's orders; and once the under-merchant's men had satisfied themselves that there were no other rafts on which the few survivors could escape, the remaining youths were also left to be dealt with another day. The mutineers returned to Batavia's Graveyard pleased with their day's work, having reduced the population of the nearby cay by nearly half. The boy Gerritsz went with them, another recruit to the under-merchant's cause.

Jeronimus wasted little time in resolving the problem of the fleeing cabin boys. A few days later he dispatched a second party to Seals' Island, on this occasion waiting until after dark to be certain of catching the surviving members of the corporal's party in their tents. Once again the mutineers were led by David Zevanck, but this time there were eight of them, including Mattys Beer, Gÿsbert van Welderen, and a youth from the small town of Bommel named Jan Pelgrom. The killers landed close to the camp without being seen and crept silently toward the tents, spreading out as they went so as to be able to enter each of them simultaneously. Then, at the assistant's signal, they attacked.

One of Zevanck's men that night was Andries Jonas, the old soldier from Luyck:*

'On the 18 July, Andries Jonas has been ordered by Jeronimus to go, together with David Zevanck and another [six] men, with the little yawl to Seals' Island, in order to kill there the remaining four women and about 15 boys who had not been killed on the previous murder of 15 July.

'Therefore Zevanck has asked whether he had a knife; Andries Jonas answered that he had a knife but it was not very sharp. Whereupon Zevanck handed him his own knife, saying, "Cut the throats of the women."

'So willingly, without objection, Andries has gone to Mayken Soers, who was heavily pregnant, has taken her by the hand and led her a little to one side and said to her, "Mayken, love, you must die," and thrown her underfoot and cut her throat; that

*Modern Liége.

being done, he saw that Jan van Bommel was trying to kill
Janneken Gist (the wife of Jan Hendricx from The Hague); therefore he went to help ... and stabbed Janneken to death with his
knife; the other two women were killed by the others.'

While this was going on, Van Welderen and Beer had crept into
the tents with three or four of the other mutineers and caught the
surviving cabin boys asleep. The mutineers set upon the youths
with daggers and clubs, bludgeoning and stabbing them where
they lay. A dozen of the boys were killed outright, or mortally
wounded and dragged down to the sea to drown, but three
managed to escape. Dodging their assailants' blows, they ran into
the darkness and disappeared along the ridge.

These boys survived until 24 July, when they foolishly emerged
within sight of Batavia's Graveyard. Cornelisz noticed them, and
sent Stone-Cutter Pietersz with three men to flush them from their
hiding places. This time the youths did not escape; the lance corporal captured them alive and herded them into his yawl. On the
way back to Batavia's Graveyard, on the under-merchant's orders,
he and Isbrant Isbrantsz forced one of the boys to throw his two
companions overboard. The survivor, a child named Claes
Harmansz, was spared. Like Gerritsz, he became a mutineer.

※

Jeronimus's actions in the latter half of July 1629 suggest a man
driven to commit ever more perverse atrocities by a burning need
for novelty and stimulation. The under-merchant apparently felt
jaded by the endless murders he had ordered, and – like some
Roman tyrant – sought out fresh diversions to assuage his
boredom. It was not as if he really needed more followers; his
position on Batavia's Graveyard was by now unassailable, and he
was never to rely upon Andries de Vries or even Andries Liebent
in the way he trusted Jan Hendricxsz or Mattys Beer. Rather, he
seems to have taken special pleasure in exploiting weakness and
corrupting youth.

De Vries, Liebent and the surgeon Jansz had already been
forced to slaughter companions and friends in order to save themselves. Now Jeronimus and his men had forced Claes Harmansz,
Isbrant Isbrantsz, and Abraham Gerritsz to become killers too.
The under-merchant was, perhaps, intrigued by the changes that

came over his followers once he had turned them into murderers; he seems to have found the conflicting emotions of guilt and exultation a fascinating study. And though he had always distanced himself from the violence that had engulfed the archipelago, he now seems to have become obsessed with the idea of experiencing the same sensations for himself.

Evidence for this contention can be found in an incident that occurred a few days after the first killings on Seals' Island. For several nights Cornelisz and his companions had had their sleep disturbed by the endless wailings of a baby, the child of a girl from the lower deck named Mayken Cardoes. Mayken had saved her infant from the wreck and nursed it devotedly, even breast-feeding when the water on the island had run out and she herself was close to dying of thirst. But for all her frantic efforts the infant proved impossible to quiet, and she was unable to prevent it from awakening the merchant and his friends.

For Jeronimus, the crying baby seemed the perfect subject for his planned experiment, and he resolved to murder it. It was typical of Cornelisz that he chose to kill with poison – an apothecary's weapon, and something he, alone of all the people in the Abrolhos, was able to prepare – and equally telling that he preferred to proceed by stealth. Mayken was brought before him and asked for details of the baby's illness. One can readily imagine her accepting the under-merchant's offer to concoct a medicine to soothe it.

The poison that Jeronimus produced, using materials that had been salvaged from the wreck, was an old alchemical compound called *mercurium sublimatum*. Cornelisz administered it on 20 July and watched with interest to observe its effect. He must have been disappointed to discover that though the potion quickly silenced the child's crying, it failed to kill it altogether, merely inducing a sort of coma 'so that it could neither live nor die.'

This failure left the under-merchant in a difficult position. It would, of course, have been easy enough for Jeronimus to have finished the helpless infant off, but for some reason he retained his old aversion to killing with his bare hands. He chose, instead, to blood another of the minor mutineers who had thus far evaded his responsibilities.

Cornelisz's chosen instrument on this occasion was another of the island's weaklings: Pelsaert's trusted clerk, Salomon Deschamps of Amsterdam. Deschamps, who was the most senior VOC officer in the Abrolhos after Jeronimus himself, was a coward who had done nothing to prevent the under-merchant from seizing control of the islands, 'permitting the evil to take its course without saying anything against it, shutting his eyes and dissimulating in order to prolong his own life.' Indeed, as soon as Cornelisz had seemed securely established, he had transferred his allegiance to the mutineers. Now the clerk was made to pay for this betrayal.

'On 20 July, at night, he was fetched out of his tent by Jacop Pietersz, who took him into Mayken Cardoes' tent, where David Zevanck, Jan Hendricxsz and Cornelis Pietersz of Utrecht were, who said to him that they were not certain of his faithfulness [and] therefore took a Young Suckling child from the lap of the foresaid mother, Mayken Cardoes, and said to him, "Deschamps, here is a Half dead child. You are not a fighting Man, here is a little noose, go over there and fix it so that we here on the Island do not hear so much wailing." Then he, Deschamps, without protest, has taken the child outside the tent and has strangled it, an act of very evil Consequence.'

Mayken Cardoes's baby was the first of the *Batavia* survivors that Cornelisz attempted to murder himself, and it would also be the last. Yet by the time Deschamps had squeezed its barely begun life from it, the infant had become the 105th person to die at the under-merchant's hands. By now fewer than 60 people were still alive on Batavia's Graveyard, and Jeronimus was close to doing what he had set out to do: 'to have murdered or destroyed all the people until the amount of 45 or less.'

※

Of all the families on the island, by far the largest was the *predikant*'s. Gijsbert Bastiaensz and Maria Schepens had been blessed with a total of eight children, seven of whom had sailed with them on the *Batavia*. In an age in which half of all the children born in Europe died before reaching adulthood, Bastiaensz had been exceptionally fortunate to lose only one child in infancy. Even more remarkably, the *predikant*'s wife, his servant girl, Wybrecht Claasen, and all seven of the children had survived the many rigours of the voyage: running aground on the Walcheren Banks, the long journey to the Abrolhos, the shipwreck, six waterless and agonising days on Batavia's Graveyard, the maid's struggle to fetch water from the hulk, and finally 20 days of terror at the hands of Jeronimus Cornelisz.

Bastiaensz enjoyed a certain status, it was true – one that had guaranteed him and his family good rations on the ship, and some protection on the island, too – but under the circumstances, the fact that he still had all his family around him must have seemed perfectly miraculous to the rest of the *Batavia* survivors: proof, if any were required, that the *predikant* truly was a man of God.

Of the minister's children, four were boys. The eldest, who had been given his grandfather's name, was called Bastiaen Gijsbertsz; he was 23 years old, and since he was sufficiently well educated and mature to do useful work, he had been given the rank of VOC assistant and spent the voyage helping Pelsaert with his clerical work. His brother Pieter Gijsbertsz was four years younger, but though certainly old enough to join Jan Company he had not done so; it is possible that – since Bastiaen was evidently unsuited to life as a *predikant* – Gijsbert's second son was destined for the clergy. The other boys were still of school age: Johannes was 13 and Roelant, the youngest child of all, was only 8.

The minister's daughters were Judick, Willemijntgie, and Agnete. Judick was the second child; she was 21 and thus of marriageable age. In so large a family she must have spent a good deal of her time helping her mother with the younger children, although Willemijntgie, at 14, was also nearly grown-up. The youngest girl, Agnete, had celebrated her 11th birthday shortly before they had reached the Cape.

On an island where women were outnumbered 9 or 10 to 1 by men, Judick could not help but attract attention, the more so because there were no more than three unmarried women on Batavia's Graveyard. Soon she was being courted by Coenraat van Huyssen, the young cadet who was by now the murderer of half a dozen people. Being good-looking and a minor member of the nobility, as well as a leading member of Cornelisz's blood council, Van Huyssen had some claim to be the most eligible of the island's many bachelors, and unwelcome though his attentions were in most respects, they at least saved the girl from being molested by the other mutineers. She did not discourage him. Matters moved swiftly, and within a month of their arrival in the Abrolhos Van Huyssen was proposing matrimony – but with an ugly caveat. Since the couple could not legally be married in the islands (the consent of the groom's parents, at home in the Dutch Republic, would be required to make the match binding), Coenraat agreed to be content with a mere engagement – so long, that is, as Judick consummated their betrothal on the spot.

The preacher and his daughter now found themselves in an impossible position. 'Coenraat van Huyssen from Gelderlandt,' scribbled Bastiaensz,

'a member of the Council of those Murderers, besought my Daughter in Holy Wedlock. But said he would make a Betrothal with her and marry her legally before all the World, [and] that he would do at the first opportunity; many words were said about this matter, too long to narrate, for Judick and I deliberated thus: that it was better to be kept legally by one Man, in such a time, than to be mis-used. Therefore he made a betrothal vow with her, and all that went with that.

'I begged that she should go and live with him the next day ... but the other Murderers, coming in front of the Tent, said that it had to happen that night and immediately, otherwise they were ready to kill us ... She has been with him in that respect, but she has not been abused, as she has told me. What could one do against it?'

As her father had predicted, Judick's relationship with Van Huyssen was enough to safeguard her from harm, but even if the mutineer's feelings for the girl were genuine, she had no power to protect the other members of her family. For two weeks now Cornelisz had eased his boredom and sated his men's increasing blood lust every second or third day. The general pattern was one of increasing violence. Drownings had given way to stabbings and cut throats, and the sheer scale of the murders had increased, too – from the 15 people killed on 9 July to the 23 dispatched on Seals' Island nine days later. In the three days since the latter massacre, however, the one incident of note had been the under-merchant's poisoning of Mayken Cardoes's child. This was not enough for some of the mutineers. The daily routine of catching, preparing, and eating food held limited appeal for men who had come to enjoy the power of taking life, and by the end of the third week of the month Zevanck and the others were anxious to kill again. The largest (indeed the only real) target left to them was the family of Gijsbert Bastiaensz.

Judick was now inviolate, and Cornelisz had decided the

predikant himself might also be worth sparing; though their theologies could not have been more different, Jeronimus could still see uses for a man of God. Maria Schepens and her six remaining children were a different matter. On the evening of 21 July, Bastiaensz and his eldest daughter were lured away from their quarters by an invitation to dine with Van Huyssen and Cornelisz in the *jonker*'s quarters. While they were being entertained with a meal of cask meat and red wine salvaged from the wreck, David Zevanck and Jacop Pietersz gathered seven of the principal mutineers. Together, they made their way to the minister's tent. It would be 'a pleasant outing,' the Stone-Cutter declared, to 'put the *predikant*'s folk out of the way.'

By now they were well-practised killers, and the murders had been carefully planned. Earlier in the evening a group of Cornelisz's men had dug a grave pit, large enough to hold eight bodies, not far from the encampment. Zevanck and Pietersz had also decided to kill the family in their tent, where there would be less chance of any of the children contriving to escape. To this end the men exchanged their swords for knives and hatchets, which were better tools for killing at close quarters.

Pietersz and Andries Jonas were the last to arrive in the survivors' camp. They found Zevanck and Jan Hendricxsz waiting; with them were Lenert van Os, Mattys Beer, Cornelis Pietersz, Andries Liebent, and a Dutch soldier called Wouter Loos. Inside the tent, the preacher's family was cooking dinner. A kettle full of sea lion's meat hung boiling over the fire.

The first men to approach were Zevanck and Hendricxsz, the most brutal of the mutineers. Zevanck crept to the entrance of the tent and called for Wybrecht Claasen. In a second or two the servant girl emerged, walking almost straight onto Hendricxsz's dagger. The German soldier stabbed her once and left her dying on the shingle. Meanwhile Zevanck forced his way into the tent with the main body of the mutineers. It was so crowded that Pietersz and Jonas, the late arrivals, had to wait outside.

Maria Schepens and her children must have known they were dead the moment they saw the axe in David Zevanck's hand, but once again the young assistant felt the need to justify his actions. There was an oil lamp hanging in the tent; he took it, lifted it above his head and called out, 'Here has been reported hidden goods of the Company that we will search for.' He paused, then added ominously: 'And we will get them.' At this, the other mutineers began to hunt through the few possessions in the tent until, after a moment or two, the lamp blew out – Zevanck no doubt extinguished it himself – and in the pitch-black crush the murdering began.

There were 14 people in the tent: 7 of Jeronimus's men and 7 members of the preacher's family, one victim to each man. The mutineers laid about themselves with hatchets. Lenert van Os caved in Maria's skull with several blows, while Mattys Beer bludgeoned Willemijntgie. Wouter Loos pushed Bastiaen to the ground 'and has beaten the eldest son underfoot with an adze, until he was dead,' while Zevanck, Van Os, and Beer between them accounted for Pieter, Johannes, and Agnete. The only child not killed or wounded in the initial flurry of blows was the youngest; eight-year-old Roelant was so small that he ducked through the legs of his attacker, Beer, and fled in terror, searching desperately for a way out of the tent. He almost got away; Beer dared not turn and swing at the boy for fear of striking one of his companions. But Zevanck and Cornelis Pietersz were standing close behind him, and one or other of them brought his hatchet down hard upon the child and killed him.

In only a few moments the killing ceased. Then the murderers became aware that one of their victims was still alive, and moaning in pain. It was Maria Schepens, 'who was not then quite dead.' Mattys Beer bent over her as she lay prostrate on the ground and finished her off with several more blows to the head. The groans stopped. It was over.

They cleared the tent. Andries Liebent made off with the meat from the dead family's kettle and took it back to his own quarters. The other murderers dragged the bodies to the pit that had been prepared and hurled them in, so that they lay huddled together in a single bloodstained mass.

It was still only midevening and the mutineers' blood was up. The group split up and went in search of other prey. Jan Hendricxsz went to the tent of Hendrick Denys, one of the Company bookkeepers, ordered him out onto the shingle, and, when he showed himself, 'battered in [his] head, with an adze, in front of his tent, so that he died immediately.' Meanwhile, Zevanck summoned Andries Jonas, who had not yet killed that night. 'Go and call Mayken Cardoes out of her tent and cut her throat,' he told him.

Cardoes guessed well enough what was happening when

Andries arrived outside her quarters. 'Mayken,' Jonas said, 'are you asleep? Come, we'll go for a walk.' It was not a request but an order, and the girl had little choice but to obey. She emerged hesitantly from her tent. 'Andries,' she begged him, 'will you do me evil?' 'No, not at all,' he said, but they had only walked a little way along the shore when he seized her without warning and forced her backward onto the coral. Fumbling for his knife, Jonas crouched over her; he reached down and tried to cut her throat, but she was struggling so violently beneath him that he could not manage it. After a few seconds he abandoned the attempt and instead leaned back, pinning her down with one hand while he tried to stab her with the knife held in the other. Desperately, Cardoes thrust out an arm and tried to seize the blade as it descended. She caught the tip of it, but the knife was travelling with such force that the blade sliced straight through the palm and emerged from the back of her hand, wedging itself firmly between the bones.

Jonas tugged hard at the haft, but the knife was stuck fast and he could not remove it. He could feel the unfortunate girl still thrashing about beneath him, attempting to free herself with her one good hand, so he let go of the knife and tried to strangle her instead. Even then he could not subdue her, but the sound of their struggles had alerted Wouter Loos, and he ran to Jonas's aid. Exhausted, wounded, and pinned against the coral, Cardoes had no chance against two soldiers. Loos stoved her skull in with an axe and they hurled the corpse into the pit that had been dug for the bodies of the minister's family. It was little more than a day since they had murdered the girl's child.

Still David Zevanck had not had enough. Back in the mutineers' camp he summoned Allert Janssen, who like Jonas had taken no part in the killing of the *predikant*'s family, and ordered him to kill the under-barber, Aris Jansz of Hoorn. Like Andries Jonas, Janssen employed a pretext to get the surgeon out of his tent and away from the camp, saying, 'Aris, come outside, we have to go and catch four small birds for the merchant.' It was by now well after dark, and Jansz can hardly have believed that this was true, but like Mayken Cardoes he was too scared to refuse. The barber-surgeon and his murderer walked down to the beach, Aris slightly ahead of Allert, and just as they reached it Janssen drew his sword and stuck his victim a sudden blow across the shoulder. At this signal a second mutineer, Cornelis Pietersz, loomed out of the darkness; he had been hiding close by, and now joined in the attack, swinging at Jansz's head. Remarkably, both men's swords were so blunt that the surgeon was hardly wounded by their blows. Instead of falling to the ground as they had expected, Jansz took to his heels and vanished into the night, splashing away into the shallows to the east of the island. Janssen and Pietersz went after him, calling one to the other as they searched and no doubt cursing their luck, but their victim had the sense to drop down and let the water hide him, and they could not find him in the darkness. After a few minutes' fruitless wading to and fro, the two mutineers managed to persuade themselves that Jansz had been critically wounded and was sure to die. 'So they said to one another, turning back, *"Hij heves al wel"'* – 'He's had it' – and set off together, dripping, to report to Zevanck.

Bleeding somewhat, but otherwise not badly hurt, Aris kept himself hidden until he was quite certain that the mutineers were gone. Then, slowly and with great care, he worked his way around the island to the beach where Cornelisz's men kept their skiffs. The boats were poorly guarded – probably Zevanck and the others had not imagined that someone might come at them out of the sea rather than along the island paths – and no one saw him as he untethered a little homemade raft and dragged it silently into the water. When he was well clear of the island, Aris clambered aboard, and began to pull for Hayes's Island to the north.

❁

Thus, by the end of the third week of July, the situation in the Abrolhos was relatively clear. Jeronimus and his gang of mutineers had secured absolute control over Batavia's Graveyard. Nevertheless, their base, the island itself, was so devoid of natural resources that their position in the longer term was not absolutely assured. They remained dependent on the rain for water and on salvaged, and thus limited, supplies for everything else, from clothing to weaponry.

Meanwhile, Wiebbe Hayes and his original party of 20 men had somehow contrived to survive on the two largest islands in the archipelago. There had been no direct contact between the under-merchant and the soldiers for more than a month, but thanks to the arrival of the survivors from Seals' Island, and then Aris Jansz, Hayes had a very good idea what the mutineers were doing and understood the danger he was in. Jeronimus, on the other hand, had no real inkling of the soldiers' situation. He realised they had been forewarned and reinforced by several refugees, but neither he nor his council knew whether Hayes's men were comfortably established on their island, or so short of food and water they were simply dying by degrees.

The under-merchant knew, however, that the situation had changed in one critical respect. Wiebbe might have no swords or guns, but now he did possess some boats. Cornelis Jansz's little homemade rafts and Aris Jansz's skiff were not a danger in themselves; they could never carry enough men for Hayes to launch a worthwhile attack. But they could make things very difficult for the mutineers if Pelsaert reached his destination and returned to rescue them.

CHAPTER 6

Longboat

'We expected nothing else but death.'
ANONYMOUS SAILOR

The *Batavia*'s longboat, with Francisco Pelsaert and Ariaen Jacobsz aboard, bobbed in the ocean swells north of the Abrolhos, steering for the South-Land. She was quite a substantial craft – a little more than 30 feet long, with 10 oars and a single mast – but though her sides had been built up with some extra planking there was still not much more than two feet between them and the ocean's surface. The boat could easily be swamped in heavy seas, and even the short voyage to the mainland over the horizon – which the skipper guessed was only 50 miles away – was not without its dangers.

Pelsaert's original intention had been to search for water on the nearest stretch of coastline and bring back enough, in barrels, to supply the rest of the survivors for several weeks at least. This, in turn, would make it possible to send a boat north to fetch help. The chief problem with the plan was that the coast of Terra Australis was so poorly mapped that neither the skipper nor the *commandeur* had any real idea where to search; the VOC's earlier encounters with the South-Land indicated that a river reached the coast about 360 miles north of their position, but locating supplies any closer than that would require luck as much as judgment, and there was no telling how long it would take to get them back to the Abrolhos.

Lurking at the back of Ariaen Jacobsz's mind was the thought that if no fresh water could be found they would have to sail the longboat straight to Java, where the Dutch trading settlement of Batavia was the one place they could be sure of finding help. The

Indies were nearly 2,000 miles away, however, and even if such a lengthy voyage was possible, it would be at least two months before any survivors in the archipelago could be rescued; by that time it seemed likely that many of them, if not all, would have died of thirst. No doubt others in the skipper's entourage had reached the same conclusion, for all 48 of the people who had been part of Jacobsz's party insisted on sailing with him. They took with them all the remaining food and water. In consequence, the longboat, which was designed for no more than 40, was dangerously overloaded.

The only people in the boat who really mattered were the sailors. All the senior officers of the *Batavia* – the skipper, the three steersmen, and the high boatswain, Evertsz – were on board, and they alone had the experience and skills required to keep a small vessel afloat on the open ocean and navigate to and from the Abrolhos. Of the other 43 passengers and crew, the great majority were surely able seamen; in addition, Jacobsz's cousin, the bos'n's mate, and Harman Nannings, the *Batavia*'s quartermaster, were probably on board. Only six of those who sailed from the Abrolhos – three men, two women, and a child – had no apparent knowledge of the sea. Zwaantie Hendricx was one; Ariaen had kept her close to him ever since the wreck and had no intention of leaving her behind now. Zwaantie was accompanied by a young mother (she is not named in Pelsaert's journals) and her two-month-old baby, who had been born somewhere in the Southern Ocean. Also on board were Hans Jacobsz, a joiner; Claes Jansz, the *Batavia*'s chief trumpeter; and Francisco Pelsaert himself.

They sighted the South-Land on the afternoon of 8 June, their first day at sea. The coast was bleak and utterly forbidding: flat; featureless; devoid of water, trees, or vegetation; and protected by an unbroken line of cliffs that stretched as far as could be seen in either direction. Huge breakers crashed endlessly against the rocks, churning the sea white with foam and making any approach to land extremely hazardous. By now night was only a few hours away, and Jacobsz did not dare remain inshore; instead, he steered back out to sea for several hours, turning east again at midnight and coming back upon the coast a few miles to the north at dawn. The sun rose to reveal an identically awe-inspiring cliffscape, and they sailed north along it for a whole day without finding anywhere to land.

Pelsaert and Jacobsz had, in fact, chanced upon the South-Land coast at its most desolate. From Houtman's Abrolhos the shoreline remains almost unremittingly hostile all the way to what is now Shark Bay, 200 miles to the north. Along the way, the cliffs rise precipitately to heights of up to 750 feet. There are almost no safe landing places, and the hinterland is parched and almost uninhabited.

A few decades later, another Dutchman, Willem de Vlamingh, sailed along this stretch of coast and described it as 'an evil place':

> 'The land here appears very bleak, and so abrupt as if the coast had been chopped off with an axe, which makes it almost impossible to land. The waves break with so great a fury that one should say that everything around must shake and become dismembered, which appears to us a truly terrible sight.'

Pelsaert was of the same opinion. The cliffs, he noted gloomily, were 'very steeply hewn, without any foreshore or inlets as have other countries.' Worse, the land behind them was uniformly unpromising: 'a dry, cursed earth without foliage or grass.' There was no sign of any water.

To make matters worse, another storm blew up toward evening on 9 June, and the longboat was caught dangerously close to the coast. Jacobsz and Pelsaert had been searching for a landing place when the wind rose in the west, and they were driven steadily toward the cliffs. For a while it seemed they would all be tipped into the surf to drown, but eventually the skipper got them clear. Even then, however, it took continued effort from the steersmen to keep the boat clear of the shore, and they passed a miserable night and the whole of the next day battling the rising seas.

By the third evening, Jacobsz and his sailors were exhausted, soaked, and chilled, and still the gale showed no sign of abating. The wind started to gust out of the northwest, setting up a dangerous chop that slapped against the built-up sides and sometimes swilled into the longboat. The little yawl they had towed from the Abrolhos was taking on water too, and as it grew dark they were forced to cut the smaller boat adrift and bail their own craft frantically. They were so tightly packed there was little room for such energetic work, and before long the situation had become so desperate that Jacobsz ordered them to tip much of their food and spare equipment overboard. Two small barrels of fresh water in the bottom of the boat were spared.

With most of the supplies gone, the boat rode a little higher in the water and there was more room to bail. Gradually the danger of swamping receded, and on the morning of 11 June the storm blew itself out. But the swell remained as high as ever, and the current pushed them ever farther north.

For three more days they searched fruitlessly for a landing spot until, after a week at sea, they had reached latitude 24 degrees south. The longboat was now about 300 miles from the Abrolhos and one-sixth of the way to Java, and their own supply of water had nearly gone. Only strict rationing – half a pint per person per day – had made it last so long, but now they had enough for no more than another day or so. There could no longer be any question of turning back. They would die themselves if they could not find water farther up the coast.

At length, on the afternoon of 14 June, Pelsaert managed to get a party of men ashore at a place where he had spotted smoke rising from the mainland, but there was nothing to be found. Next day they tried again, this time on the North-West Cape, where they found a way inside the reefs and into calmer water. Here at last there were beaches and dunes. It was the first time Jacobsz had been able to land the boat, and with many more hands available to search for water, the *commandeur* split his party into two. One group was set to digging in the dunes while the other went to hunt among the rocks inland.

The dunes yielded only brine, but the men who had ventured inland had better luck. They chanced upon the remains of an Aboriginal fire, with discarded crab shells scattered all about, and close by found dozens of tiny pools among the rocks. It was rainwater, which had fallen during the storm a few days earlier; had they reached the spot a few days earlier or later it would not have been there. As it was, they gathered up enough to quench their thirst and still fill the nearly empty barrels with another 80 *kannen* of liquid (about 17½ gallons), enough for at least another six days at sea.

There was nothing further to be found, and on 16 June they made their way back to the open sea. Pelsaert had intended to run into 'the river of Jacop Remmessens,'* in the most northerly part of Eendrachtsland, which a Dutch ship had chanced upon in 1622; it lay on the far side of the Cape, still another hundred miles away, but the wind was now blowing from the east and forcing them

---

*Present-day Yardie Creek, at the southern end of Exmouth Gulf.

away from the coast. It soon became apparent that they could not stay close to land, and as they were now more than 360 miles from the Abrolhos, with only enough water for themselves, Pelsaert and Jacobsz at last made the decision to head for Batavia. It was a serious step; there was every chance it could be interpreted as a deliberate act of desertion, and to protect himself the *commandeur* required all those on board to sign an oath signifying their agreement with his resolution. When that was done, Jacobsz swung the tiller. The longboat came about, and the skipper pointed her bow north into the Timor Sea.

There were few precedents for what the people from the *Batavia* were about to attempt: a voyage of about 900 miles across the open ocean in an overloaded boat, with few supplies and only the barest minimum of water. Jacobsz and Pelsaert had some advantages: good winds, fair weather, and a boat adapted to the open sea. But, even so, the *Batavia*'s longboat took on water continually, and none of those on board dared move too much for fear of overturning the boat. There was no shelter from the heat of the day. Before long, one of the sailors in the boat confessed, 'we expected nothing else but death.'

The men who sailed in the longboat recorded few details of the privations they endured. Even Pelsaert, who kept up his journal throughout the voyage, confined himself to brief daily notes about the weather, the boat's estimated position, and the distance run. But 160 years later, Captain William Bligh undertook a similar – though considerably longer – voyage after being cast adrift by the *Bounty* mutineers. He sailed 4,600 miles west across the Pacific with 18 men and their supplies crammed into a 10-man launch, leaving a detailed account that gives some clues as to what Jacobsz, Pelsaert, and their men must have gone through to survive.

Bligh was in command of an experienced crew of able seamen and did not have women or children to worry about. He also sailed across a part of the Pacific rich in islands, and only rarely for days on end across an empty sea. Nevertheless, his men suffered badly from overcrowding, as the people from the *Batavia* must also have done. They found it necessary to swap places in the boat every few hours and devised a system whereby men took turns on the tiller while others gingerly exchanged seats. Bligh also established a definite routine. The men in the *Bounty*'s boat were divided into three watches, as they would have been on board ship, to ensure there were always people alert to the danger of being swamped by an unexpected wave. Some of those who were off duty bailed; the others rested or slept. At noon they shot the sun and calculated their position. It seems likely Ariaen Jacobsz would have done the same.

A good captain – and William Bligh, for all his faults, was a fine one in this respect at least – also understands that men facing the likelihood of death need hope as much as they need water. Studies of shipwreck survivors have shown that men who do have hope outlive those who may be physically as strong or stronger but give way to despair. A stubborn determination to make land, perhaps see a wife or family again, has helped many sailors to survive long periods in open boats. Religion is another comfort; even the most agnostic man tends to turn to prayer in the middle of the ocean. Nevertheless, it is leadership – provided by a man who displays competence, remains confident, and tries to keep up the spirits of his men – that most often means the difference between life and death for sailors cast adrift. There were two such potential leaders in the *Batavia*'s longboat, the skipper and the *commandeur;* but from what we know of the two men – Pelsaert no sailor and still ill, Jacobsz not only an excellent seaman but loud and assertive – it seems certain that it was the skipper who performed this vital function in the longboat.

Thus Ariaen found some measure of redemption on the Timor Sea. Whether he still planned to mutiny is difficult to say. Jacobsz had no idea he was suspected of plotting against the Company, and without Jeronimus at his side the resolution he had displayed in the Southern Ocean may well have drained away. Cornelisz, as we have seen, retained some faith in him and hoped the skipper would murder Pelsaert during the voyage north, tip his body over the side, and then sail to Malacca for assistance. But though the Portuguese might indeed have supplied a rescue ship, when they heard about the VOC money chests waiting in the Abrolhos, it seems unlikely that Jacobsz could have disposed of the *commandeur* even if he had wanted to. There were, perhaps, half a dozen mutineers in the longboat; but they must have been heavily outnumbered by the loyalists. The three steersmen, for example, had never been part of Jacobsz's conspiracy and were unlikely to stand by while Pelsaert was murdered and the boat diverted to the Malay coast. Besides, it would have been impossible, in the crowded longboat, to kill the merchant without being detected, and a struggle might have tipped the boat, and its passengers, into the sea. Frightened, thirsty sailors seldom make good material for mutiny, and as they neared the Indies the chances are that Jacobsz and Jan Evertsz spent more time husbanding their remaining stores than scheming against the *commandeur*.

The voyage from the North-West Cape had taken them 11 days – long enough for the remaining stocks of food and water to run dangerously low. Most of the bread had been tipped overboard during the storm, and what was left must have been severely rationed; the people in the boat would have endured severe hunger pangs at first, and then the dull feeling of emptiness that marks the onset of starvation. Rain fell on three occasions while they were at sea, marginally reducing their dependence on the water casks, but they were forced to cut the water ration even so. Thirst tormented everyone on board, but the knowledge that the boat was making rapid progress – they were sailing up to 90 miles a day – must have helped to sustain morale during the voyage.

The Javan coast was sighted on the afternoon of 27 June. They had completed the crossing only just in time; when the longboat made its landfall, only one *kannen* of water (less than two pints) remained of the 70 they had scooped up from the rock pools of the North-West Cape. Some caution was still required – the island's southern littoral was not under Dutch control, and the local people might be hostile – but next morning they replenished their barrels from a waterfall and sailed and rowed on toward Sunda Strait, where the trade routes and the monsoon winds converged and Dutch ships congregated on their way to and from Batavia. Remarkably, all 48 of those who had left the Abrolhos in the longboat had survived the journey; even the babe in arms was still alive. Light winds delayed them, but they reached the southwest tip of Java on 3 July and found, to their intense delight, four VOC ships waiting in the Strait; one of them was the *Sardam,* the little *jacht* that had sailed with them all the way from Texel to the Cape. Four days later they were in Batavia.

❈

The VOC's headquarters in the Indies had been a town of little moment until Cornelis de Houtman arrived there one day in November 1596. It was then a community of perhaps 2,000 or 3,000 people, situated at the mouth of the Tiliwung River and protected by nothing more than a bamboo wall. The Javanese inhabitants, who called their town Jacatra, were subjects of the Sultan of Bantam, 50 miles to the west. They made their living from fishing, agriculture, and trade, and their town also boasted a small Chinese community, which controlled the arak-brewing business and a good deal of the general commerce besides. De Houtman purchased some supplies, and thereafter Dutch ships began to call regularly at the port, which was marginally healthier and a good deal cheaper than Bantam itself.

Gradually Dutch influence grew. In 1610 the local ruler, or *pangeran,* gave the VOC some land in the Chinese quarter and permission to construct a stone warehouse and a walled compound on it; within a few years, this building became one of Jan Company's largest factories, or warehouses, in the Far East. Relations between the Gentlemen XVII and the *pangeran* were generally excellent, so, in 1618, the Company built a new hospital and a little ship repair yard just outside the town. It was also decided to move most of the business traditionally transacted at Bantam along the coast to Jacatra.

At this point, to the great displeasure of the VOC, the English East India Company began to build its own warehouse outside the walls. If the Jacatran ruler's intention was to play the rival Europeans off against one another, he succeeded all too well. The Dutch attacked the English factory and burned it to the ground; the English retaliated by assembling such a substantial fleet outside the town that the whole Dutch community was forced to flee east to the Moluccas. That was far from the end of the matter, however; a few months later the VOC counterattacked in force, unleashing 2,000 troops against Jacatra, burning it down, and levelling the few buildings left standing in the ruins. The *pangeran,* who had sided with the English, was overthrown, and the old settlement was rebuilt as the fortress of Batavia.

The new town, founded on 30 May 1619, was protected by a modern castle on the coast, nine times bigger than its predecessor and built of white coral slabs. The castle had four bastions, known as Diamond, Ruby, Sapphire, and Pearl, prompting the local Javanese to nickname the settlement *kota-inten,* 'Diamond City.' The name stuck, not least because the trade that soon began to pour through the gates made it one of the wealthiest places in the Indies.

Old Jacatra disappeared; new Batavia looked Dutch. The houses were built of brick, much of it imported all the way from the Netherlands in the bilges of *retourschepen* sailing out in ballast, and they were tall and thin and roofed with tiles, just as they were in Amsterdam. The streets were lined with trees and ran in dead-straight lines, and there were churches, schools, and even canals built in the European style. The whole town, indeed, made few concessions to the tropics; most of the Dutch who lived there smoked and drank to excess, as they did at home*; there was a tremendous preoccupation with rank and social status; and despite the humidity and heat, soldiers and merchants alike still dressed in the heavy black wool clothes that were the fashion in the Netherlands. The native Javanese were not allowed within the gates.

For all this, even newcomers such as Zwaantie Hendricx could never really think of Batavia as a European town. In many respects, indeed, it was thoroughly oriental. There was an extensive Chinese quarter and a whole street packed with gambling dens, which was closed to Europeans after dark. One in four of the citizens were Chinese, and, of the remainder, two-thirds were Asian slaves. The European population amounted to about 1,200 soldiers and a few hundred merchants, clerks, and artisans; there were very few Dutch women at all, and almost all the men took local mistresses or wives. The wildlife, too, was alien. Rainforest crept up almost to the gates; there were monkeys and rhinoceroses in the jungle, and tigers sometimes stalked and killed slaves in the sugar fields outside the walls. To make matters worse, Bantamese bandits often prowled in the vicinity, attacking and robbing those unwise enough to venture any distance from the town. Batavia thus existed in a sort of splendid isolation. Newcomers arrived by sea, stayed sometimes for years without seeing anything of the country they were in, and departed the same way they had come.

The community within the walls was singularly one-dimensional. Virtually the entire white population worked directly for the VOC. Over the years, the Gentlemen XVII did make repeated efforts to entice emigrants from Europe to settle in the Indies as 'free-burghers' – private citizens who would, it was hoped, provide the sort of infrastructure a real community required – but since the newcomers suffered appallingly from

---

*A little later in the century one in seven of the entire European population of Batavia, excluding merchants and soldiers, were tavern-keepers. 'I think it no exaggeration,' writes the historian C. R. Boxer, 'to say that most of the Dutch and English males who died in the tropics died of drink, even making due allowance for the heavy toll taken by malaria and dysentery.'

disease and were never allowed to profit from the trade in spices, they made up no more than a tiny fraction of the population. The few would-be settlers who did make the journey rarely stayed for long. Drained and depressed by the muggy pall that hung limply over the whole settlement, they found the town intolerable. Disease was rife, the canals swarmed with mosquitoes, and the midday heat was so intense that even Jan Company did not require its clerks to be at their desks at noon. They worked from 6 to 11 A.M. and 1 to 6 P.M. instead.

The ruler of Batavia was the governor-general of the Indies. He was a senior merchant, sent out from the Dutch Republic by the VOC, who controlled – either directly or through local subordinates – not only the town itself, but all the Company's factories and possessions from Arabia to the coast of Japan. The governor-general was charged not only with ensuring the profitability of the spice trade but with diplomatic and military affairs as well, and his powers within Batavia itself rivalled those of any eastern potentate. A Council of the Indies, made up of eight upper-merchants of wide experience, offered advice and played some part in the decision making, but it was rare for its members to stand up to a man on whom they themselves largely depended for advancement. Since it took a minimum of 18 months to send a request to the Netherlands and receive an answer, strong governors could and did defy even the Gentlemen XVII for years.

There were only two significant restrictions on the power of an able governor. One was the law – Dutch statutes applied throughout the VOC's possessions, and legal affairs were in the hands of the *fiscaal,* a lawyer sent out from the Netherlands. The other was the ever-changing size and strength of the Company's military forces. Like every other European power active in the Eastern oceans, the Dutch were permanently short of ships and men, and each governor-general was aware that if his factories and forts ever were attacked – whether by native armies, the English, or the Portuguese – his forces were so meagre that the loss of a single ship, or a company of soldiers, might determine the outcome of the battle. The soldiers and sailors of the VOC understood this too, and were much harder to control than they had been in the Netherlands. Men fought, drank, and whored their way through five years' service in the East with little fear of punishment, and they were capable of causing considerable disruption within Batavia itself.

Only a governor of strong character could adapt to the debilitating conditions, deal with his own men and the local rulers, and still increase profits for the Gentlemen XVII; but in 1629, when the emaciated crew of Pelsaert's longboat finally stumbled ashore in Java, it happened that just such a man had charge of all the VOC's possessions in the East – a governor who was at once stern, unbending, humourless, God-fearing, honest, and austere. His name was Jan Coen, and he was the architect of the Dutch empire in the Indies.

Coen was a native of the port of Hoorn, in the North Quarter of Holland, and had served the Company since 1607, standing out so starkly among the self-serving private traders who peopled the VOC hierarchy in the East that he was promoted very swiftly. He was an upper-merchant at the age of 25 and governor-general by 1619, when he was only 32. Unlike many of the merchants serving in the East, Coen believed in using military force to expand the VOC's dominions and had no compunction in unleashing the Company's armies against both native rulers and his European rivals. He had already all but driven the English East India Company out of the Spiceries, founding Batavia along the way, and conquered the Banda Islands,* securing the world's supply of nutmeg for the Dutch. The Gentlemen XVII held him in the highest regard, even tolerating the blunt and caustic criticisms of their own tightfisted lack of ambition that were a feature of Coen's frequent letters home.

Nevertheless, as Pelsaert would have known, the governor's unprecedented ruthlessness had caused the VOC all sorts of trouble in the last decade. The most notorious of several incidents had occurred in 1623 on the spice isle of Ambon, when the VOC wrongly suspected its English competitors of plotting an attack on the Dutch factory. Fifteen East India Company merchants were arrested, along with several Japanese mercenaries. The men were tortured until they confessed – one had flames played along the soles of his feet 'until the fat dropt and put out the candles' – and then were executed. When news of the 'Amboina massacre' reached London, the outcry that erupted was so violent that the Gentlemen XVII were forced to promise that Coen would see no

---

*Coen was also capable of serious mistakes. The most spectacular came in 1621–22, when he decided to attempt the conquest of China. His tiny fleet of eight ships and just over 1,000 men got no further than the gates of Portuguese Macao, where they were comprehensively defeated.

further service in the East. Privately, however, the Company knew that it could not do without him. Within three years it had sent its most notorious servant back to the Indies, sailing under an assumed name, to begin a second term as governor-general.

Coen had returned to Batavia in September 1627 to find the city under threat. The Bantamese, whose lands lay to the west, had fallen quiet, but to the east of the Dutch enclave lay the much larger empire of Mataram, 'an oriental despotism of the traditional kind' whose sultan controlled three-quarters of Java. The VOC – with its gaze fixed firmly on the spice trade – had little interest in its neighbour, which was a purely agricultural society with a barter economy, but Mataram coveted Batavia. Its ruler, Agung, was a conqueror who dreamed of ruling huge tracts of the Indies. He had already subdued several smaller sultanates and taken the title 'Susuhunan,' which means 'He to whom everything is subject.' Now he began to plan to overthrow the Dutch.

Within a year of Coen's return, the Susuhunan attacked. In August 1628 Agung laid siege to Batavia with an army of more than 10,000 men, and the governor-general was compelled to order the evacuation of the southern and western quarters of the town. To deny Batavia to the enemy, Coen was forced to burn most of the settlement down and withdraw to the fortress, where he and his garrison endured a three-month siege that ended only when the Mataramese ran out of supplies. The siege was not lifted until 3 December, and the Dutch knew that Agung would almost certainly return the following August, when his next harvest had been gathered in. Thus, when Pelsaert's emaciated, bone-weary sailors reached their destination – having no doubt sustained themselves during their ocean voyage with visions of feasting and debauchery in the taverns of the town – they found it lying in ruins and the inhabitants preoccupied with the prospects of a fresh attack.

In these straitened circumstances, news that a brand-new *retourschip* and her cargo had gone aground on an unknown reef was a particularly devastating blow. The *Batavia,* her money chests, and Pelsaert's trade goods were together worth at least 400,000 guilders, the equivalent of about £20 million today, and the 280 people abandoned in the Abrolhos could have helped to swell Coen's depleted garrison. The merchants of Jan Company had always understood that a small proportion of their ships would inevitably be lost on voyages to and from the Netherlands, but, even so, the wrecking of the *Batavia* was a serious disaster.

Pelsaert and Jacobsz must have appreciated this. Both men would have known that their future careers, and perhaps even their liberty, now rested in the hands of the most implacable man ever to serve the VOC – someone who 'could never forget misdeeds even when they resulted from understandable human weakness, and whose heart was never softened by the sufferings of his opponents.' Only the previous month, Coen had vividly demonstrated his willingness to punish all those who transgressed his fearsome standards, no matter what their station, by flogging a girl named Sara Specx in front of the town hall. Sara was the half-Japanese daughter of the VOC fleet commander Jacques Specx, and her crime had been making love in the governor's apartments.* Because she was only 12 years old, and her lover, who was the nephew of the town clerk of Amsterdam, no more than 15, even the *fiscaal* and the Councillors of the Indies had begged Coen to show compassion; but though there was evidence to show that the intercourse had been consensual and the lovers wished to marry, the governor-general had remained unmoved. He had the boy beheaded and was only narrowly prevented from having Sara drowned. The skipper and the *commandeur* knew that they could expect no mercy from such a man.

The longboat had arrived in Batavia on a Saturday. No work was permitted in the citadel on Sundays, but as soon as the Council of the Indies reconvened on 9 July the *commandeur* was summoned and asked to account for the loss of his ship. Pelsaert cannot have relished this audience with Coen, and he delivered what can only be described as a partial account of the whole episode, emphasising that his navigators had repeatedly assured him that the ship was still well clear of land, and stressing his own determination to find water for the castaways. The decision to head for Java was presented as a regrettable necessity rather than a matter of self-preservation, and the *commandeur* was also careful to give the governor-general some cause for guarded optimism. The most precious trade goods had been landed in the archipelago, he reminded his interrogators, and even in the midst of the evacuation of the ship he had seen to it that buoys were placed at the wreck site to indicate the positions of valuables that had vanished overboard.

Jan Coen, it seems, was not overly impressed by this account,

*Coen had been so enraged when he heard of this that 'his face turned white, and his chair and the table trembled.'

but one thing did count in the Pelsaert's favour. On Coen's last voyage out to Java, the governor-general had learned all about the dangers of the South-Land's coast; he had nearly run aground on it himself. 'When we chanced upon the Land of the *Eendracht,*' Coen had written in a letter home,

> 'we were less than two miles away from the breakers, which we noticed without being able to see land. If we had come to this spot during the night we would have run into a thousand dangers with the ship and crew. The ship's position fixed by the mates was 900 to 1,000 miles away, so that land was not expected at all.'

This near disaster had occurred in September 1627, and the governor must have recognised that there were clear parallels between his own narrow escape on board the *Wapen van Hoorn** and the loss of the *Batavia.* The fierce currents of the Southern Ocean had swept both vessels much farther east than they had realised, to the confusion of their skippers, and it was only Coen's good fortune in coming onto the South-Land during the day, rather than in the middle of the night, that had saved him. Since the governor-general was, for all his harsher qualities, at least scrupulously fair, he thus forbore – for the time being – from any criticism of the *commandeur.* Instead, he offered Pelsaert one chance to redeem himself.

According to the records of the Council of the Indies,

> 'It was put forward by His Hon. to the Council, since it was apparent that it was possible that some of the people and also some of the goods might be saved and salvaged, whether ... they should be sent thither with a suitable *jacht* ... and it was found good to despatch the *Sardam,* arrived here from the Fatherland on the 7th inst.; to provide the same with provisions, water, extra cables and anchors, and to send back thither Francisco Pelsart, *commandeur* of the wrecked ship *Batavia* ... in order to dive for the goods, with the express order to return hither as soon as possible after having done everything for the saving of the people and the salvaging of the goods and cash.'

Coen's proposal was immediately endorsed by the other members of the council, Antonio van Diemen and Pieter Vlack. Directions

---

'Weapon of Hoorn.'

were given for the *Sardam* to be rapidly unloaded and prepared for the voyage south, and while this was being done the governor-general wrote out his instructions to the *commandeur*.

At first glance, the orders that Pelsaert eventually received were reasonably straightforward, but they carried undertones of threat and had been drafted carefully to ensure that the *commandeur* had no excuse for any second failure. The *Sardam* was to sail to the Abrolhos as rapidly as possible, it was explained, and once there she would save not only any survivors but also as much money and equipment as possible, 'so that the Company may receive some recompense to balance its great loss.' Time was not a consideration; Pelsaert should be prepared to spend 'three, four or more months' at the wreck site if need be. Even if he had to wait for the southern summer to arrive before completing salvage operations he should do so, establishing a temporary base on the South-Land itself if storms drove him from the islands.

The *commandeur* was to be supplied with six divers, Coen went on – two Dutchmen and four men from Gujerat – and the *Sardam*'s crew was to be kept to a minimum, apparently in the hope that a large number of survivors might yet be found. In the event that no sign of the *Batavia*'s people could be found, the *jacht* was to sail on to the South-Land and scour the coast for traces of the passengers and crew. Above all, Pelsaert was cautioned, it was his duty 'to salvage the cash, which is an obligation to the Company and on which your honour depends.' Failure to carry out these orders, it was definitely implied, would not be tolerated.

Ariaen Jacobsz had not been present at the council meeting to hear the *commandeur*'s attempt to place the blame for the disaster on his shoulders. He may still have been recovering from the rigours of their recent voyage or may simply not have been asked to attend; at any rate, it would appear that once they had arrived in the Indies, Pelsaert kept his distance from both the skipper and the boatswain, Evertsz.

The *commandeur* had evidently come to suspect both men of complicity in the assault on Creesje Jans long before the *Batavia* was wrecked. How he guessed they were involved we do not know for certain, but it certainly appears possible that Lucretia had recognised Evertsz as one of the masked men who had attacked her by his height or size, or strong North Quarter accent; and once that connection had been made, shipboard gossip, or something a little more definite than that, seems to have alerted Pelsaert to the role played by the skipper. Cornelis Dircxsz, the Alkmaar man who alone of those approached by the high boatswain had declined to have anything to do with the attack, is so carefully cleared of any involvement in the crime in the ship's journals that it is at least possible it was he who eventually informed on his companions. Whatever Pelsaert's motives and his evidence, however, it is clear that shortly after his arrival in Batavia he denounced both Jacobsz and Evertsz to his superiors. On 13 July Ariaen was suddenly arrested and thrown into the dungeons of Castle Batavia. Jan Evertsz followed him into the cells.

No record of the high boatswain's arrest survives, but it is evident the allegations that he faced were serious, and every attempt was made to extract the truth from him. Justice, in Evertsz's case, would have meant interrogation at the hands of the *fiscaal,* Anthonij van den Heuvel, or one of his subordinates. Sitting or lying, probably tightly bound, in a chamber deep within the citadel, the high boatswain would have been confronted with Pelsaert's charges and the evidence against him and asked to confirm whether they were true. Denials were rarely taken at face value, and if the case was deemed serious enough, Evertsz would undoubtedly have been tortured in an attempt to make him talk.

This procedure was perfectly legal, though Dutch law did stipulate that a confession extracted under torture was not in itself enough to secure a conviction. Instead, the prisoner would be allowed to recover his senses and then asked to confirm the admissions he had just made. Only a 'freewill confession' of this sort, made no more than a day after torture was applied, was acceptable as evidence of guilt. Naturally, however, the retraction of confessions made under duress was not the end of the matter and generally led only to the application of even harsher tortures, as Torrentius the painter had already discovered. Since the end result was almost inevitably the same, the Dutch insistence on freewill confession was thus something of a legal fig leaf.

Few men were capable of resisting the attentions of the torturer for long, and the high boatswain of the *Batavia* was not one of them. Before long a full confession of his involvement in the attack on Creesje Jans came tumbling from him. Given all that

Evertsz knew about the skipper's role in events on board the ship, and particularly his plans for mutiny, it is tempting to wonder exactly what he said during his interrogation at Castle Batavia. No evidence survives, but while it seems not at all unlikely that Jacobsz's name came up in connection with the 'very great insolences, yea, monstrous actions, that were committed on the mentioned ship,' the one surviving account – by Councillor Antonio van Diemen – confirms only that Evertsz was subsequently hung for the assault and makes absolutely no mention of Jeronimus Cornelisz. Whether this detail implies that the high boatswain was simply unaware of Jeronimus's closeness to the skipper, that he contrived not to mention the planned mutiny in order to avoid still greater punishment, or that he was even more afraid of the undermerchant than he was of being tortured is unclear.

More is known of the charges brought against the skipper. The minutes of the Council of the Indies observe that there were two of them:

> 'Because Ariaen Jacobsz, skipper of the wrecked ship *Batavia,* is notorious through allowing himself to be blown away by pure neglect; and also because through his doings a gross evil and public assault has taken place on the same ship … it has been decided by His Hon. [Coen] and the Council to arrest the mentioned skipper and bring him to trial here in order that he may answer those accusations made to his detriment.'

Unlike Evertsz, the skipper does not seem to have been put to the torture. Perhaps he was protected by his rank; perhaps the governor-general and his council were simply less convinced of his guilt than they were of the high boatswain's. In truth, however, there was really no need to rely on Pelsaert's accusations in this case. It was beyond dispute that Jacobsz bore responsibility for the faulty navigation that had piled the *Batavia* onto a reef; and as the officer of the watch on the night in question he had been doubly responsible for the disaster. Whether or not he had had anything to do with what had happened to Creesje Jans, the skipper could be held indefinitely just for hazarding his ship.

❉

The *Sardam* cleared Batavia on 15 July, a Sunday. The crew had set out one day before the date ordered by Coen, so anxious was the *commandeur* to be on his way.

Three of the men who had sailed north with Pelsaert were with him on the *jacht*. Two were steersmen, Claes Gerritsz and Jacob Jansz Hollert; their navigational skills would be needed to help relocate the Abrolhos, whose position at this time was still most uncertain. The third was the *Batavia*'s upper-trumpeter, Claes Jansz Hooft. The trumpeter was on the *Sardam* for an altogether different reason. He had left his wife, Tryntgien Fredericx, on Batavia's Graveyard and must have been desperately anxious to rescue her.

The voyage from the islands to Batavia had taken 30 days, and even though the *jacht* would be sailing against the prevailing winds, she was a fast ship and Pelsaert probably hoped to reach the wreck site around the middle of August. By then it would be 10 weeks since his ship had gone aground, and the *commandeur* must have recognised that the people he had abandoned on Batavia's Graveyard could only have survived by finding water. He knew, however, that heavy rain had fallen in the area three days after he had left – memories of the violent gale of 10 June would have been all too vivid for the people in the longboat – and he no doubt hoped to discover some, if not all, of the remaining passengers and crew alive.

The *Sardam* made reasonable time. The ship was south of Java by 17 July, and three weeks later, on 10 August, they reached latitude 27 degrees 54 minutes and found themselves less than 50 miles from Batavia's Graveyard, which lies at 28 degrees 28 minutes south. What followed was more than a month of intense frustration. In the chaos that ensued after the loss of the *Batavia*, Ariaen Jacobsz and his steersmen had obtained no more than rough bearings for the wreck site. Calculating latitude required a navigator to 'shoot the sun.' Persistent bad weather in the Abrolhos had made this very difficult, and the position given by the skipper was no more than an estimate. In consequence, Pelsaert knew only that the *Batavia* lay at about 28 degrees south, and since he had almost no idea of the wreck's true longitude, it followed that the best way of finding the *Batavia* was to zigzag east along Jacobsz's estimated line of latitude until the Abrolhos were sighted. The skipper had, however, miscalculated by about a third of a degree, placing the *retourschip* and the islands around 30 miles north of their true position. In most circumstances this would not have been an error of any moment, but when it came to searching for a few lumps of low-lying coral amid the endless swells of the eastern Indian Ocean it was a significant mistake. Pelsaert and the crew of the *Sardam* spent the last two weeks of August and the first half of September cruising fruitlessly to and fro some way to the north of Houtman's Abrolhos.

It was not until 13 September that they at last chanced on the most northerly part of the archipelago. They were then no more than 17 miles from the wreck site, but the weather soon closed in and the *Sardam* had to spend another two days lying at anchor, riding out the storm. On 15 September the winds had abated somewhat, but the *jacht* made no more than six miles into a strong southeasterly and it was not until the evening of 16 September that Pelsaert at last sighted Hayes's islands on the horizon. Night was falling and the sailors were all too aware that there were reefs about, so they anchored for the evening and got under way again at dawn. Soon the *Sardam* was only a few miles from the islands, her men lining the decks and climbing into the rigging to look for signs of life. At last, at about 10 in the morning, they found it: 'smoke on a long island west of the Wreck, [and] also on another small island close by.' Pelsaert could hardly contain his joy.

There was still someone alive on Batavia's Graveyard.

CHAPTER 7

'Who Wants to Be Stabbed to Death?'

'What a godless life is that which has been lived here.'

FRANCISCO PELSAERT

Gijsbert Bastiaensz settled himself down on the sand and stared disconsolately out to sea. It was now August in the archipelago, and the mutineers had kept him hard at work since the murder of his family some weeks earlier. The *predikant* was employed as the island's boatman, launching the mutineers' flotilla in the morning and hauling the skiffs and rafts back onto the little beach when their crews returned from a day's fishing. For the remainder of the day he was merely required to remain near the landing place, and for the most part he spent those hours on the strand, seeking consolation in his Bible.

Gijsbert had not been allowed to mourn his murdered family. The day after his wife and children had been killed, the mutineers had found him 'weeping very much,' and ordered him to stop. 'Said that I ought not to do so,' the preacher noted. 'Said, that does not matter; be silent, or you go the same way.' Nor did Bastiaensz receive, in Jeronimus's kingdom, the respect and special treatment normally accorded to a minister. He not only worked, as everybody had to work, but ate the same meagre rations as the other people on Batavia's Graveyard. And, like them, the *predikant* heard Zevanck and the others freely discuss who they would kill next and how, and he feared daily for his life:

'Every day it was, "What shall we do with that Man?" The one would decapitate me, the other poison me, which would have been a sweeter death; a third said, "Let him live a little longer, we might make use of him to persuade the folk on the other Land to come over to us." ... And so, briefly, this being the most important thing, my Daughter and I, we both went along as an Ox in front of the Axe. Every night I said to her, you have to look tomorrow morning, whether I have been murdered ... and I told her what she had to do if she found me slaughtered; and that also we must be prepared to meet God.'

Gijsbert was rarely allowed to preach. Religious affairs in the Abrolhos were now in the under-merchant's hands, and – having made himself the ruler of the island – Jeronimus felt free to drop his old pretence of piety. To his followers, he openly espoused the heretical beliefs that had once been furtively discussed at Geraldo Thibault's fencing club, so that 'daily [they] heard that there was neither devil nor Hell, and that these were only fables.' In the place of these old certainties, Jeronimus preached the heterodox doctrines of the Spiritual Libertines, which he used to justify his actions and assuage the guilty consciences of his men.

'He tried to maintain ... that all he did, whether it was good or bad (as judged by others), God gave the same into his heart. For God, as he said, was perfect in virtue and goodness, so was not able to send into the heart of men anything bad, because there was no evil or badness in Himself; saying that all he had done was sent into his heart by God; and still more such gruesome opinions.'

Even this summary of the apothecary's views, written – as it was – after the fact by someone who scarcely began to comprehend such heresies, only scratches at the surface of Cornelisz's beliefs. As a Libertine, Jeronimus held to a theology based on the central tenets of the Free Spirit as they had been set down in the fourteenth century. One of these beliefs, as written in a medieval manuscript, was that 'nothing is sin except what is thought of as sin.' Another explained that 'one can be so united with God that whatever one may do one cannot sin.'

What the other mutineers made of Cornelisz's ideas it is difficult to say. The majority of them were barely educated men, and they could not have been expected to grasp the subtleties of the Libertine philosophy. But the general thrust of the apothecary's thought was easy enough to understand; and his men had every reason to accept it, since it promised to absolve them from wrong-doing. Some of them evidently did embrace the new theology; it is certainly possible to hear garbled echoes of Jeronimus's thinking in the pronouncements of his men. Still, the under-merchant was no prophet. There is no sign that Cornelisz much cared whether he made converts, and, as we have seen, his own grasp of the Free Spirit's doctrine was incomplete. Though it seems likely that Jeronimus did think of himself as a Libertine, he also used the philosophy to further his own ends.

One of the under-merchant's aims was to strengthen his own position by removing his followers from contact with the one authority in the islands that might have had the power to restrain them: the Dutch Reformed Church. By silencing the *predikant*, Cornelisz shielded the mutineers from the fear of criticism and divine retribution; and by introducing his men to a new theology he in effect began to create a new society in the Abrolhos – one in which his followers owed personal loyalty to him and were bound together not only by their crimes, but also by their rejection of conventional authority.

Once Cornelisz had assumed control of Batavia's Graveyard, the mutineers were urged to reject the rules and laws that had until then restricted them. They were incited to blaspheme and swear – which was strictly prohibited by VOC regulations – and absolved from the requirement to attend religious services. Above all, they were encouraged to ridicule the *predikant*. On the one occasion that Bastiaensz did call on the men to pray, one mutineer shot back that they would rather sing; and when the minister beseeched God to take all those on the island 'under His wings,' he looked up to find Jeronimus's men capering about behind his tiny congregation. The mutineers were flapping the bloody, severed flippers of dead sea lions above their heads and sneering at his piety. 'No need,' they hooted, 'we are already under them.'

Jeronimus's methods did help to bind him and his men togeth-er; nevertheless, it is clear that the under-merchant did not entirely trust the mutineers. Surrounded as he was by heavily armed sol-diers, Cornelisz must have been painfully aware that he owed his position not to any military prowess – indeed, his actions all suggest that he himself was a physical coward – but to his unusual-ly clever tongue; and he may have doubted he was strong enough to resist a real challenge to his authority. So, on 12 July, he required all two dozen of his followers to sign an 'Oath of trust,' swearing loyalty to each other; and he also took oaths separately 'from the Men he wanted to save, that they should be obedient to him in every way in whatever he should order them.' A second oath, sworn on 20 August, reinforced these vows. This one was signed by 36 people, including the *predikant*. By then the mutineers' ranks had been swollen by fear.

It did not take long for a hierarchy to emerge among Jeronimus's men. In theory they were equal, 'assisting each other in brotherly affection for the common welfare,' but in fact Stone-Cutter Pietersz, the lance corporal, became the under-merchant's second-in-command. Pietersz's elevation no doubt owed a good deal to his influence among the soldiers, but since he was far junior to Cornelisz in rank, and a relatively colourless personality to boot, it was likely also because Jeronimus found him easy to manipulate. The corporal was certainly less of a potential threat than David Zevanck and Coenraat van Huyssen, who were both self-confident, if junior, members of the officer class. Zevanck had not only led but orchestrated many of the killings on Batavia's Graveyard, and Jeronimus had struggled to control Van Huyssen's hotheadedness on the ship. The apothecary may have thought it wise to keep both men somewhat at arm's length and invest more authority in the malleable Pietersz.

Cornelisz and the corporal set themselves apart from the other mutineers in several ways. They determined who would live or die, but they themselves did not kill, leaving Zevanck and Van Huyssen to carry out their orders. They were the only men to adopt new titles – Jeronimus renouncing the rank of under-merchant for that of 'captain-general' of the islands, and Pietersz promoting himself all the way to 'lieutenant-general' – and wasted no time in creating liveries to match their grandiose new ranks. Cornelisz, who had already requisitioned Pelsaert's clothing, led the way, transforming the *commandeur*'s existing finery into a series of comic-opera uniforms. 'He gave free rein to his pride and devilish arrogance,' the *Batavia* journals observed:

'The goods of the Company which they fished up … were very shamefully misused by making them into clothes embroidered with as much *passementerie** as possible, [and Cornelisz] set the example … by changing daily into different clothes, silk stockings,

*French trimming, usually of gold or silver lace.

garters with gold lace, and by putting on suchlike adornments belonging to other persons. Moreover, to all his Followers whom he could best trust, and who were most willing to murder, he gave clothes made from red *laken** sewn with two or more bands of *passementeries*. And created a new mode of Cassock, believing that such evil vain pleasure as this could last for ever.'

The other mutineers soon followed suit, each man outfitting himself according to his status. The old Company ranks still counted for something on the island – assistants and cadets seem to have been treated more respectfully than ordinary soldiers and sailors – but even among the rank and file, some mutineers were more equal than others. The men the captain-general depended on most, and summoned most frequently, were the tried and tested killers who could be relied on to tackle and subdue full-grown men. This murderous elite included Jan Hendricxsz, Gÿsbert van Welderen, Mattys Beer, and Lenert van Os. The likes of Andries Jonas, whose victims were mostly pregnant women and young boys, enjoyed a lesser status, and the dozen or so men who signed Jeronimus's oaths, but never took part in the killing, were no doubt looked down on by their more ruthless cohorts.

The elite mutineers seem to have enjoyed their work. Men such as David Zevanck and Coenraat van Huyssen had been of minor consequence on board the *Batavia;* now they revelled in their status as men of importance, possessed of the power of life and death. Others, including Jan Hendricxsz – who butchered between 17 and 20 people – and Lenert van Os – who slaughtered a dozen – were efficient killers, seemingly unburdened by conscience, who enjoyed moving among Cornelisz's inner circle. Nevertheless, killing, in itself, was not the prime motive of the rank and file. These men murdered because the alternative was to become one of the victims, and because the favour of the captain-general meant improved rations and access to the island's women.

There had not been many more than 20 females on the *Batavia* when she had left the Netherlands, and most of those were already dead – drowned, killed by thirst after the ship was wrecked, or cut down in the massacre on the rafts or on Seals' Island. The mutineers had ruthlessly exterminated those who were too old or too pregnant to interest them. The handful of young women who

*Wool of exceptional quality.

remained were gathered on Batavia's Graveyard, where Jeronimus and his men took their pick.

There were seven of them in all. Creesje Jans and Judick the preacher's daughter were the only women from the stern. The others came from the lower deck: Anneken Bosschieters, the sisters Tryntgien and Zussie Fredricx, Anneken Hardens and Marretgie Louys, all of whom were probably married to soldiers or sailors among the crew. Tryntgien's husband had found himself with Pelsaert on the longboat, and Anneken Bosschieters's had gone with Wiebbe Hayes, leaving them without protectors. Hardens's husband, Hans, was a soldier and a minor mutineer, and it is a mystery why he did not act to stop her from being corralled with the others. But he did not, and the women from the lower deck were set aside 'for common service,' which meant simply that they were available to any of the mutineers who wished to rape them.

Jeronimus's men were not entirely indiscriminate. Some of the officers behaved relatively well, and Coenraat van Huyssen, in particular, seems to have remained faithful to his fiancée, Judick. But many of the mutineers were less punctilious. It was normal for the women kept for 'common service' to have had relations with two or three of the mutineers at least, and those who had been with only one man were envied. 'My Daughter has been with Van Huyssen about five weeks,' noted Bastiaensz. 'He has protected her very well, so that no disaster has befallen her, other than that she had to remain with him; the other Women were very jealous of her, because they thought that too much honour was accorded her.'

Of all the seven women, Creesje Jans was by far the most desirable, and Jeronimus claimed her as his own. Almost as soon as he took power in the island, the captain-general had Lucretia taken to his tent, where rather than assaulting her he made every effort to seduce her. For nearly two weeks, he wrote her sonnets, poured her wine – tried everything, in fact, to persuade her that he was not a monster. Cornelisz's remarkable behaviour suggests that he wanted to possess her not just physically but mentally – and that he also possessed a great capacity for self-delusion, for she resisted stubbornly, just as she had resisted Ariaen Jacobsz, and eventually Jeronimus gave up his attempts at gallantry. The story of what happened next somehow reached the ears of others on the island:

'In the end [Jeronimus] complained to David Zevanck that he could not accomplish his ends either with kindness or anger. Zevanck answered: "And don't you know how to manage that? I'll soon make her do it." He had then gone into the tent and said to Lucretia: "I hear complaints about you." "On what account?" she asked. "Because you do not comply with the Captain's wishes in kindness; now, however, you will have to make up your mind. Either you will go the same way as Wybrecht Claasen, or else you must do that for which we have kept the women." Through this threat Lucretia had to consent that day, and thus he had her as his concubine.'

Creesje therefore yielded in the end; but she did so unwillingly. Like the women kept for common service, the girl had acted to save her life, and as long as the captain-general was happy she at least assured herself of decent food and drink, and protection of a sort. The rest of the survivors on Batavia's Graveyard – the menfolk and the boys – enjoyed no such assurance. Hungry, thirsty, ill, they lived in constant terror of their lives. Now that a good deal of the killing had been done, the mutineers' existence on the island was increasingly routine, and they began to look for fresh diversions; attracting the attention of any of Cornelisz's henchmen was unwise, and a few mutineers, perhaps unstable to begin with, became deranged.

The most extreme case was that of Jan Pelgrom, the cabin boy, whose 'gruesome life' is vividly sketched in the ship's journals. 'Mocking at God, cursing and swearing, also conducting himself more like a beast than a human being,' Pelgrom lacked any self-control, 'which made him at last a terror to all the people, who feared him more than any of the other principal murderers or evil-doers.' The boy's sudden elevation – he had been one of the lowliest of the *Batavia*'s crew, and now found himself among the most powerful – practically unhinged him, and he took to racing around the island 'like a man possessed,' spewing out challenges and blasphemies to anyone who would listen. '[He] has daily on the island run,' the journals observe, 'calling out, "Come now, devils with all the sacraments, where are you? I wish that I now saw a devil. And who wants to be stabbed to death? I can do that very beautifully."'

In this highly charged and dangerous environment, it is no surprise that the killings on the island did not cease with the murder of the *predikant*'s family on 21 July. Cornelisz and his blood council still sat in judgment on their dwindling band of subjects, and the captain-general continued to order executions.

What did change was the nature of the violence. For two weeks, Jeronimus's men had killed – ostensibly at least – to limit the drain on their supplies. In reality they had also done so to remove potential rivals and ensure that there could be no challenge to their authority, but, whatever the motive, the murders themselves had been cold-blooded and considered. The slaughter of Gijsbert Bastiaensz's wife and children changed that. The *predikant*'s family had, it would appear, been marked for death in the usual way; there were eight of them, not including Bastiaensz and Judick, and they must have been consuming a good deal of food and water. But the act of killing had roused David Zevanck and his men, and they had gone on to dispose of the unfortunate Hendrick Denys and Mayken Cardoes without orders from Jeronimus. Denys had been dispatched by Jan Hendricxsz, who was apparently in the throes of some sort of blood lust. Andries Jonas had been ordered to kill Cardoes, probably because he had taken no part in the general massacre and Zevanck wished to ensure that he shared responsibility for what had taken place that night. From this perspective, the murder of the girl can be seen as an attempt by Zevanck to assert control and ensure conformity within Jeronimus's band. So far as can be ascertained, the deaths of these later victims had not been planned; both killings were atypical, and, when they occurred, one phase of the mutiny ended and another one began.

From that day on, the captain-general killed to kill. A handful of Jeronimus's later murders were intended to settle scores or punish dissent, but increasingly they were ordered out of boredom or to defuse tension among the mutineers. There was no real need for further bloodshed; the number of survivors on the island had been satisfactorily reduced, rains continued to fall, and by now enough fish and birds were being caught to provide everyone with food. But life had become so worthless on Batavia's Graveyard that a dispensation to kill became simply another way for Cornelisz to reward his followers. In the end he and his men were slaughtering for mere entertainment.

By the last week of July, the captain-general had already begun to set himself apart from the men whose support he had depended on at first. The law that death sentences could be passed only by the council, sitting in solemn judgment, was ended; the gardener Jan Gerritsz and a sailor, Obbe Jansz – drowned by Zevanck, Van Huyssen, and Gÿsbert Van Welderen on 25 July – were the last men to be executed in this way. From then on, Jeronimus ordered further murders merely on his own authority, and in an increasingly casual and arbitrary way.

On 6 August, for example, Cornelisz found himself dissatisfied with the work done by one of his carpenters:

> 'Jan Hendricxsz was called by Jeronimus in the morning when he was standing in the tent of Zevanck, and he gave him a dagger which he carried in his own pocket, with the words, "Go and stab Stoffel Stoffelsz, that lazy dog who stands there working as if his back is broken, through the heart." Which Jan Hendricxsz did with two stabs so that he was killed immediately.'

On other occasions, Cornelisz continued to make his men murder as a test of their loyalty. Rogier Decker, a 17-year-old cabin boy, had been the under-merchant's personal servant on board the *Batavia*. As such, Decker apparently enjoyed some degree of protection on the island. He was not one of the mutineers – at least he had not signed the oath taken on 16 July – but one day 'when he was frying some fish in his tent,' Jeronimus unexpectedly appeared. The cabin boy was taken to the captain-general's tent, given a beakerful of wine for courage, and handed Cornelisz's own dagger. Jeronimus then told him to stab another carpenter, Hendrick Jansz, who could be seen nearby. Decker carried out the order without protest, but the boy knew for certain that he himself would have been killed had he refused to do it. No attempt was ever made to explain why the blameless Hendrick Jansz was chosen as Decker's victim, and perhaps there never was a reason; but now that he was blooded, the servant boy became a full-fledged mutineer, and he signed the oath of 20 August with the others.

Pelgrom did not have to be told to kill; he begged the captain-general for the opportunity. Even the boy's companions seem to have found his intense desire to be a murderer strange and perhaps a little wearing, but Cornelisz evidently approved of it. He did nothing to curb Pelgrom's daily rampages around the island and twice attempted to oblige the boy by finding him a victim.

Jeronimus's first choice was Anneken Hardens, one of the women kept for common service. Perhaps she had failed to give satisfaction or was chosen to help keep her husband, Hans, in line (the mutineers, it will be recalled, had already strangled the couple's daughter, Hilletgie). In any case, Pelgrom was brought to the under-merchant's tent one night and told that he could kill her. Andries Liebent and Jan Hendricxsz were to assist him. Jan, it seems, 'was very glad, and he went quickly,' but he was also small and weak for his age and in the end Hendricxsz and Gÿsbert van Welderen had to strangle Anneken, using her own hair ribbon, while Liebent and Pelgrom held her legs.

The cabin boy would not give up. For two more weeks he pestered Cornelisz continually, until Jeronimus at last gave way. By this time the number of people on the island had been reduced to the point where only a small group of useful artisans remained alive alongside the mutineers themselves. One of their number was Cornelis Aldersz of Yplendam, a boy kept busy mending nets. On 16 August, when almost a week had passed without a murder on the island, Jeronimus decided that they could do without him.

As soon as he heard that Aldersz was to die, Pelgrom 'begged so very much that he be allowed to do it' that Cornelisz agreed. Once again, however, the boy found himself frustrated by his puny body:

> 'Jeronimus said to him, "Jan, here is my sword, which you have to try on the Net-Maker to see if it is sharp enough to cut off his head." Whereupon he was very glad. Zevanck, hearing the same, maintained that he was too light for that. Meanwhile Mattys Beer came, who asked if he might do it, which was granted to him. So he took the sword. Jan would not willingly give it because he wanted to do it himself, but [Beer] tore it out of his hands and took it immediately to Gillis Phillipsen* in order to file it sharp. Meanwhile Jan was busy blindfolding the boy in the presence of Jeronimus, who said to [him]: "Now, be happy, sit nicely, 'tis but a joke." Mattys Beer, who had the sword under his cloak, [then] slew him with one blow, cutting off his head.'

Cornelisz, Zevanck, and Beer found this incident tremendously amusing. But Pelgrom, who had 'daily begged that he should be allowed to kill someone, because he would rather do that than eat

---

*Another soldier, and one of the minor mutineers.

or drink,' did not share in their laughter: 'When he was not allowed to cut off the head of the foresaid youngster, Jan wept.'

The decapitation of the net-maker was a mere diversion for the captain-general, a game played to pass the time one afternoon. But other murders that occurred at about the same time had a more serious purpose, for though the mutineers had won undisputed control of their little patch of coral, they could still not feel entirely secure. Even Jeronimus could not control every aspect of life on Batavia's Graveyard, and, elsewhere in the archipelago, the soldiers who had been left to die of thirst on the islands to the north were still alive. Cornelisz, like so many dictators, was consumed by the fear that his followers might either cheat or challenge him, or defect to his enemies at the first opportunity.

The first man to fall foul of the captain-general in this respect was Andries de Vries, the assistant whose life had been spared by the mutineers. Andries had unwisely formed a friendship with Lucretia Jans, who, in the first weeks of July, was still resisting Jeronimus's efforts at seduction. News of their relationship aggrieved Cornelisz; grimly, he forced De Vries to swear 'that if ever in his life he talked to her [again], he would have to die.' On 14 July, the day after he had been forced to slit the throats of the remaining sick, Andries was caught by David Zevanck calling to Creesje 'from afar.' Zevanck ran to tell Jeronimus, and the apothe-cary summoned Jan Hendricxsz, Lenert van Os, and Rutger Fredricx to his tent. The men were given a beaker of wine and a sword apiece, and at noon, in front of all the people on the island, they confronted the assistant. Andries guessed why they had come, and tried, uselessly, to save himself. What followed was in effect a public execution: 'When De Vries saw that his life was forfeit, he fled into the water. But Lenert Michielsz, following him the quickest, chiefly hacked him to death.'

A second mutineer only narrowly avoided the same fate. The *Batavia*'s senior cooper, Jan Willemsz Selyns, was a hanger-on who had played only a minor role in the killings and had perhaps failed to show the necessary enthusiasm for Jeronimus's schemes. On 5 August, Cornelisz sent Wouter Loos and Hans Jacobsz Heijlweck to dispatch the cooper in his tent; but Loos, who had felt no com-punction in hacking Mayken Cardoes to death two weeks earlier, liked Selyns, and instead of killing him he begged the captain-general to spare the artisan's life. Jeronimus, surprisingly, gave way, and nothing more was heard of the matter; but that afternoon, when the under-merchant ordered the murder of another potential defector, Heijlweck was among the four men chosen for the task, and Wouter Loos was not.

The new object of Cornelisz's suspicions was Frans Jansz. The surgeon appears to have retained a good deal of influence in the archipelago – no doubt because of his involvement in the first survivors' council – and for a while he and David Zevanck had competed for the captain-general's favour. Zevanck won this contest, becoming Jeronimus's chief executioner; but the assistant did not forget Jansz and was irritated to find him 'in the way' on more than one occasion. The surgeon, meanwhile, retained a certain degree of independence. He was not one of Jeronimus's band (that is, he did not sign the oath of 16 July); but he took part in some of its operations, and as he was still the most senior member of the *Batavia*'s crew in the islands, the mutineers could not ignore him altogether. Exactly what Jansz said, and did, in the survivors' camp after Cornelisz supplanted him was never written down and is now lost. What we do know is that the under-merchant did not trust him and decided to remove him because 'he would not dance exactly to their pipes.' The four men chosen to kill him accepted the commission eagerly. They were Lenert van Os, Mattys Beer, Heijlweck, and Lucas Gellisz.

By now they were well schooled in the art of murder. The surgeon was taken to one side 'on the pretext of searching for seals,' and when he was well away from any source of help, his executioners fell on him together. Their attack was unusually violent, indeed excessively so, and suggests a certain personal antipathy: 'Lenert Michielsz first stabbed him with a pike right through his body; after that, Hans Jacobsz [Heijlweck] smote his head with a Morning star, so that he fell down, and Mattys Beer has cleft it quickly with a sword.' Each of these blows would have been fatal on its own, but Lucas Gellisz wanted to make certain, and he 'stabbed Mr Frans in his body with a pike,' finishing him off. 'Which Gruesomeness,' it was subsequently observed, 'he could just as well have omitted, because the man was already so hacked and stabbed.' The four men watched the surgeon die, then went to tell Cornelisz that Jansz would not, after all, be running off to Wiebbe Hayes.

As it turned out, Jeronimus had every reason to fear Hayes and the soldiers he had abandoned six weeks earlier. The captain-general's scouts – like Pelsaert and the sailors in the longboat before them –

had spent very little time on the two large islands to the north of Batavia's Graveyard. They had gone ashore for perhaps an hour or two, found each in turn as rocky and barren as the rest of the archipelago, and seen no evidence of pools or wells. But the scouts had made a serious mistake in reporting to Jeronimus that the High Land could never support life. Both cays were, in fact, far richer in resources than the islands controlled by the mutineers.

The smaller of the two land masses, which lay farthest to the north, was two miles from end to end and about a mile and a half across. At its centre stood the only hill in the entire archipelago, a modest hummock rising 50 feet above the sea; in consequence it was called the High Island. Its neighbour, just under a mile away to the southwest, was larger still – more than three miles long and not far short of two miles wide. Hayes and his troops established their base there, and in time it became known as 'Wiebbe Hayes's Island.' The two isles were connected by the mile-wide muddy causeway that Wiebbe had used to cross from one to the other.

Had Pelsaert and the skipper had the sense to explore the archipelago with any thoroughness, they would surely have transferred the survivors of the wreck to Wiebbe Hayes's Island, which offered far more in the way of natural resources than Batavia's Graveyard and could have supported the whole company for months. Like the smaller islets in the archipelago, it was surrounded by rich fishing grounds and alive with nesting birds, but to the soldiers' surprise, it also turned out to be full of new and unknown hopping animals, which they called 'cats' – 'creatures of miraculous form, as big as a hare.' These were tammars, a species of wallaby indigenous to the Abrolhos, and as the soldiers soon discovered, they were easily caught and delicious cooked.

Most significant of all, the island turned out to have wells. They were not easily located, and both Pelsaert and Jeronimus's scouts might be forgiven for having failed to uncover them, but in the end Hayes's men discovered them by searching under the limestone slabs that lay scattered on the ground throughout the island. They appear to have found at least two good wells, one near the coast and the other toward the middle of the island, and possibly more; one cistern had 10 feet of water in it and an entrance large enough for a man to climb down into it. Between them they contained so much fresh water that it would hardly have been necessary to ration it.

Life on Wiebbe Hayes's Island was thus far easier than it was on

Batavia's Graveyard. 'The Lord our God fed us so richly that we could have lived there with ten thousand men for a hundred years,' wrote Cornelis Jansz, who had reached Hayes from Seals' Island, with the pardonable exaggeration of a man who had survived the desert islands of the south to find himself living in a land of plenty. 'Birds like doves we could catch, five hundred in a day, and each bird had an egg, as large as a hen's egg.' They hunted wallabies, slaughtering 'two, three, four, five, six or even more for each person,' and found fishing spots where they could haul in '40 fish as large as cod' in only an hour.

Wiebbe Hayes must have wondered why all contact with Batavia's Graveyard had ceased as soon as he and his men were put ashore on the High Island, and become still more perplexed when the signal fires he lit to announce the discovery of water went unanswered. Lacking boats, he and his men could hardly investigate, however, and they may have remained ignorant of events elsewhere in the archipelago until the second week of July, when the first parties of refugees staggered ashore with horrifying tales of murder and massacre to the south. Over the next few days, at least five different groups made the difficult passage across more than four miles of open water, sitting on little homemade rafts or swimming behind planks of wood. The new arrivals included the eight men who somehow escaped the general massacres on Seals' Island, and nearly 20 who contrived to slip away from Batavia's Graveyard itself in groups of four and five. Between them, these men more than doubled the strength of Hayes's force and kept him and his soldiers well informed concerning Cornelisz's activities.

The news that Jeronimus's men had gone to Seals' Island and massacred all the people that they found there was particularly disturbing. It must have been obvious that the mutineers would eventually turn their gaze on Wiebbe Hayes's Island, and that when they did the unarmed loyalists would find themselves at a fatal disadvantage. It was imperative that they organise themselves, construct makeshift defences, and improvise some weapons.

Wiebbe Hayes proved equal to the challenge. The soldiers' leader is a shadow figure in the *Batavia* journals, remaining out of sight on his own island while the main action develops to the south. Nevertheless he must have been an able and inspiring leader. He and his men had already survived for three weeks on the High Island and its neighbour, and they eventually found the water that Pelsaert's experienced sailors had missed. Although a private soldier, Wiebbe not only led the original expedition to the islands, but then integrated the various groups of refugees who found their way to him, so that by the middle of July he was in command of a mixed party of almost 50 people. His forces included not only VOC assistants but also company cadets who were nominally his superiors; yet there is no suggestion that any of them ever questioned his fitness to command them. This confidence was justified, for Hayes now directed the construction of makeshift weapons and defences that gave his men at least a chance against the mutineers.

With Wiebbe to rally and cajole them, the soldiers fashioned pikes from planks, tipping them with wicked sixteen-inch-long nails that had washed ashore with driftwood from the wreck. Like the mutineers, they improvised morning stars, and though swords and muskets were still lacking, there were plenty of fist-sized lumps of coral around, which could be hurled at the heads of any attackers. There is even a reference to the fact that 'guns' were assembled on the island. What these were remains a mystery, but, supplied with rope, the soldiers could perhaps have cut branches from the stunted trees that dot the interior and turned them into catapults for larger rocks.

While the soldiers worked, Hayes selected his defensive positions. He recognised that the geography of the archipelago and the pattern of the shallows meant that the mutineers would have to approach his island across the mudflats that guarded the whole southern shoreline. This limited the risk of a surprise attack. A lookout post built midway along the coast, at the apex of a bay, provided him with a forward base and a clear field of observation. With sentries posted at intervals along the coast, it would have made sense to position the bulk of his troops farther inland, close to the wells, where they could rest and feel relatively secure.

With the arrival of the last party of refugees, Hayes found himself in command of 46 men and a boy. Collectively, these Defenders, as they now became known, gave him a significant numerical superiority over the mutineers that offset, at least in part, the inferiority of his weapons. The best troops included a group of Dutch and German soldiers, and Hayes had his two cadets, Allert Jansz and Otto Smit, to help command them. These men could probably be depended on, but the ranks of the Defenders also included a party of half a dozen French troops whose loyalty to the VOC, and thus general reliability, was perhaps more suspect. The balance of Hayes's men were gunners, sailors, and civilians of limited military experience. It was impossible to say how well these men would fare in the face of a determined attack by well-armed mutineers.

Nevertheless, with his preparations complete, Hayes may have felt a certain optimism. He had numbers on his side; he could hardly be surprised; and his Defenders were well fed and well supplied with water. Morale was relatively high. He and his men also had sheer desperation on their side. It was only too plain, from the descriptions of the refugees, that Cornelisz would come, and that he would kill them all if given the chance. Surrender, even a negotiated peace, were hardly options. They would fight, when they fought, to the death.

Wiebbe Hayes was a competent soldier and a good leader. It was the Defenders' good fortune that Jeronimus Cornelisz was neither. The captain-general had no military experience and, it would appear, little grasp of strategy. As soon as it emerged that Hayes and his men were still alive, Cornelisz must have known that they would have to be dealt with, for fear that they would alert a rescue ship. Yet it was not until the last week of July that Jeronimus resolved to move against them. By then Wiebbe had had at least two weeks to make his preparations; he and his men were a much more formidable enemy than they might have been a fortnight earlier.

Perhaps Cornelisz understood this. Probably he had become aware that the Defenders outnumbered the mutineers, and certainly he recognised the difficulty of launching an assault without the advantage of surprise. For these reasons the captain-general decided to begin his campaign by exploiting the well-known antipathy between the soldiers and the sailors of the VOC in order to divide Hayes's party.

He wrote a letter, warning of treachery. The sailors on Wiebbe Hayes's Island, Jeronimus alleged, had plotted to betray their comrades. 'They have in their possession (unknown to you) a Compass, in order to go thus secretly with the little skiff to the High land.*' To 'maintain justice, and punish the evil-doers,' he

*In this instance, the phrase appears to denote Australia.

urged the soldiers to hand over all the sailors on the island for punishment: 'Give to our hands Lucas the steward's mate, Cornelis the fat trumpeter, Cornelis the assistant, deaf Jan Michielsz, Ariaen the gunner, squinting Hendrick, Theunis Claasz, Cornelis Helmigs and other sailors who are with Your Hons.*' If they would also return a boat – the one Aris Jansz had taken during his escape from Batavia's Graveyard a few days earlier – the apothecary added, the soldiers and the mutineers could still be the very 'greatest and truest brothers and friends' – and, indeed, look forward to enjoying 'still more bonds and mateships.'

In composing this devious epistle, Cornelisz displayed his absolute conviction that his actions in the Abrolhos were not only justified, but sanctioned by law. He wrote as the head of the ship's council, and apparently in the hope, if not the expectation, that his orders would be obeyed. He explained that the refugees who had saved their lives by fleeing to Wiebbe Hayes's Island were in fact 'evil-doers who deserved death on account of mutiny,' and he even commented on the 'particular liking and trust' he had for Hayes himself. This was more than the self-delusion he had shown in wooing Creesje Jans. The letter was a product of Jeronimus's certainty that he was the legally ordained leader of all the *Batavia* survivors and the conviction that his actions were inspired by God.

As his emissary, Jeronimus chose Daniel Cornelissen, the young cadet who had helped to drown several of the first victims of the mutiny. On 23 July the youth was rowed to Hayes's Island, where he somehow made contact with the half dozen French soldiers among the Defenders. These men had been selected as the letter's addressees, apparently in the hope that they would be better swayed by Cornelisz's mendacity than the Dutch. But even the Frenchmen did not believe in the mutineers' sincerity, and rather than receiving Cornelissen as an ambassador, they seized him and took him captive. The cadet was bound and brought to Hayes, who confiscated the letter and imprisoned him.

False diplomacy had failed. Now Jeronimus tried violence. Two or three days after Daniel Cornelissen's disappearance, during the

---

*Some of these men have been met before. 'Lucas the steward's mate' was Lucas Gerritsz, whom Allert Janssen had attacked on his way to the liquor stores when the *Batavia* was wrecked. 'Cornelis the assistant' was Cornelis Jansz, and 'Ariaen the gunner' may have been Ariaen Ariaensz, who had tapped a barrel of wine with Abraham Hendricx at the beginning of July and set the whole mutiny in motion.

last week of July, Zevanck and Van Huyssen gathered 20 men and attempted to subdue Wiebbe by force. As Hayes had calculated, the mutineers' boats were spotted while they were still well out to sea, and their crews had to slip and stumble their way across seaweed-strewn mudflats to reach the shore. The Defenders came to meet them with their homemade weapons, and there was some sort of encounter on the beach. Exactly what occurred was not recorded, but it appears that the mutineers' reconnaissance was unsuccessful. Zevanck and Van Huyssen may have been surprised to meet with concerted resistance from a group of well-fed, well-armed men; in any case, they withdrew before either side could inflict casualties on the other, and scrambled back to their own camp to gather reinforcements. Taken by surprise themselves, they needed new ideas and a fresh approach. Unfortunately, they had neither.

Zevanck and Van Huyssen returned to Wiebbe Hayes's Island on 5 August. On this occasion they brought with them their entire gang, but they had not improved their tactics. Once again the men from Batavia's Graveyard made a long drawn-out approach across the mud; once again the Defenders were prepared for them. Hayes's troops met the mutineers in the shallows, 'up to their knees in water,' and prevented them from reaching land. The mutineers showed no more stomach for a fight than they had the previous week; again there were no casualties on either side. The second assault on Hayes's Island was as unsuccessful as the first.

After that the captain-general made no more attacks on the Defenders for a while, and the civil war in the Abrolhos lapsed into an uneasy truce, which lasted for the best part of a month. A few of the Defenders had family on Batavia's Graveyard, but Wiebbe Hayes showed no inclination to counterattack Cornelisz's men, and in retrospect his caution seems perfectly justified; secure though they were in their well-prepared positions, Hayes's troops would have been badly exposed to Jeronimus's swords and pikes in more open fighting. For their part, the mutineers now knew that they could not inflict serious casualties on Wiebbe's men without taking greater risks themselves. Some sort of new plan was evidently required.

The problem became urgent at the end of August, for time had turned against the mutineers. Each passing day increased the risk of the long-awaited rescue ship appearing, and as the wet season in the Abrolhos neared its end, their supplies of water dwindled. The more impulsive members of the captain-general's gang – Van Huyssen and Andries Liebent among them – grumbled at the strict rationing they were expected to endure; they knew by now that the Defenders had abundant food and drink and declared that they would rather fight to take Wiebbe's island than live in increasing misery on their own.

Under pressure to take action, Jeronimus himself began to plan a third attempt to ambush Hayes. Manipulative by nature, the captain-general greatly preferred deceit to frontal assaults. Rather than launch a third attack, he conceived the idea of a bogus offer of peace – 'to come to an accord with them, in order, under the cloak of friendship, to surprise them by treason at an opportune time.' He would go, he said, to Wiebbe's island bearing gifts.

Cornelisz's scheme was more subtle than those of Van Huyssen and Zevanck, but hardly well thought out. He knew that Hayes's troops required blankets and fresh clothing – after three months in the islands, their shirts and breeches were torn and dirty, and their shoes, which had been cut to pieces on the coral, had been replaced with rough clogs carved from planks of driftwood – while his men needed fresh water. There was cloth to spare on Batavia's Graveyard, and he hoped that Wiebbe might exchange fresh meat and water for clothing and red wine. A parlay on the beach would give his men the chance to talk to the Defenders, sow seeds of dissension, and then, perhaps, persuade some of them to come over to the mutineers, 'under cover, as friends, in order to help murder the others'; but Jeronimus never explained how the mutineers were to bribe their counterparts, or arrange a betrayal without Wiebbe realising what was going on. Cornelisz's cunning had once been an asset to the mutineers but now his inability to think things through, coupled with an invincible belief in his own rightness, would cost them dearly.

The parlay took place on 2 September. The day before, Gijsbert Bastiaensz had been sent to Wiebbe Hayes's Island with proposals for a peace treaty. The Defenders had received him kindly and expressed guarded interest in the plan; a time had been agreed for negotiations to take place. Now Jeronimus assembled his entire company – 37 men and all their women – on a small islet opposite the Defenders' main position and about 400 yards away across the mudflats. That done, he crossed to Hayes's Island with only a small group of his most trusted lieutenants, leaving the remainder of the mutineers behind him.

What persuaded Cornelisz to take such an insane risk? The overtures that had been made on 1 September seemed to have been positively received, and the captain-general was confident that Wiebbe and his men were genuinely desperate for the clothing. He had returned from the reconnaissance of the previous day 'saying joyfully to his folk that they now quite certainly had those [people] surely in his hands.' Possibly he was also convinced, by the ragged appearance of Hayes's troops, that the Defenders were not much of a threat. But knowing Jeronimus, it seems likely that he was also fatally overconfident. The captain-general had complete faith in his own powers of persuasion and perhaps did not understand that the loyalists mistrusted every word he said. Having seen Zevanck and Van Huyssen fail to overwhelm Hayes by force, it may have seemed to him that he was teaching his companions a lesson in how to handle malcontents. And, of course, he retained the absolute conviction that his God was protecting him.

Cornelisz arrived on Wiebbe Hayes's Island with a bodyguard of five: David Zevanck, Coenraat van Huyssen, Gÿsbert van Welderen, Wouter Loos, and Cornelis Pietersz. His men struck the Defenders as 'very skinny of hunger and thirst,' but, even in this diminished condition they were still dangerous, having committed 25 or 30 murders between them. They bore the promised supplies of *laken* and red wine. A party of Defenders came to meet them, and the bales of cloth were opened on the beach. While the men drank wine and passed samples of the cloth about, Wiebbe and Jeronimus conversed. The captain-general monopolised the negotiations, 'deceiving [him] with many lies, saying he would harm none, that it had only been on account of the Water that he had fought against them, [and] that there was no need to distrust him because some had been killed.' While Hayes was thus occupied, however, Zevanck and the other mutineers were 'walking hither and thither,' trying to strike up conversations with individual Defenders. As Cornelisz had instructed, they attempted to suborn Wiebbe's men, promising them 6,000 guilders a man, and a share in the salvaged jewels, if they would change sides.

It proved to be a fatal mistake. The Defenders had anticipated treachery, and they were ready for it. Rather than listening to Zevanck and his companions, they fell upon them suddenly, and Jeronimus paid dearly for setting foot on Hayes's Island without adequate protection. Hopelessly outnumbered, his bodyguard surrendered with hardly a fight. Cornelisz was taken prisoner and bound. Only Wouter Loos escaped, tearing himself free from his captors and making off in the mutineers' skiff before he could be recaptured.

David Zevanck and his companions now had less than two minutes to live. A quarter of a mile away across a muddy channel, the remaining mutineers had realised too late what was happening. They seized their arms and made ready to attempt a rescue, but Hayes and his men saw them coming and backed away, dragging their new prisoners with them. As the Defenders reached their positions and turned to face another attack, Wiebbe took rapid stock of his situation. The advantage he had enjoyed in numbers had probably all but evaporated, for it must have required at least two men to guard each of the struggling mutineers and prevent their fleeing after Loos. Moreover, his enemies' blood was up, and it would probably remain so while there was a chance for them to save their leaders. The logic was inescapable: he gave the order to kill the prisoners.

Jeronimus alone was spared; he was too important, both as a ringleader and a potential hostage, to be dispatched. But Zevanck, Coenraat van Huyssen and Gÿsbert van Welderen were slaughtered where they stood, along with the unfortunate Cornelis Pietersz. The executions occurred in plain view of the other mutineers as they swarmed down to the beach of their little islet, and they had the desired effect. It was plain that the Defenders were well prepared to meet an attack, and any assault would only result in the death of Cornelisz himself. Shocked and demoralised by the unexpected turn of events, the remaining mutineers pulled back instead and retired in some confusion to Batavia's Graveyard.

In the space of perhaps five minutes, the balance of power in the Abrolhos had shifted for good. The mutineers had lost their leader and his principal lieutenants, while Hayes had won the first real victory in the indecisive island civil war, immeasurably strengthening his men's morale. The Defenders had secured the wine and clothing they had coveted, for the mutineers' supplies had been abandoned on the beach when they were captured. Individual survivors were also affected by what had happened; Judick Gijsbertsdr, for instance, had lost both of her protectors; her father, left by chance among the loyalists by the swift collapse of his diplomacy, remained on Hayes's Island, while her husband-*manqué* Coenraat, run through by Wiebbe Hayes's nail-tipped pikes, lay dead on the beach.

Of all the *Batavia*'s people, none experienced a more dramatic reversal of fortune than Jeronimus Cornelisz. When he stepped ashore that day, the captain-general was the undisputed master of the survivors, gleefully wielding the power of life and death. His absurd costume of gold-trimmed *laken* had marked him as a man of great self-regard and consequence, compared with whom the ragged Defenders seemed to be no more than a rabble. Half an hour later, though, Cornelisz had at last experienced for himself something of the terror he had inflicted on Batavia's Graveyard. He had been deposed, deprived of his authority, tightly bound, and no doubt harshly treated, too; worse, the aura of invincibility that had once surrounded him – and in which he himself certainly believed – had been unceremoniously stripped away.

The captain-general's humiliation was compounded by the quarters that the Defenders found for him. For three months Jeronimus had dwelled in a large tent packed with looted clothes and treasure, taking his pick of the salvaged food and drink. Now he was hurled into a limestone pit some way inland and made to help feed Hayes's men. Into the hole the Defenders tossed the birds they caught, for their prisoner to pluck for them, and at the bottom lived Cornelisz, spattered with guts and feathers. For every nine birds that rained down on him, eight had to be surrendered to Wiebbe Hayes. The ninth he was allowed to keep, as 'salary.'

Still smarting from the disastrous setback of 2 September, the remaining mutineers regrouped on Batavia's Graveyard and elected a new leader. The only remaining member of Cornelisz's council – Stone-Cutter Pietersz, the ineffectual and unpopular lance corporal – was passed over. In his place, the 32 survivors of the under-merchant's band elected Wouter Loos.

Loos was a professional soldier who came from the southern Dutch town of Maastricht. He was considerably younger than Jeronimus, being about 24 years old, but unlike Cornelisz and his cohorts he did possess some military ability; this, in the aftermath of a devastating defeat, no doubt helps to explain his election. He had long been one of Cornelisz's favourites and had participated in several murders, but unlike the captain-general Loos took no great pleasure in killing for its own sake. Under his command, the massacres on Batavia's Graveyard ceased, and the remaining people on the island* ceased to live in constant terror of their lives.

Nevertheless, in most respects Wouter's regime differed little from Jeronimus's. Strict rationing remained in force. The women from the lower deck were still 'kept for common service,' and Loos himself shared Creesje's tent, though he would always insist that he had neither touched nor slept with her. Judick Gijsbertsdr was also treated well after her lover Coenraat's death; that is, she was left alone, and no other mutineer was permitted to possess her.

Like Cornelisz, Loos required the other mutineers to swear an oath of loyalty to him. This document, which was signed on 8 September, closely resembled the allegiances demanded by Jeronimus. At about the same time, a new ship's council was elected. Nothing is known of its composition, but it was, in any case, entirely ineffectual, since Loos's one real strategy was to continue the war against Wiebbe Hayes. He was encouraged in this by his men's escalating complaints concerning rationing, but – since it was by now apparent that the Defenders were too strong and too well organised to be easily overrun – it is by no means clear exactly what Wouter hoped to gain by returning to the attack. The most likely explanation is that he planned to inflict sufficient damage to win concessions from the Defenders, particularly with regard to the supply of food and water. It is also possible that he hoped to raise the morale of his dwindling band by reminding them that they had a common enemy. In any case, Loos was determined to proceed. On Hayes's Island, Bastiaensz was still trying to negotiate a truce – 'I had made up a script,' he noted, 'that they should have peace with each other, and that they [the mutineers] should not do any harm to the good ones.' But Wouter had no interest in such niceties. 'They tore that in pieces,' Gijsbert wrote, 'and have come at us.'

The fourth attack on Wiebbe Hayes's Island began at about 9 o'clock on the morning of 17 September and continued in a desultory fashion for about two hours, for the sides were not well matched. The committed mutineers by now were rather less than 20 strong, and the deaths of Zevanck, Pietersz, Van Huyssen and Van Welderen had deprived them of four of their best men. Of those who remained, only Loos and seven or eight other soldiers had much military experience. They were supported by a rather

*By now they numbered 47: 31 mutineers, 6 women, and 10 other men and boys.

smaller number of gunners and sailors who were also useful fighting men, but the other active mutineers were either ill or little more than boys. The camp followers – another dozen or so men who had taken the oath of loyalty demanded by their new captain-general – had played no real part in events thus far, and some at least had signed under duress. Given the opportunity, some, if not all, of this last group might well defect to Wiebbe Hayes. They were certainly not trustworthy, and if they were included in the raiding party, they would all have to be watched. Some or all of them may in fact have been left behind on Batavia's Graveyard.

The Defenders, on the other hand, still numbered 46 or 47 fighting men. Half of them were soldiers and the rest were able-bodied sailors; they were better fed and rested, and they also had the advantage of the higher ground. In the circumstances, it is hardly surprising that Loos's plan was to balance the odds by depending on his muskets. The mutineers had managed to drag two guns from the wreck, and each of them, properly handled, could fire one round a minute. By keeping the action at long range they might hope to pick off the Defenders one by one. Hayes's men, it seems safe to assume, simply took cover, perhaps sheltering behind slabs of coral. Neither side dared engage the other at close quarters, and so the action sputtered on intermittently throughout the morning.

By 11 o'clock the situation had begun to change. Four Defenders had been hit; three had severe flesh wounds, though only one, Jan Dircxsz, an 18-year-old soldier from Emden, had sustained a mortal injury. The mutineers, however, had suffered no losses at all, and it therefore seemed that Loos's strategy was working. By keeping the action at long range, he slowly but surely had begun to even the odds against him. In a few more hours, with a little more application by his musketeers, he might hope to inflict more telling casualties; and if he did that, eventually the Defenders would surely have to break cover to attack him. When they did, Loos appears to have thought, everything would come down to the matter of hand-to-hand combat, and his superior weapons might prevail. Some sort of resolution might be possible by midafternoon, and ...

It was then that Pelsaert and the rescue ship sailed over the horizon.

CHAPTER 8

Condemned

'The justice and vengeance of God made manifest.'

GIJSBERT BASTIAENSZ

Pelsaert steered the *Sardam* as close to the islands as he dared, tacking cautiously through the treacherous maze of shallows to the north. It was difficult work, and it was not until midday that the *jacht* came to anchor in a natural deep-water channel on the south-east side of the High Island, still two miles away from Wiebbe Hayes's Island and about four from Batavia's Graveyard. She was on the edge of further shallows there, and the *commandeur* could go no deeper into the archipelago.

Pelsaert had arrived in the Abrolhos not knowing whether he would find the *Batavia*'s people alive or dead. The sight of smoke rising from the islands in the group had caused him to hope – as Cornelisz had once predicted – that some, if not all, of them might still be saved. As soon as the *Sardam* had dropped anchor, he had one of the ship's boats loaded with supplies of bread and water and rowed for the nearest land, which happened to be a corner of the High Island. It was not far away, and as the *Sardam*'s men strained at their oars, the *commandeur* examined the beaches and the interior of the island for any sign of life. There was none to be found but, even so, he leapt ashore as soon as the boat grounded in the shallows, still confident that survivors would be found. The oarsmen followed – and as they did so, Pelsaert glanced back out to sea and saw a wonderful sight. 'A very small yawl with four Men' was heading toward him as swiftly as her crew could manage. The men in the boat were still too far away for the *commandeur* to determine who they were, but he could now at least anticipate that the *Batavia*'s story would turn out well.

✹

The sudden appearance of the *jacht*, coming as it did at the height of the climactic battle between the Defenders and the mutineers, had had a dramatic effect on the men fighting on both sides. For Wiebbe Hayes it seemed to be, quite literally, the product of divine intervention. Salvation had arrived when everything seemed lost, and he and his men greeted the ship's arrival with frantic relief. For Loos and the other mutineers, Pelsaert's return meant something altogether different: not life, but death; not rescue, but the certainty of retribution. All their plans had depended on dealing with Hayes's men before the appearance of a rescue ship; now that strategy lay in ruins, and when the ship was seen they broke off the action almost at once and retired in some confusion to their camp. Hayes, meanwhile, ran for his own boats in order to warn the *commandeur* of what had happened in the archipelago.

While Pelsaert tacked slowly through the shallows, the mutineers on Batavia's Graveyard were debating what to do. Wouter Loos – who had never held the men in thrall as Jeronimus had – lacked the captain-general's demonic singleness of purpose. Without the advantage of surprise, the fight had gone out of him. But other members of Cornelisz's band, including Stone-Cutter Pietersz, Jan Hendricxsz, and Lucas Gellisz, were not yet ready to surrender. 'Come on,' Jan Pelgrom urged, 'won't we now seize the *jacht*?' Loos demurred – 'No, I have given up the idea,' he replied – but Pelgrom found plenty of support for his idea, and within minutes a group of heavily armed mutineers were tumbling into the most seaworthy of their boats and pulling as quickly as they could for the High Island.

The Defenders and the mutineers raced to be the first to reach the *Sardam*. Wiebbe Hayes kept his skiffs on the north side of his island, safe from capture by the mutineers; to reach them he had to cross almost two miles of rough ground, thick with nettles and riddled with the burrows of nesting birds, and then row the best part of three miles from his mooring to the *jacht*. The mutineers' boat splashing up from the south had an almost identical distance to travel. Neither party knew exactly where the other was, or who would be the first to find the *jacht*, and Pelsaert, on the High Island, was as yet unaware of either Jeronimus's treachery or the danger he was in. The outcome of the mutiny itself thus hung in the balance.

Wiebbe Hayes's task was to find Pelsaert, persuade him to believe his undeniably amazing account of what had happened in the islands, and then warn the people in the *Sardam* before the murderers could surprise them. The mutineers' one hope was to get aboard the *Sardam* and attack before her crew realised they were in danger. Jeronimus had been quite right to predict that the rescue *jacht* would be only lightly manned, to leave room for large parties of survivors; she had left Java with a crew of only 26, and perhaps a quarter of those men were with Pelsaert in the boat. The remaining sailors, finding armed mutineers among them, might yet be overwhelmed; and if they were, Jeronimus's gang would control the one means of escape from the Abrolhos. The Defenders would have to come to terms or be abandoned, and the mutineers might thus secure the freedom of their captain-general. As for Pelsaert – still standing on the beach trying to discern who was in the fast-approaching boat – his difficulty would lie in deciding whom he should believe.

It was a while before the *commandeur* at last made out the identity of the people in the yawl. They came 'rowing round the Northerly point,' he later recalled, 'and one of them, a man named Wiebbe Hayes, sprang ashore and ran towards me, calling from afar: "Welcome, but go back on board immediately, for there is a party of scoundrels on the islands near the wreck, with two sloops, who have the intention to seize the *jacht*."' The Defenders' leader had just sufficient time to gasp out a brief summary of events in the archipelago before the *commandeur*, suddenly alert to the danger he was in, made off to warn the *Sardam*. As he jumped into his boat, Pelsaert ordered Hayes to bring Cornelisz to him, 'bound'; then he pulled like fury for the *jacht*.

Hayes and his men had won their race with the mutineers, but not by much. Pelsaert was still some distance from the *Sardam* when he 'saw a sloop with people rowing come round the Southerly point of the High Island.' It was the mutineers' boat, coming on with steady strokes, and the *commandeur* had barely enough time to scramble up the sides of the *jacht* and alert the crew before the sloop pulled alongside. One look at the 11 men on board – dressed in their ostentatious *laken* uniforms, dripping with gold and silver braid and crewing a vessel filled with swords and cutlasses – was enough to convince Pelsaert that Hayes's story was true. At his command, the swivel guns on the *Sardam*'s poop were levelled at mutineers' boat and men with pikes lined the deck. Thus reinforced, the *commandeur* felt ready to repel boarders. He hailed the boat, demanding: 'Wherefore do you come aboard armed?'

Even now, Jan Hendricxsz and the other cutthroats in the sloop were not quite ready to surrender. 'They answered me that they would reply to that when they were on the ship,' Pelsaert recalled, but by now he was thoroughly alarmed and would not permit any such thing. A brief standoff ensued, the men in the boat refusing to lay down their arms and the *Sardam*'s men threatening to open fire, and it was only when it at last became apparent to the muti-neers that their cause was hopeless that they threw their weapons overboard and clambered, unarmed, onto the *jacht*. Each man was seized the moment that he stepped on board, securely bound, and locked up in the forecastle.

Pelsaert began the process of interrogation that same afternoon, at once anxious and appalled to discover the true extent of the dis-asters that had engulfed the archipelago. Most of his information came from 'a certain Jan Hendricxsz from Bremen, soldier,' who immediately and freely confessed to having killed '17 to 20 people' on the orders of Jeronimus. Hendricxsz had been one of the first men to join the conspiracy on the *Batavia,* and he possessed an inti-mate knowledge of all Cornelisz's stratagems and plans. Under questioning by the *commandeur,* the German mutineer soon revealed not only the terrible details of the murders and massacres in the Abrolhos, but the original plot to seize the ship, and the skipper's role in it, which Pelsaert had long suspected but never had confirmed. Armed with this information, the *commandeur* then had the other mutineers brought before him, one by one, confronting each man with statements of his guilt:

'We learned from their own confessions, and the testimony of all the living persons, that they have drowned, murdered and brought to death with all manner of cruelties, more than 120 persons, men, women and children as well, of whom the principal murderers amongst those still alive have been: Lenert Michielsz van Os, soldier, Mattys Beer of Munsterbergh, cadet,* Jan

*Pelsaert here confuses the ranks of these two mutineers. Van Os was the cadet, and Beer the soldier.

Hendricxsz of Bremen, soldier, Allert Janssen of Assendelft, gunner, Rutger Fredricx of Groningen, locksmith; Jan Pelgrom de Bye of Bommel, cabin servant, and Andries Jonas of Luyck, soldier, with their consorts.'

Other names were also mentioned. Those of councillors David Zevanck, Coenraat van Huyssen, and Jacob Pietersz cropped up several times in the course of the interrogations. Nevertheless, the evidence of Jan Hendricxsz and his fellow mutineers seemed conclusive on at least one point. Jeronimus Cornielsz had been the cause of all the trouble.

Hayes brought Jeronimus aboard late that same afternoon. The captain-general arrived under close guard. Stripped of his men and all his power, he was reduced to something of a curiosity. Even now, however – dishevelled, tied up, stinking of decomposing birds, with his red cloth finery in tatters – Cornelisz plainly retained something of his weirdly compelling aura, the hypnotic fascination that had bound the mutineers together and made men willing to kill for him. Nor had two weeks of plucking feathers in a limestone pit deprived him of his facile tongue, his agile mind, or his ingenuity. Francisco Pelsaert, a less clever and a much less complex man, hardly knew what to make of his former deputy. 'I looked at him with great sorrow,' wrote the *commandeur,*

'such a scoundrel, cause of so many disasters and of the shedding of human blood – and still he had the intention to go on ... I examined him in the presence of the [*Sardam*'s] council, and asked him why he allowed the devil to lead him so far astray from all human feeling, to do that which had never been so cruelly perpetrated among Christians, without any real hunger or need of thirst, but solely out of bloodthirstiness.

'[Jeronimus] answered, that one should not blame him for what had happened, laying it on David Zevanck, Coenraat van Huyssen, and others, who have been killed, that they had forced him and willed him to do it; that also one had to do a great deal to save oneself; denied that he had ever had the intention to help in the plan to seize the ship *Batavia,* and as to the idea of seizing any *jacht* that might come, he said Zevanck had proposed this, to which he had only consented on account of his own safety without meaning it. For, firstly, he believed that they would never

> be delivered; [and secondly] that skipper Ariaen intended to throw the *commandeur* overboard [from the longboat] ... In this manner he tried to talk himself clean, with his glib tongue telling the most palpable lies, making out that nowhere had he had a hand in it, often appealing to the [other mutineers], who would say the same thing.'

Unable to penetrate this barrage of untruths for the time being, Pelsaert halted the interrogation at dusk. There were other things to do: salvaging the wreck and subduing the remaining mutineers, who were still on their island. Cornelisz was returned to his prison in the forecastle, and next morning, before dawn, Pelsaert took the *Sardam*'s boat to Wiebbe Hayes's Island, where he armed 10 of the Defenders with swords and muskets. At daybreak he sailed to Batavia's Graveyard, 'where the rest of the scoundrels were, in order to capture and secure them.' Half a dozen mutineers had stayed on the island, including Wouter Loos, Lenert van Os, and Mattys Beer; but when they saw a boatload of fully equipped soldiers disembarking on the beach, even these hardened men surrendered without a fight. Pelsaert had them securely bound and immediately began to search the island for the Company's valuables, and in particular the casket of jewels he had landed on Traitors' Island three and a half months earlier. He was pleasantly surprised to discover his hoard intact, down to and including the Great Cameo of Gaspar Boudaen – 'these were all found,' he wrote later, 'except a ring and a gold chain, and the ring has been recovered hereafter.' In the course of hunting for the valuables, the *commandeur*'s search parties also found fresh evidence of the mutiny in Jeronimus's tent. From various bundles of papers they recovered copies of the oaths that the mutineers had sworn to Cornelisz and Loos and the promises that the women kept for common service had been forced to make. These and other incriminating documents were handed to Pelsaert.

The *commandeur* must have encountered Lucretia Jans during this short stay on Batavia's Graveyard, but he makes no mention of their meeting in his account of the mutiny. Creesje had spent the last two weeks sequestered with Wouter Loos and had been treated comparatively decently since Jeronimus's capture, but having lived through shipwreck, extreme thirst and repeated rape, she was a different woman from the lady Pelsaert had known aboard the *Batavia*. There must also have been other reunions at about this time – Jan Carstensz, one of Hayes's men, with his wife Anneken Bosschieters; Claes Jansz the trumpeter with his Tryntgien; the *predikant* with his daughter Judick – but the awkwardness, and what was said, and how they explained themselves one to the other, are likewise passed over without comment in the journals; they can only be imagined.

That evening, with the search complete, Pelsaert rowed over to the wreck. It was unusually calm, and the *Sardam*'s boat was able to approach the site without much danger. There was little enough to see:

> 'We found that the ship was lying in many pieces, [and that] all above water had been washed away except a small piece of bulwark ... A piece of the front of the ship was broken off and thrown half on the shallow; there were also lying 2 Pieces of Cannon, one of brass and one of iron, fallen from the mounts. – By the foreship was lying also one side of the poop, broken off at the starboard port of the gunners' room. Then there were several pieces of a greater or lesser size that had drifted apart to various places, so there did not look to be much hope of salvaging much of the money or the goods.'

The upper-merchant nevertheless drew comfort from a statement made by Reyndert Hendricxsz, the *Batavia*'s steward and one of the unwilling mutineers. He had been employed as a fisherman and, venturing out to the wreck one day, had seen several of the money chests lying on the bottom. These, it seemed, should still be there, and Pelsaert resolved to search for them on the next calm day.

In the meantime, the *commandeur* continued his interrogation of the prisoners. Pelsaert was legally bound, under Dutch law, to administer justice as quickly as possible, and to that end he assembled the *Sardam*'s council and then enlarged it with two men from the *Batavia* in order to form a Broad Council, which alone had the power to try criminal cases. The members of the *Sardom*'s *raad* were the *commandeur* himself, the *jacht*'s skipper, Jacob Jacobsz Houtenman,* Sijmon

---

*'Wooden man,' a prototype surname adopted to distinguish him from his many namesakes; his was one of the most common names in the Dutch Republic at this time.

Yopzoon, the high boatswain, and Jan Willemsz Visch, who was probably the *Sardam*'s provost. The *Batavia*'s representatives were Claes Gerritsz, the upper-steersman, and his deputy, Jacob Jansz Hollert; on at least one occasion Gijsbert Bastiaensz was drafted onto the council, too, to take the place of someone unavoidably detained. Rather more remarkably, the clerk tasked with recording the proceedings was none other than Salomon Deschamps, who was both a mutineer and a murderer. Nor did Deschamps merely write up the interrogations and the sentences as they were made; he himself signed many of the council's resolutions and thus helped to pass judgment on his former comrades. It is possible that Pelsaert remained unaware of the assistant's guilt until late on in the proceedings – certainly the clerk would have glossed over his involvement in the killings – but it is hard to believe that the mutineers themselves were so discreet. Perhaps the *commandeur* had an unreasoning trust in his old colleague; more probably, however, Deschamps was the best scribe available, and the appointment was simply a matter of necessity.

Once the proceedings were under way, the prisoners were kept together on Seals' Island, where they were less likely to cause trouble than on board the *Sardam,* and the interrogations took place largely on Batavia's Graveyard itself. The *commandeur* dealt with the mutineers one by one – asking questions, noting answers, and often calling witnesses to confirm the truth of what he had been told. Most of Jeronimus's men were examined several times, over several days, so that the information they provided could be used to question others. It would appear, from the summaries prepared by Salomon Deschamps, that statements were also taken from some of the survivors from the island, as well as the Defenders, but very little of this evidence found its way into the record. Practically all of the surviving accounts come from the mouths of mutineers.

The proceedings on the island were conducted in accordance with Dutch law, but they were not trials in the modern sense and the mutineers did not have lawyers, nor any right to call witnesses in their own defence. Pelsaert's chief difficulty lay in securing reliable testimony from the accused, for the statutes of the United Provinces were quite specific on the question of what constituted evidence: a man could only be condemned to death on the basis of his own confession, freely given. Since few men would openly admit to capital crimes, however, the Broad Council did have the right to resort to torture when a prisoner refused to answer questions or there was good reason to doubt the veracity of his evidence. As we have seen, confessions extracted under torture were not in themselves admissible as evidence of guilt, and any statements given in this way had to be put to the prisoner again, to be confirmed 'of freewill,' within a day of being made. Some men recanted all that they had said when this was done. But since the denial of evidence given under duress led only to further interrogation, it was not unusual for testimony obtained in the torture chamber to be confirmed later in the day by men who would say anything to avoid further pain and suffering.

Jeronimus himself was the first man to be bound for torture. The under-merchant had indignantly denied his guilt when he had been brought before Pelsaert on the *Sardam,* but his testimony had been so undermined by the freewill confession of Jan Hendricxsz that the *commandeur* had little compunction in examining him more closely as soon as the Broad Council had been assembled on Batavia's Graveyard – 'in order,' as he said, 'to learn from him the straight truth, as he tries to exonerate himself with flowery talk, shoving dirt onto persons who are dead and cannot answer for themselves.'

Had Cornelisz been imprisoned in the Netherlands, he would probably have been stretched on the rack, just as Torrentius the painter had been a little less than two years earlier. But racks were cumbersome and expensive pieces of equipment, and throughout the Dutch dominions in the East the preferred method of interrogation was the water torture, which was almost equally effective and far easier to apply. Water torture required neither specialised equipment nor expert torturers; at its most basic, all that was needed was a funnel, which was forced into the prisoner's mouth. Where time and resources permitted, however, it was more usual for the man in question to be stripped to the waist and strapped, spread-eagled, into an upright frame – a door frame was sometimes used. An outsized canvas collar, which extended from his neck up to his eyes or a little higher, was then slipped over his head and fastened under his chin in such a way that liquids poured into it had nowhere to escape. The torturer then climbed a ladder by the frame, carrying a large jug, and the interrogation began.

Water was poured slowly over the prisoner's head, trickling down into the collar until it formed a pool around his chin. Failure to answer questions satisfactorily led to more liquid being added, until the man's mouth and finally his nostrils were submerged. From then on, he had to drink in order to breathe; but each time he reduced the level of the water the torturer would add more from the jug, so that the interrogation proceeded with the prisoner alternately gulping down the water and gasping for breath.

If the man persisted in his denials, and the torture became protracted, the sheer quantities of water that he consumed would bloat him hideously, 'forcing all his inward partes [and] coming out of his nose, eares and eyes,' as a contemporary English writer observed, and 'at length taking his breath away and bringing him to a swoone or fainting.' When this happened, the prisoner would be cut down and forced to vomit so that the torment could begin again. After three or four applications of the torture, the man's body would be 'swollen twice or thrice as big as before, his cheeks like great bladders, and his eyes staring and strutting out beyond his forehead,' and he would generally be ready to confess to anything that he was asked to.

Few men endured the water torture for this long, and Cornelisz was not one of them. It took some days, and several applications of the torment, but gradually the under-merchant was driven to confess not only to his plot to seize the rescue *jacht,* but also to the part that he had played in planning mutiny on the *Batavia* herself. Yet still he wriggled like a worm on a hook. Where there was little chance of misleading anyone, Jeronimus confessed freely to his crimes. He knew that Pelsaert had found copies of the oaths the mutineers had sworn to him, and he made no effort to deny that they existed. But where he could – where no other evidence existed – Cornelisz continued to blame Ariaen Jacobsz or David Zevanck for decisions that had actually been his own. Jan Hendricxsz, Lenert van Os, and Allert Janssen were brought in to confront him, at which he belatedly confessed to ordering the murders of three dozen people; but at no point did the apothecary admit to any involvement in the deaths of men killed by Zevanck, Van Huyssen, or Gÿsbert van Welderen. Then, on 28 September, when his interrogation was finally concluded, he suddenly recanted everything – 'saying they [the witnesses] are lying, also that all he has confessed he has confessed because he has been threatened with torture; also that he knew nothing of the seizing of the ship *Batavia*' – and Pelsaert found himself confronted with the possibility that he would have to start the whole procedure once again.

'Therefore,' noted the *commandeur,*

'on account of his unsteady and variable confessions, practising crooked means – though by all people accused in his own presence in order to prove the same to be lies – have again and for the last time threatened him with torture and asked why he mocked us, because he has confessed and told everything freely several times.'

Cornelisz replied with a further lie: he had wished, he said, to delay matters sufficiently to be taken to Batavia 'in order to speak again to his wife' – although he knew, as Pelsaert perhaps did not, that she was still in the Dutch Republic. Then, when the *commandeur* read out his statements and confessions 'before all the people on the Island,' Jeronimus complained that a small detail was still incorrect: 'Something was in it of which Assendelft,* Jan Hendricxsz and others accused him wrongly.' It was yet another delaying tactic; the law compelled Pelsaert to recall both witnesses to double-check their stories, which in turn meant a respite of perhaps an hour while the men were brought over from Seals' Island.

At last, when the men concerned had been fetched and reconfirmed their testimony, the exasperated *commandeur* confronted Cornelisz directly, demanding to know why he 'mocked the Council through his intolerable desperation, saying one time that they spoke the truth, another time that they all lied.' From Pelsaert's voice, or manner, the under-merchant finally understood that he was now beaten. Further evasion, he could see, would only result in vigorous torture; and so a truth of sorts emerged. 'Confesses at last,' noted Deschamps at this point in his summary, in his best Italian hand, 'that he did it to lengthen his life.'

Rather than endure any further torment, Jeronimus now agreed of free will that all his testimony was true, and late in the afternoon of 28 September he signed his statements and confessions. 'He well knows that all he has done is evil enough,' Pelsaert observed in conclusion, 'and he desires no grace.'

Cornelisz's fellow mutineers were more easily entrapped. A few, such as Jan Hendricxsz, largely spared themselves the agonies of the water torture by confessing freely to their sins. Others,

---

*Allert Janssen. Assendelft was the gunner's hometown.

including Rutger Fredricx and Mattys Beer, tried to conceal at least some of their crimes, in the hope of lessening their punishment. They were put to the torture in an attempt to get at the truth. Andries Jonas suffered more than most for his blind insistence that he had remained outside the *predikant*'s tent on the night the family were murdered; the *commandeur* suspected that Jonas was concealing his role in the affair, and the soldier was half-drowned twice before his persistent denials were believed. But none of the captain-general's gang escaped without enduring at least a little pain. Even Hendricxsz was tortured once, when he tried to pretend that he knew nothing of his leader's plan to seize the *jacht*.

Jeronimus, meanwhile – once he had been forced into confession – betrayed his fellow mutineers without compunction. He had never cared remotely about how other people felt, and now he saw no reason to risk further torture simply to help men who had sworn loyalty to him. When Rutger Fredricx begged his captain-general to confirm that he, Fredricx, had been given a direct order to kill Andries de Vries, Cornelisz obliged – but added maliciously 'that he certainly believes that Rutger has done more than he has confessed, because he was always very willing to offer his services if anyone had to be put out of the way.' Next, the under-merchant gave a lengthy statement implicating Lenert van Os in eight murders, the first massacre on Seals' Island, and the slaughter of the *predikant*'s family, naming in addition Jan Hendricxsz as the killer of Stoffel Stoffelsz and Mattys Beer as the murderer of Cornelis Aldersz. Then he mentioned Lucas Gellisz as Lenert van Os's accomplice in the killing of Passchier van den Ende and Jacob Hendricxen Drayer, and named Rogier Decker as the murderer of Hendrick Jansz. Perhaps Pelsaert would have got to the truth anyway; but Jeronimus's willingness to recall places, names, and dates must certainly have aided the investigation, and it quickly broke down the remaining bonds of loyalty among the mutineers. Before long each man was blaming his companions, and the whole truth about the mutiny emerged.

Seven of the mutineers were examined in this first round of interrogations. They were the worst of the murderers – Jan Hendricxsz, Andries Jonas, Mattys Beer, Lenert van Os, Allert Janssen, Rutger Fredricx, and Jan Pelgrom – and only Andries Jonas, at the end of his interrogation, blurted out, apparently spontaneously, 'that he has been very willing in murdering, and does not know how he wandered so far from God.' The other six gave neither reasons for their crimes nor the least show of remorse.

It would have made little difference if they had. The Broad Council's verdicts, when they were delivered on 28 September, were very nearly as severe as Pelsaert could make them, and the *commandeur* seems to have made no allowance whatsoever for the men who had cooperated more or less freely with his investigation. Each case had been judged strictly on its merits.

All of the *retourschip*'s survivors, and the *Sardam*'s crew, were assembled on Batavia's Graveyard to witness the sentencing. The surviving members of Cornelisz's gang were present too. It was nearly evening by the time Pelsaert was ready to proceed and the leading mutineers shuffled forward to hear the verdicts on their cases.

The captain-general was the first man to be called. 'Because Jeronimus Cornelisz of Haarlem, aged about 30 years, apothecary, and later under-merchant of the ship *Batavia,* has misbehaved himself so gruesomely,' Pelsaert intoned,

'and has gone beyond himself, yea, has even been denuded of all humanity and has been changed as to a tiger ... and because even under Moors and Turks such unheard of, abominable misdeeds would not have happened, we, the undersigned persons of the Council ... in order to turn us from the wrath of God and to cleanse the name of Christianity of such an unheard of villain, have sentenced the foresaid Jeronimus Cornelisz that he shall be taken to a place prepared to execute justice, and there first cut off both his hands, and after that punish him on a gallows with a cord until death follows – with confiscation of all his goods, Moneys, Gold, Silver, monthly wages, and all that he may have to claim here in India against the VOC, our Lord Masters.'

It was the maximum penalty available under Dutch law. And so the *commandeur* continued: Jan Hendricxsz, Lenert van Os, Allert Janssen and Mattys Beer were sentenced to have their right hands removed before they were hanged; the other three mutineers – Jan Pelgrom, Andries Jonas and Rutger Fredricx – received a slightly lesser punishment. Presumably because their crimes had been less extensive, these men were to go to their deaths unmutilated, but in each case they, like all the others, suffered the confiscation of their goods and died knowing that Jan Company, not their families, would inherit whatever meagre worldly possessions they left behind.

Pelsaert had not yet finished. In the course of his investigation, the *commandeur* had also formed opinions of the remainder of the mutineers. Nine of them, he now announced, were to be taken to Java for interrogation – 'or to punish them on the way, according to time and occasion.' They were Wouter Loos, Stone-Cutter Pietersz, Hans Jacob Heijlweck, Daniel Cornelissen, Andries Liebent, Hans Frederick, Cornelis Janssen, Rogier Decker, and Jan Willemsz Selyns – by no means all of them minor figures in the tragedy. Nineteen other men, who had signed Jeronimus's oaths and had been held on suspicion of active involvement in the mutiny, were freed 'until later decision, unless something detrimental arises.' Most of them had done little more than pledge allegiance to Cornelisz – their numbers included relative nonentities such as the steward, Reyndert Hendricxsz, Gillis Phillipsen, the soldier who had sharpened the sword used to decapitate the netmaker Cornelis Aldersz, and the doubly bereaved Hans Hardens. Bastiaensz the *predikant* was also cleared, at least provisionally. But several of these men had been closer to Jeronimus than Pelsaert yet appreciated. Among those who were now released was Olivier van Welderen, who was more than capable of causing further trouble.

At least the *commandeur* could rely on Wiebbe Hayes. The Defenders' leader, who was still a private soldier, was now promoted to the rank of sergeant at a salary of 18 guilders per month – twice his former wage. He was thus placed in charge of all the surviving soldiers, who had been without a commanding officer since the *Sardam*'s arrival in the archipelago, a move that no doubt helped to reinforce their sometimes doubtful loyalty to the Company. Hayes's principal lieutenants on his island, the cadets Otto Smit and Allert Jansz, were both made corporals at a salary of 15 guilders. These promotions were the only ones that Pelsaert offered to the 48 loyalists who had helped preserve the VOC's interests in the Abrolhos.

The *commandeur* had other matters on his mind. His chief priority was now to salvage what he could from the wreck site, but he also had to keep his men supplied with food and water and ensure that

Cornelisz and the mutineers were kept securely under guard. The salvage work was proving difficult – fierce winds and high seas had kept Pelsaert's divers from the wreck on seven of the eight days that he spent on the interrogations – and by the end of September the only goods recovered were two money chests and a box of tinsel. Though the same weather conditions at least kept the mutineers safely imprisoned on Seals' Island, the members of the Broad Council were also uncomfortably aware that these cases full of silver coins, which had already helped to spark one mutiny, might yet cause trouble on the voyage back to Java.

It was the last consideration that caused the *commandeur* to wonder if it would be wise to transport Cornelisz and his men all the way back to the Indies to be executed. There were more than enough mutineers about to cause trouble on a ship the *Sardam*'s size, and now that the most brutal of them were under sentence of death they had very little to lose by plotting further violence. The thought of traversing nearly 2,000 miles with Cornelisz alive and waiting for a chance to exploit the least sign of dissent was not a pleasant one, and Pelsaert rapidly concluded that 'it would not be without danger for the ship and the goods to set off to sea with so many corrupt and half-corrupted men.' The latter, he reasoned, 'could easily become wholly corrupted by the richness of the salvaged wealth,' and he and his men could still go the way of the skipper of the *Meeuwtje*. The safer option was to carry out the hangings in the Abrolhos, and it was soon decided that it would be safest if the ringleaders were dispatched next day, 29 September. To reduce the risk of moving groups of desperate men about the archipelago, the place of execution was to be Seals' Island.

The *commandeur* did not announce this date in passing sentence, and Jeronimus continued to dream up ways to buy himself more time. His next ploy was to request a stay of execution, 'because he desired to be baptised and so that he could meanwhile have time to bewail his sins and think them over so that at last he might die in peace and in repentance.' This, he cynically calculated, might buy him several weeks of life; but though Pelsaert was pious enough to agree to a brief postponement, he was not prepared to allow the under-merchant more than an extra 48 hours to confront his demons. At dusk on 28 September the executions of the seven prisoners were moved back to Monday, 1 October, but once again the date itself was not revealed to the condemned men.

Jeronimus Cornelisz, who had kept the people of Batavia's

Graveyard in fear of sudden death for two long months, found he could not stomach the agony of wondering how long he had left to live. The apothecary begged Gijsbert Bastiaensz to reveal the date of his execution, and when the preacher could not or would not tell him, he became quite agitated. In the end 'the *predikant* put him at ease for that day [28 September], and he behaved himself as if he had some solace, and was more courageous,' but next morning this veneer swiftly fell away and again Jeronimus pleaded to be told how many days he had, saying that he could not otherwise properly prepare himself for death.

This time, Pelsaert told him. 'Tut – nothing more?' Cornelisz muttered in disgust. 'Can one show repentance of life in so few days? I thought I should be allowed eight or fourteen days.' Then his self-possession left him and he altogether lost his temper, raging:

> 'I see well [you] want my blood and my life, but God will not suffer that I shall die a shameful death. I know for certain, and you will all see it, that God will perform unto me this night a miracle, so that I shall not be hanged.'

And that, the *commandeur* noted with concern, 'was his tune all day.'

Whether or not Jeronimus really believed, at this point, that his God would intervene to save him is an interesting question; it would not have been out of character for him to have entertained such thoughts. But Pelsaert plainly guessed that the apothecary's boasts meant that he intended to commit suicide. He issued special orders to the guards, demanding extra vigilance and warning them not to allow anyone to smuggle the prisoner anything that he could use in such an attempt.

Security was, however, still a problem in the Abrolhos. Although the mutineers were kept safely away from the other survivors, they were not in any modern sense in prison on Seals' Island. There were no thick-walled cells to lock them in; their quarters were merely tents, and it was impossible to prevent so many men from mixing with their guards. In these circumstances, and especially when Pelsaert was still unaware of the real extent of the mutineers' support, it was unusually difficult to ensure that the prisoners were kept isolated. Jeronimus had already been able to write two letters to his friends back in the Netherlands, full of tall tales of the conspiracies against him and outraged assurances of his innocence; these he had smuggled to Jacob Jansz Hollert, the *Batavia*'s under-steersman, in the hope that he would send them home. As it happened, Hollert had given the letters to Pelsaert instead, and they had been opened by the Broad Council and found to be 'contrary to the truth, in order to cover up his gruesome misdeeds.' But if it was possible for Cornelisz to pass notes out of his tent, it was also easy enough for him to receive contraband. At some time prior to 29 September the apothecary had obtained some poison, which was perhaps a remnant of the batch that had been mixed to dispose of Mayken Cardoes's child; and, that night, he took it – either in fulfilment of his own prophecy, or because he had at last despaired of divine intervention.

The effect was not at all what he had hoped. The poison, Pelsaert wrote, was not strong enough to do its job, for although it 'started to work at about one o'clock in the morning, so that he was full of pain and seemed like to die,' it left Jeronimus writhing in hideous agony without actually killing him. 'In this great anxiety,' the *commandeur* noted with just a trace of satisfaction,

> 'he asked for some Venetian theriac. At last he began to get some relief ... but he had to be got out of his prison certainly 20 times during the night, because his so-called miracle was working from below as well as from above.'

By morning on 30 September, a Sunday, Cornelisz was sufficiently recovered to be called from his tent to hear the preacher's sermon with the other prisoners. He alone, however, refused to join the party, vowing to have nothing at all to do with the minister. This refusal to seek solace in religion less than a day before the scheduled executions struck the *commandeur* as remarkable, and it was only now, at the end of the whole story, that Pelsaert finally began to comprehend the true significance of the under-merchant's heresy. Jeronimus's strange ideas had cropped up from time to time during his interrogation, particularly in connection with the suppression of Bastiaensz's preaching on the island, but they had become so bound up with his litany of lies, half-truths, and self-deception that the members of the Broad Council seem to have largely disregarded them, seeing the captain-general's theology as little more than another of the devices that he used to control his men. The other councillors were bluntly practical men, of strictly orthodox religious views. Confronted with the reality of the murder, rape, and pillage that had gone on in the archipelago they did not feel compelled to explore a merely ideological charge of heresy.

The *commandeur,* who had a better education than the rest and at least some imagination, was perhaps the only man in the Abrolhos who – at this late remove – finally understood not only how Cornelisz's beliefs had helped to mould the shape and nature of the mutiny, but also that these views were in themselves only a part of a larger and more complex personality – a personality he plainly believed was evil. In his journals, Pelsaert recoils almost visibly from this recognition, just as a snail that has been prodded by a twig retreats into its shell. And, like the snail, the *commandeur* had no more than an incomplete understanding of what it was that had touched him. It was as though he had just seen a truth that had lain masked by the easy denunciations of the official record: 'Godless,' 'evil-minded,' 'innately corrupt.' 'See how miraculously God the Lord reveals godlessness before all the people,' the *commandeur* had written piously of Jeronimus's refusal to come to church; but what he really meant was that he had caught a glimpse – as it were from the corner of his eye – of someone living far beyond the bounds of conventional morality.

Time was now fast running out for all the mutineers. The first day of October dawned so grimly stormy that the planned executions had to be postponed; the seas were so high that it was dangerous to make the generally easy voyage across the deep-water channel to Seals' Island. But this respite was only temporary; the next day it was calmer, and a group of carpenters went over to begin building the gallows. Seals' Island is the only place in the vicinity of Batavia's Graveyard where the soil is deep enough to support such structures; there is a good landing place on the west side of the channel, toward the southern end of the islet, and a ridge just inland with enough sand and guano-encrusted earth on it to sink the posts. The carpenters used spare lumber from the *Sardam,* and perhaps the *Batavia*'s driftwood, too, and when they had finished they had put up two or three large scaffolds, with room enough for seven men.

Once that work was done, the prisoners were summoned. Pelsaert was there to supervise the execution of justice, and Bastiaensz to console the men and save their souls, if that were possible. There, too, was Creesje Jans, who had not talked to Jeronimus since his capture nearly a month earlier. An hour before the executions were due to begin, and in the hearing of some of the Defenders, she at last came close enough to the captain-general to catch his eye. Pelsaert was not present to record this last brief encounter; but Wiebbe Hayes was there, and he listened while Creesje reproached her former captor in the strongest terms. 'She bitterly lamented to the said Jerome,' the newly promoted sergeant noted later, 'over the sins he had committed with her against her will, and forcing her thereto. To which Jerome replied: "It is true, you are not to blame, for you were in my tent 12 days before I could succeed."'

Creesje was not the only person on Seals' Island anxious to confront Cornelisz before he died. The other condemned mutineers, who had once been the captain-general's creatures, had greatly resented his betrayal of them under interrogation, and they now loudly demanded that Jeronimus be strung up first, 'so that their eyes could see that the seducer of men [had] died.' This request reflected their desire for revenge, of course, but also a real fear that if they died first the apothecary might yet talk his way out of punishment. They crowded round the under-merchant as he was dragged toward his execution – Hendricxsz and Van Os, Jonas and Allert Janssen, Fredricx and Beer – and they hooted and hissed at him. They saw him kneel before the hangman so that his hands could be removed (a contemporary print suggests that the amputations were crudely performed, with a hammer and a chisel). And at the very end, they gathered beneath the gallows to watch as he ascended.

The assembled people on the island saw one last drama played out on the scaffold. 'They all shouted at each other,' Pelsaert recalled. 'Some evil-doers shouted "Revenge!" at Jeronimus, and Jeronimus shouted at them. At last he challenged them, as well as the council, before God's Judgement Seat, that he wanted to seek justice there with them, because he had not been able to get it here on Earth.'

The *predikant* witnessed the same bizarre exchange. 'If ever there has been a Godless Man,' he wrote,

'in his utmost need, it was he; [for] he had done nothing wrong, according to his statement. Yes, saying even at the end, as he mounted the gallows: "Revenge! Revenge!" So that to the end of his life he was an evil Man.'

Then Gijsbert Bastiaensz, who had more cause than most to hate Cornelisz, added a last thought. 'The justice and vengeance of God has been made manifest in him,' he scrawled, 'for he had been a too-atrocious murderer.'

CHAPTER 9

'To Be Broken on the Wheel'

'And so he died stubborn.'

FRANCISCO PELSAERT

Jeronimus took quite some time to die.

A gallows, in the seventeenth century, consisted of little more than two braced uprights, 10 to 15 feet high, joined by a thick horizontal beam from which men were strangled slowly at the end of a short rope. Two hundred years before the invention of the trapdoor and the drop, the only other piece of equipment that an executioner required was a ladder to prop against one of the uprights. The prisoner was driven up the ladder, arms tied, legs free, the noose already around his neck. The hangman tied the other end of the rope securely to the beam and then, with little ceremony, thrust one knee into the small of the condemned man's back and launched him into space. The fortunate few died quickly of a broken neck, but in most cases the fall was not enough to guarantee an instant death and the man was strangled by the noose instead. This could be a lengthy process, lasting for up to 20 minutes, and most prisoners remained conscious for a good part of the time. The convulsive kicks and struggles of the dying man were reckoned good sport by the crowds who attended the public executions popular in Europe. Those lucky enough to secure a spot close to the scaffold could also witness the unpleasant aftermath of a slow hanging: uncontrolled voiding of bladder and bowels and, in some cases, involuntary erection at the moment of death.

Attempts were sometimes made to hasten the condemned man's end; friends might be allowed to tighten the noose by pulling at his legs, while, in France, the executioner was required to swing out onto the crossbeam 'and, placing his feet in the loop formed by the bound hands of the patient, by dint of repeated vigorous shocking terminate his sufferings.' It seems unlikely that such interventions were allowed in Jeronimus's case, but unless tourniquets had been applied, the amputation of his hands would have led to loss of consciousness and death before the noose could do its work. The maximum allowable blood loss for a man of normal weight – around 160 pounds – is roughly two and a half pints. Cornelisz, who had lived on the sparse island diet for the best part of three months, almost certainly weighed a good deal less than that. He would have lost consciousness quite quickly, and died after losing around two pints of blood.

As was the custom, the *predikant* accompanied the condemned men to the scaffold in the hope that some, at least, would confess their sins. Jeronimus refused to talk to him and went to his death without the least show of remorse. 'He could not reconcile himself to dying,' Pelsaert noted grimly, 'or to penitence, neither to pray to God nor to show any face of repentance over his sins … And so he died stubborn.' Cornelis Jansz, who witnessed the execution, was likewise shocked by Cornelisz's refusal to admit his guilt, even as he stood bleeding by the gallows. Only a confession – and genuine contrition – could even begin to atone for the captain-general's many sins, and Jeronimus's resolve, the Defender thought, must have been rooted in his heretical beliefs. 'He died,' Jansz wrote, 'as he had lived, not believing there exists Devil or Hell, God or Angel – the Torrentian feeling had spread thus far.'

The other mutineers had less faith and were not so brave. Both Mattys Beer and Andries Jonas found that their courage failed them on their way to the scaffold, and each made a stumbling confession to cleanse their consciences and buy a few moments more of life. Beer admitted to the murder of another four men and a boy, killed one night 'in the presence of Jeronimus' with such anonymous efficiency that he did not even know their names. Jonas, whose victims had almost all been women and children, dredged up the memory of one further killing – that of 'still another Boy' who had died more or less by chance during one of the periodic massacres on Batavia's Graveyard. It had been a particularly merciless crime:

'On a certain night when some other Men were murdered, the

Boy, out of fear and because he was ill, came creeping on his hands and feet into their tent, which Jacop Pietersz Cosyn* had seen, [and said], "Andries, you must help to put the boy out of the way." Whereon he had gone outside, dragged the Boy out of the tent, and cut his throat with his knife.'

The other condemned mutineers – Jan Hendricxsz, Lenert van Os, Allert Janssen, and Rutger Fredricx, who had between them bludgeoned, drowned, or stabbed almost 40 of the *Batavia* survivors – went to their deaths more quietly, though all, in Pelsaert's view, 'died also very Godless and unrepentant.' The one exception was Jan Pelgrom, the half-mad cabin boy, who was only 18 years old and could not reconcile himself to death. On his way to the scaffold he succumbed to hysteria, 'weeping and wailing and begging for grace, and that one should put him on an Island and let him live a little longer.' Remarkably, given the boy's awful record, the *commandeur* gave way to Pelgrom's pleas, agreeing to spare him on account of his age. At the foot of the gallows Jan's death sentence was commuted to marooning 'on an island or the continent, according to occasion occurring,' and he was returned to the temporary prison.

Nothing is said in the *Batavia* journals as to what happened to the corpses of the other prisoners, but it was usual, in the Netherlands, for the bodies of executed prisoners to remain on view as a warning to others. In Haarlem condemned men from throughout North Holland were hung just outside the city walls and their remains were not cut down until the scaffold was required again. Even then the corpses would be strapped to wooden poles arranged nearby so that they remained on display. In the Abrolhos, therefore, the bodies of Cornelisz and his men were in all likelihood left dangling from the gallows when the execution party rowed back to the *Sardam*.

The next day there was a violent gale. By this time it was spring in the archipelago; thousands of mutton birds had returned to the islands to fill the night with their unearthly wailing, and high winds frequently interfered with Pelsaert's salvage operations. The storm persisted until 4 October; then there was one day of fair weather, during which a brass cannon on the wreck was brought back to Batavia's Graveyard. After that the weather closed in with a

*The lance corporal and member of Cornelisz's council also known as 'Stone-Cutter.' 'Cosyn' *(cosijn),* his other nickname, means 'window-frame.'

vengeance, and for two weeks the monsoons prevented much work being done out on the reef. Even after that, the weather was only good enough for salvage 'one day in 15 to 20,' in the opinion of the *Sardam*'s council.

In the circumstances, Pelsaert's Dutch and Gujerati divers did well to salvage as much as they did. Working without any protective gear in intensely dangerous waters, and with the ever-present danger of being dashed to pieces against the reef, the six men brought up seven of the Company's lost money chests, quantities of loose coin, and a good deal of Pelsaert's silverware, together with some boxes of tinsel. Three more chests were recovered later, but the other two had to be left in the Abrolhos 'with heart's regret.' One was located, sitting on the bottom, but it could not be salvaged because one of the heavy guns had fallen onto it and pinned it to the reef.

While this salvage work was under way, the *commandeur* set parties of sailors and Defenders to work on the islands of the archipelago, scouring the ground for anything of value to the VOC. Cornelisz's stores of purloined jewels and clothing were recovered, together with the remaining rations and some trade goods, but Pelsaert – acutely conscious of what the wreck of the *Batavia* had already cost the Company – insisted that even the most insignificant detritus be recovered. The men sent to pick over the islands of the archipelago dutifully salvaged every single item they could find, from sea-soiled linens to rusted old barrel hoops and nails.

It was hardly necessary work, and on 12 October the merchant's determination to retrieve every piece of VOC property resulted in a pointless accident that cost the lives of five more men. Jacob Jacobsz, the *Sardam*'s skipper, had been ordered to sail a small boat out to the reef to recover any flotsam that had become stranded there. The main object of the expedition was the recovery of a small barrel of vinegar that had been spotted on the coral on the preceding day, after which the boat was to carry on and search some of the outlying islets in the archipelago for driftwood and other objects from the wreck. Jacobsz took with him not only his quartermaster, Pieter Pietersz, and one of the *Sardam*'s gunners, but also two men who had been on the *Batavia*: Ariaan Theuwissen, a gunner, and Cornelis Pieterszoon, the *retourschip*'s under-trumpeter. The latter was almost certainly the same 'Cornelis the fat trumpeter' named in the letter sent by Jeronimus to the Defenders at the end of July, who had survived both that attempt at betrayal and three attacks by the mutineers. The men had orders to return to the *Sardam* that evening if possible, but to stay out all night if that proved necessary. In the event, they did not come back, and on the afternoon of 13 October Claes Gerritsz, on the *jacht,* caught a last glimpse of Jacobsz's yawl well out to sea, about nine miles from the ship. Soon afterward the wind began to rise and banks of rain swept in. The curtain of sea mist quickly swallowed up the boat and hid it from view.

That was the last anyone saw of Jacob Jacobsz and his men. Two days of storms prevented Pelsaert from launching a search for the missing yawl until 16 October, when a boat commanded by Jacob Jansz Hollert searched all the outlying islands without success; and though several columns of smoke were seen rising from the mainland on 4 November, giving rise to definite hopes that the men might have made a landfall there, a brief search of the Australian coast revealed no sign of the crew. The five sailors had to be given up for lost.

So obsessively did Pelsaert search for wreckage that his salvage work was not completed until the middle of November, six weeks after Jeronimus's execution. During this time the hundred soldiers and sailors under his command had to guard the 30 survivors of the group that had signed oaths of allegiance to Cornelisz. The most dangerous of the surviving mutineers – they included Daniel Cornelissen and Hans Jacob Heijlweck, both of whom had killed several men – were still kept, bound hand and foot, in isolation on Seals' Island. The remainder, though, were not confined, and since there were at least a score of them the possibility of another uprising could not entirely be discounted. In the circumstances it is hardly surprising that Pelsaert decided to deal with another six of the remaining mutineers before leaving the Abrolhos.

The men concerned were Wouter Loos, Lucas Gellisz, Rogier Decker, Abraham Gerritsz, Claes Harmansz, and Salomon Deschamps, Pelsaert's clerk, whose role in the death of Mayken Cardoes's child had finally emerged. Loos, who was the only major figure in the group, was charged with allowing himself to be 'made Captain of a troop of Murderers' and attacking Wiebbe Hayes and his Defenders, but not, at first, with any killings. The other five had all confessed to murder, but in each case Pelsaert and the members of the Broad Council observed that there had been extenuating circumstances. Deschamps, Gerritsz, and Harmansz, who had been forced to kill by Zevanck and his men, were all found to have acted under duress, and each was spared the death sentence. Decker and Gellisz were still more fortunate. Both had killed men in cold blood, 'without any protest,' as the *commandeur* noted in Decker's case, and even 'to show good faith,' as he observed of Gellisz's involvement in the bloody murder of Frans Jansz. Yet Decker was spared on account of his youth, and Gellisz apparently for no better reason than that the council wished to show him mercy. Instead of death, each of the five mutineers was sentenced to be dropped from the yard or keelhauled, followed by '100 strokes before the mast' and, in Lucas Gellisz's case, the confiscation of six months' wages.

Compared with what Jeronimus had suffered, these punishments were merciful, and Wouter Loos – who had, after all, succeeded Jeronimus in overall command of the mutineers – was treated even more leniently. Rebellion against Jan Company in itself meant an automatic death sentence at the time, but for some reason Pelsaert attached comparatively little weight to Loos's role as Cornelisz's successor. In addition, the *commandeur* noted only in passing that Loos had indeed been guilty of 'several murders,' though he had actually killed two people – Bastiaen Gijsbertsz and Mayken Cardoes – tied up at least two others so that they could be drowned, and bore a good deal of responsibility for the death of Jan Dircxsz, the Defender, in the final assault on Hayes's Island. Nor was any mention made of the prominent part Loos had played in the plot to entice the *Sardam*'s crew ashore and murder them. Pelsaert's view was that Loos had actually 'committed more with his tongue, by means of advice, than with his hands,' and certain factors may have weighed in the soldier's favour: he had saved the life of Jan Willemsz Selyns, refused to launch an attack on the *Sardam,* and no one had died on Batavia's Graveyard after he assumed command of the captain-general's gang. On the whole, however, it is hard to avoid the conclusion that Loos was treated with leniency simply because he was not Jeronimus Cornelisz. The mutineers' last leader was sentenced not to death but to be marooned, with Jan Pelgrom the cabin boy, somewhere on the South-Land's coast.

❈

The *Sardam* sailed for the Indies on 15 November 1629 carrying 77 survivors from the *Batavia*. Of this total, 45 had fought with Wiebbe Hayes; three, including Pelsaert, had reached Java in the longboat and returned on board the *jacht*; and the other 29 had been members of Cornelisz's band, unwilling associates, or concubines of the mutineers. Only five of the survivors were women – Creesje Jans was one of them – and just one was a child. Among the men, fewer than half a dozen of those who had survived Batavia's Graveyard had done so without throwing their lot in with the mutineers or signing one of Jeronimus's oaths of obedience. These people – none of them are named – were almost certainly artisans: carpenters, cooks, or coopers whom even Cornelisz could see were more valuable alive than dead. Every other man, woman, and child who had survived the wreck had been murdered in the six weeks from 4 July to 16 August. The killings on the islands had ceased for no other reason than that the mutineers had run out of victims.

The gales of the preceding weeks had at last given way to beautiful spring weather, and the *jacht* made excellent progress along the coast of the Great South-Land. She dropped anchor at Batavia on 5 December, a little under three weeks after leaving the Abrolhos. The return journey was thus accomplished in less than a third of the time that Pelsaert had taken to sail from the Indies to the archipelago two months earlier.

Only two incidents of any significance occurred during the voyage. On the morning of 16 November, less than a day after leaving Batavia's Graveyard, Pelsaert spotted smoke rising on the South-Land. The weather was considerably more moderate than it had been on his first trip along the coast, and – hoping that the smoke might come from a signal fire lit by Jacob Jacobsz and the men who had gone missing in the *Sardam*'s boat – the *commandeur* managed to put in at an inlet on the coast, not quite 50 miles north of the Abrolhos. No trace of the missing sailors could be found, but the place was evidently inhabited – the landing party found plenty of naked footprints, though 'the Blacks kept themselves hidden and did not show themselves to anyone' – and there was fresh water in a gully.* It struck Pelsaert that this would be a good spot to carry out the sentences on Jan Pelgrom and Wouter Loos, and later in the day the two mutineers were rowed ashore and abandoned on a gently shelving beach close to the stream. Pelgrom

---

*The spot has been identified as Wittecarra Gully, which lies just south of the mouth of the Murchison River near modern Kalbarri.

and Loos thus became – improbably – the first white settlers in Australia, nearly 160 years before the arrival of the British convicts of the First Fleet of 1787.

Once again, the mutineers had been exceptionally fortunate. Despite its later – and romantic – reputation, marooning frequently meant little more than a slow death. Many maroons were abandoned on waterless cays, much like those in the Abrolhos, with nothing but a water bottle and a gun; once the water was all gone, they were expected to shoot themselves. Pelgrom and Loos received a good deal more – a boatload of equipment, materials to barter with the natives, access to a good supply of water, and even instructions from the *commandeur* on how best to ingratiate themselves with the people they encountered. Their prospects of survival were not bad.

The second incident of note did not take place until the end of November, by which time the *Sardam* was almost within sight of the coast of Java. Eight of the mutineers on board had still not been told what their sentences would be. The members of this group now begged Pelsaert to review their cases and pronounce judgment immediately, before they reached Batavia. It was an unusual request, not least because the men's petition was supported by the remainder of the crew, and it was almost certainly made because the surviving mutineers knew of the light sentences handed out to Deschamps, Gellisz, Loos, and their companions and suspected that they would be treated more leniently by Pelsaert than they would by the unforgiving Council of the Indies. In this they were undoubtedly correct.

The members of Pelsaert's Broad Council took some time to debate the men's request. On one hand they suspected Governor-General Coen would probably wish to try the mutineers himself. On the other, they may have felt some slight compassion for the men, and wondered – as Pelsaert noted in his journals – if it might be better 'not to trouble further the Hon. Lord Gov. Gen. in his many duties, as we fear that the Javanese war is causing him enough heartburning, although [we] hope such is not so.' In the end a compromise was reached. Seven of the rebels were brought up from below to hear their sentences. The eighth was the last surviving member of Jeronimus's council: the unfortunate lance corporal, 'Stone-Cutter' Pietersz, who was the one major mutineer still in Pelsaert's custody. He was kept bound and chained to await the pleasure of the governor-general.

The first man called before the council was Daniel Cornelissen. The enthusiastic young cadet had killed four men and helped to kill three more before he was captured by Wiebbe Hayes; he was sentenced to be keelhauled three times and then severely flogged, and was also to suffer the confiscation of his last year's wages. Hans Jacob Heijlweck, who had brained the surgeon with a morning star, was also guilty of murder, and he received a similar sentence. So did Cornelis Janssen, the sailor, who had killed no one. His crimes were plotting mutiny on board the *Batavia,* helping to assault Creesje Jans, and looting the *commandeur*'s cabin after the wreck.

Three more of those who had sworn loyalty to Jeronimus – the soldiers Andries Liebent and Hans Frederick, and Isbrant Isbrantsz, an assistant – had assisted in the murders, though Liebent and Fredrick had killed willingly, while Isbrantsz had acted under duress. Their punishment was to be dropped three times from the mast, then flogged; Liebent and Frederick were also fined six months' wages. Jean Thirion, a soldier who had hacked open one of the VOC's money chests on the wreck, was sentenced to be keelhauled, flogged, and fined a similar amount.

Two prisoners still had to be dealt with. The last remaining member of Cornelisz's gang, Olivier van Welderen, seems to have been suspected of a good deal, including, perhaps, membership of the group of mutineers that had formed on the *Batavia*. But illness had confined Van Welderen to his tent on Batavia's Graveyard for weeks on end, and he had played no direct part in any of the events on the islands. Pelsaert plainly felt he had retained a good deal of influence over his murderous brother Gÿsbert, but Olivier remained steadfast under questioning and confessed to nothing more than sleeping with Zussie Fredericx, one of the married women kept 'for common service.' It did him little good; his punishment – 'that he shall be dropped three times from the mast, and be flogged with 100 strokes' – was identical to that handed out to men guilty of far more.

The last man to be sentenced on the *Sardam* was a French soldier, Jean Renou of Miombry, who had never been part of Jeronimus's gang. He had, in fact, been one of the Defenders and had served loyally throughout the siege of Hayes's island. The Frenchman's crime was a peculiar one; he was charged not with murder or mutiny but with slander – which was, thanks to the huge importance that the Dutch attached to their personal honour, an almost equally serious offence at this time. The particulars of the case, as set out by Pelsaert, were that Renou had defamed Zussie Fredericx by recounting to a whole tent full of people how she had willingly given herself to three men, including Renou himself and Wiebbe Hayes, during a short visit to Hayes's Island. This allegation, the *commandeur* agreed, was 'a matter of very evil consequence,' not least because Renou had announced that Zussie 'did him evil' as a result, no doubt by infecting him with a venereal disease. The Frenchman, Pelsaert said, deserved stern punishment for besmirching a married lady's name.

It may appear surprising that the *commandeur* was much concerned with the honour of one woman at such a time – and a sailor's wife at that. Probably Pelsaert's real motive was quite a different one: to protect the reputation of the new hero, Wiebbe Hayes. In doing so, he sentenced the loose-tongued Renou to be dropped three times from the mast and flogged – the same punishment that Liebent and Frederick had just received for their part in the murder of two people. The only difference between them was that Renou was allowed to keep his wages.

A good deal had changed in Batavia since Pelsaert had last seen the town. It was now the monsoon season, and the climate, never pleasant for a European, was at its most unbearable. Batavia was still hot, but with the onset of the rains it had been drenched as well. On average, almost six feet of rain fell within the walls during the summer months, and in the intervals between the storms the weather became unpleasantly humid and seemed to breed fever.

At least the military situation had improved while the *commandeur* had been in the Abrolhos. Coen's foreboding that he faced a second siege had come true toward the end of August, when the Susuhunan of Mataram returned to invest Castle Batavia with a substantial army. But only six weeks later, on 2 October – the same day that Jeronimus and his followers had been hung on Seals' Island – Agung had given up the siege 'with dishonour,' as the VOC's Batavia Day Book put it, 'and in an ignominious manner.' Hampered by lack of food, the Javanese troops had abandoned their positions overnight and streamed back into the forests before the Dutch became aware that the enemy was fleeing. The successful conclusion of the siege marked the end of Jan Company's war with Mataram, which had put a considerable dent into the Indies trade and devastated the town and its surroundings. Both soon recovered; indeed the environs of Batavia reverted to jungle so swiftly that before long the governor-general was offering money for every rhinoceros killed in the immediate vicinity. By 1700 this bounty was being paid out about 30 times a month.

The other great change had taken place within the walls of Castle Batavia itself. Coen had not lived to see the triumph of his armies. The governor-general had collapsed and died, aged 42, on 21 September – the day before Jacques Specx and the remainder of the VOC's autumn fleet (of which Pelsaert's squadron had once formed a part) came to anchor in the roadstead outside the town. The cause of death was apparently heart failure. Coen had been ill before, with dysentery, but his death was sudden and so unexpected that it gave rise to some startling rumours. The most popular attributed his seizure to the arrival of Specx, whose daughter, Sara, Coen had only recently had flogged before the town hall. It was said that Coen had been promenading on the balcony of his quarters on the afternoon before his death when he saw the autumn fleet appear on the horizon. 'There is Sir Specx, my successor,' he is supposed to have prophesied, before dropping dead from the fear of what Specx would do to him when he discovered what had happened to his daughter.

Whether he truly died this way or not, Jan Coen's last prediction did come true. Jacques Specx was appointed governor-general of the Indies three days after his predecessor's death. It thus fell to him, and to the *fiscaal*, Antonij van den Heuvel, to consider the case of the surviving *Batavia* mutineers, who were landed from the *Sardam* late in the first week of December and – it seems safe to assume – taken at once to the appalling dungeons beneath the citadel, where Ariaen Jacobsz was still confined pending further investigation of his own role in the mutiny.

There were 14 of them in all: the eight men whom Pelsaert had just dealt with, another five, including Salomon Deschamps and Lucas Gellisz, whose cases had been considered in the Abrolhos, and finally the lonely figure of Stone-Cutter Pietersz – once lieutenant general of Jeronimus's band but now a mere lance corporal once again – who had still not been heard at all. At least some of those who had come before the *Sardam*'s council had already been punished by the time the *jacht* reached Batavia (there is some doubt whether Pelsaert had dealt with Daniel Cornelissen and the others sentenced at the end of November), but even those men could not be certain they would be released. The governor-general of the Indies enjoyed absolute power within his dominions, and he could do with them as he liked.

The men were left to rot in prison while Specx and his councillors considered how to handle the *Batavia* affair, and their cases were not finally decided until the end of January. Pelsaert's leniency seems to have struck Specx as quite excessive, and as the mutineers had feared, the governor-general had no compunction in setting the *commandeur*'s verdicts to one side. On 31 January 1630, the survivors of Cornelisz's gang were brought up from the cells and told they faced much sterner punishments for the crimes they had committed on Batavia's Graveyard.

Five more mutineers were hanged. The worst of them, Daniel Cornelissen, had his right hand amputated before the sentence was carried out. Hans Jacob Heijlweck joined him on the gallows, and so did Lucas Gellisz. Salomon Deschamps, the pathetic clerk who had been forced to strangle Mayken Cardoes's half-dead baby, died alongside them; the *commandeur* had protected him in the Abrolhos, but even Deschamps's long acquaintance with Pelsaert was not enough to save him from the vengeance of the Council of the Indies.

The identity of the fifth man to hang has never been certain. When the time came to pass sentence on the minor mutineers, Specx and his Council seem to have found themselves torn between the urge to punish all of Jeronimus's men and the feeling that the youngest and most impressionable of them might deserve some mercy. Confronted with Rogier Decker, who was 17, and Abraham Gerritsz, the 15-year-old runaway whom Pelsaert had picked up in Sierra Leone, they ruled that only one should die. The manner in which the matter was decided was a torment in itself. The boys were to

'draw lots which of the two shall be punished with the Cord, and he who shall draw himself free from Death shall be severely flogged, with a Halter around his neck.'

Andries Liebent, Hans Frederick, and Olivier van Welderen also received new sentences. The three 'delinquents' (Pelsaert's word) were tied to a pole and flogged severely, after which they were put in chains and sent away from Batavia to endure three years of exile;

Frederick – who had helped to kill three men – was made to wear a heavy wooden halter around his neck as well. In the circumstances none is likely to have survived their exile long enough to return a free man. The young sailor Cornelis Janssen was flogged and branded as a looter and a mutineer. Claes Harmansz, who was just 15, was flogged as well. Isbrant Isbrantsz, who was an officer and the one mutineer to consistently protest that he had acted under duress, was the only man treated with real leniency. His sentence was to stand, 'with a halter round his neck,' to watch the execution of justice.

The worst punishment of all was reserved for Stone-Cutter Pietersz. Like Jeronimus himself, the lance corporal had played little active part in the killing on Batavia's Graveyard, though he had taken part in the massacre of the survivors on Seals' Island and helped to organise the murder of the *predikant*'s family. He had, however, played an active part in plotting the mutiny on the *Batavia,* and as one of Cornelisz's councillors he had helped to determine who should live and who should die. Because Hayes and Pelsaert had, between them, denied the authorities in Java the chance to punish David Zevanck and Coenraat van Huyssen, much less Jeronimus himself, Pietersz was now made to pay for all their sins, for though he played a lesser role in the mutiny than any of those men, his guilt could hardly be denied. On the last day of January 1630, 'Lieutenant-General' Pietersz was taken out to be 'broken from under upwards, and the body put upon a Wheel.'

Breaking on the wheel, as it was generally known, was the most painful and barbaric method of execution practised in the Dutch Republic and was, in effect, a form of crucifixion. In Pietersz's case the condemned man, stripped to a pair of linen drawers, would have been led out to a scaffold on which had been assembled a huge cart wheel – still fitted with an axle – a bench, some ropes, and a thick iron bar. He would have been lashed, spread-eagled, to the bench and positioned so that the executioner had easy access to his limbs. Taking up the heavy bar, and with great concentration, this man would have proceeded to smash the bones in the prisoner's arms and legs, starting with the fingers and the toes and working slowly inward. The aim was to completely pulverize each limb, so that when Pietersz was lifted from the bench onto the wheel, his upper arms were broken in so many places that they could be twisted and bent to follow the circumference of the wheel, while his legs were wrenched backward from the thighs, forced right around the outer rim, and tied off with the heels touching the back of the head. The latter operation was difficult to complete without allowing the broken femurs to protrude, but a skilled executioner took pride not only in ensuring that his victim remained fully conscious throughout the operation, but also in crushing his bones so thoroughly that the skin remained intact. As a further refinement, it was common for the condemned man's ribs to be stoved in with several further blows, so that every breath became an agony.

Once the grisly operation had been concluded, Pietersz's wheel would have been hoisted upright and the axle thrust deep into the ground close by the scaffold so that the Stone-Cutter's final moments could be witnessed by the assembled crowd. Death – generally as the result of internal bleeding – might take hours; in a place such as Batavia, the dying man's pain and distress would have been exacerbated by the cloying heat and the swarms of flies and mosquitoes that would have filled his eyes and mouth. The strongest men sometimes survived into a second day, and Pietersz, a brawny army veteran, may not have lapsed into unconsciousness until the early hours of February 1630.

The lance corporal thus lived to be the last of Jeronimus's close confederates from the island, and, when he died, the mutiny on Batavia's Graveyard in some respects died with him. It had cost the lives of two in every three of the people who had sailed from Texel 15 months earlier – at least 216 men, women, and children from a total complement of 332, which was a slightly higher proportion of deaths than that suffered by the passengers and crew of the *Titanic* almost three centuries later. Even today, the massacres on Houtman's Abrolhos remain the bloodiest page in the history of white Australia.

It only remains to trace the fate of the survivors.

1629 proved to be a disappointing year for the Gentlemen XVII. In addition to the loss of the brand-new *Batavia,* with most of her cargo and two chests of silver valued at 44,788 guilders, another ship from Pelsaert's flotilla, the *'s Gravenhage,* had been disabled by bad weather in the Channel and required costly and extensive repairs. A third *retourschip,* the *Wapen van Enkhuizen,** had

* *Weapon of Enkhuizen.*

blown up off the coast of Sierra Leone on 12 October when fire reached her powder magazine. The survivors – there were only 57 of them, many terribly wounded – were picked up by the *Leyden,* which herself lost her skipper and her upper-merchant in an attempt to fight the fire, plus another 170 men – more than half her crew – from disease on the outward voyage. The survivors were eventually forced to put in to the port of Sillebor, in Sumatra, for a month to nurse the sick, which greatly irritated the Gentlemen and cost the *Leyden*'s remaining officers all chance of earning bonuses for the speed of their voyage out.

Even so, none of these disasters put more than a dent in Jan Company's profits for the year, and thanks to Hayes and Pelsaert and the *Sardam*'s men, even the loss of the *Batavia* could be viewed with some equanimity by Antonio van Diemen. 'The 5th of this month returns here to anchor from the Southland the yacht *Sardam,*' Van Diemen wrote in December,

> 'bringing with them 74 souls from the wrecked ship *Batavia* together with 10 chests of Cash, amongst them the chest No.33 with nine sacks of ducats. Item, the Cash with Jewels to the value of 58,000 guilders and some wrought silverwork, three barrels of Cochineal* and other baggage … Thanks be to the Almighty for this, we would not have expected it to come out so well.'

An attached list of the goods retrieved mentions 32 items, from money chests and cannon to a 'pack of old linen.' Toward the bottom of the page, one of the minor pieces listed is 'a small cask filled with vinegar,' of the sort that had cost the lives of the five men in the *Sardam*'s boat. Its value was so insignificant that Van Diemen did not bother to assess it.

Not many of those who outlived Jacob Pietersz and his fellow mutineers fared well.

One of the few who did was Johannes van der Beeck. Torrentius, in whose name Jeronimus had been accused of murdering some 115 men, women, and children, served only 2 years of his 20-year sentence for heresy. He was housed in relatively

---

*A valuable scarlet dye, made from the crushed bodies of insects.

comfortable surroundings, granted a good ration of wine, and was permitted to receive and entertain visitors in his cell. His wife, Cornelia – from whom he had been separated for 14 years – was among those who called on him. She received permission to stay with him for up to two weeks at a time.

Torrentius still had some powerful friends, both in the Netherlands and overseas. They included the *stadholder,* or governor, of the Dutch Republic, Prince Frederik Hendrik of Orange himself, who tried unsuccessfully to get the painter released soon after he was sentenced. Another of Van der Beeck's admirers was King Charles I of England, who seems to have been untroubled by his heresies. In 1630 the King wrote to Holland to inquire if Torrentius could be sent to England. Frederik Hendrik agreed to pardon him, very much against the wishes of the burgomasters of Haarlem, and Charles, in turn, promised that the painter 'will not be allowed to exercise his godless tongue, but only his art.' The English ambassador, Sir Dudley Carleton, sent to bring Van der Beeck to the English court, formed a relatively favourable impression of the painter, portraying him as 'neither so Angelical as his friends proclaim him, nor yet so Diabolical as his adversaries does publish him.' Torrentius's pardon was signed on 11 July 1630, four days after the first ships of the Indies fleet reached Rotterdam with news of the *Batavia* disaster, and thus before his supposed role in inspiring Cornelisz's mutiny became generally known. Whether his release would have been agreed had the ships arrived a few weeks earlier is an interesting question.

Van der Beeck was at the English court from 1630 until 1641 or 1642. He seems to have given – in the words of Horace Walpole – 'more scandal than satisfaction.' He painted relatively little. Eventually, his royal pension cut off by the Civil War, he crept back into Holland incognito. He had run out of money, but his elderly mother helped to support him. The painter died in February 1644, either forgiven or forgotten by the Calvinist authorities, for the great heretic of Haarlem was buried within the walls of Amsterdam's New Church, in consecrated ground.

Most of Torrentius's paintings were confiscated and burned by the public hangman during and after his trial, and the few that he produced in England were soon lost. For many years it was thought that none of his works had survived, but just before the outbreak of the First World War a single masterpiece was rediscovered. It is a still life, showing a flagon and a jug flanking a wineglass and a bridle, which had once been owned by Charles I. The painting had disappeared after the royal collection was auctioned off in 1649, and somehow found its way back to the Netherlands. It was in the Dutch Republic around 1850, its provenance long since forgotten, and eventually came into the possession of a grocer named J. F. Sachse, of Enschede. It miraculously survived a great fire that razed the city in 1862 and was finally recovered and identified in 1913 – by which time Sachse's children were using it as the cover for a barrel of currants. After that it was restored. The painting now hangs in the Rijksmuseum in Amsterdam.

❈

Jacques Specx lived on to die, in 1652, as replete with wealth and honour as a lifetime in the spice trade could make a man. He returned to the Republic late in 1632, having been a quarter of a century in the East; since leaving home in 1607, aged 18, he had spent no more than 12 months in the Netherlands and devoted most of his energies to opening up the Dutch trade with Japan. On his way home he seized the uninhabited island of St. Helena in the Company's name, and for a few years the isle became a popular refuelling station for Dutch spice ships on their homeward voyage. Eventually, however, pirates and privateers learned that it was a rich hunting ground, and by the 1660s a sharp increase in the loss of ships had forced the VOC to abandon their new possession.

Home at last, Specx became a director of the Company – one of the Gentlemen XVII – in 1642 and held the post for the last nine years of his life. He died at the ripe age of 63; his voyages had made him rich, and he bequeathed his children a considerable inheritance, including several portraits of himself made by artists of the stature of Rembrandt van Rijn.

Specx's half-Japanese daughter, Sara, whom Coen had flogged for her supposed immorality, fared less well. After her father's return to Batavia she was nursed back to health, but because she was Eurasian he was nevertheless compelled to leave her behind in Java upon returning to the Netherlands. (Dutch law at this time forbade Eurasians to enter the Republic. The intent was to encourage men who had fathered families in the East to remain there, thus easing the VOC's perpetual shortages of manpower.) The girl, who was 15 when this happened, remained in the East and seems to have been well cared for in her father's absence. A few years later she made a good marriage to a *predikant* named Georgius Candidius. The groom was 20 years her senior, and the union endured for less than 12 months before Sara Specx died at the Dutch factory in Formosa, of unknown causes, around the end of 1636. She was only 19 years old.

❁

Perhaps half a dozen active mutineers slipped through Pelsaert's net before they could face charges for their crimes. Four of them – Dirck Gerritsz, Jan Jansz Purmer, Harman Nannings, and the bos'n's mate – were sailors who seem to have been among the crew of the longboat. Three of them had taken part in the assault on Lucretia Jans, which had cost Jan Evertsz his life, but their names only emerged when the other members of their party were interrogated in the Abrolhos. By the time the *commandeur* returned to Java, the men had dispersed, and there is no record that any of them were ever brought to trial.

Luckier still was Jan Willemsz Selyns, the *Batavia*'s upper-cooper, who seems to have led something of a charmed life. He had taken part in the awful massacre of women and children on Seals' Island on 18 July, when almost 20 people died, and was thus at least an accessory to murder. Then, on 5 August, he had come under suspicion as a potential defector to Wiebbe Hayes and only survived Jeronimus's attempt to kill him when Wouter Loos personally intervened on his behalf. Later, he had been a member of the boat's crew that set off to capture the *Sardam* and murder half her crew, and he had thus been held on board the *jacht* for further questioning. Many of those with whom he shared a cell – Jacop Pietersz and Daniel Cornelissen among them – were executed for their crimes, and all the other members of the group had at least been flogged and keelhauled, but so far as can be ascertained Selyns entirely escaped punishment. Perhaps he simply died of natural causes en route to Java, but Pelsaert's journals make no mention of this, and it seems more likely that he somehow convinced the *commandeur* of his innocence.

The fate of a sixth man, Ryckert Woutersz, is still a greater mystery. The disgruntled gunner, whose loose tongue had revealed Jeronimus's plans soon after the wreck, had certainly schemed to seize the ship and taken part in the attack on Creesje, but his name does not appear on the lists of suspects compiled by Pelsaert and he was never accused of any crime. At some point the gunner simply disappears, and it seems likely that it was Cornelisz who dealt with him, arranging for his throat to be slit one night in the Abrolhos as payment for his treachery. There is no proof of this, however, so perhaps Woutersz did somehow contrive to stay alive and found his way to Batavia with the other survivors of the under-merchant's brief and bloody reign.

Francisco Pelsaert reverted briefly to his womanising ways. Almost as soon as he had disembarked in Java – and certainly long before he finished his report to the Councillors of the Indies – the upper-merchant contrived to form a close liaison with a married woman named Pieterge, who was the wife of a certain Willem Jansz. Pieterge's husband was away from Batavia, and the woman took full advantage until, in December 1629, she and two female friends were caught by the local *predikant* carousing in the 'young, rash' company of *de gentlemen* Croock, Sambrix, and Pelsaert. Pieterge and Pelsaert received stern warnings from the cleric, and the whole affair was reported to Batavia's Church Council. The preacher's notes leave little doubt that the relationship was a sexual one, which would probably have continued for some time had it not come to the attention of the Church.

The warnings had the required effect, however, and the affair seems to have been over by the end of January 1630, when Pelsaert was summoned before the Council of the Indies to present his credentials. This interview must have caused him some concern. The Council might have been expected to deal harshly with a man who had not only failed to keep good order on his ship, but also abandoned several hundred people to Jeronimus's mercies while he himself sailed to Java to fetch help. However, the prompt recovery of almost all of the *Batavia*'s trade goods and the capture of the under-merchant and his men stood to Pelsaert's credit, and in the end the *commandeur* was neither greatly criticised nor heaped with praise. Instead he was dispatched to Sumatra as second-in-command of a military expedition to Jambi, a pepper port placed under siege by the Portuguese. He spent the months of May and June 1630 helping to lift the blockade.

The Jambi adventure kept the *commandeur* occupied while he

waited for the September monsoon winds that would finally take him back to Surat. The silver 'toys' designed to please the Great Mogul and the cameo he had shipped to the East on behalf of Gaspar Boudaen were all destined for the court at Lahore, and Pelsaert must have been keenly aware that only the successful completion of this part of his mission was likely to restore him to full favour with the Gentlemen XVII. In the meantime, all he could do was put his own version of events in the Abrolhos in writing for his employers, the directors of the chamber of Amsterdam.

The *Batavia* journals, which contained a lengthy account of the events of the mutiny, reached Amsterdam in July 1630. The Gentlemen XVII read them and were unimpressed by the *commandeur*'s actions and behaviour. By then, however, it was far too late for them to make their displeasure known. Pelsaert was already dying, most probably exhausted by the same illness that had all but killed him on board the *Batavia* during the journey from the Cape.

That fever, it appears, had never quite abated, and the *commandeur* had spent much of his time on board the *Sardam* in his bunk, 'wholly ill and reduced to great wretchedness.' He must then have enjoyed a brief remission, during which he took part in the Jambi expedition, but by the middle of June his health had collapsed again, and he was struck down by a long and terminal illness that ended, the records of the Company attest, with his death some time before mid-September. He was then about 35 years old and had spent almost half his life in the service of the VOC.

Francisco Pelsaert thus survived his nemesis, Cornelisz, by no more than 11 months, and his career, which in the summer of 1628 had seemed to hold great promise, never recovered from the wrecking of his ship. In some respects, indeed, the *commandeur* was fortunate to have died at the moment that he did. The markets of India, which he had professed to understand better than any other Westerner, had changed fundamentally with the death of the Emperor Jahangir in 1627; the Great Mogul's successor, Shah Jahan, did not share his taste for Western fripperies. The VOC came to the unwelcome realisation that there was no longer any market for Pelsaert's gold and silver toys. They had cost, it will be recalled, around 60,000 guilders, and so far as the Councillors of the Indies were concerned, blame for the debacle rested squarely with the late *commandeur,* who had pressed ahead with his commissions even after news of Jahangir's death had reached him in the Netherlands.

There can be little doubt that this second failure, coming so soon after the loss of the *Batavia,* would have put an end to Pelsaert's career. As it was, the high officials of the Company in Java – to whom the thankless task of finding buyers for the trade goods fell – complained bitterly about the impossibility of getting a good price for them. The plate, which the *commandeur* had confidently predicted would yield a 50 percent profit, was eventually disposed of in India – after six months' fruitless haggling – for a 'vile price' in 1632, but no amount of effort could persuade the Moguls to show any interest in Gaspar Boudaen's Roman cameo, the fabulous jewel that Jeronimus had displayed to seduce the mutineers with dreams of unimagined luxury. It had accompanied Pelsaert's toys to India, but no buyer could be found, and by 1633 it was in Batavia again. After years of being peddled unsuccessfully in Asia, it was put up for auction in Amsterdam in 1765. In 1823 the jewel was purchased by King Willem I for 5,500 guilders. It can now be seen in the royal coin collection in Leiden.

While all this was going on, the remnants of Pelsaert's fragile reputation had finally been destroyed by the revelation that the *commandeur* had been deeply involved in illegal private trade. Soon after his death, a search of Pelsaert's baggage had turned up a variety of jewels and other goods valued at almost 13,500 guilders. These, the Company suspected, were to be sold for private profit, which was strictly forbidden, and Pelsaert no doubt expected to receive a commission for his part in the transactions. Upon investigation it emerged that a number of the items – including a second agate cameo, this one brand-new and engraved with a likeness of the Great Mogul – belonged to Gaspar Boudaen, who was eventually compelled to appear before the Gentlemen XVII of Amsterdam to beg, unsuccessfully, for their return. Others were the property of a second merchant, Johannes Dobbelworst. All these goods were confiscated by the VOC.

Pelsaert's early death thus cost his family most of the fortune he had laboured to amass. Barbara van Ganderheyden, the *commandeur*'s elderly mother and the chief beneficiary of his will, did eventually receive his outstanding salary, together with the sum of 771 guilders – the value of her son's personal possessions. The Company, however, banked the 10,500 guilders it earned from the sale of the confiscated jewels, and although Van Ganderheyden was eventually promised compensation amounting to 3,800 guilders, the VOC made it clear that this amount would only be paid in full and final settlement of all the claims the Pelsaert family might have against it.

Even then, the payment took forever to come through. Van Ganderheyden applied for her money in 1635, but it was evidently not forthcoming, for she repeated the request in 1638. Pelsaert's mother was dead by the end of the latter year, probably aged somewhere in her middle sixties. It seems probable that she never saw any of the money her son had worked so hard for.

❁

Wiebbe Hayes, whom Pelsaert had promoted to the rank of sergeant at a salary of 18 guilders a month, received further recognition and reward upon his arrival in Batavia.

He was commissioned as an officer in the Company's army and made a standard-bearer. It was an astonishing promotion for a man who had left Amsterdam as a common soldier, but certainly no less than he deserved. As a standard-bearer, Hayes's salary was increased again, to 40 guilders a month – roughly equivalent to that previously enjoyed by Jeronimus Cornelisz – and he was promised the chance of further promotion 'according to opportunity and merit.'

The Defenders were rewarded, too. All Hayes's common soldiers became cadets, with a salary of 10 guilders a month – a gesture that was not quite as generous as it sounds, since they already earned 8 or 9 guilders a month as privates. His sailors had their pay increased to the same figure. In addition, the Council of the Indies awarded all those who had 'shown themselves faithful and piously resisted evil' in the Abrolhos an additional gratuity of two months' wage, a bonus worth somewhere between 10 and 20 guilders a man. The two dozen sailors of the *Sardam,* who had helped Pelsaert to put down the mutiny, were given 100 pieces of eight (worth about 240 guilders in total) to share among themselves.

Hayes himself was not heard from again after landing in Batavia. There is no trace of him in the records of his home town, Winschoten, but the archives there are so incomplete it cannot be said with any certainty whether he lived to return there. Perhaps he moved elsewhere and married, or took up residence in a crowded town such as Amsterdam, which he could now certainly afford. It is equally possible, however, that Jeronimus's captor died somewhere in the Indies, perhaps in battle, but more likely manning an outpost on some distant island, of some unknown tropical disease.

❧

Toward the end of December 1629, Gijsbert Bastiaensz sat down to write a letter to his family at home. Remarkably, his narrative of the mutiny – rambling and almost incoherent in places, and hurriedly composed to catch the fleet returning to the Dutch Republic – survived to become the only independent account of events on Batavia's Graveyard. It shows the *predikant* still far from recovered from his tribulations in the archipelago ('we have just come out of such a sorrow that the mind is still a little confused,' he wrote) and seeking consolation in religion. 'Having yielded myself to the providence of the Lord, who tries his children for his benefit,' Bastiaensz concluded, '[I] through the Grace of God have gained some strength and power, for I could hardly stand on account of weakness.'

As it happened, the *predikant*'s trials were not yet over. His role in the Abrolhos incident had come to the attention of Jacques Specx and the Council of Justice at Batavia, who wanted to know not only whether he had done all he could to oppose Jeronimus and his godless henchmen, but exactly how a minister of the Reformed Church had come to swear an oath of allegiance to a heretic. All the papers relating to Bastiaensz's actions were turned over to the public prosecutor, who spent almost four months looking into the case, and it was not until the spring of 1630 that the *predikant* was cleared of any wrongdoing by the Batavian Church Council. Even then, the governor-general remained suspicious; between 18 and 22 April, he clashed on three separate occasions with the church authorities over their desire to proclaim Bastiaensz's innocence from the pulpit. Specx plainly thought the *predikant* had displayed fatal weakness in the Abrolhos. Had a better man been assigned to the *Batavia,* he told the leaders of the Church Council, 'things might not have gone the way they did.'

So Bastiaensz was called to account for his equivocal behaviour on Batavia's Graveyard and emerged with his reputation barely intact. The Church Council's support at least meant that he could now preach anywhere in the lands under its jurisdiction, and it only remained to find him a suitable church. There was some talk of

sending him to Surat, but it came to nothing, and it was only after a
long while in Batavia that Bastiaensz was dispatched to the remote
Banda Islands to minister to the troops guarding the world's
supply of nutmeg. The *predikant* remained in Java long enough to
complete two years' mourning for his dead wife and marry, in July
1631, Maria Cnijf, the widow of the Bailiff of Batavia. Shortly
thereafter he departed for the Bandas, where he survived for at
most 18 months before being struck down and killed by dysentery
in the spring of 1633.

Gijsbert Bastiaensz, who had experienced so much on
Houtman's Abrolhos, now lies buried in an unknown grave on
another long-forgotten island. News of his death was not forward-
ed to Batavia until the summer of 1634. Plainly it was not regarded
as an event of any great significance.

❊

Of the handful of people from Batavia's Graveyard who did live to
see the Dutch Republic once again, Judick Gijsbertsdr suffered
more than most.

The *predikant*'s one surviving child had sailed on the *Batavia* as
the eldest daughter of a family of nine. She arrived in Java a little
more than a year later with only her father for company, quite destitute, and having survived scurvy and shipwreck, the brutal
murder of her mother, two sisters, and four brothers, and two
months as the 'fianceé' of Coenraat van Huyssen. She was one
month shy of her 22nd birthday, and her troubles were far from
over.

Judick's immediate concern would have been her precarious
financial position. Her father's investigation by the Church
Council of Batavia kept him from working for several months
after their arrival, and since the family had lost almost all of their
possessions in the wreck, Bastiaensz and his daughter probably
found it hard to make ends meet. Judick would have found it expe-
dient to marry, and though her father's poverty and her own loss
of virginity might have rendered her an unattractive prospect in
the United Provinces, the marriage markets of the Far East
worked quite differently. White women were a rarity in Java, and
pretty, single European girls were rarer still. The merchants and
soldiers of the town coveted new arrivals 'like roasted pears,' and
the *predikant*'s daughter would have had no shortage of suitors.

Sadly, good fortune eluded her even then. Within a few weeks of her arrival Judick had met and married a certain Pieter van der Hoeven – whose profession is not recorded – and so, she must have hoped, secured her future; but he died within three months of their wedding day, adding widowhood to her recent tribulations. She completed a full year's mourning before marrying again, this time to Helmich Helmichius of Utrecht, whom she accompanied to the Spice Island of Ambon. Judick's new husband – a *predikant* of absolutely no distinction – was probably an acquaintance of her father's. This time the marriage lasted for a while, but in 1634 the bloody flux struck down Helmichius, as it had claimed Gijsbert Bastiaensz the year before, leaving the girl orphaned and twice-widowed.

Even the VOC was moved by this new misfortune, and on the orders of the Council of the Indies Judick received 600 guilders to compensate her for her widowhood and general suffering. This substantial payment – the equivalent of perhaps £30,000 today – enabled her to return to Dordrecht with her second husband's estate still intact. She was back in her hometown by October 1635, when, aged 27 and in robust health, she made a will naming two uncles and an aunt her 'universal heirs.' From this it would appear that neither Judick's relationship with Coenraat van Huyssen nor her two marriages had produced surviving issue. The will does, however, show that she was at last comfortably off. She left in excess of a thousand guilders to be distributed to her relatives, the poor committee of the Reformed Church of Dordrecht, and a religious institution in the town.

There is no record of Judick Gijsbertsdr's death in the archives of Dordrecht. She may well have married for a third time and moved away from her home town or been caught in the great epidemic of bubonic plague that swept through the city in 1636, throwing normal recordkeeping into temporary disarray. Without further clues it is impossible to say.

❉

Creesje Jans, who had travelled 15,000 miles to rejoin her husband, reached Batavia at last only to discover he was dead. Having survived so much, she now found herself alone in a ruined town where she had no business and few friends.

Her husband, Boudewijn van der Mijlen – it will be recalled –

had been sent in September 1627 to Arakan, a Burmese river port, to purchase slaves for the Dutch settlements in Java. He had orders to remain there indefinitely, and there is no record that he ever did return to Batavia; certainly he was dead by July 1629, when 'Lucretia Jans of Amsterdam' is mentioned as his next of kin in the records of the town. He had been in his late twenties, and Creesje had just turned 28 when she discovered she had been widowed.

The woman capable of arousing enormous passion in suitors as diverse as Jeronimus and Ariaen Jacobsz thus found herself without a man. Life in the seventeenth century was harsh, and it was rare to reach maturity without losing a father or a mother, a sibling, or a spouse. Creesje Jans had nevertheless endured far more than was usual even in that age, and it seems inconceivable that she would not have been profoundly marked by her experiences and loss. Still, she had unusual courage and strength of spirit, and she evidently remained a fine prospective wife, for in October 1630 she married a certain Jacob Cornelisz Cuick. The couple lived on in Batavia until about 1635 – probably the time it took for Cuick to see out his contract with the VOC – and then returned together to the Netherlands, where they were both still alive in 1641.

Creesje's motives for remaining in Batavia and remarrying can only now be guessed at. Unlike Judick Gijsbertsdr, she had money – her own and that of her first husband, whose arrears of pay, in a remote outpost such as Arakan, may well have totalled several hundred guilders. She was still beautiful, had assets, and could certainly have contracted a good marriage with a senior Company official. The man she had made her new husband was, however, a soldier, and a mere sergeant at that. He had fought during the Susuhunan's siege but lacked the social status and the prospects Van der Mijlen had enjoyed. Creesje's choice therefore requires some explanation.

The answer appears to lie in the church records of Cuick's home town, Leyden, where Creesje and her husband stood as godparents to no fewer than four children of Pieter Willemsz Cuick and his wife Willempje Dircx between September 1637 and December 1641. Reading between the lines, it seems likely that this Pieter Cuick was Jacob the soldier's brother, and at least possible that his wife, Willempje, was none other than Lucretia's stepsister – the same Weijntgen Dircx with whom she had lived in the Herenstraat in Amsterdam almost 20 years before.

Once allowance has been made for the extravagant variations in the spelling of proper names that were all too common at this time, therefore, it would appear that Creesje's second husband may have been her own stepbrother-in-law. This discovery may well explain Creesje's willingness to marry, as it were, beneath herself. Alone and friendless in an unknown town far from everything she knew, it would have been natural to seek out any familiar face. Jacob Cuick, whom Creesje may perhaps have known and liked in Holland, could well have seemed a better choice than a stranger who could not begin to understand her extraordinary tribulations.

Lucretia Jans and her new husband disappear from sight after 1641. They do not seem to have dwelled in Leyden, where no further trace of their existence can be found, and perhaps went to live in Amsterdam, where the surviving records are so enormous and so poorly organised that it is difficult to search for them. It can be said with some confidence that no Jacob Cornelisz Cuick was ever interred there, but one tantalising clue can still be found to his wife's fate: at the beginning of September 1681, a Lucreseija van Kuijck died in Amsterdam and was buried there on the sixth day of the month. If this Van Kuijck was really Creesje of the *Batavia,* she had survived into her late seventies and outlived her suitors and her persecutors alike – some small recompense, perhaps, for the suffering she had endured.

❁

While Creesje Jans tried to make a new life in the Indies, Ariaen Jacobsz remained rotting in the dungeons of Castle Batavia. The skipper had been confined there since the middle of July 1629, arrested on the strength of Pelsaert's accusations, and held – along with Zwaantie Hendricx – on suspicion of plotting mutiny.

From the beginning, Jacobsz resisted all attempts to make him talk. His physical stamina must have been immense; that he survived not only the sea voyage to Batavia in an open boat but a long spell in a squalid prison, doubtlessly interspersed with none-too-gentle questioning, was a remarkable achievement. Zwaantie, too, was interrogated about her actions on the ship, but little progress seems to have been made during the time that Pelsaert was absent in the Abrolhos.

Even the problem of exactly who had arranged for Evertsz and his men to attack Lucretia Jans was never resolved to the Company's entire satisfaction. 'The skipper,' Specx conceded in a note to the Gentlemen XVII,

'was very much suspected that [this] had happened with his knowledge, yea, even with his aid and at his instigation; about this he, and a certain other female who had been the servant of Lucretia, have been examined by the *fiscaal* and brought before the Council of Justice, but through the obscurity of the case no verdict has yet been given.'

From these comments, it appears that Ariaen had consistently proclaimed his innocence, and that Antonij van den Heuvel had failed to extract anything resembling a confession even after the *commandeur*'s return from Batavia's Graveyard with fresh evidence and accusations. 'We do not think that [Jacobsz] is wholly free,' the governor-general concluded cautiously,

'being certain that if he had publicly maintained authority and justice as well as he secretly undermined both, many of the committed insolences would not have happened aboard the ship, nor would the previous actions have remained unpunished.'

But without some sort of confession, the true extent of the skipper's involvement in the mutiny could never be known.

The problem confronting the Councillors of the Indies was thus a simple one. They certainly believed Jacobsz to be guilty, at least to some degree, of the charges ranged against him. But they also felt that Pelsaert shared the blame for what had happened on the *Batavia* and afterward, not least for his lax handling of the skipper. All that was certain, Van Diemen concluded, was that 'a completely Godless and evil life has been conducted on the mentioned ship, of which both the skipper and Pelsaert are greatly guilty, may the Almighty forgive their sin.' Because of this, the Councillors clearly thought that it would be unwise to take the *commandeur*'s allegations entirely at face value; and since the only other evidence against Jacobsz came from the mouths of now-dead mutineers, only a full confession could establish Ariaen's guilt. In the absence of any such admission, the existing stalemate could endure indefinitely.

The case against the skipper was thus reduced to a simple test of will, and to everyone's frustration, Ariaen remained in prison as late as June 1631, the charges still unproven despite the belated application of torture. 'Jacobsz,' Van Diemen noted in frustration, 'skipper of the wrecked ship *Batavia,* is still imprisoned, although [he] has several times requested a relaxation and a return to the fatherland; on the strong indictment of having had the intention to run off with the ship [he] has been condemned to more acute examination.' In the meantime, the Councillor suggested, the Gentlemen XVII might wish to examine the papers pertaining to the case and 'give an order in this matter.'

What happened to Ariaen when he was tortured again (for that is what Van Diemen's comments meant) remains a mystery. No further reference to the skipper has been found in the records of the VOC, and, frustratingly, all the transcripts of his interrogation – which might have shed a good deal of light on events on the *Batavia* – have vanished, too. It seems unlikely that Jacobsz was released, and if he had been executed one might expect to find some reference to the fact in the record. More probably he died of injury or illness in his cell. The skipper had already survived two years in the malarial dungeons under Castle Batavia – an achievement equal in its own way to his voyage in the longboat – but it would be almost two years more before a reply could be expected from the Gentlemen XVII, and that was more than even he was likely to endure.

Zwaantie Hendricx, Creesje's loose-moralled servant, likewise disappears from the records of Jan Company. The likelihood is that she, too, perished in the fortress, dying some time between December 1629, when she was definitely in custody, and June 1631, by which time Jacobsz was being held alone. Just possibly, however, she walked free for lack of evidence, to make her own way in the Indies.

If so, the girl would soon have found herself in an uncomfortable position. She had no employment; there was little demand for expensive European maids in a settlement supplied with abundant native labour; and her marriage prospects were far worse than those of Judick and Lucretia. With Ariaen locked up and likely to remain so, though, Zwaantie would have had little option but to wed; had she then remained in Batavia she, like every other emigrant, would have had a less than even chance of seeing the Netherlands again. Imprisoned, she could hardly have survived – but even free the odds are that she died in Java, a wife but not, perhaps, a much-changed woman.

❄

Half a world away from the squalid dungeons of Castle Batavia, off one of the cramped and crowded streets that twisted their way through Haarlem's poorer quarters, ran a narrow little alleyway called the Cornelissteeg. The houses there were small and poorly appointed, and the people who dwelled in them were mostly artisans – water carriers, carpenters, singers, and the like. It was to this wretched accommodation, far from the luxuries of the Grote Houtstraat, that Belijtgen Jacobsdr came to live after her husband sailed on the *Batavia*.

Jeronimus's wife had fallen a long way. Only a few months earlier she had been a respectable and – to all appearances – prosperous member of Haarlem's upper middle class. Now she had lost her home, her business, and her husband. VOC officers could have a portion of their wages paid to their next of kin, so Jacobsdr would not have starved; nevertheless, she would hardly have been human had she had not resented the abrupt change in her circumstances.

Matters were made worse by Heyltgen Jansdr. Belijtgen's former wet nurse continued to harass her long after Jeronimus was gone. As late as the summer of 1630 Heyltgen and her husband, Moyses Starlingh, came down to the Cornelissteeg one afternoon while Belijtgen was out and began to hurl torrents of abuse at her front door in front of her astonished neighbors. In the course of this tirade, Heyltgen was heard screaming her familiar insults; Jeronimus's wife, the nurse called out, was a pig and a whore riddled with syphilis, and if she dared to leave her home Heyltgen would 'cut her face and trample on it.' Receiving no response from the empty house, the wet nurse and her husband returned that same evening. Belijtgen was still not home, and Moyses tried to break down her door, loudly announcing he would wait for her inside. According to the neighbours, whose testimonies were recorded the next day, Starlingh was in a violent mood, and they feared that he would loot the property if he got in.

Heyltgen's tirade must imply that the old dispute over Cornelisz's son had still not been resolved, though it was now almost 18 months since Jeronimus had buried the boy. Whether or not Belijtgen Jacobsdr had taken legal action over her dead child cannot be said for certain, since Haarlem's judicial archives are very incomplete. The one trace of what may be the same dispute occurs in the city burgomasters' records, which often concern themselves with the resolution of petty quarrels between members of the lower classes. The relevant *memorial,* issued on 6 July 1629, concerns a wet nurse and a mother – neither, unfortunately, is named – who were told to make their peace in a dispute over a child. Both women were bound over, and the nurse was ordered to pay to the mother seven shillings' compensation. If the parties concerned were indeed Belijtgen and her tormentor, it must be assumed that the burgomasters' attempts at arbitration had no lasting effect – and observed that the compensation paid seems minimal in the extraordinary circumstances. But such, perhaps, was the price of an infant's life in the early seventeenth century.

What happened next remains unknown; the fracas in the Cornelissteeg is the last sign of Belijtgen's life in Haarlem. Three weeks later, on 7 July 1630, news of the *Batavia* tragedy reached the Dutch Republic on the ship *Wapen van Rotterdam,** and within days the details of the mutiny were circulating in pamphlets and printed laments. Cornelisz's bloody role in the affair thus became notorious, and one can imagine that his wife found it impossible to remain in Haarlem.

Did Belijtgen return to wherever she called home? There is no way to know for certain. The meagre remains of her unfortunate existence provide no resolution for her story; like her enigmatic husband, she lived and died in history's penumbra – a shadow figure whose origins and motives remain unknown, and whose real character and hopes, and loves and fears, can now only be guessed at.

❁

Upon the coral islets of the Abrolhos, all sign of the *Batavia* and her crew soon disappeared.

The wooden hulk of the *retourschip,* already battered almost beyond recognition by the sea, did not take long to vanish beneath the waves. Caught between the ceaseless pounding of the breakers and the reef, Pelsaert's flagship disintegrated plank by plank until her upperworks had been reduced to so much flotsam and the remaining contents of the hold were scattered all across the ocean bed. Within a year or two, the only indication she had ever been

* *Weapon of Rotterdam.*

there was the broken wreckage of her masts and spars, washed up on the rocky beaches of the archipelago.

The islands of the Abrolhos bore witness for a little longer to the Dutchmen who had lived and died there. In their frantic search for anything of value to the VOC, Pelsaert and his men had picked Batavia's Graveyard almost clean of debris. But on Wiebbe Hayes's Island, a few scraps of sailcloth fluttered on the scrub, and the remains of the Defenders' dwellings still testified to their stubborn refusal to surrender.

There were less tangible signs of human intrusion, too. Beneath the surface of the island, the freshwater lenses that had floated in the waterholes and saved the lives of Hayes's men had been drained off by thirsty Dutchmen, leaving the water in a number of ancient wells so brackish it was all but undrinkable. The animal population had been substantially reduced, and several colonies of tammars and sea lions – which had survived in unchanging balance for several thousand generations – had been hunted almost to extinction during the Defenders' three-month war with Cornelisz's band.

Then there were the seven bodies on Seals' Island. The dead mutineers had been left to dangle from the makeshift gallows that the *Sardam*'s carpenters had thrown up for them, and by the time the ropes – rotted by salt-laced gales of rain – finally sagged and snapped, the island birds would have all but picked the corpses clean. Before long the gallows would have toppled and fallen too, leaving little more than piles of bones and wood to bleach and crumble slowly on the strand.

Across the deep-water passage between the islands, on the deserted and infertile skeleton of Batavia's Graveyard itself, an altogether stranger change occurred. When the survivors of the wreck had landed, they had found the isle a barren place. Its sandy soil was too poor to support much life, and, scoured clean by the wind, it had long been all but devoid of vegetation. In the early 1630s, however, new patches of undergrowth sprang up among the coral outcrops, establishing themselves where the soil was deep and clear of birds' nests and debris. For a decade or more, the northern portion of the island bloomed.

The explanation for this unexpected fertility lay a foot or two beneath the surface, where the bodies of Jeronimus's victims rested in their shallow graves. As they decomposed, the remains of Hendrick Denys, Mayken Cardoes, the *predikant*'s family, and all the rest released their nutrients into the earth, providing freshly fertile ground for the spores of tea-tree scrub and dandelion, and the site of each burial pit was soon marked by a little wreath of stubborn greenery. Slowly, over many years, the plants consumed the cadavers, enveloping them in a dense black mass of probing roots. They fed off them until they were quite gone, and – in doing so – transformed death into life, and burial into rebirth.

On the Shores of the Great South-Land

'They shall be put ashore as scoundrels and death-deserving delinquents, in order to know once, for certain, what happens in this Land.'

FRANCISCO PELSAERT

Wouter Loos and Jan Pelgrom, the two mutineers whom Pelsaert had marooned on 16 November 1629, were never heard from again.

Their immediate prospects of survival were fair. Wittecarra Gully, at the southern end of Gantheaume Bay, is one of the few places on the Western Australian coast where water can always be found. In the southern winter a small stream flows down the gully into salt marshes along the shore, and though the water in the gully is brackish and unpalatable by the coast, and dries up altogether in the summer, a spring about two miles upstream would have provided a steady supply of fresh water – even during the dry season – for anyone prepared to venture inland. The more substantial Murchison River is only a few miles to the north, and though food is not abundant in the region, the availability of water attracted many Aborigines to the area. The local people belonged to the Nanda culture and were cultivators, growing yams and living in huts grouped into permanent villages. Had they wished to, they could have helped Loos and Pelgrom and kept them alive.

The exact fate of the two mutineers would have been decided by their first and most important decision: whether to stay where they were, or take their boat and attempt to sail north along the coast. It would have been pointless for them to make for the Indies; the Dutch colonies were too far away to be reached in so small a craft, and in any case they would have been executed the moment they stepped ashore. Their only real alternative was to head for a point on the coast, at about latitude 24 degrees south, where the *commandeur* had seen men on the shore on 14 June. That spot was almost 200 miles away to the north. Neither Loos nor Pelgrom could navigate or were in any way accomplished sailors, and their boat (which Pelsaert described as a *champan*) would appear to have been one of the jerry-built small craft constructed on Batavia's Graveyard from driftwood. An ocean voyage – had they attempted it – would almost certainly have killed them.

Had the mutineers remained where they were, however, they could not have avoided making contact with the local people for long. Pelsaert had foreseen this eventuality and had taken care to provide the men with beads and 'some Nurembergen' – the cheap wooden toys that the German town of Nuremberg was famous for even then – 'as well as knives, bells and small mirrors' made of iron and copper, which the Dutch knew, from their experience with the Bushmen of the Cape, were highly prized by 'savages.' Loos and Pelgrom were advised not to be too ready with their limited supplies of gifts – 'give to the Blacks only a few until they have grown familiar with them' – but to treat the local people with trust and consideration. 'If they will then take you into their Villages,' the *commandeur*'s instructions went on,

> 'to their chief men, have courage to go with them willingly. Man's luck is found in strange places; if God guards you, you will not suffer any damage from them, but on the contrary, because they have never seen any white men, they will offer all friendship.'

Whether or not the two mutineers took Pelsaert's advice is a matter for conjecture. Loos, who had shown in the Abrolhos that he possessed both courage and the skill of leadership, was perhaps intelligent and mature enough to have stood some chance among the Nanda. The hotheaded Pelgrom, on the other hand, was younger and considerably less stable and may well have proved a liability. The two men had been marooned without weapons of any sort and would have been easy prey for the Aborigines, whom they would have needed in order to find food. Without the goodwill of the local people they would surely have died shortly after they were put ashore, either violently or of slow starvation.

The portents for friendly cooperation between Dutchmen and Aborigines were not good. A *jacht* named *Duyfken,* which was the first Dutch ship to land men in Australia – and probably the first

Western vessel to sight the continent, so far as can be ascertained – had explored the east coast of the Gulf of Carpentaria in the summer of 1606 and lost half her crew to an attack by natives. Her successors, the *Arnhem* and the *Pera* of 1623, provoked open hostility among the people of the Cape York peninsula by repeatedly attempting to seize some of the local hunters and carry them off on board the ships. The *Arnhem* lost 10 men to a surprise attack during this reconnaissance, including her skipper and an assistant who was 'torn to pieces' by the Aborigines.

The northern coast was so removed, both geographically and culturally, from the western seaboard that it is extremely unlikely that the Nanda had any direct knowledge of these earlier encounters, but the early history of mistrust and hostility between Dutch sailors and native Australians was such that Loos and Pelgrom were unlikely to receive a warm reception. The European tendency, which the two mutineers would almost certainly have shared, was to view the Aborigines as violent, primitive, and treacherous; the Australian view (at least in the northeast of the country, where early traditions survived long enough to be recorded) was that the whites were *munpitch* – mischief spirits associated with the bodily remains of the recently deceased. It would be hard to imagine a less promising basis for mutual trust.

Nevertheless, Pelsaert had given Loos and Pelgrom some hope of eventual salvation by clearly stating in their instructions that they should 'look out keenly' between the months of April and July, 'the time that the ships make the South-Land there' in the hope of rescue, and later Dutch ships were occasionally instructed to watch out for signs of the mutineers and to take them on board if the men themselves desired it. In 1636 a certain Gerrit Thomasz Pool was given command of two *jachten,* the *Cleen Amsterdam* and the *Wesel,* and a commission to explore the whole known coast of Australia; his sailing instructions reminded him that 'Francisco Pelsaert having AD 1629 put ashore two Dutch delinquents, who had in due form of justice been sentenced to forfeit their lives, you will grant passage to the said persons, if they should be alive to show themselves.' Pool was killed in New Guinea, however, long before he could reach the Western Australian coast, and although Abel Tasman – sent to circumnavigate the continent* in 1644 – was also furnished with specific

*He gave his name to Tasmania.

instructions regarding the wreck of the *Batavia,* the two mutineers, and the VOC's missing chests of money, he too turned back before reaching the Abrolhos.

Tasman's orders made it clear that the Company's main interest in the *Batavia* mutineers was the hope that they would have acquired valuable information about the interior resources of the red continent; the old tales of Beach and its limitless reserves of gold had not yet been relegated to the realms of legend. It is interesting to speculate on what the great navigator might actually have found had he ever reached the spot where the two men had been put ashore. Pelgrom and Loos would have been no more than 33 and 39 years old in 1644 – assuming they had survived at all – and in 1697 the Dutch explorer Willem de Vlamingh found a well-made clay hut, with sloping roofs, by Wittecarra spring. It had been built in quite a different style to those usually found in the area, and it has since been suggested (on no sure evidence) that it must have been built by Dutchmen. If that is the case, it was almost certainly constructed by the two *Batavia* mutineers, and a landing party seeking water might conceivably have encountered Cornelisz's men.

🌸

In the event, no real attempt was ever made – by Jan Company or anyone else – to discover what had become of the two mutineers, but Loos and Pelgrom did not remain alone in Australia for long. During its 200-year history, the VOC lost 1 in 50 of its ships outward bound, and nearly 1 in 20 on the return voyage, a total of 246 vessels. At least 3 of these ships, and possibly many as 8 or 10, were wrecked along the western coast. A minimum of 75 more Dutchmen, and perhaps as many as 200, are known to have been cast up on the South-Land as a result.

The first of these disasters occurred in 1656, when the *Vergulde Draeck,** a *retourschip* from Amsterdam, ran aground on a reef three miles off the coast and about 50 miles north of the present-day city of Perth. Sixty-eight members of the crew reached land, and three men from a rescue ship were subsequently abandoned in the same area when they ventured into the bush in search of them and became lost. At least a few of these men probably survived for

---

Gilt Dragon.

some time, for a variety of apparently Dutch artifacts – from ship's planking to an incense urn with a Chinese dragon entwined around its stem – have turned up inland from the wreck site since the ship ran aground.

The *Vergulde Draeck* was followed by the *Zuytdorp,** which vanished in 1712 with all 200 of her crew. Her fate only became clear in the 1920s, when a wreck site was discovered between Kalbarri and Shark Bay, a little to the north of the Abrolhos. The ship had been forced against the same unbroken line of cliffs that had defeated Pelsaert's attempts to find a landing spot almost 80 years earlier; she was swept onto the rocks stern first, heeled over, and quickly broke into three sections. With her bottom torn out, heavy guns and cargo wrenched loose and rolling about inside the hull, and her masts either snapped or felled, the majority of the crew were most likely crushed to death before she finally came to rest, or drowned in the heavy surf trying to get ashore. Nevertheless, about 30 men appear to have survived to make their way onto the cliffs, some of them crawling along the stumps of masts or tangles of rigging to reach land, and a few may have found their way to Wale Well, an Aboriginal encampment about 30 miles north of the wreck site with a permanent population of 200. In 1990 a team exploring the vicinity of the well with metal detectors recovered an old Dutch tobacco box lid, made of brass and engraved with a drawing of the town of Leyden, which could have belonged to a survivor from this ship.

The third and last *retourschip* known to have been lost in Australian waters was the *Zeewijk,* which went aground in the far south of Houtman's Abrolhos in June 1727. About two-thirds of the crew of 158 survived to set up camp in the islands while a dozen men, led by the upper-steersman, attempted to sail to Batavia in the *Zeewijk*'s longboat. The longboat never arrived, and though the remainder of the crew eventually built themselves a sloop from the wreckage of their ship and successfully sailed to Java, the mystery of what had become of the longboat's men still remains. It is just possible that they too were blown onto the South-Land.

By 1728, then, sailors from at least three *retourschepen* had been cast up on the Australian coast. These men found themselves stranded in an utterly alien environment, distant from everything they knew and held dear, and with absolutely no prospect of ever

*South Village. This ship was named after a place in Zeeland.

seeing Batavia, let alone the Netherlands, again. Few of them would have had any understanding of exactly where they were; the sheer extent of the unknown land, its harshness, its people, and its unique wildlife were all quite unknown in this period, and few of the survivors would have had any good idea of just how far away they were from safety, or of the enormous physical barriers separating them from their destination. The majority of them probably died close to the spot where they had come ashore, running out of food or water, or murdered by the local people while awaiting a rescue ship that never came. Some no doubt came to grief trying to make their way north – in the 1790s, escaping prisoners from the English penal colonies near Sydney believed that it was possible to walk from New South Wales to China in only a few weeks, and rank-and-file Dutch seamen of the seventeenth and eighteenth centuries would seldom have been any better informed than that. But perhaps the most intriguing possibility of all is that a few of the survivors swallowed up in the heart of the great red continent found acceptance with the Aborigines, married into their tribes, and lived out long, undreamed-of lives somewhere inland – 15,000 miles from the windmills and canals of Holland.

Hints that at least some of the men cast ashore did survive in the Australian interior have surfaced from time to time during the last 200 years. In the early days of the Swan River colony – the first permanent British settlement in Western Australia, established in 1829 – reports were received of tribes of light-skinned Aborigines living along the coast. These stories resemble those of the 'white Indians' often said to have been encountered in the American interior, which are generally written off as travellers' tales. Still, in a handful of cases the evidence is at least intriguing. The explorer A. C. Gregory reported meeting, in 1848, a tribe in the Murchison River area 'whose characteristics differed considerably from the average Australian. Their colour was neither black nor copper, but that peculiar yellow which prevails with a mixture of European blood.' Gregory was disappointed to discover no evidence that they possessed technology unknown to other Aborigines. Thirteen years later the *Perth Gazette* reported encounters with 'fair complexioned' natives with 'long light coloured hair flowing down their shoulders.' Men of this sort could be met with along the Gascoyne, Murchison, and Ashburton Rivers, according to a station hand named Edward Cornally; and other nineteenth-century writers also suggested that fair hair was commonplace among the Nanda peoples. Daisy Bates, a controversial Australian writer who actually lived for four decades among various Aboriginal tribes in Western and Southern Australia in the late nineteenth and early twentieth centuries, made similar observations of the people of the Gascoyne and Murchison valleys. 'There is no mistaking the heavy Dutch face, curly fair hair and heavy stocky build,' she believed. Other supposedly European characteristics, such as blue eyes, great height, and a propensity to baldness, have also been attributed to the people of the same tribes.

It is difficult to know what weight to give such purely anecdotal tales, and if Bates and the other early observers were correct, the men they saw were more probably descendants of men from the *Vergulde Draeck* or *Zuytdorp* than the offspring of Loos and Pelgrom. Nevertheless, the accumulated evidence does suggest at least the possibility that these ill-matched mutineers lived on in the South-Land's interior. The two men were thus, at least in a symbolic sense, every bit as much the founders of modern Australia as were Captain Cook and the British convicts who settled there from 1787. And, if they did survive long enough to befriend the west coast Aborigines, they may have taken local wives and outlived Pelsaert and Hayes, fathering sons whose children's children still live, unknowing, in Australia today.

❁

For many years, the location of both the *Batavia*'s wreck site and the islands where Cornelisz had established his short-lived kingdom remained almost as mysterious as the fate of the Dutch sailors washed up on the South-Land. This was hardly surprising. The Abrolhos were scarcely ever visited; the wreck itself had already all but vanished beneath the waves by the time Pelsaert left the islands; and even in the seventeenth century there would have been relatively little sign that the murderous events described in the *commandeur*'s journals had ever taken place.

The *Batavia*'s story itself was too bloody and dramatic to be forgotten quickly; it was kept alive, in the Dutch Republic at least, by books and pamphlets in the seventeenth century, and in travel narratives and histories of the Indies in the eighteenth. Ariaen Jacobsz's feat in navigating the ship's longboat all the way to Java was remembered, too – though ironically the little boat's progress from the Abrolhos to the Sunda Strait was marked as the 'Route de

Pelsart' on the world maps drawn by Guillaume de l'Isle between 1740 and 1775. Nevertheless, by the early nineteenth century recollections of the events of 1629 had faded. Jeronimus Cornelisz was little more than a half-forgotten nightmare, and the *Batavia*'s wreck site had been completely lost.

It was not until 1840, when Houtman's Abrolhos were finally charted by a Royal Navy hydrographic survey, that public interest in the *Batavia* was rekindled. The surveying work was conducted by Lieutenant Lort Stokes, RN, sailing in Charles Darwin's old ship HMS *Beagle,* and it was only at this late date that the archipelago was definitely shown to fall into three distinct groups, stretching north to south for a total of about 50 miles. Stokes had read accounts of the voyages of the Dutch East India Company and was aware that both the *Batavia* and the *Zeewijk* had been lost somewhere in the Abrolhos, so his interest was naturally piqued by the discovery of ancient wreckage on a large island in the southernmost group. 'On the south-west part,' he wrote,

> 'the beams of a large vessel were discovered, and as the crew of the *Zeewyck* ... reported having seen the wreck of a ship in these parts, there is little doubt that the remains were those of the *Batavia* ... We, in consequence, named our temporary anchorage Batavia Road and the whole group Pelsart Group.'

The island on which the ancient wreckage was discovered was given the name Pelsart Island, and the spot at which the timber was discovered – the debris consisted of 'a heavy beam of timber with a large iron bolt through it, [which] on the slightest touch soon dwindled down to a mere wire from corrosion,' together with 'a row of small glass demijohns* which, having stood there for the past 210 years, were half buried in the soil that had been accumulated around them and filled to about the same depth with the debris of insects and animals that had crawled in and perished' – was called Wreck Point. Proceeding north, Stokes named the middle islets the Easter Group, because he came upon them on Easter Sunday, 1840, and the most northerly part of the archipelago the Wallabis, after the marsupials that were found only on the two largest islands in the group.

Thus – at least so far as the public was concerned – the mystery

---

*Bottles with a narrow neck and substantial circumference.

of the *Batavia*'s last resting place had been solved, and the identification of Pelsart Island as the place where Cornelisz and the others had been wrecked was generally accepted for a further century. It was only when full accounts of the mutiny began to appear in English – a translation of one seventeenth-century pamphlet on the subject was published by a Perth newspaper in 1897 – that the first doubts arose, as the geography of the Pelsart Group made it impossible to fix the positions of Seals' Island, Wiebbe Hayes's Island, or the High Island at all satisfactorily if Pelsart Island was assumed to be Batavia's Graveyard. In 1938 a newspaper expedition led by a journalist named Malcolm Uren attempted to tackle this conundrum by positing that Gun Island, the most northerly island in the Pelsart Group, had actually been Jeronimus's headquarters. Even this explanation, however, seemed to stretch the facts set out in the *commandeur*'s journals to breaking point, and Uren and his colleagues were forced to consider the possibility that the wreckage seen by the *Zeewijk*'s men might not have come from the *Batavia* at all. It could have been part of one of several Dutch *retourschepen* that had gone missing in the Indian Ocean over the preceding decades – perhaps the *Ridderschap van Holland** (1694), the *Fortuyn†* (1724), or the *Aagtekerke‡* (1726).

The confusion persisted until the early 1960s, when the *Batavia*'s wreck site was finally rediscovered. The first person to recognise that the ship must lie elsewhere in the Abrolhos was a novelist, Henrietta Drake-Brockman, whose thoughts on the subject were published between 1955 and 1963. Drake-Brockman's interest in the *Batavia* stemmed from her early friendship with the Broadhurst family, which had long held concessions allowing it to mine for guano on the Abrolhos. In the course of their excavations, the Broadhursts had unearthed an extensive collection of Dutch artifacts in the Pelsart Group of islands – old bottles, pots and cooking utensils, as well as a pistol and two human skeletons – which they thought must have come from the *Batavia*. Cornelisz's story had enthralled Drake-Brockman as a child, and when she grew up she undertook her own research, corresponding with archives in the Netherlands and Java. It was Drake-Brockman who was the first to point out that, since Francisco Pelsaert had clearly seen and described wallabies during his time in the Abrolhos, the

---

*'Knighthood of Holland.'
†'Fortune.'
‡She was named after a village in Zeeland.

Batavia must have been wrecked in the Wallabi Group, almost 50 miles north of the position suggested by Lort Stokes. The approaches to the group were guarded by three large coral shoals, the Morning, Noon, and Evening Reefs. The novelist initially suggested that the wreck of the *Batavia* would be found somewhere on Noon Reef, in the middle of the group.

Drake-Brockman's views, which were first advanced in an article published in 1955, were not widely accepted at first. But in the years following the Second World War, the Abrolhos became an important crayfishery, and fishermen began to set up temporary homes on the islands of the Wallabi Group. In 1960 one of them, O. 'Pop' Marten, was digging a posthole on Beacon Island, an islet two miles east of Noon Reef, when he uncovered a human skeleton. A visiting doctor confirmed that the bones were human, and before long two policemen had arrived from Geraldton, on the mainland, and taken the remains away in a cardboard box for examination. At about the same time, Marten found a 'pewter utensil' lying near his posthole. It turned out to be the bell of a trumpet made by Conrat Droschel, a seventeenth-century German instrument maker who had lived in Nuremberg. The pewter bore an inscription that not only named Droschel, but also gave the date that the trumpet had been made: MDCXXVIII, or 1628. It was the first clear evidence that unexceptional Beacon Island was actually Batavia's Graveyard.

Marten's finds aroused a certain degree of interest. Hugh Edwards, a Perth newspaperman who was also an experienced skin diver, mounted a small expedition to the islands, searching unsuccessfully for evidence of the wreck along the reefs, and other fishermen working in the Abrolhos were alerted to the possibility that the wreck of a famous East Indiaman might be close nearby. But it was only three years later, in June 1963, that the wreck of the *Batavia* was positively identified.

The discoverers were Dave Johnson, another Abrolhos fisherman, and a diver from Geraldton named Max Cramer. Johnson had actually stumbled across the wreck late in 1960, while setting lobster pots. Over the next three years he returned to the site several times and searched it from the surface using a water glass, locating a quantity of ballast blocks and what looked like the remains of cannon scattered on the bottom. Digging a hole one day near the asbestos-walled shack he had built on Beacon Island, he also found another human skull. Johnson kept these discoveries to himself until Cramer and his brother arrived in the Abrolhos to hunt for the wreck. Then he decided to share his information and took the divers out to the wreck site in his boat. On 4 June 1963 – 334 years to the day since the *retourschip* had gone aground in the archipelago – Max Cramer became the first man to dive on the *Batavia*.

She lay on the southeastern end of Morning Reef, about two miles from the spot suggested by Henrietta Drake-Brockman, in 20 feet of water. With the help of Johnson and about 20 other Abrolhos crayfishermen, Cramer managed to salvage a large bronze cannon. It bore the mark of the VOC and the letter 'A,' indicating that it had once belonged to the Company's Amsterdam chamber. This discovery was enough to persuade most people that the right ship had been found. Hugh Edwards organised another expedition, this one with the backing of the Western Australian Museum and the Royal Australian Navy. Soon Morning Reef began to yield its secrets.

The salvage divers found the *Batavia* lying in a shallow depression in the reef. All of her upperworks had gone, and what remained of the hull was thickly covered by coral concretion. 'Over the years,' wrote Edwards,

'the sea had dug a grave for the old ship. It started with the gully grooved when her keel ran up into the coral with the crash that threw Francisco Pelsaert from his bunk on that June 4th morning before daylight. The sea had enlarged, scoured, and eaten at the edges of the gash until, by the time that we arrived, there was hollowed a hole in the shape of the ship, 200 feet long, and 12 feet deep. Now the main wash of the waves passed with eddies and swirls and white, confused foam over the top of the hole, and the skeletal *Batavia* lay partly protected from the main surges and the storms ... In the bottom of this hollow lay the bronze cannon, the spiked, 12-foot anchors – she had been carrying eight spares, as well as bow and stern anchors – and wonderful buried things, which we would excavate from beneath the protecting crust of reef which covered what remained of the crushed and flattened hull.'

It took more than a decade to complete the work of salvaging the wreck, but in the end a huge quantity of material was recovered from the reef and the surrounding islands. The most spectacular finds included a large portion of the stern, still almost intact after more than three centuries in the sea; 15 more of the cannon that Jan Evertsz and his men had tipped overboard on 4 June 1629; and the 137 giant sandstone blocks, carried as ballast, that together made up a portico for the castle at Batavia. A wide variety of other artifacts were also salvaged: apothecary's jars and a surgeon's mortar, probably once the property of Frans Jansz; stinkpots, grenades, and shot for the guns; the heel of a silk stocking; and coins from the money chests Pelsaert had left behind. There were more personal items, too: a quantity of Ariaen Jacobsz's navigation instruments; some of the silverware the *commandeur* had ordered specially to sell to the Emperor of India, including a triangular salt cellar and a set of silver bedposts; and an engraved stamp that had once been used to seal correspondence. It bore the initials 'GB' and must once have belonged to the *predikant,* Gijsbert Bastiaensz. Today, these pieces can be seen among the *Batavia* artifacts on display in the Western Australian Maritime Museum in Fremantle. The centrepieces of the collection are the *retourschip*'s stern – raised, carefully conserved, and reconstructed – and the castle portico, reassembled for the first time in nearly 400 years into a gateway more than 25 feet high.

On rough days, when diving on the wreck was impossible, the members of the Edwards expedition scoured the islands of the Wallabi Group for more evidence of the *Batavia* survivors. They had limited success. There was virtually nothing to find among the coral rubble, but Edwards and his companions did identify Long Island as Pelsaert's Seals' Island, and a year later, on West Wallabi, about five miles due west of Beacon, they succeeded in locating the remains of Wiebbe Hayes's dwellings.

As early as 1879, a surveyor named Forrest had noted the existence of two rectangular 'huts' on the island, and both can still be seen today. One was just inland from the sea, close to a feature known as Slaughter Point and in a commanding position overlooking the approaches from Batavia's Graveyard and Seals' Island. The other was further inland, in the middle of a flat limestone plain toward the centre of the island. Both 'huts' are built from coral slabs, which lie piled in a half-haphazard fashion to a height of about three feet. The structure closest to the sea has an internal wall, which divides it into two 'rooms' of roughly equal size. It is quite large – almost 30 feet from end to end – and (at 6 feet) broad enough to allow the average Dutchman of Pelsaert's time to lie stretched out inside it. With sailcloth added as a roof, the 'hut' could conceivably have housed somewhere between 12 and 20 men. The inland structure is more simply built. It has one room, nearly square in shape, and – unlike its companion – it has an entrance on one side. Although its setting seems desolate at first glance, it has actually been placed only a few yards from one of the island's largest wells.

Excavations at the coastal site unearthed fragments of Rhenish stoneware, iron fishhooks, and a ladle that had been crudely fashioned from a sheet of lead. One piece of ancient pottery bore the shield of Amsterdam and established that this building, at least, had been the work of Wiebbe Hayes. It had been positioned with a soldier's eye, guarding the middle of a bay, so that attempts to approach it could have been detected while the attackers were still miles away. Once they had come ashore, Jeronimus's mutineers would still have had to scale a small rock face, six feet high, to leave the beach and reach the structure. Hayes and his men, who occupied the high ground, would have had a good chance of defending it.

All this has led to the suggestion that the coastal 'hut' was actually a fort, built to protect the Defenders from the muskets carried by the mutineers. Certainly its coral walls are nowhere broken by a doorway, and the building seems to have been permanently manned. Nearby, the explorers found two fire pits and a large quantity of charred animal bones from wallabies and sea lions – enough, they reckoned, to have fed a group of 40 men for about three months.

The inland structure is the more controversial of the two. It is built on bedrock, making it impossible to excavate, but careful sifting of the surface debris around it has failed to turn up any evidence of Dutch occupation. Some have argued it was built only in the late nineteenth century; Lort Stokes, in 1840, took water from the well nearby without apparently noticing any sign of a building, and old fishermen, questioned in the 1960s, recalled seeing the hut in use by guano diggers around 1900. Those who prefer to think it dates from the seventeenth century point out that surveyor Forrest noted its existence in 1879, before organised guano mining on West Wallabi began. One piece of circumstantial evidence seems to connect it to Hayes: although the inland structure cannot be seen from its companion near the coast, a cairn of coral slabs has been discovered midway between the two. Both structures are clearly visible from its summit, so perhaps the cairn was built to permit signals from the coastal fort to be sent inland. Whatever the truth, though, and no matter what the controversy concerning the inland hut, the provenance of the coastal structure now seems well understood. The untidy pile of coral slabs is, in fact, the first evidence of European habitation in Australia.

In the Netherlands, the rediscovery of the *Batavia* led to a resurgence of interest in the East Indiaman. One of those inspired by the story of the ship was Willem Vos, a master shipwright specialising in the construction of wooden sailing boats. In the 1970s, when archaeologists from the Western Australian Maritime Museum were salvaging the *Batavia*'s stern from Morning Reef, Vos conceived the idea of building a full-sized reconstruction of the *retourschip,* a project that would provide employment for young craftsmen and help to keep alive traditional skills that were fast being lost.

The *Batavia* herself had been built in a little more than six months. It took Vos almost a decade simply to lay the keel of his replica East Indiaman. The early years were spent raising money – the *Batavia* reconstruction cost more than 15 million guilders, or £4,600,000, in excess of 150 times the price of the original – and scouring archives for contemporary plans and drawings. Working out how the VOC had built its ships proved to be at least as difficult as finding backers for the project; Dutch shipwrights of the seventeenth century put together all their craft – even East Indiamen – by rule of thumb, without the benefit of plans. *Retourschepen* generally conformed to the same general dimensions, which were laid down by the Gentlemen XVII, but each ship was unique and differed from its consorts in a myriad of small ways.

Eventually, Vos acquired copies of Dutch shipbuilding treatises compiled in 1671 and 1697, and these, together with earlier drawings, supplied sufficient information to plan the reconstruction with some certainty. The new *Batavia*'s keel was laid in October 1985 in a purpose-built yard in Lelystad, built on land reclaimed from the Zuyder Zee. Construction proceeded hesitantly at first, but gradually the modern shipwrights became more expert and, in the process, rediscovered many lost techniques that helped to illuminate the working methods of Jan Rijksen, the architect of the original *Batavia*. Vos and his men were thus able to provide useful information for the archaeologists struggling to reassemble the salvaged stern section in Australia – 'the archaeology of reconstruction and experiment,' it has been termed – receiving details of the *retourschip*'s actual construction in return.

The second *Batavia* was launched in April 1995 and has already attracted well over four million visitors. She is perfectly seaworthy, and though she lacks the passengers, crew, and much of the equipment that would make her as packed and busy as her predecessor, going aboard provides fine insights into what life on board an East Indiaman was like. The confined spaces, the darkness below decks, the squalor of the open latrines, and the impossible discomforts of the orlop deck all come vividly to life; and, in winter, the lack of heat and proper light are only too apparent. The thought of spending between six and nine months living on her, sleeping on deck, eating cask meat, and drinking stagnant, green-tinged water is not a pleasant one.

In the years since 1960, digging on Beacon Island had revealed more skeletons. The remains of as many as 19 of the 70 or so people who are known to have died on Batavia's Graveyard have been uncovered from three main sites. Persistent rumors suggest that local fishermen have stumbled across other graves but prefer simply to rebury any bones they find.

The known remains are telling enough. Jeronimus's victims did not die well. With only one exception, their bodies were thrown into grave pits and buried carelessly. Many bore not just the unmistakable signs of violence, but scars inflicted by illness, injury, and malnutrition earlier in life. These skeletons bear mute testament to the privation and desperation that drove men and women to travel to the Indies in the 1620s.

Three of the bodies are male, and one is female; the rest are so undeveloped or so badly damaged that their sex cannot be determined. Seven, at least, were found in a single grave pit, into which their bodies had been tipped with little ceremony so that they lay huddled close together just below the surface. Two others, adult males, had been interred side by side a little way away, and a third – the remains of an 18-year-old – also lay nearby. This last corpse is said to have been found with a musket ball lying inside the chest cavity. If so, it ought to be the body of Jan Dircxsz, the Defender shot in the mutineers' final assault on Wiebbe Hayes's Island and the only person reported to have died of gunshot wounds throughout the whole course of the mutiny.

Together, the *Batavia* corpses represent a broad cross section of the *retourschip*'s passengers and crew: the oldest is that of a man (or, perhaps, a heavyset woman) aged about 40 or 45, and the youngest a child who was no more than five or six when his or her life was ended. Several of the skeletons show signs of scurvy, and many of the teeth have been scratched and scoured by the sand that found its way into the rough island diet. The young child's teeth have been worn down by constant grinding brought on by severe stress.

Of all the bodies, the most complete and best preserved is one recovered during the original *Batavia* expedition. It was found by the east corner of Dave Johnson's house on Beacon Island, buried face up in about 15 inches of soil. The remains are those of a tall man – he was only just under six feet in height – who had been somewhere between 30 and 39 when he died.* He must have come from a relatively poor family: the skeleton still shows growth-arrest lines of the sort caused by bouts of malnutrition, and the teeth and jaw are badly diseased, perhaps as the result of scurvy. Bony excrescences cover parts of the pelvis; they seem to have been caused by a severe blow inflicted just below the stomach some years before his death. The victim's injuries had been badly treated; the man who bore them would have been in constant pain.

A detailed examination of this skeleton, carried out in 1999 by Dr. Alanah Buck, a forensic scientist from the Western Australian Centre for Pathology and Medical Research in Perth, showed that the victim had died after being struck over the head by a right-handed assailant who had stood almost directly in front of him to deliver the attack. A single vicious blow, apparently inflicted with a sword, had left a two-inch cut mark on the victim's skull. The resultant concussion may have been severe enough to kill; at the very least the wound would have caused unconsciousness and profuse bleeding. As there are no traces of damage to the bones of the forearm of the sort typically inflicted on a man who dies pro-tecting his head and face, it would appear that the victim was unable to defend himself. He may have been restrained by several of Cornelisz's men, or taken by surprise. If he survived the initial assault at all, he was most likely stabbed to death or had his throat cut while he lay stunned.

The dead man's identity remains something of a mystery. One possibility is that he was Jacop Hendricxen Drayer, who was killed because Jeronimus thought him half-lame and thus useless. The

*Edwards's team had thought him less than 20 and speculated that the body might have been that of Andries de Vries.

skeleton shows that the victim's pelvic injury had never healed properly, and the man who bore it would certainly have limped. But the wounds found on the body do not tally with those mentioned in Pelsaert's journal, which describes how Jan Hendricxsz 'struck two knives to pieces' on Drayer's chest, and two more in his neck, before cutting his throat. This skeleton shows no sign of the nicks and scratches to the ribs and vertebrae that such a violent assault must surely have caused.

The remains of three other *Batavia* skeletons, examined by Buck and a forensic dentist, Dr. Stephen Knott, suggest that many of Jeronimus's victims underwent still more terrifying deaths. One man in his early 30s had been struck a massive upward blow with a wooden club or axe handle. The impact had been absorbed by two of his front teeth; one of the canines had been forced more than an inch up through the jaw and into the nasal cavity. The right upper incisor next to it had been smashed and twisted up through 90 degrees, so the cutting edge now faced straight out from the mouth. The victim had then been finished off with another blow to the side of the head, heavy enough to open up the sutures joining the fused skull plates and cause immediate unconsciousness and death.

The second victim was a girl aged 16 or 18 who had suffered severely from the effects of malnutrition in her youth. She had been struck a glancing blow across the top of her skull with a sharp, light-bladed instrument – possibly a cutlass. The attack probably came from behind, and the blade sliced off a thin sliver of skull. The girl would have been knocked unconscious but not killed; possibly she had been fleeing her assailant, who was unable to get in a lethal blow, or perhaps the man trying to kill her hesitated for some reason as he struck her. This interpretation of events might suggest that the victim was Mayken Cardoes and the attacker Andries Jonas, but the *Batavia* journals state that Cardoes was finished off by Wouter Loos, who caved her skull in with an axe, and these remains bear no sign of such an assault. In the absence of any other obvious wounds it is not possible to say how the girl, whoever she was, actually died; she may have been strangled, stabbed, or drowned. All that can be said for certain is that, once again, there are no signs she was able to protect herself.

The skull of the third victim, now on display in the maritime museum at Geraldton, displays the most extensive wounds of all. It too was dug up close to Johnson's house – so close, in fact, that the remainder of the skeleton still lies in the foundations. The skull appears to be that of a man in his late thirties who had been hit a sweeping, horizontal blow across the back of his head with a small axe. The blow cut right through the bone, forcing fragments into the brain, and this initial assault could well have proved fatal in its own right, but as the victim fell forward – or was pushed – his attackers had made certain he was dead by delivering two more blows. Both were aimed at the middle of the occipital region, breaking through the thickest part of the skull and exposing the brain membrane. Death would have followed quickly, almost certainly as the result of heavy loss of blood.

The Geraldton skull has been tentatively identified as that of Hendrick Denys, the assistant clubbed to death by Jan Hendricxsz on the same night that the *predikant*'s wife and children were murdered; the wounds match those mentioned by Pelsaert in the journals, and Denys could well have been in his late thirties, as was the owner of the skull. In the autumn of 1999, Stephen Knott built up a clay approximation of the victim's face using established forensic techniques. The reconstruction shows the heavyset, strong-jawed face of a once-handsome man, reduced somewhat in stature by emaciation. The features have been deliberately made rather regular; modelling a dead man's nose, ears, and lips can only be a matter of guesswork, and since the Geraldton skull lacks a jaw, another Beacon Island mandible has been substituted for it. Nevertheless, Knott's work had revealed, for the first time, the near likeness of a man who sailed with Pelsaert and Cornelisz on the *Batavia*. Without his seventeenth-century hair and clothing, Denys – or whoever he once was – has acquired an oddly contemporary look. It is difficult to imagine him as he must have been on the night of 21 July 1629: cold, hungry, scared, unarmed, and hiding in his tent from a man wielding an axe.

Pelsaert gave conflicting accounts of the final death toll in Houtman's Abrolhos. In his report to the Gentlemen XVII, written midway through December 1629, he suggested that Jeronimus and his followers had killed 124 men, women, and children, and in another letter 'more than 120.' A more detailed but undated note, preserved in the VOC archives, reduces this figure to 115: 96 men and boys who were 'employees of the VOC,' 12 women, and 7 children.

The latter total is probably more correct, but it is horrifying enough.* The dead were often those least able to defend themselves – all but two of the children from the *Batavia* were killed, and almost two-thirds of the women – and the protracted slaughter in the Abrolhos was without parallel in the history of the VOC. Worst of all, perhaps, the victims were mostly dispatched by people whom they knew, acting on the orders of men whose reasons, even today, seem almost impossible to comprehend.

Pelsaert was inclined to blame the skipper for a good deal of what took place in the archipelago. He saw Jacobsz as the main instigator of the planned mutiny on the *Batavia* and Cornelisz as the man who edited Jacobsz's thoughts and deeds, and 'moulded their similar intelligences and feelings into one.' Nevertheless, the skipper could hardly be held personally responsible for what took place in his absence, and even the *commandeur* had to agree that it was Jeronimus who had organised and led the slaughter in the Abrolhos. Pelsaert seems to have been tormented by his inability to understand what drove Cornelisz to such a course of action, and in his journals he several times refers to the under-merchant as a 'Torrentian' or an 'Epicurean,' as though this explained his actions. It would be interesting to know exactly what the *commandeur* meant by these terms, since he does not define them, but the writer seems to employ the two words interchangeably to indicate a man who thinks that self-gratification is the highest good and indulges his impulses and whims irrespective of the rights of others. Because the journals contain no transcripts of the interrogations, it is impossible to know whether Cornelisz himself ever claimed to be a disciple of Torrentius, and the words *Torrentian* and *Epicurean* may simply have been vague labels applied by Pelsaert – a sort of shorthand that conveyed more in 1629 than it does now. On the other hand, Antonio van Diemen also thought that Jeronimus had been 'following the beliefs of Torrentius' in the archipelago, and though the councillor could have picked up this opinion from the *commandeur,* an anonymous sailor from the *Batavia* did observe that Cornelisz was 'claimed to have been a follower of Torrentius' while he was still on Batavia's Graveyard.

If Jeronimus did indeed attempt to live by Torrentius's

*Pelsaert's journals cannot solve the mystery; a total of 108 deaths are mentioned in its pages, but the *commandeur* does not include Abraham Hendricx or the dead Defender, Dircxsz, among the casualties and is never precise about the number of sick people killed by Andries de Vries on 13 July.

philosophy, all that can be said with any certainty is that he badly misrepresented his friend's opinions. Not much is really known of Torrentius's clearly heterodox views, though – as we have seen – he was, perhaps, an Epicurean himself, and probably a Gnostic. It would certainly be wrong to identify the painter with the Rosicrucians or the Libertines; Torrentius may not have believed literally in the stories in the Bible, and denied (as did Cornelisz) the reality of hell, but there is no evidence that he shared Jeronimus's belief that everything that a man did, including murder, might be ordained by God. It would be unfair to place the blame for what happened in the Abrolhos at his feet. Indeed, all attempts to explain the *Batavia* mutiny in terms of philosophy are doomed to failure, for they cannot explain why the under-merchant was so indifferent to the suffering of others. The answer to that question seems to lie within Jeronimus's mind itself.

We know far too little about the Haarlem apothecary to reconstruct his character completely. Nothing at all has survived concerning Jeronimus's childhood; his adult years in Haarlem are illuminated only by his infrequent dealings with solicitors; and the records of the voyage of the *Batavia,* though far more detailed, are inherently unreliable. The Cornelisz of Pelsaert's journals is undoubtedly a monster, but his personality, as revealed to us, is filtered through Deschamps's summaries of Pelsaert's questioning. Much of what the under-merchant had to say in his own defence was not recorded, and some of the testimony was extracted under torture. Jeronimus, moreover, had every reason to mislead his interrogators when he could, and it would be unwise to take anything that he said at face value. In most respects, therefore, Jeronimus Cornelisz remains a mystery today, just as he was in 1629.

Little is definitely known, for instance, about his personality. He was obviously intelligent; he could not have qualified as an apothecary if he did not have a good memory and a sharp mind. He was well educated, and his languages were good – he must have spoken not only Dutch but Latin, and perhaps Frisian, too. He had a quick tongue, and he could often be good company: 'Well spoken,' Pelsaert called him, and skilled at getting on with people; the sort of man who would make a good companion on a long ocean voyage.

But Cornelisz used his superficial charm to ingratiate himself with others and then to manipulate them. Gijsbert Bastiaensz's account of the under-merchant's execution agrees with Pelsaert's in stating that the other mutineers condemned their former leader as a 'seducer of men,' and there can be no question that Jeronimus was adept at using others to achieve his aims. Yet he was also weak and thoroughly incompetent in key respects. He shrank from the prospect of physical violence – his only victim on Batavia's Graveyard was a defenceless baby – and he put up no resistance when he himself was captured. He was a poor judge of other people's character; at home in Haarlem he had hired an insane midwife and a diseased wet nurse for his wife, and in the Abrolhos he badly underestimated Wiebbe Hayes. Moreover, Cornelisz showed little enthusiasm for making detailed plans and rarely thought ahead in any but the most general terms. It may be that this weakness first manifested itself in his mismanagement of his failed apothecary's shop, but it was certainly in evidence on Batavia's Graveyard, where the mutineers neglected to guard their boats, gave Hayes's Defenders more than two weeks to prepare for an attack, and failed to bring their superior weaponry to bear on them with decisive effect. Jeronimus's strategy was disastrous, yet he displayed such a bloated sense of his own self-worth that he promoted himself to the post of captain-general, dressed in outlandish uniforms, tried to seduce Creesje Jans, and ventured – fatally – onto Wiebbe Hayes's Island with such a tiny bodyguard that he was captured without difficulty.

Other facets of the under-merchant's personality are not mentioned in the journals but may be inferred nonetheless. Cornelisz appears to have been impulsive and easily bored; many of the murders that took place in the Abrolhos, particularly the later ones, were ordered on a whim. The sufferings of others had no apparent effect on him; he stood and watched as people died, ignoring all their pleas for mercy. Freed of normal constraints by the wreck and the departure of the ship's officers, Jeronimus took to living by his own moral code. It may well be that he adopted the tenets of the Libertines not out of any religious conviction, but because they mirrored the feelings he already had.

Seen from this perspective, Jeronimus Cornelisz was almost certainly a psychopath: a man devoid of conscience and remorse, living his life free from the shackles of normal self-restraint. Though years of casual usage have stripped the word of much of its meaning – so that any violent criminal now tends to acquire the label – true psychopaths are not evil men incapable of self-control.

On the contrary, they are always chillingly in command of their emotions. What they actually lack is empathy: the capacity to either understand or care what other people feel.

Dr. Robert Hare of the University of British Columbia, who developed the 'Psychopathy checklist' widely used today to diagnose the syndrome, notes that:

'Most clinicians and researchers know that psychopathy cannot be understood in terms of traditional views of mental illness. Psychopaths are not disorientated or out of touch with reality, nor do they experience the delusions, hallucinations or intense subjective distress that characterise most other mental disorders. Unlike psychotic individuals, psychopaths are rational and aware of what they are doing and why. Their behaviour is the result of *choice,* freely exercised.'

A psychopath, in other words, understands the distinction between right and wrong. He robs or hurts or kills not because he does not know what he is doing but because he does not care that his actions have consequences for other people. A convicted psychopath thus goes not to a mental hospital, but to prison.

The psychopath's inability to feel guilt is his most distinctive trait. Ordinary criminals operate within the parameters of a well-defined code of conduct; they may reject everyday society, but they are still constrained by a sense of what is right and wrong. Such men may, for example, never hurt a woman or a child, or go to prison rather than betray a colleague to the authorities. Psychopaths simply do not think this way. A man afflicted with the syndrome will transgress all accepted boundaries if it benefits him to do so. He will rob his parents and abandon his own wife and child without feeling remorse.

Other relevant symptoms of psychopathy include glibness and superficiality, impulsive behaviour, and the lack of any sense of responsibility. Psychopaths are deceitful and manipulative people; they like to exercise power over others. Most possess good social skills and can be highly persuasive, even though they also lie 'endlessly, lazily, about everything.' They remain characteristically unperturbed when their deceits are exposed; if one lie is disposed of, they will simply spin another, often unrelated, to take its place. They lack the capacity to plan ahead, preferring grand fantasies to realistic short-term goals. Above all, as Hare explains, 'psychopaths have a narcissistic and grossly inflated view of their self-worth and importance, a truly astonishing egocentricity and sense of entitlement, and see themselves as the centre of the universe, as superior beings who are justified in living according to their own rules.'

A psychopath behaves this way because he lacks the range and depth of feelings that other men experience. He appears cold and unfeeling. Though he may well be capable of brief outbursts of emotion, 'careful observers are left with the impression that he is play-acting and that little is going on below the surface.'

Plainly Jeronimus displayed many of these symptoms. His practised tongue and agile mind, his grandiose plans, and his manipulations were all characteristic of the psychopath. He appears to have been impulsive and was frequently betrayed by his inability to plan ahead. At no point in Pelsaert's account of the mutiny, moreover, is there any indication that Cornelisz felt genuine remorse for what he had done. On the contrary, Jeronimus continued to justify his actions all the way to the gallows.

True, not everything that the captain general said or did fits the psychopathic profile. Few psychopaths would have waited for nearly two weeks to impose themselves on Creesje Jans, and most would have actively participated in the slaughter that occurred in the Abrolhos. But Pelsaert's journals and the *predikant*'s letter are patchy sources at best, and they may neglect to mention other incidents that might confirm the diagnosis. All in all, the evidence points strongly to the conclusion that Jeronimus was psychopathic.

Why he was a psychopath is much harder to explain. There is little consensus, even today, as to whether such men are born or made. Some psychologists believe that psychopathy is actually a form of brain damage, others that it manifests itself in early childhood, the consequence of a wretched upbringing. All that can be said with any certainty is that the syndrome was considerably less common in the seventeenth century than it is now. Modern estimates imply that as many as 1 in every 125 present-day Americans are psychopaths of one sort or another – a total of two million across the country, and 100,000 in New York alone. But the same surveys suggest that China has many fewer psychopaths than the United States, and that psychopathy flourishes best in societies where stress is laid on individual freedom and instant gratification. If this is true, the syndrome is unlikely to have been common in the Dutch Republic of the Golden Age, which placed such powerful emphasis on conformity and the notion of good citizenship. Most of the people on the *Batavia* would surely never have encountered someone in whom the major traits of psychopathy were present to such a remarkable degree. Cornelisz was an exceptionally unusual character for his time.

Even before he boarded the *retourschip,* moreover, Jeronimus would have been beyond help. There has never been a 'treatment' for psychopathy, for those who suffer from the syndrome 'don't feel they have psychological or emotional problems,' says Hare.

'They see no reason to change their behaviour to conform to societal standards with which they do not agree. [They] are not "fragile" individuals. What they think and do are extensions of a rock-solid personality that is extremely resistant to outside influence... Many are protected from the consequences of their actions by well-meaning family members or friends; their behaviour remains relatively unchecked and unpunished. Others are skilled enough to weave their way through life without too much personal inconvenience.'

Even if Jeronimus had somehow survived the journey east, therefore, his behaviour would not have changed. He would have remained cold, calculating, and ruthless for the remainder of his life. Psychopaths may learn to modify their behaviour, having recognised that they can make their own lives easier by doing so, but they do not 'recover.' They never get better. They cannot be cured.

🐛

One unanswered question still remains: what drove Jeronimus to act as he did on the *Batavia*? From what we now know of his psychopathy, there is no reason to suppose that the apothecary boarded the *Batavia* with the already-formed intention of seizing the ship. He is much more likely to have conceived the idea quite impulsively, and in all probability it was indeed Jacobsz's grumbling, at the Cape of Good Hope, that first put the thought of mutiny into his head.

Pelsaert was therefore right, in one respect, to think of Ariaen as the key figure in the story. Sailing with another skipper, or on a different ship, Cornelisz would almost certainly have reached the

Spiceries without undue incident – and, once there, he could well have been successful. His psychopathy might not even have been noticed by the self-serving servants of the Company, for though Jeronimus would no doubt have tried to cheat and lie to his employers, most of them were cheats and liars, too. A psychopath, indeed, would have enjoyed certain advantages over the petty criminals who infested the Indies; given the opportunity, he would steal more ruthlessly and recklessly than any ordinary man, and with such single-mindedness that he would soon amass a fortune if not stopped. Jeronimus might, perhaps, have overreached himself and been detected and disgraced. But since he would not have had to kill anyone to achieve his aims, he would at least have avoided the appalling death awaiting him in Houtman's Abrolhos.

Nearly 400 years have passed since then, but the islands have hardly changed in all that time. Visions of the past persist in places such as these. At dusk on an October evening, with a full moon sailing in the sky, it is still possible to glimpse Jeronimus Cornelisz in the shadows on Seals' Island. His body hangs there, swinging in the southwest wind that first brought him to the archipelago; the noose's knot is tight under his ear and the head has snapped grotesquely to one side. The rope groans and creaks its way across the gallows tree, but the noise it makes cannot be heard. It is drowned out by the ceaseless shrieking of the mutton birds.

Notes

General

The wreck of the *Batavia* was one of the more sensational events of the seventeenth century, and it attracted considerable contemporary interest. A number of pamphlets on the subject were published, some when news of the disaster first reached the United Provinces, and others two decades later when there was a surge of interest in travel literature in the Netherlands. The most popular of these pamphlets were published in several editions and must have achieved a relatively wide circulation. Consequently, the events of the mutiny remained fairly well known, in the United Provinces at least, for 30 or 40 years afterward.

During the second half of the seventeenth century, the *Batavia*'s story was gradually forgotten, and references to the mutiny become progressively scarcer. Interest did not revive until the late nineteenth century, when the Abrolhos became a centre of the guano trade and excavations on the islands began to turn up artifacts that were thought to have come from the ship (but which, it eventually emerged, in fact came from later, less well known wrecks); and after that, publications on the subject began to appear in Australia as well as the Netherlands. The rediscovery of the wreck of the *Batavia* in 1963, which coincided with the publication of one of the key historical works on the subject, significantly increased interest in the subject, though even in the last 40 years the *Batavia* story has remained little known outside the two countries most closely connected with it. In the last quarter of a century the wreck site has been thoroughly excavated, adding substantially to our knowledge of the ship. Several accounts of the *Batavia*'s story have been published in Dutch and German over the last eight years, but none in English, and this is the first book to make use of freshly discovered information from provincial archives across the Netherlands.

Eye-Witness Accounts

The accounts of the *Batavia* disaster that have come down to us are unusually detailed for such a relatively early period. Moreover, the evidence that does survive covers the ship's story from several different perspectives. We have accounts, however fragmentary, written by people who sailed to the Indies in the ship's longboat, by a VOC merchant who was hunted down by the mutineers but escaped, and by another man who survived Batavia's Graveyard. Most important, we have the confessions of the mutineers themselves, written down during or just after their interrogations.

We are fortunate this is the case. The Dutch archives covering the country's Golden Age are still voluminous, but the material they contain largely concerns the doings of the moneyed classes, and records of those who owned no property and had little money – those, in other words, who made up the great majority of the *Batavia*'s passengers and crew –

are largely nonexistent. Nor were there newspapers to record sensational events or reporters to take an interest in the experiences of the *Batavia*'s survivors. Taken together, Francisco Pelsaert's detailed summaries of the evidence he heard on Batavia's Graveyard make up one of the most complete accounts of a single mutiny that survives in any language, for it was comparatively rare for a large group of mutineers to be captured and tried together.

Pelsaert's version of events is contained within the *commandeur*'s MS journal of the *Batavia*'s maiden voyage, which has been preserved among the VOC papers now in the Algemeen RijksArchief in The Hague. The journal has been bound up among the volumes of correspondence received annually from the Indies and now occupies folios 232r–317r of the volume known as ARA VOC 1098. An earlier volume of Pelsaert's, which concerned the outward voyage of the *Batavia* from Amsterdam to the Abrolhos, was thrown overboard by the mutineers and lost when the *commandeur*'s cabin was ransacked after the wreck. The surviving account covers the period from the wreck on 4 June 1629 to Pelsaert's final return to the East Indies in December of the same year.

The journals vary considerably from page to page in content and tone. In places they are little more than a traditional ship's log; elsewhere they become a personal account of the author's experiences in the aftermath of the mutiny. The bulk of the manuscript, however, consists of lengthy summaries of Pelsaert's interrogation of the *Batavia* mutineers, followed by what appear to be more or less verbatim transcripts of the verdicts handed down to the guilty men.

The journals have been assembled in roughly chronological order. However, it is evident from the arrangement of the documents that they were not written contemporaneously. Each of the major mutineers is dealt with separately, the account of his interrogation in the third week of September being immediately followed by the verdict passed on him on the 28th of the month, after which the account moves back to the interrogation of the next man, and so on. At one point in this compilation [ARA VOC 1098, fol. 278v], the writer has crammed in some additional testimony concerning the mutineer Mattys Beer, made on the day of his execution, in a blank he had previously left at the bottom of one of the pages. This may indicate that the journals were written up in their current form between the passing of the sentences on 28 September and the hanging of the principal mutineers on 2 October. On the other hand, the sheer bulk of the testimony is such that it is perhaps more likely that all the accounts were taken down in rough during the interrogations, and then copied into journals later, while salvage operations were proceeding or even during the survivors' voyage to the Indies, which occupied the period from mid-November to 5 December. In that case it may be that the compiler simply mislaid Beer's final confession when he was writing up his account of the mutineer's examination and was forced to interpolate this evidence when it eventually emerged from the pile of papers on his desk.

It would, anyway, be unwise to treat Pelsaert's journals as a spontaneous, contemporary account of the *Batavia* mutiny. A good deal of care must have gone into their compilation, and they were unquestionably edited in the course of the work. Thus the summaries of the various interrogations are just that – summaries, put into the third person – and not word-for-word transcripts of what each prisoner actually said.

Owing to the quirks of the Dutch legal system, which placed overwhelming significance on confessions, there is virtually no room in the journals for evidence from ordinary passengers who witnessed the extraordinary events that took place on the Abrolhos; in particular, it is noteworthy – though unsurprising – that none of the *Batavia*'s women were heard. It is, furthermore, entirely possible that other material – perhaps a good deal of material – has been omitted altogether, either because it seemed irrelevant or because it cast some of the protagonists in an unfavourable light. Finally, it is important to remember that the journals were compiled to be read by the directors of the Amsterdam chamber of the VOC. It was these gentlemen who would determine the future career – if any – of Pelsaert and the other officers of the *Batavia*. It would be naive to suppose that they were not written with this thought very much in mind.

Some idea of the degree of editing that may have occurred during the writing-up emerges from a study of the journal's authorship. The *commandeur*'s report is not in Pelsaert's own cramped and unconfident hand, which is known from a single surviving letter in the VOC archives [ARA VOC 1098, fol. 583r–4r], and throughout much of it Pelsaert himself is referred to in the third person. It would appear, therefore, that the *Batavia* journals were actually written by one of the *commandeur*'s clerks, almost certainly Salomon Deschamps, who was himself one of the unwilling mutineers. This contention is supported by the fact that the handwriting in the journal matches that in the VOC's copy of Pelsaert's *remonstrantie* on Mogul India, which Deschamps is known to have compiled. It is therefore noteworthy that although the lists of Cornelisz's followers, copied into the journal, are given – as was the custom – in descending order of rank, the name of the relatively high-ranking Deschamps always appears at the bottom of the lists. From this it would appear that the hapless clerk was doing what he could to distance himself from the mutineers [R 42–7]. It is, thus, not strictly accurate to refer to Pelsaert's journal as 'his,' though for the sake of simplicity I have often done so.

The only other account of the mutiny that still exists in manuscript form comes to us at third hand in the form of a collection of anecdotes concerning Dutch journeys to the Indies, preserved among the municipal archives of Harderwijk, a small port in Gelderland. This MS [Gemeente Archief Harderwijk, Oud Archief 2052, fol. 30–7] contains some details of events on the Abrolhos – such as the story of Wybrecht Claasen's swim to the wreck for water, and the anecdote of Cornelisz being imprisoned in a limestone pit and forced to pluck birds – that do not appear in any other sources. It seems likely that the anonymous compiler had them from a member of the *Batavia*'s crew. From internal evidence, it would appear that these anecdotes were written down in about 1645 [R 22–8, 57].

Four further eyewitness accounts were printed and preserved in various contemporary and near-contemporary pamphlets. The most important of these was produced, anonymously, by Isaac Commelin, an Amsterdam bookseller whose *Origin and Progress of the United Netherlands Chartered East-India Company,* published in 1645, helped to start the Dutch vogue for accounts of voyages to foreign lands.

Commelin (1598–1676) followed up this success with *Ongeluckige Voyagie, Van 't Schip* Batavia *(The Unlucky Voyage of the* Batavia*),* a densely packed pamphlet, illuminated with copper-plate engravings, that included not only the details of Cornelisz's mutiny but also accounts of two other voyages. The book was first published by the Amsterdam printer Jan Jansz in 1647 and was closely based on Pelsaert's unpublished journals, rearranged and transposed where necessary to the third person from the first. It includes one short interpolation [OV (1647) pp. 59–60], in the form of a purported statement by Wiebbe Hayes that does not appear among the VOC archives. This rather puzzling piece of evidence is discussed in the notes to chapter 8; suffice it to say here that it seems more likely than not that it is authentic.

How Jansz obtained sight of Pelsaert's manuscript, which should have been filed among the papers of the Amsterdam chamber, remains something of a mystery; but the pamphleteer is known to have had close contacts with several of the VOC's directors, and Commelin's earlier publications had already featured accounts based on official sources, which he must have purchased, clandestinely or otherwise, from employees of the Company. In any event, *The Unlucky Voyage* was a considerable success and was republished several times over the next two decades, keeping the *Batavia*'s name before the Dutch public. Commelin's work was also swiftly pirated by other publishers, as was common at the time; in 1648 Joost Hartgers of Amsterdam brought out his own edition of the text, supplementing Pelsaert's text with a lengthy letter by Gijsbert Bastiaensz that described events on Batavia's Graveyard from the *predikant*'s perspective. The original MS of the letter is now lost, but it appears, from internal evidence, to be authentic. Two years later Lucas de Vries of Utrecht published a third variant, including in his edition a list of the rewards given to the *Batavia*'s loyalists. (C. R. Boxer's 'Isaac Commelin's "Begin ende voortgangh"' in *Dutch Merchants and Mariners in Asia 1602–1795,* pp. 2–3, 5, and DB 4–5, 78–9, contain further information about Commelin, Jansz, and the various editions of *The Unlucky Voyage*.)

The other three surviving accounts have the advantage that they appeared shortly after news of the *Batavia* mutiny first reached the Netherlands, but they are considerably shorter. The first, a typical 'news song' of the period, was published as *Droevighe Tijdinghe van de*

Aldergrouwelykste Moordery, Geschiet door Eenighe Matrosen op 't Schip Batavia ['Sad tidings of the most horrible murder done by some sailors of the ship *Batavia*'], an anonymous pamphlet containing a short explanatory preface and a song of 16 verses. The news song contains no information not available from other sources, but the information in it is so detailed that it is reasonable to suppose that the publisher had his information direct from a *Batavia* survivor [R 227–30]. The other two accounts appear in the anonymous pamphlet *Leyds Veer-Schuyts Praetjen, Tuschen een Koopman ende Borger van Leyden, Varende van Haarlem nae Leyden* ['Conversation on a canalboat between a merchant and a citizen of Leyden, travelling from Haarlem to Leyden']. One is an anonymous letter dated December 1629, written by someone who accompanied Pelsaert to Java in the *Batavia*'s longboat and returned with him to the Abrolhos. This letter includes the statement that Cornelisz was a Frisian, a fact that is nowhere mentioned in Pelsaert's journals but that appears, from the research undertaken for this book, to be correct. It has been suggested that Claes Gerritsz, the *Batavia*'s upper-steersman, was the author; this is quite probable, but there is no evidence [R 49, 61]. The second letter, dated 11 December 1629, is the work of someone who was originally on Seals' Island and later escaped to join Wiebbe Hayes. It, too, is anonymous, but it is fairly certainly the work of the assistant Cornelis Jansz [R 48].

Other Contemporary Sources

Background information on the main characters in the *Batavia*'s story has been drawn from the contemporary records of the Dutch Republic. All cities kept registers of baptisms, marriages, and deaths, and on the whole these still exist in either town or provincial archives. Where they do, it is usually possible to discover basic biographical information about local citizens, though in some cases – the baptismal records, which are Reformed Church documents and thus take no account of the birth of Catholics, Mennonites, and members of other religious minorities, are a case in point – the records can appear misleading.

Archives full of solicitors' papers also survive for many cities, and these often offer rich pickings for historians. Contemporary Dutchmen were so obsessed with upholding their personal honour (for reasons that are discussed later) that almost anyone with any property or money occasionally resorted to solicitors to make a record of some controversial incident for possible use in a future legal action. The legal records therefore provide odd snapshots of the lives of people whose personal histories would otherwise have been completely lost. The incidents they record are, by definition, hardly representative of their subjects' ordinary existence, but they were important nonetheless, and if the records' contents can be somewhat sensational, it is also often possible to deduce a good deal from casual asides.

Books

The first noteworthy book on the *Batavia* was Henrietta Drake-Brockman's *Voyage to Disaster,* published in Australia in 1963. Though it is chaotically organised, lacks any significant narrative, and is also poorly indexed, it does print a tremendous amount of original material, including – critically – the first full translation of Pelsaert's journals into English. Drake-Brockman also conducted a good deal of research into contemporary Dutch archives – a laborious business for someone living in Western Australia years before the introduction of the Internet and e-mail. It is impossible not to admire Drake-Brockman's results, and if the author discovered little about Cornelisz himself, she had great success in fleshing out the histories of Ariaen Jacobsz, Creesje Jans, and other major characters in the story. Forty years after its first publication, *Voyage to Disaster* remains an essential source book for all those interested in the *Batavia*.

More recently, a Haarlem scholar, Vibeke Roeper, reedited Pelsaert's journals for publication in the Netherlands by the Linschoten Society. Her scholarly edition, *De Schipbreuk van de* Batavia, usefully prints a number of documents from the VOC archives that escaped Drake-Brockman and her collaborators.

Hugh Edwards, who helped to discover the *Batavia*'s wreck site, wrote the first narrative history of the whole incident. His *Islands of Angry Ghosts* is particularly valuable for its firsthand accounts of the early excavation of the wreck and the grave pits on Beacon Island. More recently Philippe Godard has gone over much of the same ground in a privately published volume, *The First and Last Voyage of the* Batavia. It adds little that is new, but very usefully prints hundreds of colour photographs of the islands, the artifacts, and the documents in the case.

A Note on Citation

A large proportion of the existing primary source material on the *Batavia* has been published over the years – the first official documents by H. T. Colenbrander and W. Ph. Coolhaas, *JP Coen: Bescheiden Omtrent Zijn Bedrijf in Indië* (The Hague: Martinus Nijhoff, 7 vols., 1920–52), and the journals themselves, with extensive supporting material including Coolhaas's sources, by Roeper and Drake-Brockman. Most readers will find it easier to obtain one of these books than to visit archives in the Netherlands and so, in referring to the primary sources, I have also added references to the printed editions as appropriate. These appear in the notes as [R], for Roeper, and [DB], for Drake-Brockman, followed by the relevant page numbers. Drake-Brockman has been my main source simply because my mother tongue is English; as it is by 30 years the older of the two works, it seems worth noting that Marit van Huystee, a Dutch linguist working for the Western Australian Maritime Museum, gives it as her opinion that its translations, by E. D. Drok, are excellent in almost every respect.

Prologue: Morning Reef

The details of the *Batavia*'s last hours at sea and of the aftermath of the
wreck have been principally drawn from Pelsaert's own account, JFP 4–8
June 1629 [DB 122–8]. I have made a few minor conjectures, based on
standard Dutch nautical practice in this period – for which see Jaap
Bruijn, F. S. Gaastra, and I. Schöffer, *Dutch-Asiatic Shipping in the 17th and
18th Centuries* (The Hague: Martinus Nijhoff, 3 vols., 1979–1987) and C. R.
Boxer, 'The Dutch East Indiamen: Their Sailors, Navigators and Life on
Board, 1602–1795,' *The Mariner's Mirror* 49 (1963).

The Dutch watch system Boxer, 'The Dutch East Indiamen,' p. 93.

Ariaen Jacobsz It has not been possible to discover much information about the
skipper of the *Batavia*. Drake-Brockman, in *Voyage to Disaster,* pp. 61–3,
records the essential details of his career from 1616 onward. The surviving
records of his hometown, Durgerdam, are meagre. We know he was (or had
been) married, and that his wife was a Dutch woman – one of the *Batavia*'s
under-steersmen was his brother-in-law, according to JFP 19 Sep 1629 [DB
162] – but although the Durgerdam marital registers survive for this period,
no reference to the marriage of an Ariaen Jacobsz could be found.

Already been a servant Records of Jacobsz's service have not been traced back
before 1616, when he was promoted to the post of high boatswain; Drake-
Brockman, op. cit., p. 61. But this was a senior rank, and to reach it would
almost certainly have required up to 10 years' sea service, and quite possibly
much longer. Jacobsz's age is likewise unknown, but the records of his
service, together with comments that he made to Jeronimus Cornelisz at the
Cape (see chapter 4), imply he was significantly older than the upper-
merchant, Pelsaert – who was 34. He was probably in his mid-40s in 1629, and
it is not impossible that he was 50.

Jacobsz's culpability for the wreck Pelsaert's declaration to the Council of Justice,
Batavia, 20 July 1629, ARA VOC 1098, fol. 223r–224r [R 214]. There is no
reason to doubt Pelsaert's statement that Jacobsz ignored the lookout's warnings, since the skipper himself signed his declaration to confirm its truth.

Difficulty of identifying reefs in the dark It should not be assumed that Ariaen
Jacobsz and Hans Bosschieter were uniquely negligent in allowing the *Batavia*
to run aground. It was notoriously difficult to spot low-lying reefs by night,
and the records of the period contain many similar instances of ships coming
to grief after dark. The VOC ship *Zeewijk,* which was wrecked in the Southern
Abrolhos in 1727, was also lost because members of her crew made the same
mistake as Jacobsz: '... We asked the look-out, who had sat on the fore-yard, if
he had not seen the surf, and he answered that he had seen the same for even
half an hour before, but had imagined it was the reflection of the moon.' Louis
Zuiderbaan, 'Translation of a journal by an unknown person from the Dutch
East Indiaman *Zeewijk,* foundered on Half Moon Reef in the Southern
Abrolhos, on 9 June, 1727' (typescript, copy in Western Australian Maritime
Museum), entry for 9 June 1727. Similarly, the Spanish maritime historian

Pablo Pérez-Mallaína cites a virtually identical incident that occurred when the New Spain fleet of 1582 neared Veracruz one night: '[One] ship was commanded by an impulsive and imprudent master who wanted to be the first to enter Veracruz, but in the darkness he was surprised by a strange brightness, first attributed to the light of the dawn but which finally proved to be the deadly whiteness of a reef, against which the ship crashed and broke into pieces. "And because for half an hour [the master] saw the sea whitening, like to foam of waves breaking, he asked the sailors to be on guard ... and they all said it was the light of day."' Pérez-Mallaína, *Spain's Men of the Sea: Daily Life on the Indies Fleets in the Sixteenth Century* (Baltimore: Johns Hopkins University Press, 1998), p. 179.

Timing of the wreck Pelsaert, in JFP 4 June 1629 [DB 122], gives the time as 'about two hours before daybreak,' which, after making allowance for the time of year and prevailing local conditions, Drake-Brockman (op. cit., p. 122) put at about 4 A.M. I think it must have been slightly earlier, given that the watch would have changed at 4 and that it seems most unlikely Jacobsz would have stood the early morning watch.

'First a coral outcrop ...' Pelsaert's declaration, 20 July 1629 [R 212–4].

'Flung to the left ...' Excavation of the ship in the 1970s revealed that the *Batavia* had settled on her port (i.e., left-hand) side. The wreck was found in a shallow depression some 800 yards east of the southwest corner of Morning Reef at a spot where there is a noticeable drop of about six feet to the seabed at the stern. Hugh Edwards, *Islands of Angry Ghosts* (New York: William Morrow, 1966), pp. 134–5; Jeremy Green, *The Loss of the Verenigde Oostindische Compagnie Retourschip* Batavia, *Western Australia 1629: an Excavation Report and Catalogue of Artefacts* (Oxford: British Archaeological Reports, 1989), p. 5.

Another 270 people ... This figure assumes 50 of the *Batavia*'s 150 sailors were on watch. The ship had originally set sail with 332 people (List of those on board the *Batavia*, ARA VOC 1098, fol. 582r [R 220–1]), but 10 had died *en voyage* – rather a low total for the period, as will be seen.

Actions after the wreck JFP 4 June 1629 ⊕ 122–3). For the various dimensions of the *Batavia*, see Willem Vos, Batavia *Cahier 1: De Herbouw van een Oostindiëvaarder: Bestek en Beschrijving van een Retourschip* (Lelystad: np, 1990).

'What have you done ... ?' JFP 4 June 1629 [DB 123].

'The smallest of the Batavia's eight anchors' This anchor was eventually recovered by marine archaeologists from a position some distance from the wreck. A woodcut in OV shows a cable run out through one of the *Batavia*'s stern gunports. This ancient method of hauling a ship off rocks is still sometimes used today. It is known as 'kedging off.'

The sounding lead Dutch leads were about 18 inches long and cast with a hollow, bowl-shaped end. This would have been filled with sticky tallow, which would bring up traces of mud or sand where the bottom was soft. In unknown waters the lead was swung regularly from the bows and the results reported to the officer of the watch by loudly singing out the depth. For the details of the soundings, see Governor-General in Council, Batavia, 9 July 1629, in H. T. Colenbrander, *JP Coen: Bescheiden Omtrent zijn Bedrijf in Indië,* V, pp. 756–7 [DB 44].

'*Dutch East Indiamen were built strong...*' Boxer, 'The Dutch East-Indiamen,' p. 82.

View of the Abrolhos from the wreck site Hugh Edwards, 'Where Is Batavia's Graveyard?,' in Jeremy Green, Myra Stanbury, and Femme Gaastra (eds.), *The ANCODS Colloquium: Papers Presented at the Australia-Netherlands Colloquium on Maritime Archaeology and Maritime History* (Fremantle: Australian National Centre of Excellence for Maritime Archaeology, 1999), pp. 88–9.

'*The largest island*' This was East Wallabi (Pelsaert's 'High Island' in the journals), which, with a 50-foot hill as its highest point, is visible from considerably farther off than any other island in the Wallabi Group.

'*The great Yammer...*' JFP 4 June 1629 [DB 124].

'*There was no order to the evacuation...*' In truth, the men of the *Batavia* were no better and no worse than the other sailors of their day. In the 1620s – and indeed for the next 200 years – perhaps only 1 in every 7 people could swim, and it was rare indeed for the crew of any vessel to remain disciplined in the aftermath of a shipwreck. Skippers were much more likely to save themselves than they were to remain at their posts until the last of their men had been rescued. Sailors frequently commandeered the ship's boats for themselves and left their passengers to drown. There was no recognised emergency drill for the men to follow. The concept of 'women and children first' did not exist, and the very idea of carrying lifeboats sufficient to save all passengers and crew on a vessel the size of an East Indiaman was regarded as preposterous. See the numerous examples cited by Edward Leslie, *Desperate Journeys, Abandoned Souls: True Stories of Castaways and Other Survivors* (London: Papermac, 1991). For the contemporary Spanish view, see Pérez-Mallaína, op. cit., pp. 214–5.

Death of a dozen people by drowning Pelsaert's declaration, 20 July 1629, ARA VOC 1098, fol. 223r–224r [R 212–4].

Food and water from the wreck JFP 4 June 1629 [DB 124–5]. There was much more food than water – 66 gallons of bread (the Dutch measured their food supplies by volume) to 17 ¼ gallons of water, according to Pelsaert's journal (ibid.) and his declaration on arrival at Batavia.

Value of the jewels taken from the wreck The total was first calculated, with an exactness entirely typical of the VOC, at 20,419 guilders and 15 stuivers. (There were 20 stuivers in one guilder.) This figure was later revised upward to 58,000 guilders, for reasons that are not clear (see chapter 5). Antonio van Diemen to Pieter de Carpentier, 30 November–10 December 1629, ARA 1009 [DB 42, 49].

'*It won't help at all...*' JFP 4 June 1629 [DB 124].

Indiscipline below Interrogation of Allert Janssen, JFP 19 Sep 1629 [DB 194–6]; interrogation of Lenert Michielsz Van Os, JFP 23 Sep 1629 [DB 185–6]; interrogation of Mattys Beer, ibid. [DB 189]; verdict on Cornelis Janssen, JFP 30 Nov 1629 [DB 242]; verdict on Jean Thirion, ibid. [DB 243].

Further actions after the wreck JFP 5–8 June 1629 [DB 125–8].

Houtman's Abrolhos J. A. Heeres, *The Part Borne by the Dutch in the Discovery of Australia 1606–1765* (London: Luzac, 1899), pp. 14–8; Günter Schilder, *Australia*

Unveiled: The Share of Dutch Navigators in the Discovery of Australia (Amsterdam: Theatrum Orbis Terrarum, 1976), pp. 75–6.

Naming Batavia's Graveyard Green, Stanbury, and Gaastra, op. cit., p. 99.

'It was better and more honest...' JFP 5 June 1629 [DB 125–6].

Chapter 1: The Heretic

The full history of Jeronimus Cornelisz has never been written before and has had to be pieced together from fragmentary references in surviving Dutch archives – in particular the Old Solicitors' Archive, Haarlem, and the Municipal Archive, Leeuwarden. The most useful general study of Dutch Anabaptism is still Cornelis Krahn, *Dutch Anabaptism: Origin, Spread, Life and Thought, 1450–1600* (The Hague: Martinus Nijhoff, 1968), but James Stayer's *Anabaptists and the Sword* (Lawrence, KA: Coronado Press, 1976) deals specifically with the Anabaptists' attitudes to violence and relations with the state. For details of the Torrentian scandal, I have relied on Govert Snoek's unpublished Ph.D. thesis, *De Rosenkruizers in Nederland: Voornamelijk in de Eerste Helft van de 17de Eeuw. Een Inventarisatie,* and the biographies of A. Bredius, *Johannes Torrentius* (The Hague: Martinus Nijhoff, 1909) and A. J. Rehorst, *Torrentius* (Rotterdam: WL & J Brusse NV, 1939). On the peculiar story of the Rosicrucian order and their supposed beliefs, I turned to Snoek and to Christopher McIntosh, *The Rosy Cross Unveiled: The History, Mythology and Rituals of an Occult Order* (Wellingborough: The Aquarian Press, 1980), and on the social structure of Haarlem in the 1620s to the work of Gabrielle Dorren, particularly 'Communities Within the Community: Aspects of Neighbourhood in Seventeenth Century Haarlem,' *Urban History* 25 (1998). No history of medicine in the Netherlands is as detailed as Brockliss and Jones's recent *The Medical World of Early Modern France* (Oxford: Clarendon Press, 1997), and I have used this work, with some caution, as a guide to the equivalent 'world' of the Dutch Republic.

Life expectancy in the Indies Jaap Bruijn, F. S. Gaastra, and I. Schöffer *Dutch-Asiatic Shipping in the 17th and 18th Centuries* (The Hague: Martinus Nijhoff, 3 vols., 1979–1987), I, 170; Giles Milton, *Nathaniel's Nutmeg: How One Man's Courage Changed the Course of History* (London: Hodder & Stoughton, 1999), p. 242.

'A great refuge...' Quoted in Bruijn et al., *Dutch-Asiatic Shipping,* I, 151. The VOC's soldiers were 'louts from the depths of Germany,' it was commented, and according to a saying current in the Holy Roman Empire at the time, 'Even a man who has beaten his father and mother to death is too good to go to the East Indies.' C. R. Boxer, *The Dutch Seaborne Empire 1600–1800* (London: Hutchinson, 1965), p. 135; R. van Gelder, *Het Oost-Indisch Avontuur: Duitsers in Dienst van de VOC, 1600–1800* (Nijmegen: SUN, 1997), p. 149.

'Cornelisz came originally from Friesland...' Earlier authorities have generally been content to label Jeronimus a Haarlemmer, assuming he was born in the

town where he lived immediately prior to joining the *Batavia*. However, one passing contemporary reference does describe him as a Frisian (anonymous *Batavia* survivor's letter, printed in Anon., *Leyds Veer-Schuyts Praetjen, Tuschen een Koopman ende Borger van Leyden, Varende van Haarlem nae Leyden* (np [Amsterdam: Willem Jansz], 1630) [R 236]. This suggestion appears to be confirmed by the extensive Frisian links uncovered in the course of research for this chapter.

Distinctness of Friesland P. H. Breuker and A. Janse (eds.), *Negen Eeuwen Friesland-Holland: Geschiedenis van een Haat-Liefdeverhouding* (Zutphen: Walburg Pers, 1997), pp. 15–17, 20, 30–1, 42–3, 120–1.

Cornelisz's possible origins in Leeuwarden or Bergum Jeronimus was one of the heirs of Griete Douwes, a widow who died in Bergum, and was possibly apprenticed to a Leeuwarden apothecary named Gerrit Evertsz, as will be seen. See ONAH 129, fol. 63 and below. Griete Douwes's son, Sijbrant, who was with Jeronimus co-heir to her fortune, also seems to have had some involvement with the local apothecaries; see RAF HTI 89, fol. 83v. It seems likely that Cornelisz and his family were somehow related to the Douwes family, either as business partners or through marriage. The marital records of Bergum are unfortunately absent for the period 1618–1674, and Cornelisz, possibly for reasons that will be discussed, does not make an appearance in the baptismal registers of the town. Nor does he appear in Leeuwarden's *Burgerboek* (citizen book) or the marital registers of that city. It is, in short, impossible to say with any certainty that he came from this area of Frisia – merely that his relationship with Griete Douwes and Gerrit Evertsz suggests it. On the population of Leeuwarden at this time, see Jonathan Israel, *The Dutch Republic: Its Rise, Greatness and Fall, 1477–1806* (Oxford: Oxford University Press, 1998), p. 332.

Elementary schools Ibid., pp. 686–90.

Latin schools Ibid., pp. 43–5. Jeronimus must surely have attended one of these establishments, since a good knowledge of Latin was one of the main prerequisites of a career as an apothecary.

Wealth of London apothecaries Harold Cook, *The Decline of the Old Medical Regime in Stuart London* (Ithaca, NY: Cornell University Press, 1986), pp. 48–9.

Diseases and the intercessory saints Brockliss and Jones, *The Medical World of Early Modern France,* pp. 44, 74–5. For St. Fiacre, see *The Catholic Encyclopaedia,* vol. 6 (New York: Robert Appleton Company, 1909).

The Dutch guild system Paul Zumthor, *Daily Life in Rembrandt's Holland* (London: Weidenfeld & Nicholson, 1962), pp. 141–3.

Gerrit Evertsz For his dates and occupation, see CLE I, fol. 2; CLE II fol. 297, 441; HLE 23, fol. 233. For his status, see ALE 1611–1624, fol. 206, 270, 280, 437, 540, 719. All in GAL. For his appointment as Cornelisz's agent in Friesland, see ONAH 129, fol. 63. Cornelisz was disputing the actions of Sijbrant Douwes, who had apparently sold his mother's lands in Bergum to a certain Goossen Oebes of Lutgegeest without the approval of his co-heir.

Cornelisz's apprenticeship Apothecaries in Haarlem served apprenticeships of three years and were not permitted to become masters before the age of 25 – at least according to the regulations of 1692, which are the earliest to have survived. See D. A. Wittop Koning, *Compendium voor de Geschiedenis van de Pharmacie van Nederland* (Lochem: De Tijdstroom, 1986), p. 131. Cornelisz would have been 25 in 1623–24.

The medical trinity in early modern Europe Brockliss and Jones, *The Medical World of Early Modern France,* esp. pp. 9–10, 164–5, 175, 188–9, 191. The great majority of what Brockliss and Jones say applies equally to the situation in the Netherlands.

The scarcity of physicians Haarlem, in 1628, had nine doctors for a population of 40,000 people. A. T. van Deursen, *Plain Lives in a Golden Age: Popular Culture, Religion and Society in Seventeenth Century Holland* (Cambridge: Cambridge University Press, 1991), p. 237.

Ingredients of potions See Brockliss and Jones, *The Medical World of Early Modern France,* pp. 160–2; Cook, *The Decline of the Old Medical Regime in Stuart London,* p. 134; Sarah Bakewell, 'Cooking with Mummy,' *Fortean Times* 124 (July 1999): 34–8. The whole notion that real 'mummy' was made of human flesh was, incidentally, a mistake. The original 'mummy' was a black, bituminous substance called *mumia,* which was thought to have healing properties and was popular in ancient Persia. The Greeks thought it was used by the Egyptians for embalming and slowly, over the centuries, the original meaning of the word was forgotten. Embalmed Egyptian bodies became known as 'mummies' and were associated with the alleged healing properties of *mumia.*

Theriac Gilbert Watson, *Theriac and Mithridatium: A Study in Therapeutics* (London: The Wellcome Historical Medical Library, 1966), pp. 4–5, 98, 102–4; Charles LeWall, *Four Thousand Years of Pharmacy: An Outline History of Pharmacy and the Allied Sciences* (Philadelphia: JB Lippincott, 1927), pp. 215–8; Brockliss and Jones, *The Medical World of Early Modern France,* p. 160. Analysis of surviving recipes suggest that theriac would have possessed mild antiseptic qualities, thanks to its balsemic ingredients, which may account for its great popularity.

John Evelyn, the noted diarist, records witnessing the preparation of Venice treacle in 1646. The medicine, he wrote, was mixed annually in an event that had 'all the character of a great proprietary ceremony and public festival. All the public squares and the courtyards of hospitals and monasteries in Venice were transformed for the occasion into great open-air theatres, adorned with rich damasks, with busts of Hippocrates and Galen, and with the great majolica jars destined to receive the precious medicament. Grave and important personages, sumptuously robed, moved to the applause of the crowds in an atmosphere of rejoicing and expectation.

'In some cities the preparation was preceded by exhibiting the ingredients to the public for three consecutive days so that anybody could examine them. On the fourth day the actual making of the theriac was preceded by a benediction given by the highest ecclesiastical authority and by a panegyric delivered by the leading physician of the city. Only the leading pharmacists, who were vested with the office of *Triacanti* (theriac-makers), were allowed to make the theriac, and always under the eye of the chief physicians.'

Sale of groceries and poisons Wittop Koning, *Compendium voor de Geschiedenis van de Pharmacie van Nederland,* pp. 90, 172, 206.

296 · BATAVIA'S GRAVEYARD

Haarlem S. Groenveld, E. K. Grootes, J. J. Temminick et al., *Deugd Boven Geweld. Een Geschiedenis van Haarlem 1245–1995* (Hilversum: Verloren 1995), pp. 144, 172–4, 177.

Cornelisz's house on the Grote Houtstraat ONAH 130, fol. 219v. For gapers, see Witlop Koning, *Compendium voor de Geschiedenis van de Pharmacie van Nederland,* pp. 97–8. Cornelisz does not appear among contemporary lists of Haarlem property owners, hence the supposition that the building was rented.

Cornelisz's popularity His neighbours were prepared to testify to his character and honesty before solicitors, which, as we will see, was certainly not true for every citizen of Haarlem.

Cornelisz's citizenship of Haarlem ONAH 129, fol. 78v. The Haarlem *poorterboecken,* which would have contained additional details concerning Jeronimus's life in the city, have not survived.

Belijtgen Jacobsdr, her pregnancy, her illness, and her maidservant Ibid.; ONAH 99, fol. 131 ONAH 130, fol. 159, 198. For her age, see ONAH 130, fol. 219v, where she is obliquely referred to as a 'young mother'; this would hardly have applied in this period had she been Cornelisz's age, 29 or 30. For the appearance of Dutch women, see Van Deursen, op. cit., pp. 81–2. For the contemporary incidence of death in childbirth, see Brockliss and Jones, op. cit., p. 62.

Cathalijntgen van Wijmen ONAH 131, fol. 12. The remains of the afterbirth were finally removed by a 'wise woman' who was the mother of Belijtgen's maidservant five days after the birth. ONAH 99, fol. 134v.

Belijtgen as an assistant in the apothecary shop See ONAH 130, fol. 159, where Jacobsdr is described as sitting in the shop on 28 April 1628.

Breast-feeding in the Dutch Republic Simon Schama, *The Embarrassment of Riches: An Interpretation of Dutch Culture in the Golden Age* (London: Fontana, 1991), pp. 538–40.

Burial of Cornelisz's son GAH, burial registers 70, fol. 83v.

Syphilis in infants Congenital syphilis is a well-recognised condition that affects about 70 percent of children whose mothers are infected with the disease and have not been treated. *T. pallidum,* the bacterium that causes the condition, infects the foetus through the placenta and the child is born with syphilis. The symptoms may not be visible at first and may take up to five weeks to manifest themselves. Early indications of the disease include bloody snuffles in the first weeks of the baby's life, the appearance of a syphilitic rash after one to two weeks, and fissures on the lips and anus.

It was once thought that diseased wet nurses could infect their charges with syphilis through their milk; indeed Ludwig II, the notorious 'Mad King of Bavaria,' was popularly supposed to have been given syphilis by his nurse. This method of transmission is now thought to be a myth. Nevertheless, medical literature acknowledges the possibility that a very young infant may be infected with the disease by a third party shortly after birth. Transmission is by contact with open sores on the infected person's body. Luger studied the case of three syphilitic infants reported from Vienna in 1968. His findings were that the disease could not have been transmitted venereally but was probably the product of crowded conditions and insanitary housing.

Eisenberg et al. had already reported 20 similar cases of asexually acquired syphilis from Chicago. H. Eisenberg, F. Plotke, and A. Baker, 'Asexual Syphilis in Children,' *Journal of Venereal Diseases Information* 30 (1949): 7–11; A. Luger, 'Non-Venereally Tranmsitted "Endemic" Syphilis in Vienna,' *British Journal of Venereal Diseases* 48 (1972): 356–60; K. Rathblum, 'Congenital Syphilis,' *Sexually Transmitted Diseases* 10 (1983): 93–9.

'... *this was a very serious concern.'* Not only was it the case that in the Dutch Republic at this time, women infected with venereal diseases by their husbands were considered to have grounds for separation (Schama, op. cit., p. 406); in Haarlem, in the 1620s, it was difficult to survive at all without the goodwill and respect of one's neighbours.

Like many other cities in the United Provinces, Haarlem was a town full of strangers. The population had grown by a third since 1600, swollen by refugees who had fled from the Southern Netherlands during the war with Spain. Others, including Jeronimus and perhaps his wife, had arrived from other parts of the Republic, bringing with them a variety of religious views, social mores, and degrees of wealth. For the 10,000 immigrants who had moved to the city, most of who had no family or friends to whom they could turn in times of trouble, it was particularly important to be able to rely on assistance from the *gebuurte,* or neighbourhood.

Haarlem recognised almost 100 such neighbourhoods, and the Grote Houtstraat, where Cornelisz lived, contained no fewer than five. Honour mattered greatly in these miniature societies. Without it, it was impossible to obtain credit, and – since the presence of disreputable people brought discredit on their neighbors – any loss of honour was a matter of concern for the whole *gebuurte.* It is only in this context that the frantic efforts that Jeronimus and Belijtgen made to clear themselves of the suspicion that they were infected with syphilis can be properly understood. See Gabrielle Dorren, 'Burgers en Hun Besognes. Burgemeestersmemorialen en Hun Bruikbaarheid als Bron voor Zeventiende-Eeuws Haarlem,' *Jaarboeck Haarlem* (1995): 58; idem, *Het Soet Vergaren: Haarlems Buurtleven in de Zeventiende Eeuw* (Haarlem: Arcadia, 1998), pp. 12–3, 16, 22–3, 27–9; idem, 'Communities Within the Community,' pp. 178, 180–3.

Economic conditions in the Dutch Republic in the 1620s Israel, op. cit., pp. 478–9.

The disgrace of bankruptcy Schama, op. cit., pp. 343–4; Geoffrey Cotterell, *Amsterdam: The Life of a City* (Farnborough: DC Heath, 1973), p. 118.

Loth Vogel ONAH 99, fol. 159v. There is no surviving record of any person of this name in the Haarlem birth, marriage, or burial registers. However, the historian Gabrielle Dorren notes the existence of an Otto Vogel, an extremely wealthy corn merchant from Amsterdam who settled in Haarlem in the hope of improving the health of his sickly wife. This Vogel was in Haarlem by 1604 and resisted several efforts by local dignitaries to force him to become a full citizen of his adopted town. Eventually, Vogel became so irritated by this pressure that he threatened to leave the town, taking with him his – unnamed – brother. It seems possible that this brother may have been Cornelisz's Loth. 'De Eerzamen. Zeventiende-Eeuws Burgerschap in Haarlem,' in R. Aerts and

H. te Velde (eds.), *De Stijl van de Burger: Over Nederlandse Burgerlijke Cultuur vanaf de Middeleeuwen* (Kampen: Kok Agora, 1998), p. 70.

The case against Heyltgen For the condition of Belijtgen, see the testimony of Gooltgen Joostdr, 3 May 1628 (ONAH 130, fol. 159); Aeffge Jansdr, Ytgen Hendricxdr, Grietgen Dircksdr, and Wijntge Abrahamsdr, 18 June 1628 (ONAH 130, fol. 198); Maicke Pietersdr van den Broecke, 6 July 1628 (ONAH 130, fol. 219); Willem Willemsz Brouwerius (Cornelisz's physician), 8 August 1628 (ONAH 99, fol. 131); Aeltgen Govertsdr, 9 August (ONAH 99, fol. 134); and Aecht Jansdr and Ytgen Henricxdr, 11 August 1628 (ONAH 99, fol. 134v). For Heyltgen, see the testimony of Jannitge Pietersdr, Willem Willemsz, Grietgen Woutersdr, Hester Ghijsbertsdr, Jannitgen Joostsdr, and Elsken Adamsdr, 27 July 1628 (ONAH 60, fol. 99); Elsken Adamsdr, 11 August 1628 (ONAH 99, fol. 135v).

Aert Dircxsz ONAH 60, fol. 99. Asked by one Cornelia Jansdr who Dircxsz was, Heyltgen is alleged to have replied: 'A dirty whore hunter.' In the context of the dispute, this might well be taken to suggest that her former lover carried a venereal disease.

Heyltgen's response ONAH 99, fol. 131; ONAH 130, fol. 159.

'She twisted the scanty evidence' Aeltgen Govertsdr, who had given a statement to the solicitor Sonnebijl at the wet nurse's request, later disputed the accuracy of the deposition he produced in her name. She had, she said, protested at the time, to which Sonnebijl's wife, who was also present, had rejoined: 'Well, woman, one cannot write perfectly – do you think my husband hasn't got a soul to lose?' ONAH 99, fol. 134. Unfortunately the Sonnebijl archive has not survived, denying us Heyltgen's side of this long-running dispute.

Heyltgen's reappearance in the Grote Houtstraat ONAH 130, fol. 159.

Cornelisz comes to terms with Vogel ONAH 99, fol. 159. The solicitor on this occasion was Willem van Triere.

Cornelisz as an Anabaptist There is no definite proof of Jeronimus's Anabaptist antecedents, though V. D. Roeper (ed.), *De Schipbreuk van de* Batavia, *1629* (Zutphen: Walburg Pers, 1994), p. 14, and Philip Tyler, 'The *Batavia* Mutineers: Evidence of an Anabaptist "Fifth Column" Within 17th Century Dutch Colonialism?' *Westerly* (December 1970): 33–45 have previously speculated that he had a background in the Mennonite community. The fact that he appears to have been unbaptised (for which see JFP 28 Sep 1629 [DB 211]; there is also no trace of any baptism in the surviving records of Leeuwarden, Bergum, or Haarlem) is obviously suggestive. Perhaps more significantly, the Haarlem archives indicate that his wife, Belijtgen, was herself an Anabaptist (in ONAH 130, fol. 159 Heyltgen Jansdr describes her, among other insults, as 'a Mennonite whore'). Definite proof is unlikely ever to emerge; the records of the Haarlem Mennonites go back no further than the second half of the seventeenth century. But I am inclined to feel that there is an excellent chance Cornelisz came from Anabaptist stock.

Anabaptist numbers in Leeuwarden Israel, op. cit., p. 656.

Religious toleration and persecution Ibid. pp. 372–83.

Anabaptist origins and views William Estep, *The Anabaptist Story: An Introduction to*

Sixteenth-Century Anabaptism (Grand Rapids, MI: William B. Eerdmans, 1996), pp. xi, 14–28, 171; Stayer, *Anabaptists and the Sword,* p. 290; Norman Cohn, *The Pursuit of the Millennium: Revolutionary Millenarians and Mystical Anarchists of the Middle Ages* (Oxford: Oxford University Press, 1970), p. 253; Israel, op. cit. pp. 84–95, 656; Van Deursen, *Plain Lives in a Golden Age,* pp. 307, 311.

Anabaptist millenarianism and the siege of Münster Krahn, *Dutch Anabaptism,* pp. 114–5, 120–4, 130, 135–50; Stayer, op. cit., pp. 191–3, 227–80; Cohn, op. cit., pp. 259–61.

Anabaptist revolutionaries in Amsterdam and Friesland Krahn, op. cit., pp. 148, 154; Israel, op. cit. pp. 92–6, 655–6.

The emergence of the Mennonites Israel, op. cit., pp. 85–90.

The Batenburgers and their successors Jan van Batenburg was born around 1495, and became mayor of a town in Overijssel. During the early 1530s, he converted to Anabaptism and found himself the leader of a large number of his coreligionists in Friesland and Groningen. He had Münsterite sympathies, but in 1535 one group of his followers urged him to announce himself as 'a new David' and before long he had established a new and wholly independent sect, which quickly became the most extreme of all the early Anabaptist movements.

The Batenburgers believed that every man and everything on earth was owned, in a literal sense, by God. They also believed that they were God's chosen children. It followed, in their theology, that everything on earth was theirs to do with what they pleased; indeed, killing 'infidel,' by which they meant any man who was not a member of their sect, was pleasing to their God. Those who joined the sect after 1535 – when the Münsterite leadership had declared the door to salvation to be closed – could never be baptised, they thought, but these men and women would nevertheless survive the coming apocalypse and be reborn in the coming Kingdom of God as servants of the Anabaptist elite. The Batenburgers also shared the views of the radical Münsterites on polygamy and property; all women, and all goods, were held in common. A few Batenburger marriages did occur, and Van Batenburg himself retained the right to present a deserving member of his sect with a 'wife' from the group's general stock of women. However, such unions could be ended just as readily, and on occasion the prophet did order an unwilling wife to return to servicing the remainder of the Batenburger men.

Van Batenburg seems to have commanded the loyalty of at least several hundred men. Members of his sect were required to swear oaths of absolute secrecy, however, and had to endure a painful initiation designed to ensure they would be able to resist torture if they were ever captured, so the true extent of his following never emerged. The Batenburgers did not gather openly in public and had their leader's dispensation to pose as ordinary Lutherans or Catholics, going to church and living apparently normal lives in the lands along the borders of the Holy Roman Empire and The Netherlands for several years after the fall of Münster. They recognised one another by secret symbols displayed on their houses or their clothing, and by certain ways of styling their hair. It was only after Van Batenburg himself was captured and burned at the stake that they came together at last, infesting the Imperial marches for at least another decade under the leadership of a Leyden weaver called Cornelis Appelman. By now the group had been reduced to a core of no more than 200 men, most of whom were joined by bonds of family or marriage.

Appelman remained active until his own capture in 1545. He was if anything more extreme than Van Batenburg, giving himself the title of 'The Judge' and killing any of his followers who refused to join his criminal activities, or proved themselves lax in killing, robbing or committing arson. Like Van Batenburg, he preached and practised polygamy, with the additional refinement that the women of his sect could leave their husbands at any time should they decide to marry a man further up the Batenburger hierarchy. Appelman himself murdered his own wife when she refused him leave to marry her daughter, and subsequently killed the girl as well.

After the Judge's death, the Batenburger sect fragmented into several tiny groups, one of which, the Children of Emlichheim, was active in the middle 1550s. Its sole creed appears to have been revenge against the infidel; on one notorious occasion its members stabbed to death 125 cows that belonged to a local monastery. The last of the Batenburger splinter groups, and also the largest, was the 'Folk of Johan Willemsz.' This sect persisted until about 1580, living by robbery and murder in the countryside around Wesel, on the Dutch-German border. It was when Willemsz himself was burned at the stake that the remnants of the group found their way to Friesland. L. G. Jansma, *Melchiorieten, Münstersen en Batenburgers: een Sociologische Analyse van een Millenistische Beweging uit de 16e Eeuw* (Buitenpost: np, 1977), pp. 217–35, 237, 244–75; Jansma, 'Revolutionairee Wederdopers na 1535' in MG Buist et al. (eds.), *Historisch Bewogen. Opstellen over de radicale reformatie in de 16e en 17e eeuw* (Groningen: Wolters-Noordhoff, 1984), pp. 51–3; S. Zijlstra, 'David Joris en de Doperse Stromingen (1536–1539)', in ibid., pp. 130–1, 138; M. E. H. N. Mout, 'Spiritualisten in de Nederlandse reformatie van de Zestiende Eeuw,' *Bijdragen en Mededelingen Betreffende de Geschiedenis der Nederlanden* 111 (1996): 297–313.

Giraldo Thibault's fencing club Govert Snoek, *De Rosenkruizers in Nederland: Voornamelijk in de Eerste Helft van de 17de Eeuw. Een Inventarisatie* (unpublished Ph.D. thesis, University of Utrecht, 1997), pp. 164–73. The Amsterdam club shut down in 1615, when Thibault moved temporarily to Cleves, so Cornelisz could not have attended it himself. However, Thibault returned to the Dutch Republic in 1617 and apparently settled in Leyden, where he died in 1626. It is possible, though there is certainly no proof, that Jeronimus could have met the fencing master there; in any case, the point is that he may well have attended some intellectual salon run along similar lines.

Guillelmo Bartolotti Israel, op. cit., pp. 345, 347–8.

Cornelisz and Torrentius Cornelisz's association with Torrentius was taken for granted in the *Batavia* journals, which occasionally refer to him as a 'Torrentian.' For a discussion of this point, see epilogue.

The extent of the Torrentian circle Snoek, op. cit., pp. 78–9.

Schoudt and Lenaertsz Ibid., pp. 89–90, 91, 94; ONAH 99, fol. 159; Bredius, *Torrentius,* p. 42. Lenaertsz witnessed the legal document that Cornelisz had drawn up to transfer all his worldly goods to Loth Vogel, a matter so humiliating that he would surely have called on only a close friend to countersign it.

'... apothecaries sold the paints...' Roeper, op. cit. p. 14.

'Disciple' Antonio van Diemen to Pieter de Carpentier, 30 November–10 December 1629, ARA VOC 1009, cited in Henrietta Drake-Brockman, *Voyage to Disaster* (Nedlands: University of Western Australia Press, 1995), p. 50. It should be admitted here that there remains no direct evidence that the two men were acquainted, and Jeronimus's name does not appear in the process file concerning Torrentius's eventual arrest and trial. Nevertheless, in a town with an elite the size of Haarlem's – perhaps 1,000 men – it would actually be remarkable if two men of such distinct views were not known to one another.

Torrentius Bredius, *Johannes Torrentius,* pp. 1–3, 12, 22–6, 29–31, 34–5, 45–6, 49, 58; Rehorst, *Torrentius,* pp. 11–4, 15–6, 78–80; Zbigniew Herbert, *Still Life with a Bridle* (London: Jonathan Cape, 1993), pp. 82–100; Snoek, pp. 60, 67–8, 71, 80–3, 87, 90, 101, 171. He was born in Amsterdam in 1589. Torrentius's father is famous for having been the first inmate of Amsterdam's new prison; his mother, Symontgen Lucasdr, remained loyal to him throughout his imprisonment and exile and survived him.

According to testimony collected by the painter's irate father-in-law, Torrentius was well able to pay for his wife's upkeep but chose not to. He always dressed in silk, velvet, and satin and owned a horse or two. On one occasion he offered to take Cornelia back, but only, he said, so that he could 'feed her one day and hit her three days.'

Van Swieten Bredius, op. cit., p. 25.

Epicurus One of the principal philosophers of the Hellenistic period, Epicurus (ca. 341 B.C.–ca. 270 B.C.) was a materialist who taught that the basic constituents of the universe are indivisible atoms, explained natural phenomena without resorting to mysticism, and rejected the existence of the soul. As a corollary, he believed the main point of life was pleasure. Epicurus himself was no hedonist, believing instead that true happiness stemmed from control of one's desires and in overcoming fear of death. His followers, however, soon acquired a reputation for debauchery, and his views were naturally anathema to the Calvinist ministers of Holland.

Torrentius's Gnostic views Snoek, op. cit., pp. 80–2.

Jeronimus's philosophy JFP 28 Sep 1629 [DB 153]; verdict on Andries Jonas, JFP 28 Sep 1629 [DB 203]; verdict on Jan Pelgrom, JFP 28 Sep 1629 [DB 209]; JFP 30 Sep 1629 [DB 212].

Antinomianism, the Free Spirit and the Libertines Cohn, *The Pursuit of the Millennium,* pp. 149–51, 156, 166–7, 170, 172–3, 178, 182–4, 287, 301.

'... a state where conscience ceased to operate...' Ibid., pp. 148, 151, 178.

Descartes McIntosh, *The Rosy Cross Unveiled,* p. 71. The philosopher was then a resident of Amsterdam.

Rubens Snoek, op cit., p. 142.

Rosicrucian cells The suggestion that the Rosicrucians were active in Paris appeared in books and posters distributed throughout the French capital in 1623. Ibid., pp. 61–2, 108. Reports in several books that there were Rosicrucian cells in The Hague and Amsterdam appear to be the product of a nineteenth-century hoax. Ibid., pp. 182–4; McIntosh, op. cit., p. 69.

The Rosicrucian debate in the United Provinces Snoek, op. cit., pp. 62–3, 103–8; Herbert, op. cit., p. 86.

Investigation of the Rosicrucians Snoek, op. cit., pp. 62–4; Bredius, op. cit. pp. 17–18.

'... *the Calvinist authorities were anxious to convict* ...' Bredius suggests the trial of Torrentius was staged to stress the orthodoxy of Haarlem's ruling elite and bolster the city's case to be considered the leader of the strictly Calvinist cities of the province of Holland at a time when several of its neighbours were still indulging liberal, Arminian views. Op. cit., p. 28.

The banishment of the Torrentian circle Snoek, op. cit., pp. 79–80. The coincidence of dates is not exact; Torrentius's followers were supposed to leave the city no later than 19 September, but Jeronimus Cornelisz may have lingered longer than that, and certainly either remained in, or returned to, Haarlem as late as 9 October, when the city records show he visited one of his solicitors.

Chapter 2: Gentlemen XVII

The story of the Dutch East India Company is of considerable importance to both the Netherlands and many of the nations of the Far East, and it has been extensively documented and well studied. Statistical information concerning the VOC's shipping and its voyages to the East is summarised and elaborated upon, in English, in the three volumes of Jaap Bruijn et al., *Dutch-Asiatic Shipping in the 17th and 18th Centuries* (The Hague: Martinus Nijhoff, 1979–1987). Dutch speakers will turn also to Femme Gaastra's general study *De Geschiedenis van de VOC* (Zutphen: Walburg Pers, 1991), which is more complete and up-to-date than any English language equivalent. Kristoff Glamann's earlier *Dutch-Asiatic Trade 1620–1740* (Copenhagen: Danish Science Press, 1958), though now in many respects outdated, also remains of interest. For details of the construction of Dutch East Indiamen, see Willem Vos's and Robert Parthesius's five-volume series, the Batavia *Cahiers* (Lelystad: np, 1990–93), which fully documents Vos's recent reconstruction of a full-sized *retourschip* of the *Batavia*'s time. This valuable and extremely practical project has resulted in the rediscovery of many early shipbuilding techniques, and the *Cahiers* deal with many questions that would otherwise have to remain unanswered, given the absence of relevant documentation from the period. On the life of Francisco Pelsaert, I have relied largely on the introductory section to D. H. A. Kolff's and H. W. van Santen's recent edition of the *commandeur*'s Mogul chronicle and *remonstrantie*, published as *De Geschriften van Francisco Pelsaert over Mughal Indië, 1627: Kroniek en Remonstrantie* (The Hague: Martinus Nijhoff, 1979).

The growth of Amsterdam Jonathan Israel, *The Dutch Republic: Its Rise, Greatness and Fall, 1477–1806* (Oxford: Oxford University Press 1998), pp. 114–6, 328–32; Geoffrey Cotterell, *Amsterdam: The Life of a City* (Farnborough: DC Heath, 1973), pp. 18–24. Another problem was the boggy ground, which meant that each new house within the city walls could only be constructed on foundations made of 42-foot wooden piles, each of which had to be driven to the bottom of the marsh by hand. A huge number of piles were required; the royal palace on the Dam itself rests on 13,659 of them. See William Brereton, *Travels in Holland, the United Provinces etc...1634–1635* (London: Chetham Society, 1844), p. 66. The inaccessibility of Amsterdam explains why, for all its enormous commercial success in the seventeenth and eighteenth centuries, Rotterdam is now the principal Dutch port.

Development of Dutch trade Jonathan Israel, *Dutch Primacy in World Trade, 1585–1740* (Oxford: Clarendon Press, 1989), pp. 6–17, 45–8. There were other factors, the most important of which may have been the protracted blockade of Antwerp instituted by the United Provinces in the 1570s. Dutch warships intercepted shipping all along the coast and halted river traffic to the city. After 1584 the main land approaches also fell into rebel hands, reducing the city's trade enormously and contributing to the further growth of Amsterdam.

The spice road Bruijn et al., *Dutch-Asiatic Shipping,* I, pp. 2, 189–92; Bernard Vlekke, *The Story of the Dutch East Indies* (Cambridge, MA: Harvard University Press, 1946), pp. 57–62; Glamann, op. cit., pp. 13, 16–17, 74–5; Giles Milton, *Nathaniel's Nutmeg: How One Man's Courage Changed the Course of History* (London: Hodder & Stoughton, 1999), pp. 3–4.

Population of cities London, with a population of about 230,000, Paris, with approximately 300,000, and Madrid, whose population was somewhere in between, were considerably bigger; Paris was comfortably the largest city in Europe throughout the seventeenth century. The only other European cities with a population comparable to Amsterdam were Lyons, Naples, and Rome. Antwerp's population halved as a result of the Revolt, and a large proportion of the 40,000 or so people who left the city made for the towns of the United Provinces. The Dutch Republic was in fact by far the most heavily urbanised country in Europe in Cornelisz's time; by 1600, one Dutchman in four lived in a town with more than 10,000 inhabitants, while the comparable figure in England was only 1 in 10. Israel, *The Dutch Republic,* pp. 115, 219.

Spain and Portugal in the East Determining exactly where the boundary between Spanish and Portuguese interests fell on the far side of the world was no easy matter in an age where there was no reliable way of measuring longitude while at sea. There were several disputes between the powers before the Spanish king sold his claim to the Spiceries to Portugal for the sum of 350,000 ducats in 1529. For Francis Xavier's views, see Vlekke, op cit., p. 62.

Jan Huyghen van Linschoten Throughout his stay in the Indies, Van Linschoten, who had a lively and curious mind, had made it his business to gather information about Portugal's colonies in the East. He appears to have come across the rutters during his sojourn in the Azores. Charles Parr, *Jan van Linschoten: The Dutch Marco Polo* (New York: Thomas Y. Cromwell, 1964), pp. xvi–xvii, 6,

19, 33, 45–8, 80, 176, 180, 189. It was, incidentally, on Van Linschoten's recommendation that the Dutch concentrated their efforts on the island of Java, where there were no Portuguese trading posts.

Reinier Pauw Israel, *The Dutch Republic,* pp. 344–8. Later, Pauw (1564–1636) was to become a prominent politician and the leader of the strict Calvinist faction that brought down the regime of Johan van Oldenbarnevelt, the advocate of Holland, and had him beheaded in 1619.

The early history of Dutch trade with the East Israel, *Dutch Primacy in World Trade,* pp. 61, 67–9; Vlekke, op. cit., pp. 62–3; Milton, op. cit., pp. 28–9, 52–65.

The Compagnie van Verre and the Dutch first fleet 'Far-Lands Company' is a more literal translation. Israel, *Dutch Primacy,* pp. 67–8; Bruijn et al., *Dutch-Asiatic Shipping,* I, pp. 1–5, 59; Milton, op. cit., pp. 52–65; Vlekke, op. cit., p. 67.

Cornelis de Houtman Miriam Estensen, *Discovery: The Quest for the Great South Land* (Sydney: Allen & Unwin, 1998), p. 62; Milton, op. cit., p. 59.

'... the surviving members ...' The crews of the *Eerste Schipvaart* experienced appalling mortality rates; only one in three returned alive.

Expeditions of 1598–1601 Israel, *Dutch Primacy,* pp. 67–9; Bruijn et al., *Dutch-Asiatic Shipping,* I, pp. 3–4; Vlekke, op. cit., p. 70.

The creation of the VOC The proposition of a joint stock company was a unique solution made possible only by the fact that the United Provinces was a federal republic. A precedent had, however, been set a few years earlier with an attempt to create an eight-strong cartel of companies involved in the Guinea trade. This attempt was unsuccessful, as in the end the companies of Zeeland had elected to retain their independence. Israel, op. cit., pp. 61, 69–71; Bruijn et al., *Dutch-Asiatic Shipping,* I, pp. 4–5. The price of the monopoly and of state support was not cheap; the first charter, which ran for 21 years, cost the VOC 25,000 guilders. It was renewed for a similar period at no charge in 1623, the Company's reward for its assistance in the wars with Spain, but by the end of the century a 40-year renewal cost the VOC a further three million guilders. Glamann, op. cit., p. 6. The goods that Jeronimus and his colleagues were required to buy and sell became more varied as the Company evolved. Spices remained the staple of the Indies trade, but over the years the VOC expanded its operations to deal in cottons and silks from India and China, dyestuffs, and even copper and silver from Japan. Profits were good here, too; cotton, for example, typically sold at 80–100 percent more than it had cost in the Indies, and margins of up to 500 percent were not unheard-of.

The Gentlemen XVII See Bruijn et al., *Dutch-Asiatic Shipping,* I, pp. 15–9.

Spices Glamann, op. cit., pp. 13, 16–24, 74–6, 91–3, 134; Vlekke, op. cit., pp. 57–61; Milton, op. cit., pp. 3, 18, 58, 80.

The Dutch in the Indies, 1602–1628 Israel, *Dutch Primacy,* p. 73; Vlekke, op. cit., pp. 75–7.

'... this frothy nation ...' Cited by John Keay, *The Honourable Company: A History of the English East India Company* (London: HarperCollins, 1993), p. 34.

'The places and the strongholds ...' C. R. Boxer, *The Dutch Seaborne Empire 1600–1800* (London: Hutchinson, 1965), pp. 45–6. The governments of Europe

reciprocated with scorn, and when, years later, the Dutch envoy to the court of Charles X of Sweden ventured a remark about the freedom of religion, the king is said to have pulled a golden rixdollar from his pocket and brandished it in the diplomat's face, remarking: 'Voilà votre religion.'

'These butterboxes ...' Quoted by Israel, *Dutch Primacy,* p 105.

Jacob Poppen Israel, *The Dutch Republic,* pp. 347–8.

Pay of merchants In the second half of the century an upper-merchant's salary was typically 80–100 guilders a month, or perhaps 1,100 a year, less than the earnings of a typical merchant at home in the Netherlands. Under-merchants earned half that, and assistants only a quarter as much, so that only the provision of free board and lodging while in the service of the Company made theirs a living wage. Boxer, *The Dutch Seaborne Empire,* pp. 201, 300.

The life and times of Francisco Pelsaert The identity of Francisco Pelsaert's father is not known, but his mother was Barbara van Ganderheyden. She married twice and had three children – Anna Pelsaert, who was born around 1588, Francisco, and Oeyken, who was five years younger than her brother and thus born around 1600. The children took their surname from Barbara's second husband, Dirick Pelsaert, who was a man of German stock. Dirick came originally from Aachen, but his marriage to Barbara was of short duration, and contemporary records attest that her three offspring were *voorkinderen* – 'forechildren' – that is, the children of an earlier marriage, the details of which have not yet been traced. Barbara's father, Dirick van Ganderheyden, who brought Pelsaert up, earned a good living as administrator of the estates of various noble widows, heiresses, and monasteries in the Southern Netherlands. He died in the autumn of 1613 and was buried in Antwerp, though it seems he had not lived there. His cousin was Hans van Ghinckel of Middelburg, who secured Pelsaert his introduction to the VOC. Kolff and van Santen, *De Geschriften,* pp. 4–7.

Joining the VOC Unusually, Pelsaert was required to lodge a surety of 1,000 guilders with the Company before he was accepted. Probably this was because – being less than 25 years of age – he was still a minor by the standards of the time. Kolff and Van Santen, *De Geschriften,* p. 7.

Inaccuracies concerning Pelsaert's antecedents, relations, and personal history have crept into the record as a result of erroneous statements by the genealogist H. F. Macco, whose *Geschichte und Genealogie der Familen Peltzer* (Aachen, np, 1901), p. 323 incorrectly states that the *commandeur* was brother-in-law to the important VOC director Hendrik Brouwer. The 'Francoys Pelsaert' mentioned as Brouwer's relative, who came from Eupen, appears to have been an entirely different person; Kolff and van Santen, *De Geschriften,* p. 7. Unfortunately Macco's error had already been perpetuated by Henrietta Drake-Brockman in her *Voyage to Disaster* (Nedlands, WA: University of Western Australia Press, 1995), pp. 13–14, and from there it entered the *Batavia* literature generally.

Pelsaert in India As they evolved, the VOC's trading bases overseas were divided into three quarters. The governor-general of the Indies took direct responsibility for the Spice Islands themselves, which were by far the most important

of the Company's possessions and made up the 'Eastern Quarter.' The factories in Japan, China, and Formosa made up the 'Northern Quarter,' and Surat,
which was established in 1606, became the administrative centre for the
'Western Quarter,' which included the trading centres of Persia and the
Coromandel Coast. Pelsaert took control of the factory at Agra in 1623–4 on
the death of his predecessor, Wouter Heuten. His first caravan to Surat (1623)
included 146 packs of cloth, 15 packs of indigo, and three female slaves. Kolff
and van Santen, *De Geschriften,* pp. 7–12, 13, 17–9, 25–8; Drake-Brockman, op.
cit., pp. 11, 15–20, 21n.

Agra Pelsaert stayed in the city some half a dozen years before the Mogul
emperor Shah Jehan began the construction of its most famous monument,
the Taj Mahal.

'… *one of the Company's more vigorous and efficient servants*…' Drake-
Brockman, op. cit., pp. 21–7.

Pieter van den Broecke He lived from 1585 to 1640 and wrote a journal, still
extant, which is an important source for the history of Dutch trade in West
Africa and northern India. He owed some of his success, in turn, to the spon-
sorship of Gerard Reynst, who eventually became governor-general of the
Indies. By 1626–7, Van den Broecke and Pelsaert had, however, fallen out
spectacularly over the latter's suspicion that his friend planned to claim much
of the credit for Pelsaert's achievements in India. Van den Broecke's fame
rests on his journal, but recent research into his years with the VOC have
shown that while well regarded as a diplomat, he was notorious for the poor
state of his accounts, which were slipshod and impenetrable. Whether this
failing was the consequence of genuine ineptitude or a deliberate attempt to
conceal private trading is difficult to say. K. Ratelband (ed.), *Reizen naar West-
Africa van Pieter van den Broecke, 1605–1614* (The Hague: Martinus Nijhoff, 1950),
pp. xxii–xxxiv, xliii–xlv; Kolff and van Santen, *De Geschriften,* p. 48; W. P.
Coolhaas (ed.), *Pieter van den Broecke in Azië* (The Hague: Martinus Nijhoff,
1962), p. 4.

'… *reports sent to the Netherlands*' Kolff and van Santen, *De Geschriften,* pp. 53–7.
Pelsaert's genuine interest in the local people was exceptionally unusual. As
one historian notes, 'The average man going to the Indies had no training and
no knowledge of foreign languages. What he knew of Asia before leaving
Amsterdam was very little, usually based on hearsay – or he knew nothing at
all. His contract with the VOC obliged him to serve in the East for some years
only… his expectations were limited to the issue of money-making during a
temporary sojourn abroad. Both this and his socio-educational background
would make it extremely unlikely for him ever to get in touch with his Asian
environment and to develop an interest in the cultural specifics of Asia.' Peter
Kirsch, 'VOC – Trade Without Ethics?' in Karl Sprengard and Roderich Ptak
(eds.), *Maritime Asia: Profit Maximisation, Ethics and Trade Structure c. 1300–1800*
(Wiesbaden: Otto Harrassowitz, 1994), p. 198.

Eurasian couples in the east and infant mortality L. Blussé, 'The Caryatids of
Batavia: Reproduction, Religion and Acculturation Under the VOC,' *Itinerario*
7 (1983): 57, 65; Jean Gelman Taylor, *The Social World of Batavia: European and*

Eurasian in Dutch Asia (Madison, WI: University of Wisconsin Press, 1983), pp. 8, 12, 14–6.

'... *dalliances with slaves*...' Kolff and van Santen, *De Geschriften,* pp. 19–21, 24, 31; Ratelband op. cit., pp. 91–2; Coolhaas, op. cit., p. 5.

The oil of cloves incident Kolff and van Santen, *De Geschriften,* pp. 32–3; for the properties and uses of oil of cloves, see M. Boucher, 'The Cape Passage: Some Observations on Health Hazards Aboard Dutch East Indiamen Outward-bound,' *Historia* 26 (1981): 35.

'*There are no Ten Commandments south of the equator*' Cited in Boxer, *The Dutch Seaborne Empire,* p. 205.

Private trade 'The result was that everyone from Governor-General to cabin boy traded on the side, and everyone else knew it,' Boxer says. '[The men's] superiors in the East normally had no inclination to give their subordinates away, as they themselves were almost invariably deeply implicated.' Ibid., pp. 201–2. The English East India Company, despite an ostensibly more liberal system (from 1674, employees were allowed to ship as much as 5 percent of the chartered tonnage on their own account), in fact fared little better; see Keay, op. cit., pp. 34–5, Ralph Davies, *The Rise of the English Shipping Industry in the Seventeenth and Eighteenth Centuries* (Newton Abbot: David & Charles, 1971), p. 147.

'*There was no esprit de corps*...' Kirsch, op. cit., p. 199.

Huybert Visnich Ibid., p. 200.

Pelsaert as a money lender He avoided detection simply by adding the interest he was owed to the price of the indigo he purchased, thus leaving no trace of his activities in the factory's accounts. Without detailed knowledge of local market conditions, neither the Gentlemen XVII nor Pelsaert's superiors at the VOC factory in Surat were in any position to question the prices he paid. Kolff and van Santen, *De Geschriften,* pp. 33–4.

The Amsterdam one-way system Geoffrey Cotterell, *Amsterdam: The Life of a City* (Farnborough: DC Heath, 1973), p. 86.

Cornelisz's selection procedure Boxer, *The Dutch Seaborne Empire,* p. 51; Kirsch, op. cit., pp. 198–9; Bruijn et al., *Dutch-Asiatic Shipping,* I, p. 147. 'To be ranked as an assistant, merchant or upper-merchant did not mean very much,' Kirsch observes. 'Whatever the rank, it had little or nothing to do with abilities or morals. It was a label only, won by practical experience of acting as a profit-maximiser.'

Adriaan Block He lived from 1581/2 until 1661 and was the brother-in-law of Isaac Massa (1586–1643), another wealthy merchant who built a fortune trading with Russia and who belonged to Thibault's Fencing club. Govert Snoek, *De Rosenkruizers in Nederland, Voornamelijk in de Eerste Helft van de 17de Eeuw. Een Inventarisatie* (Ph.D. thesis, University of Utrecht, 1997), pp. 72–4, 164.

Merchants and assistants Difficult as it generally was to recruit both officers and men, it was unusual for the Company to go so far as to hire a novice as an under-merchant. The position was a relatively senior one and was generally awarded to men who boasted at least half a dozen years of faithful service to the company in the lesser position of assistant, or clerk. On many smaller ships, an under-merchant would be the most senior VOC officer on board, and it would fall to him to direct the skipper and barter for trade goods with the experienced native merchants of the east. For this reason, even men who came from good families tended to join the VOC as assistants if they were without influence, and they learned the trade of merchant by watching their superiors for a period of years. Francisco Pelsaert started as an assistant and served at that rank for four or five years before receiving promotion to under-merchant (Kolff and van Santen, op. cit., pp. 6–7). He was, however, much younger at this time than was Cornelisz, who was not in any case unique. Some men were even more greatly favoured than he; Pieter van den Broecke, who had years of experience in Africa, actually joined the company as an upper-merchant on the recommendation of Gerard Reynst, the son of a prominent soap-boiler and a future Governor-General of the Indies. Ratelband, op. cit., pp. XXXI, XXXIV.

The Peperwerf and the building of the Batavia The island of Rapenburg has long since become part of the city of Amsterdam and now exists only as a street name and a square. The yards there dated to 1608, before which the Amsterdam chamber of the VOC contracted with private shipbuilders for its vessels. Even after that date the six chambers built their own ships to their own specifications, and there were subtle – indeed sometimes considerable – differences between the vessels built in the different yards.

No records survive concerning the construction or the cost of the *Batavia* herself, though she was built in compliance with a directive of 17 March 1626. Given that average building times were then 8 or 12 months, it would appear to have taken the VOC another 12–18 months to lay her down. Like all Dutch East Indiamen, she was built not to a detailed set of plans, but by rule of thumb. The ship was made of green timber – Dutch shipwrights found sea-soned wood too hard to work with. Measurements are given in English feet, which were slightly bigger than the Amsterdam feet the original shipwrights worked in (one Amsterdam foot = 11 inches, or 28 cm). In terms of labour, construction required about 183,000 man hours. P. Gretler, 'De Peperwerf,' in R. Parthesius (ed.), Batavia *Cahier 2: De Herbouw van een Oostindiëvaarder* (Lelystad: np, 1990), pp. 58–64; Willem Vos, 'Een Rondleiding Door een Oostindiëvaarder,' in Batavia *Cahier 4: Een Rondleiding door een Oostindiëvaarder* (Lelystad: np, 1993), pp. 3–45; A. van der Zee, 'Bronmen voor Oostindiëvaarders: Het VOC-Boekhoundjournaal,' in R. Parthesius (ed.), Batavia *Cahier 3: De Herbouw van een Oostindiëvaarder* (Leylystad: np, 1990), p. 61; Jeremy Green, Myra Stanbury, and Femme Gaastra (eds.), *The ANCODS Colloquium: Papers Presented at the Australia-Netherlands Colloquium on Maritime Archaeology and Maritime History* (Fremantle: Australian National Centre of Excellence for Maritime Archaeology, 1999), p. 71; Bruijn et al., *Dutch-Asiatic Shipping*, I, pp. 37–9, 93; Philippe Godard, *The First and Last Voyage of the Batavia* (Perth: Abrolhos Publishing, nd, c. 1993), pp. 56–66; C. R. Boxer, 'The Dutch East-Indiamen: Their Sailors, Their Navigators and Life on Board, 1602–1795,' *The Mariner's Mirror* 49 (1963): 82; H. N. Kamer, *Het VOC-*

Retourschip: Een Panorama van de 17de- en 18de-Eeuwse Scheepsbouw (Amsterdam: De Bataafsche Leeuw, 1995), pp. 30–8, 218–9.

Batavia The name is taken from that of the ancient, and semimythical, tribe of Batavians, who had occupied the Netherlands 1500 years earlier and – in legend at least – were supposed to have fought exceptionally bravely against the Romans.

'...*30 guns*...' Bert Westera, 'Geschut voor de Batavia,' in Robert Parthesius (ed.), Batavia *Cahier 2: De Herbouw van een Oostindiëvaarder* (Lelystad: np, 1990), pp. 22–5.

'...*the most complex machines yet built*...' Pablo Pérez-Mallaína's observation, made of sixteenth-century Spanish merchantmen, applies equally to the Dutch East Indiamen of the next century. 'A multi-decked ship... formed a floating collection of the incredible successes achieved by human ingenuity to that time. [Such ships were] veritable showcases of the technological developments of western Europe. They were the most complex machines of the epoch.' *Spain's Men of the Sea: Daily Life on the Indies Fleets in the Sixteenth Century* (Baltimore: Johns Hopkins University Press, 1998), p. 63.

Fluyt and jacht Jaap Bruijn and Femme S. Gaastra, 'The Dutch East India Company's Shipping, 1602–1795, in a Comparative Perspective,' in Bruijn and Gaastra (eds.), *Ships, Sailors and Spices: East India Companies and Their Shipping in the 16th, 17th and 18th Centuries* (Amsterdam: NEHA, 1993), p. 185; Davies, op. cit., p. 49.

'...*in as little as six months*...' Eight to 12 months was perhaps closer to the average, but still a remarkable achievement.

'...*the VOC flogged its ships*...' Bruijn et al., *Dutch-Asiatic Shipping*, I, 27–8, 95.

'*virtually no demand for European goods*...' The only significant exports at this time were lead and mercury.

The prefabricated gateway This gateway, salvaged and restored, can be viewed in the Western Australian Maritime Museum in Fremantle. See Marit van Huystee, *The Lost Gateway of Jakarta* (Fremantle: Western Australian Maritime Museum, 1994) and the epilogue for additional details.

Coinage on board Especially the fabled *stukken van achten*. These 'pieces of eight,' which came from Spanish mines in South America, could be counted on to contain silver of a fixed purity and value, but with the renewal of the war against Spain in the early 1620s, supplies of this superior coinage dried up, and the VOC was forced to export less well regarded Dutch and German coinage instead. The enduring clamour for silver posed particular problems for the Gentlemen XVII in the 1620s. The occasional spectacular naval victory might secure substantial quantities of freshly minted reals for Jan Company; indeed, in 1628 Admiral Piet Hein captured the entire annual Spanish treasure fleet off the coast of Cuba. But the *Batavia* sailed before this fortune made its way into circulation, and carried a heterogeneous collection of coins from the principalities of northern Germany (a region that, thanks to the notorious economic madness known as the *kipper- und wipperzeit* [ca. 1600–1623], had acquired an unenviable reputation for producing clipped coins and debased coinage). Glamann, op. cit., pp. 41–51; Phillip Playford, *Carpet of Silver: The*

Wreck of the Zuytdorp (Nedlands, WA: University of Western Australia Press, 1996), pp. 10, 43–5. For the *kipper- und wipperzeit*, see Charles Kindleberger, 'The Economic Crisis of 1619 to 1623,' *Journal of Economic History* 51 (1991). Jan Company's success in opening up the Indies trade eventually caused significant problems for the Dutch economy. So much silver was shipped out to the East that the States-General was forced to pass a law forbidding more than two-thirds of the bullion coming into the country to be re-exported. Stan Wilson, *Doits to Ducatoons: The Coins of the Dutch East India Company Ship* Batavia, *Lost on the Western Australian Coast 1629* (Perth: Western Australian Museum, 1989), pp. 3–11.

The need for diplomacy Kolff and van Santen, op. cit., p. 11.

Pelsaert's return from India Ibid., pp. 29, 37–41; confession of Jeronimus Cornelisz, JFP 19 Sep 1629 [DB 163–4]; Henrietta Drake-Brockman, *Voyage to Disaster* (Nedlands, WA: University of Western Australia Press, 1995), pp. 32–3.

Wollebrand Gheleijnsen de Jongh De Jongh (1594–1674) was head of the VOC settlement at Burhanpur and much less experienced in India than Pelsaert. He came originally from Alkmaar and served the VOC from 1613 to 1648. In the nineteenth century he became famous in the Netherlands as a character in a popular historical novel, but he has since been forgotten. Kolff and van Santen, op. cit., pp. 28–9.

Jacobsz and the Dordrecht Drake-Brockman, op. cit., p. 61.

Chronicle and remonstrantie Ibid., pp. 21–32; Kolff and van Santen, op. cit., pp. 1–2, 44.

Pelsaert in the United Provinces The plate showed scenes that would be familiar to the Muslim emperors – one example, recovered from the wreck site and now on display in the Western Australian Maritime Museum, is a one-foot silver jar portraying an Islamic purification ceremony. Cf. V. D. Roeper (ed.), *De Schipbreuk van de* Batavia, *1629* (Zutphen: Walburg Pers, 1994), pp. 10, 13.

'... designed to the upper-merchant's own specifications ...' Drake-Brockman, op. cit., p. 36.

'... travelling via the East Indies ...' The prevailing winds in the Indian Ocean meant that, in normal circumstances, it was actually faster to sail to India via Java than it was to go directly there, battling adverse winds and currents on the voyage from the Cape of Good Hope to Surat.

Jacques Specx He was born in Dordrecht in 1589, the son of an immigrant from the Southern Netherlands, and sailed for the Indies as an under-merchant in December 1607. Specx travelled to Japan and opened up a new trade there, becoming the first head of the Dutch factory on the island of Hirado (1610–13 and 1614–21). Recalled to the Netherlands in 1627 to brief the Gentlemen XVII in person on Japan, he was appointed to command the main autumn fleet sailing to the Indies in the autumn of 1628. W. P. Coolhaas, 'Aanvullingen en Verbeteringen op Van Rhede van der Kloot's *De Gouveneurs-Generalen Commissarissen-Generaal van Nederlandsch-Indië (1610–1888),*' *De Nederlandsche Leeuw* 73 (1956): 341; F. W. Stapel, *De Gouveneurs-Generaal van Nederlandsch-Indië in Beeld en Woord* (The Hague: Van Stockum, 1941), p. 19.

Chapter 3: The Tavern of the Ocean

No detailed accounts survive of the first leg of the *Batavia*'s journey east. The ship's journal and letters home, left under a 'post office stone' at the Cape of Good Hope, seem to have been lost and certainly never reached the Netherlands; and Pelsaert's own papers were thrown overboard by rioting sailors in the Abrolhos. Because of this, some of the details in my account have been drawn from general Dutch experience, and a description of a typical passage in the late 1620s constructed from sources such as Jaap Bruijn et al., *Dutch-Asiatic Shipping in the 17th and 18th Centuries* (The Hague: Martinus Nijhoff, 3 vols., 1979–1987) and Bruijn's 'Between Batavia and the Cape: Shipping Patterns of the Dutch East India Company,' *Journal of Southeast Asian Studies* 11 (1980).

Dordrecht The proper name of the ship was the *Maeght van Dort* (which means *Virgin of Dordrecht*), but she seems usually to have been known simply by the diminutive.

'Autumn was the busiest time of year...' Three main fleets sailed to Java every year – one in April, another in September, and the last at Christmas. The Christmas fleet had always been the largest. Its crews were expected to endure the miseries of the Dutch winter, but by the time they neared the equator there were generally fresh winds to carry them across the doldrums, and the fleet arrived in the East in good time to be unloaded and repaired before the return voyage began in November. Ships that left at Easter enjoyed better weather in European waters, but less favourable conditions once they reached the Atlantic. The third, September, sailing occurred while the Dutch were enjoying their great autumn festivals, and the ships that departed at this time of year were known as the *kermis,* or fair, fleet. The *kermis* fleet was a recent innovation, and in 1628 only two ships a year were sent east this early in the autumn. From this it will be seen that the fleet commanded by Jacques Specx and Francisco Pelsaert fell outside the normal run of VOC operations. Bruijn et al., *Dutch-Asiatic Shipping,* I, 62–3; Bruijn, 'Between Batavia and the Cape' p. 252.

Initial impressions of the ship R. van Gelder, *Het Oost-Indisch Avontuur: Duitsers in Dienst van de VOC, 1600–1800* (Nijmegen: SUN, 1997), p. 149. In his account of the Georgian Royal Navy, N. A. M. Rodger recounts a British boy's first impressions of being 'registered in a wooden world' a little more than a century later, which were quite similar. Life on board was quite different to life ashore in almost every aspect; sailors had their own society, manners and dress, the boy observed. 'Nor could I think what world I was in, whether among spirits of devils. All seemed strange, different language and strange expressions of tongue, that I thought myself always asleep or in a dream, and never properly awake.' *The Wooden World* (London: Fontana, 1988), p. 37.

The Great Cabin It measured approximately 20 feet by 15 and enjoyed good head room, though – like every cabin in the stern – its steeply sloping floor made it treacherous in any sea.

Creesje Jansdochter For her use of the diminutive, see GAA, baptismal registers 40, fol. 157 (30 January 1622), which records the birth of her first son.

The life and times of Gijsbert Bastiaensz For his marriage, see GAD, marital registers 17 (1604–1618) for 10 February 1604. On the burial of his child, see GAD, burial registers 1692 for September 1613. Neither the name nor the sex of the child are specified in the register, but the only candidates for the burial are Pieter Gijsbertsz (baptised March 1610) and Hester (baptised July 1612), for whom see GAD baptismal registers 3 (1605–1619). Since a passing reference in JFP (Sentence on Jeronimus Cornelisz, 28 Sep 1629) mentions another child, Willemijntgie, as the 'middle daughter' of the family, it would appear that only three girls were alive at that time, and that Hester must therefore have been the child buried in 1613. For the horse-mill, see GAD, TR 747 fol. 95. The mill was acquired from Neeltgen Willemsdr, widow of the miller Cornelis Gillisz, on 7 May 1604. For the land Gijsbert acquired for grazing horses, see ONAD 23, fols. 252–252v, which records that the *predikant* had rented five *morgen* (a *morgen* is two and a quarter acres) from Walvaren van Arckel in the nearby village of Dubbeldam. Bastiaensz also owned some additional property through his wife in the Steechoversloot, the Dordrecht street where he and his family lived; see GAD 766, fol. 99v. For the *predikant*'s service as one of the 10 elders on the church council in Dordrecht, see GAD NKD 3, fol. 38v; NKD 3, fol. 115; ibid., fol. 158v; ibid., fol. 248; NKD 4, fol. 48. Records suggestive of Gijsbert Bastiaensz's status in the community are relatively abundant. His name appears 15 times in the indexes to the solicitors' records of Dordrecht; for his services in witnessing notarial acts, see, e.g., ONAD 3, fol. 21v; for his work as a member of a 1616 arbitration committee, see ONAD 53, fol. 63; and for his duties as an executor of the will of Willem Jansz Slenaer, in September 1618, see ONAD 54, fol. 23v.

'His scant surviving writings …' The *predikant*'s only known written legacy is the letter he penned in December 1629 describing his experiences on the *Batavia*, published in the second (1649) edition of the pamphlet *Ongeluckige Voyagie, Van 't Schip Batavia*. This document is hereafter referred to as LGB.

'Gijsbert Bastiaensz was later to confess …' LGB.

Dordrecht noted for its orthodoxy Israel, *The Dutch Republic*, p. 382.

Maria Schepens For the history of the Schepens family, see GAD, Familie-archief 85, a notebook relating to the ancestors of Matthijs Balen. This book, which lacks pagination, contains a section on the genealogy of the Schepenses. From this it appears that Maria was the last of 12 children born as a result of her father's two marriages, the first betrothal being to Elisabeth van Relegem of Brussels, in 1555, and the second to one Judith Willemsdr in about 1570–2. Pieter Schepens came from Beringe in the province of Liège and was thus probably a member of the diaspora that resulted from the persecution of the non-Catholic population of the Southern Netherlands by the Spaniards. His daughter Maria's birth date is not known, but it was probably around 1580–1. Her eldest half-brother, Gerard Schepens (1556–1609), was also a Calvinist minister, though he did not join the Reformed Church until he was 16 years old. Gijsbert Bastiaensz stood as godfather to Gerard's daughter Catharina in

November 1609. Gerard's son Samuel followed his father into the Reformed Church. It is also interesting to note that one of Maria's many cousins was Emanuel Sweerts, a leading exporter of tulip bulbs who lived in Amsterdam.

The difficulties of recruitment In fact, no more than 900 *predikanten* served in the East in the whole 200-year history of the VOC. C. R. Boxer, *The Dutch Seaborne Empire 1600–1800* (London: Hutchinson, 1965), pp. 114–7.

Bastiaen Gijsbrechtsz and his family Gijsbrechtsz was probably born some time in the 1550s, since he married in April 1575. His wife was named Haesken Jansdr. The couple had at least five children. Gijsbert, the eldest, would appear to have been born in 1576. His sister Elisabeth followed in 1580/1, but she must have died young since a second daughter of the same name was baptised in February 1588. A second son, Cornelis, was born early in 1583, and a third, called Huich or Hugo, in February 1595. Bastiaen Gijsbrechtsz died in Dordrecht at some point before 5 April 1606; his wife survived him and was not buried until April 1624. It would appear probable that she and Gijsbrechtsz moved away from Dordrecht for a while between 1588 and 1595, since there is a long gap between the births of the second Elisabeth and Hugo, and a will of Haesken's dated 1606 mentions two further children – a son named Willem and another daughter, Agnete – who cannot be traced in the town records. Yet another son, Jan, is mentioned in a will of Hugo Bastiaensz, which was drawn up in July 1614, and he is referred to again, along with an otherwise unknown sister, Sara, in the preamble to Gijsbrecht Bastiaensz's letter from Batavia, LGB. This takes the possible total of Bastiaen Gijsbrechtsz's children to nine. Alternatively, he may have been Haesken's second husband, and several of her children may have been fathered by the first. GAD, baptismal registers 1 (1574–1587), 2 (1587–1604); burial registers 1697. For Haesken's will, see ONAD 3, fol. 423 and for Hugo's see ONAD 20, fols. 240r–240v. Gijsbert Bastiaensz himself also goes unrecorded in the Dordrecht baptismal registers. For his age, see ONAD 27, fol. 23.

The near-bankruptcy of Bastiaensz The mill and grounds were purchased from Bastiensz's creditors on 7 January 1629 by Jan Cornelisz and Maerten Pietersz, millers. GAD TR 766, fol. 99v.

'He applied to be a preacher in the Indies' Bastiaensz appeared before the Classis of Amsterdam, which handled the affairs of the colonial church, on 11 September 1628. He passed his examination and was immediately dispatched to the Indies. GAA, ANHK (Records of the Classis of Amsterdam) 3, fol. 91–92v.

Boudewijn van den Mijlen His last child was conceived in May 1624 (GAA baptismal registers 40, fol. 294) and he was in Batavia by September 1627 (Drake-Brockman, *Voyage to Disaster,* p. 65n, citing W. P. Coolhaas, *JP Coen: Bescheiden Omtrent zijn Bedrijf in Indië,* VII, p. 1174), which implies a departure from the Netherlands no later than the autumn of 1626. The history of the Van den Mijlen family is recorded by J. H. van Balen in his *Geschiedenis van Dordrecht,* though no mention can be found there of a child named Boudewijn. The Van den Mijlens were influential members of the regent (ruling) class of the United Provinces. One branch of the family had roots in Dordrecht, but no trace has been found of any cadet line in Woerden.

'*She was an orphan ... died in infancy*' Creesje's early life has already been pieced together by Drake-Brockman, op. cit., pp. 63–9, using Dutch archival sources. Drake-Brockman was, however, unaware of the existence of Jans's children. Their brief lives are recorded in the town archives: GAA baptismal registers 6 (Old Church), fol. 60; 40 (New Church), fols. 157, 294. There is no record of the children's deaths in the burial registers of the town, though this is not unusual when the infants in question died very shortly after birth. While it is not impossible that one or more survived and was entrusted to the care of relatives (perhaps that of Lucretia's elder sister, Sara, who was the godmother to two and was her only surviving relative) when the *Batavia* departed, the fact that Creesje remained in the East after her husband's death (see chapter 10) strongly suggests they were dead before she ever sailed.

The life and times of Lucretia Jans Her father was Jan Meynertsz, who was buried on 16 August 1602. City tax records show that at the time of his death he and his wife had only one child, who must have been Lucretia's elder sister, Sara. Meynertsz's widow, Steffanie Joostendr, remarried in 1604 after observing an appropriate period of mourning. Her second husband, Dirck Krijnen, was a widower and a captain in the Dutch navy. He brought a daughter, Weijntgen, from his first marriage to join the household. Steffanie died in May 1613 and was buried, like her first husband, in Nieuwe Zijds chapel. She was laid to rest in her own tomb, a sign that she must have possessed considerable wealth. Dirck Krijnen appears to have been dead by 1620, as by that date Creesje's affairs were in the hands of Amsterdam's Orphan Chamber, and she had acquired a guardian in the shape of a sexton named Jacob Jacobsz, who also helped to officiate at her marriage. Her sister, Sara, married twice and had five children. Their affairs have been recorded in some detail because the two girls eventually became the heirs of their mother's uncle, Nicholas van der Leur, and inherited a considerable sum of money. Under Dutch law the inheritance was administered by the Orphan Chamber of the City of Amsterdam. The house in which Creesje was born, then known as The White Angel, still stands and the current address is 113 Nieuwendijk, Amsterdam (Drake-Brockman, op. cit., pp. 63–9, 273). For Creesje's marriage, see GAA marriage registers 969 (Old Church 1619–20), fol. 433, which also records her current address as the Herenstraat. At this time it was in theory possible for Dutch women to get married at the age of 12, but in practice the average age at which they wed in Amsterdam was 24 to 28 and though half of the city's brides were aged 20 to 24, 18 was regarded as the age of sexual maturity. Creesje was thus very much a youthful bride. Gabrielle Dorren, *Eenheid en Verscheidenheid: De Burgers van Haarlem in de Gouden Eeuw* (Amsterdam: Prometheus/Bert Bakker, 2001), p. 41; Simon Schama, *The Embarrassment of Riches: An Interpretation of Dutch Culture in the Golden Age* (London: Fontana, 1987), p. 436.

'*... to Arakan ...*' Drake-Brockman, op. cit., p. 65n, citing Coolhaas, op. cit. p. 1186.

Jan Pinten Confession of Allert Janssen, JFP 19 Sep 1629 [DB 196].

Sick bays Bruijn et al., *Dutch-Asiatic Shipping*, I, p. 161.

Sailors' attitude to soldiers' deaths Charles Parr, *Jan van Linschoten* (New York: Thomas Y. Cromwell, 1964), p. xxxii.

Gabriel Jacobszoon and his wife Confession of Andries Jonas, JFP 24 Sep 1629 [DB 201].

Jacop Pietersz, his origins and nicknames Interrogation of Jeronimus Cornelisz, JFP 19 Sep 1629 [DB 165]; death sentences pronounced 28 Jan 1630, ARA VOC 1099, fol. 49.

Coenraat van Huyssen For his appearance, nobility, and origins in Gelderland, see LGB; for his family background, see W. J. d'Ablaing van Giessenburg, *De Ridderschap van de Veluwe* (The Hague: Martinus Nijhoff, 1859), p. 78 and *De Ridderschap van het Kwartier van Nijmegen* (The Hague: Van Stockum, 1899), pp. 157, 164; A. P. van Schilfgaarde, *Register op de Leenen van her Huis Bergh* (Arnhem: Gouda Quint, 1929), pp. 253–4. There is a considerable gap in the Den Werd fief records for the period 1560–1656, which makes it impossible to state with certainty that Coenraat van Huyssen was a member of this family, but it seems likely that he was.

The Van Welderens and Nijmegen The Van Welderens were a distinguished family and had lived in Nijmegen since at least 1500. The family had produced several members of the knighthood of Gelderland, as well as a number of well-respected military officers of the rank of colonel and above. The name Gÿsbert was common in the family, but neither the *Batavia* mutineer nor his brother, Olivier, can be identified in the surviving genealogy. It is possible that the two Van Welderens were bastard sons who had been forced to seek their fortunes in the Indies. Van Welderen collection, Centraal Bureau voor Genealogie, The Hague; verdict on Olivier van Welderen, JFP 30 Nov 1629 [DB 245].

Soldiers and seamen Boxer, *The Dutch Seaborne Empire,* pp. 69–73; Van Gelder, op. cit., pp. 148–55.

Hammocks Although they were not yet in widespread use, at least some of the *Batavia*'s men had hammocks, including the High Boatswain, Jan Evertsz, and several of the soldiers. Confession of Allert Janssen, JFP 19 Sep 1629 [DB 195].

Pelsaert's flotilla Bruijn et al. pp. 2, 60–3.

The distance from the Texel to Batavia Bruijn, 'Between Batavia and the Cape,' p. 259. This calculation takes account of the fact that Dutch ships never sailed the shortest possible route between the two points, in order to take full advantage of favourable winds.

Record passages See Bruijn et al., *Dutch-Asiatic Shipping,* I, 56 and F. J. Tickner and V. C. Medvei, 'Scurvy and the Health of European Crews in the Indian Ocean in the Seventeenth Century,' *Medical History* 2 (1958): 41.

Unlucky voyages For the *Westfriesland,* see A. J. C. Vermeulen, 'Onrust Ende Wederspannigheyt: Vijf Muiterijen in de Zeventiende Eeuw,' pp. 33–4, in Jaap Bruijn and E. S. van Eyck van Heslinga (eds.), *Muiterij, Oproer en Berechting op de Schepen van de VOC* (Haarlem: De Boer Maritiem, 1980). For the *Zuytdorp,* see Phillip Playford, *Carpet of Silver: the Wreck of the Zuytdorp* (Nedlands, WA: University of Western Australia Press, 1996), pp. 45–55.

Cargo and cargo capacity Stern cabins were also used to stow the most valuable cargo on the voyage home. Kristoff Glamann, *Dutch-Asiatic Trade 1620–1740* (Copenhagen: Danish Science Press, 1958), p. 24, notes that one VOC constable had to share his tiny cabin with a chest of nutmeg cakes, two small cases of birds' nests, a pot of civet, and 15 bales of tea. See also H. N. Kamer, *Het VOC-retourschip: Een Panorama van de 17de- and 18-de-Eeuwse Scheepsbouw* (Amsterdam: De Bataafsche Leeuw, 1995), pp. 24–30; Bruijn et al., *Dutch-Asiatic Shipping*, I, pp. 43, 179–87; list of retrieved cash and goods from the wreck, ARA VOC 1098, fol. 529, published by V. D. Roeper (ed.), *De Schipbreuk van de Batavia, 1629* (Zutphen: Walburg Pers, 1994), pp. 218–9; Marit van Huystee, *The Lost Gateway of Jakarta* (Fremantle: Western Australian Maritime Museum, 1994). Some authorities estimate the cargo capacity of a *retourschip* of the *Batavia*'s size as high as 1,000 tons.

Seasickness M. Barend-van Haeften, *Op Reis met de VOC: De Openhartige Dagboeken van de Zusters Lammens en Swellengrebel* (Zutphen: Walburg Pers, 1996), p. 53.

Seasickness in pigs Pablo Pérez-Mallaína, *Spain's Men of the Sea: Daily Life on the Indies Fleets in the Sixteenth Century* (Baltimore: The Johns Hopkins: University Press, 1998), p. 132.

Latrines Bruijn et al., *Dutch-Asiatic Shipping*, I, 161; Boxer, *The Dutch Seaborne Empire 1600–1800*, p. 76; Van Gelder, op. cit., p. 159; on the layer of filth in the bilges, see Philip Tyler, 'The *Batavia* Mutineers: Evidence of an Anabaptist "Fifth Column" within 17th century Dutch Colonialism?' *Westerly* (December 1970): p. 44.

Smells Van Gelder, op. cit., p. 159; N. A. M. Rodger, *The Safeguard of the Sea* (London: HarperCollins, 1997), p. 408; J. J. Keevil, C. S. Lloyd, and J. L. S. Coulter, *Medicine and the Navy, 1200–1900* (4 vols., Edinburgh, 1957–1963), I, p. 183; M. Barend-van Haeften and A. J. Gelderblom (eds.), *Buyten Gaets: Twee Burleske Reisbieven van Aernout van Overbeke* (Hilversum: Verloren, 1998), p. 94.

'Fuming like hell ...' Pérez-Mallaína, op. cit., p. 140.

Tedium Cf. Barend-van Haeften, op. cit., pp. 35, 61, 66.

Food It has been said that the proportion of salt to meat in naval stores was so high that when it was cooked in brine the salt content actually fell. The salting itself had to be done with rock salt; modern free-flowing table salts seal the meat too quickly, leaving it badly cured and with a bitter taste. Also on the menu on an East Indiaman were oatmeal, butter (which turned rancid very quickly), and Dutch cheese – the last made from the thinnest of skinned milk and so hard that sailors were known to carve spare buttons from it. C. R. Boxer, 'The Dutch East-Indiamen: Their Sailors, Their Navigators and Life on Board, 1602–1795,' *The Mariner's Mirror* 49 (1963): 94–5; Sue Shepherd, *Pickled, Potted and Canned: The Story of Food Preserving* (London: Headline, 2000), pp. 26–8, 34, 44–8, 54–6, 67, 85, 196–7, 198–9; N. A. M. Rodger, *The Wooden World*, pp. 82, 92. For contemporary views of potatoes, see Paul Zumthor, *Daily Life in Rembrandt's Holland* (London: Weidenfeld & Nicholson, 1962), p. 71. On the occasional lethality of the hold, see *The Wooden World*, p. 106.

Wine, beer, and water Bruijn et al., *Dutch-Asiatic Shipping*, I, 160; Boxer, *The Dutch Seaborne Empire*, pp. 74–5; Willem Vos, 'Een Rondleiding Door een Oostindiëvaarder," *Batavia Cahier 4: Een Rondleiding door een Oostindiëvaarder* (Lelystad: np, 1993), p. 4; see also Pérez-Mallaína, op. cit., pp. 141–3, 149.

'About as hot as if it were boiling' Comment by Governor-General Gerard

Reynst, made on board ship off Sierra Leone in 1614 and quoted by Boxer, *The Dutch Seaborne Empire,* p. 74.

Pass-times Jeremy Green, *The Loss of the Verenigde Oostindische Compagnie Retourschip* Batavia, *Western Australia 1629: An Excavation Report and Catalogue of Artefacts* (Oxford: British Archaeological Reports, 1989), p. 177; Van Gelder, op. cit., pp. 165–6; M. Barend-van Haeften, *Op Reis met de VOC,* pp. 66, 72.

'Sir Francis Drake ...' N. A. M. Rodger, *The Safeguard of the Sea,* p. 325.

Scarcity of possessions For example, among the dead of the *Belvliet* (1712), Mattys Roeloffsz left an estate comprising 'a little tobacco, a few short pipes, and some odds and ends, which altogether was sold by public auction ... for 2 guilders and 10 stuivers' and gunner Steven Dircksz 'a linen undershirt and underpants, a blue-striped undershirt and pants, a watchcoat, an old mattress, an old woollen shirt, two white shirts, a blue shirt, a pair of new shoes, an old English bonnet, a handkerchief, a pair of scissors and a knife,' together worth 16 guilders, 18 stuivers. It is unlikely many of the men on the *Batavia* took with them more than that. Playford, *Carpet of Silver,* pp. 51–2; see also Barend-van Haeften, *Op Reis met de VOC,* pp. 60, 63.

Cornelisz discusses his ideas LGB.

Ports of call Bruijn et al., *Dutch-Asiatic Shipping,* I, 60–1.

Sierra Leone Adam Jones (ed.), *West Africa in the Mid-Seventeenth Century: An Anonymous Dutch Manuscript* (London: African Studies Association, 1994); Joe Alie, *A New History of Sierra Leone* (London: Macmillan, 1990), pp. 13–37; V. D. Roeper (ed.), *De Schipbreuk van de Batavia, 1629* (Zutphen: Walburg Pers, 1994), p. 15.

Abraham Gerritsz Verdict on Abraham Gerritsz, JFP 12 Nov 1629 [DB 232]; list of people on board the *Batavia,* nd (1629–30), ARA VOC 1098, fol. 582r. [R 220].

The Wagenspoor, the equator, and the Horse Latitudes Bruijn et al., *Dutch-Asiatic Shipping,* I, p. 65 contains a description of the 'cart-track.' Van Gelder, op. cit., pp. 60, 165–6, discusses fun and games; Green, op. cit., p. 163, describes the recovery of some of the *Batavia*'s pipes and tongs; the *Batavia*'s likely route is detailed by Jaap Bruijn and Femme S. Gaastra, 'The Dutch East India Company's Shipping, 1602–1795, in a Comparative perspective,' in Bruijn and Gaastra (eds.), *Ships, Sailors and Spices: East India Companies and Their Shipping in the 16th, 17th and 18th Centuries* (Amsterdam: NEHA, 1993), p. 191 and Bruijn, 'Between Batavia and the Cape,' p. 255. For trapped animals, dried faeces, and melted candles, see M. Barend-van Haeften and A. J. Gelderblom, op. cit., pp. 70–1. On the fear of fire at sea – it was a principal danger in the age of sail – see Pérez-Mallaína, op. cit., p. 180. On washing in urine, see Rodger, *The Safeguard of the Sea,* p. 107. On rats, see ibid., p. 70. On lice, see ibid., p. 132, *Ships, Sailors and Spices* p. 203, Barend-van Haeften and Gelderblom, op. cit., p. 53 and Van Gelder, op. cit., p. 159. On the Danish cockroach-hunt, see M. Boucher, 'The Cape Passage: Some Observations on Health Hazards Aboard Dutch East Indiamen Outward-Bound,' *Historia* 26 (1981): 24.

Scurvy On the variety of contemporary treatments for scurvy, see, for example, the English surgeon John Woodall's book *The Surgeon's Mate* (1617). 'The use of the iuice of Lemons,' Woodall wrote, 'is a precious medicine and well tried, being sound and good ... It is to be taken in the morning, two or three spoonfuls ... and if you add one spoonefull of Aquavitae thereto to a cold stomacke, it is the better.' But the same surgeon also saw scurvy as 'an obstruction of the spleen, liver and brain,' and recommended an egg flip as a certain prophylactic. Other passages in his book suggest that any astringent would be of equal facility in battling the disease – barley water with cinnamon water was another cure proposed. J. J. Keevil, C. S. Lloyd, and J. L. S. Coulter, *Medicine and the Navy, 1200–1900* (4 vols., Edinburgh, 1957–1963), I, pp. 220–1. One reason for the VOC's reluctance to investigate fruit juices as a possible cure was the contemporary belief that citrus juices dangerously thickened the blood. F. J. Tickner and V. C. Medvei, 'Scurvy and the Health of European Crews in the Indian Ocean in the Seventeenth Century,' *Medical History* 2 (1958). See also Boucher, op. cit., pp. 26, 29–31; for the number of the *Batavia*'s dead, see Pelsaert's list of people embarked on board the ship, ARA VOC 1098, fol. 582r [R 220–1].

Sharks Van Gelder, op. cit., pp. 167–8.

Homosexuality Pérez-Mallaína, op. cit., pp. 164, 170–1; CR Boxer, 'The Dutch East-Indiamen,' pp. 98–9.

Women on board On the number of women, see Pelsaert's list of people embarked on board the ship, ARA VOC 1098, fol. 582r [R 220–1]. They included Lucretia and her maid, Zwaantie Hendrix; the *predikant*'s wife, Maria Schepens, three of her daughters, and her maid, Wybrecht Claasen; a widow, Geertie Willemsz; a young mother called Mayken Cardoes; and a pregnant girl named Mayken Soers, who were probably the wives of noncommissioned officers or men among the soldiers or the crew; a French or Walloon girl, Claudine Patoys; Laurentia Thomas, the corporal's wife; Janneken Gist, Anneken Bosschieters, and Anneken Hardens, all of whom were married to gunners; two sisters, Zussie and Tryntgien Fredericxs (Tryntgien was the chief trumpeter's wife); and the wives of the cook, the provost, Pieter Jansz, and Claes Harmanszoon of Magdeburg. On the VOC's policy toward women, and encouragement of affairs with the women of the Indies, see L. Blussé, 'The Caryatids of Batavia: Reproduction, Religion and Acculturation under the VOC,' *Itinerario* 7 (1983): 60–1, 62–3, 65, 75; Taylor, *The Social World of Batavia*, pp. 8, 12–14. The quotation from Jan Coen is cited by Taylor, p. 12. The quotation from Jacques Specx is cited by Boxer, 'The Dutch East-Indiamen,' p. 100.

Ariaen and Creesje Confession of Jeronimus Cornelisz, JFP 19 Sep 29 [DB 161].

The fleet at the Cape of Good Hope The identity of the ships that arrived in company at the Cape is revealed in a letter written by an anonymous survivor of the *Batavia* on 11 December 1629 and published in the pamphlet *Leyds Veer-Schuyts Praetjen, Tuschen een Koopman ende Borger van Leyden, Varende van Haarlem nae Leyden* (np [Amsterdam: Willem Jansz], 1630).

The Cape of Good Hope The English and Dutch left records of these visits in the shape of 'post-office stones' – slabs of rock that they picked up on the sea shore and engraved with the names of their ships, their skippers, and the date of their arrival. Post-office stones had two functions. They marked the spots along the beach where the crew of each East Indiamen deposited ships' papers and letters for their families at home, wrapped in waxed cloth to keep out the rain until a vessel homeward-bound could find them and take them back to Europe. And they proved the men had at least reached the Tavern of the Ocean safely – a matter of importance at a time when it was all too common for ships to vanish without trace on the passage out or home. Often the evidence of a post-office stone was all there was to show whether a vessel had been lost in the Indian Ocean or the Atlantic. Cf. R. Raven-Hart, *Before Van Riebeeck: Callers at South Africa from 1488–1652* (Cape Town: C. Struik, 1967), pp. 116, 207. On the situation at the Cape in 1629, the Hottentots and the wildlife, see ibid., pp. 14–21, 23, 38, 95, 120, 122–4, 175; Bruijn and Gaastra, *Ships, Sailors and Spices*, p. 192; Boxer, *The Dutch Seaborne Empire 1600–1800*, pp. 242–6. For the fleet's dates of arrival and departure, see Bruijn et al., *Dutch-Asiatic Shipping*, II, 60. For Pelsaert's landing and the skipper's drunkenness, see Confession of Jeronimus Cornelisz, JFP 19 Sep 1629 [DB 161] and Pelsaert's 'Declaration in short [of] the origin, reason, and towards what intention, Jeronimus Cornelissen, undermerchant, has resolved to murder all the people, with his several plans, and in what manner the matter has happened from the beginning to the end,' JFP nd [DB 162–3]. (In the former, the *Assendelft* is mentioned as one of the ships that Jacobsz visited, but in the latter the vessel in question becomes the *Sardam*. I prefer the original account.) For the average duration of visits to the Cape in the 1620s, see Bruijn et al., *Dutch-Asiatic Shipping*, I, 69. The other vessel in the *Batavia* convoy, the Hoorn chapter's *jacht, Klein David,* was bound for Pulicat in India and does not appear to have called at Table Bay. Bruijn et al., *Dutch-Asiatic Shipping*, II, 60–1.

Jacobsz's dressing-down According to Pelsaert's journals, the skipper 'excused himself that on the one hand he had been drunk, and on the other hand that he did not know that one would take a thing like that so seriously.' 'Declaration in Short,' JFP nd [DB 248].

'"By God…"… It was a while before the apothecary spoke… "And how would you manage that?"' Ibid. and Confession of Jeronimus Cornelisz, JFP 19 Sep 1629 [DB 162].

Chapter 4 Terra Australis Incognita

The only surviving material concerning the beginnings of the *Batavia* mutiny can be found in Pelsaert's journals. Much of the information was extracted under torture and – given the potential impact that the mutiny was likely to have on the *commandeur*'s career – it is unfortunate that there is a total lack of corroboration. The accuracy of the testimonies recorded thus remains open to question; nevertheless, the account that emerges from the journals is internally consistent and – in places – so outrageous that it seems unlikely to be outright invention.

The beginnings of the Batavia *mutiny* 'Declaration in short [of] the origin, reason, and towards what intention, Jeronimus Cornelissen, undermerchant, has resolved to murder all the people ...,' JFP nd [DB 248–51]; interrogation of Jan Hendricxsz, JFP 17 Sep 1629 [DB 178].

'In his journal ...' 'Declaration in Short' JFP nd [DB 249–51].

Ariaen Jacobsz's guilt It has been suggested, by Philippe Godard, in *The First and Last Voyage of the* Batavia (Perth: Abrolhos Publishing, nd, c. 1993), pp. 81–5, that Jacobsz was innocent of the crime of mutiny and that events on the *Batavia* were solely the work of Jeronimus Cornelisz and his associates. It is true that the Dutch authorities were later unable, even with the application of torture, to conclusively establish the skipper's involvement in the plot, and it is undoubtedly hard to explain why a full-fledged mutiny did not break out on board soon after the *Batavia* left the Cape, when the ship was still within easy reach of havens such as Madagascar and Mauritius. Some have also found it incredible that the skipper should allow Pelsaert to survive the open boat voyage he and Jacobsz undertook after the wrecking of the ship. See chapters 6 and 9 for a further discussion of these points. The case in favour of Jacobsz's guilt, which I tend to accept, lies in the allegations made by known mutineers during their later interrogations. Jacobsz was accused of plotting mutiny by Jan Hendricxsz and Allert Janssen as well as Jeronimus Cornelisz, and whispers of his complicity reached both the *predikant* and the *commandeur*. None of these men, with the exception of Pelsaert and Cornelisz, had much to gain by implicating the skipper, and their accounts are strikingly consistent. In the absence of records of Jacobsz's interrogation at Batavia, which seem to have been lost, the matter will remain for ever unresolved. Interrogation of Jan Hendricxsz, JFP 19 Sep 1629 [DB 178]; verdict on Allert Janssen, JFP 28 Sep 1629 [DB 198]; Specx to Gentlemen XVII, 15 Dec 1629, ARA VOC 1009, cited by Drake-Brockman, *Voyage to Disaster,* pp. 62–3.

'Though it was common for the masters of East Indiamen to chafe ...' As Jan Coen, the greatest of all governors of the Indies, observed of the VOC's skippers, '"The months go by," they say,' '"[and] at sea we are lords and masters, whereas we are only servants in India ... let us see if we cannot pick up a rich prize."' Cited by C. R. Boxer, 'The Dutch East-Indiamen: Their Sailors, Their Navigators and Life on Board, 1602–1795,' *The Mariner's Mirror* 49 (1963): 90.

Jeronimus Cornelisz's reasons for not returning to the United Provinces We do not know what sort of relationship Cornelisz enjoyed with Belijtgen Jacobsdr, or whether he loved her. The period following the death of a young child is naturally a traumatic one for any parents, and in addition to the normal feelings of guilt and despair, there may well have been recriminations between the parents concerning the choice of a wet nurse for their son and the reasons for the poor state of their business. In Cornelisz's absence, Belijtgen was evidently impoverished and she was forced to move to an alleyway in a much less desirable part of Haarlem (see chapter 9). It is not unreasonable to suppose that husband and wife may have parted on bad terms.

Conditions for mutiny Jaap Bruijn and E. S. van Eyck van Heslinga (eds.), *Muiterij, Oproer en Berechting op de Schepen van de VOC* (Haarlem: De Boer Maritiem, 1980), pp. 7–8, 21–2, 26. For an equivalent study of Spain's Indiamen, see

Pablo Pérez-Mallaína, *Spain's Men of the Sea: Daily Life on the Indies Fleets in the Sixteenth Century* (Baltimore: Johns Hopkins University Press, 1998), pp. 211–2. The VOC experienced at least 44 mutinies during its two centuries in business, beginning with one on board the *Middelburg* in 1611. The *Batavia* mutiny was by far the bloodiest of them all. The rebellion that bore the closest resemblance to it occurred on board the ship *Westfriesland* in 1652. This mutiny was led by the upper steersman, Jacob Arentsen, who, thanks to his deficient navigation, had been passed over for promotion when the skipper died. Arentsen gathered 60 men around him and plotted to kill the other officers and sail the ship to Italy. Details of the plot leaked to the loyal officers on board; the upper-steersman was shot and four of his confederates thrown overboard. In this case, as in that of the *Batavia,* the presence of women on the ship was held to be a partial cause of the trouble. On the *Windhond,* in the eighteenth century, another group planned to seize the ship and turn pirate, and in this case they actually succeeded. *Muiterij,* pp. 22, 31–4.

The Meeuwtje mutiny Ibid., pp. 28–31.

Discipline on board Boxer, 'The Dutch East-Indiamen,' pp. 98–9; C. R. Boxer, *The Dutch Seaborne Empire 1600–1800* (London: Hutchinson, 1965), p. 71. Nevertheless, knife fights certainly did occur, and not just in the service of the VOC. One authority on the Spanish treasure fleet has estimated that half of all Iberian sailors bore the scars of such an encounter. Pérez-Mallaína, op. cit., pp. 220–1.

Keelhauling and dropping from the yard Bruijn and van Eyck van Heslinga, op. cit., pp. 23–4; Pérez-Mallaína, op. cit., p. 206.

'A man in whom Jacobsz had full confidence ...' Another of the skipper's relatives, a brother-in-law, also served on the *Batavia.* He was one of the two under-steersman. Pelsaert's journal is not precise on this point, but the skipper must have meant either Gillis Fransz or Jacob Jansz. In any event, the man was not told of the plan to mutiny, Jacobsz confiding to Jeronimus that he could 'put little trust' in him. Confession of Jeronimus Cornelisz, JFP 19 Sep 1629 [DB 164].

Jan Evertsz Research in Monnickendam has revealed no new information about the high boatswain of the *Batavia.* He does not feature in the town's scant surviving notarial archives, and Monnickendam's registers of birth, marriage, and death do not begin until 1641, 1643, and 1650, respectively. It is possible, however, that a thorough search of the VOC archives at The Hague might reveal some details of his early service with the Company.

The office of boatswain Pérez-Mallaína, op. cit., p. 82. The high boatswain's badge of office was usually a whistle, which he used to coordinate the activities of the crew. Although officers, many of the men who held the post were functionally illiterate, at least in English service. It has been calculated that in 1588 only one English boatswain in three could sign his name. N. A. M. Rodger, *The Safeguard of the Sea* (London: HarperCollins, 1997), p. 309.

'As the master is to be abaft the mast ...' Cited by K. R. Andrews, *The Last Voyage of Drake and Hawkins* (London: Hakluyt Society, 2nd series vol. 142, 1972) and quoted by Rodger, op. cit., p. 309.

Recruitment of the mutineers There is very limited evidence as to the mechanics of the recruitment. Under torture, Allert Janssen later confessed that 'Jeronimus has come to him on the ship and has made a proposal to him, whether he would take a hand in the seizing of the ship.' Cornelisz, himself bound and made ready for torture, confirmed it. Janssen himself also mentioned his relationship with Jacobsz. Confession of Allert Janssen, JFP 19 Sep 1629 [DB 194–5]. For further, fragmentary, details, see confession of Jeronimus Cornelisz, JFP 19 Sep 1629 [DB 161–2]; confession of Jan Hendricxsz [DB 162–3]; further confessions of Hendricxsz and Janssen, JFP 28 Sep 1629 [DB 196–7]; verdict on Allert Janssen, JFP 28 Sep 1629 [DB 198] (which mentions in passing his killing of a man in the United Provinces). Ryckert Woutersz was the man who betrayed the plot after the wreck (see chapter 5). It is worth pointing out that under later interrogation Cornelisz changed his story on many occasions, at first denying that he knew anything of the planned mutiny until after the ship was wrecked, but the considerable weight of evidence against him is compelling.

'Seducer of men' JFP 2 Oct 1629 [DB 213].

Van Huyssen, Pietersz, and the mutiny Confession of Jeronimus Cornelisz, 19 Sep 1629 [DB 162]; confession of Jan Hendricxsz, JFP 19 Sep 1629 [DB 162–3].

Separation of the ships Drake-Brockman has written (*Voyage to Disaster*, p. 40) that the *Batavia* separated from the other ships in the convoy in a storm, but she gives no reference and I have not been able to find any confirmation in the primary sources. Indeed, according to the *predikant*, the *Batavia* simply 'wandered away' from the other ships; LGB. An anonymous sailor from the ship wrote that the other four ships in the fleet 'drifted away'; letter of 11 Dec 1629 in Anon., *Leyds Veer-Schuyts Praetjen, Tuschen een Koopman ende Borger van Leyden, Varende van Haarlem nae Leyden* (np [Amsterdam: Willem Jansz], 1630) [R 232–3]. Possibly Drake-Brockman was thinking of the storm that separated the vessels on the first day out from the Texel.

'... the little warship Buren ...' She was only half the size of the *Batavia* and was possibly one of the new breed of fast frigates, which the Dutch had just introduced to help combat the Spanish-backed pirates of Dunkirk. Bruijn et al., *Dutch-Asiatic Shipping*, II, pp. 60–1; Rodger, op. cit., p. 390.

'... somewhere between eight and 18 ...' Confession of Jan Hendricxsz, JFP 19 Sep 1629 [DB 162–3].

'Without taking any thought ...' This quotation, and some of the background material in this section of the book, is drawn from Pelsaert's 'Declaration in short, of the origin, reason, and towards what intention Jeronimus Cornilissen, under merchant, has resolved to murder all the people, with his several plans, and in what manner the matter has happened from the beginning to the end,' JFP nd (Dec 1629?) [DB 248–54].

'... readily accepted the caresses of the skipper ...' Ibid.

'... who has done his will with her ...' Confession of Allert Janssen, 19 Sep 1629 [DB 196].

'He took from her the name and yoke of servant ...' 'Declaration in Short,' JFP nd (Dec 1629?) [DB 250].

'I am still for the Devil…' Confession of Jeronimus Cornelisz, JFP 19 Sep 1629 [DB 164].

Pelsaert's illness No details of the symptoms survive, and there are only the vaguest hints that it was the recurrence of a fever Pelsaert had experienced before. Drake-Brockman, *Voyage to Disaster,* p. 32, speculates that it was malaria. This is not unlikely, but it is no more than a guess.

Frans Jansz Research in the archives of Hoorn has failed to reveal any definite trace of this man, whose name, unfortunately, was one of the most common in the Dutch Republic at this time. The solicitors' archives of the city, though indexed, are extremely incomplete for the period up to 1660.

Barber-surgeons The duality of their role was perhaps best expressed in their equipment. Frans Jansz took with him a set of matching brass bowls, which fitted together as a pair. One, which had a semicircle matching the diameter of a man's neck cut from one side, was for shaving his patients. The other, which had a semicircle matching the diameter of an arm, was for bleeding them. The bowls were recovered from the seabed in the Abrolhos in the 1970s. Jeremy Green, *The Loss of the Verenigde Oostindische Compagnie Retourschip* Batavia, *Western Australia 1629: an Excavation Report and Catalogue of Artefacts* (Oxford: British Archaeological Reports, 1989), pp. 95–6.

'… they would not cut veins instead of nerves…' G. A. Lindeboom, 'Medical Education in the Netherlands 1575–1750,' in C. D. O"Malley (ed.), *The History of Medical Education* (Berkeley, CA: University of California Press, 1970), p. 201.

Health care on board Sick parades were held on the main deck twice daily, immediately before or after morning and evening prayers. The provost summoned the sick by striking his baton against the mainmast and chanting

Kreupelen en blinden	Cripples and blind men
Komt laat U verbinden	Come and be bandaged
Boven bij den grooten mast	Gather by the mainmast
Zult gij den Meester vinden	Where you will find the master

Surgeons were naturally vulnerable to all manner of infectious diseases, and part of their standard equipment was a brush with which to remove any lice that might leap from their patients' sick beds onto their own clothes. M. Boucher, 'The Cape Passage: Some Observations on Health Hazards Aboard Dutch East Indiamen Outward-bound,' *Historia* 26 (1981); Jaap Bruijn and Femme S. Gaastra, 'The Dutch East India Company's Shipping, 1602–1795, in a Comparative Perspective,' in Bruijn and Gaastra (eds.), *Ships, Sailors and Spices: East India Companies and Their Shipping in the 16th, 17th and 18th Centuries* (Amsterdam: NEHA, 1993), p. 202; Iris Bruijn, 'The Health Care Organization of the Dutch East India Company at Home,' *Social History of Medicine* 7 (1994): 371–2. By the second half of the seventeenth century, the typical staff of a *retourschip* was three surgeons, so the *Batavia* was in effect understaffed.

Sea exams Iris Bruijn, op. cit., p. 371. These examinations were easier to pass than the equivalent exam for surgeons intending to work on land, and were deliberately made so in order to attract candidates to the service of the VOC. Not every chamber insisted on them in any case, though at least one – the Zeeland chamber – introduced them as early as 1610.

Jan Loxe Cited by Boxer, 'The Dutch East-Indiamen,' p. 97. For a while, late in the century, VOC surgeons were required to keep journals and submit them to the Gentlemen XVII on their return. This archive provides rich detail concerning the day-to-day activities of surgeons in the service of Jan Company.

Amputations The contemporary English surgeon William Clowes set out the approved method of amputating a limb as follows:

- The surgeon should secure a good strong operating table.
- One assistant should sit astride the patient, holding both arms.
- Another should sit on the leg concerned athwart the thigh, holding it in place and applying a tourniquet to deaden sensation and staunch blood flow.
- Specially sharpened saws, double-edged amputation knives, and scalpels were to be used to cut through bone and tissue, muscle, and sinew.
- Severed blood vessels were to be stoppered with plugs or powder, the vessels stitched, and the wound packed.

As little as 4 oz. of blood, Clowes added, might be lost by this method. J. J. Keevil, C. S. Lloyd, and J. L. S. Coulter, *Medicine and the Navy, 1200–1900* (4 vols. Edinburgh, 1957–1963), I, p. 133.

The sea surgeon's apothecary's chest Ibid., pp. 32, 200; Iris Bruijn, op. cit., p. 367.

Treatment of malaria Laurence Brockliss and Colin Jones, *The Medical World of Early Modern France* (Oxford: Clarendon Press, 1997), p. 160n.

Sick bays and sick visitors Bruijn et al., *Dutch-Asiatic Shipping*, I, p. 161. The recovery of those in the sick bay must usually have owed more to the better food they received there than to the quality of the medical treatment. Boxer, 'The Dutch East-Indiamen,' p. 97; Pérez-Mallaína, op. cit., p. 183.

'Uncircumcised idiots' Boxer, *The Dutch Seaborne Empire*, p. 136.

13 May 'Declaration in Short,' JFP nd (Dec 1629?).

Zwaantie's pregnancy Interrogation of Allert Janssen, JFP 19 Sep 1629 [DB 194–7].

'The skipper and Jeronimus' Ibid.

The assault on Creesje Jans Ibid.; verdict on Cornelis Janssen, alias Bean, [DB 241–3] JFP 3 Dec 1629 [DB 241–3]; letter of an anonymous survivor, December 1629, published in *Leyds Veer-Schuyts Praetjen, Tuschen een Koopman ende Borger van Leyden, Varende van Haarlem nae Leyden* (np [Amsterdam: Willem Jansz], 1630).

'We have an assault upon our hands' Interrogation of Allert Janssen, JFP 19 Sep 1629 [DB 194–7]. The men were assured by Evertsz that the attack was no more than a 'trick,' which may have lessened any concerns they had about participating. See also Antonio van Diemen to Pieter Carpentier, 15 Dec 1629, ARA VOC 1009, cited by Drake-Brockman, *Voyage to Disaster,* pp. 62–3. This letter refers to statements and enclosures concerning the assault on Creesje, which have, very unfortunately, been lost. There is thus no direct

statement in the few surviving letters that mention the case or in the *Batavia* journals to suggest an actual assault, though the whole attack had obvious sexual overtones. Committed as it was in an exposed position, close to the Great Cabin and almost next to the steersman's position, the blackening of Lucretia Jans can hardly have lasted for more than a few seconds, however. There would have been no time for a serious sexual assault or rape.

'Innate and incankered corruptness' That at least was Pelsaert's view, though the boy actually killed no one during the mutiny and eventually received a relatively light punishment. Verdict on Cornelis Janssen of Haarlem, JFP 3 Dec 1629 [DB 241–3].

Cornelis Dircxsz Interrogation of Allert Janssen, 19 Sep 1629 [DB 195]. 'I will not have anything to do with it, for surely something else will follow on that,' the gunner is reported to have said. 'Not at all,' Evertsz is recorded as answering. 'I shall take the consequences, whatever comes from it.' Unhappily for the high boatswain, this was all too true; see chapter 6.

'... very violently and in the highest degree ...' 'Declaration in Short,' JFP nd ?Dec 1629 [DB 250].

'This has been the true aim ...' Ibid.

'... the commandeur *was merely biding his time ...'* 'So that when the *Commandeur* should put the culprits of this act into chains,' Pelsaert's journal continues, 'they would jump into the Cabin and throw the *Commandeur* overboard, and in such a way they would seize the ship.' 'Declaration in Short,' JFP nd ?Dec 1629 [DB 250].

The plan to turn pirate For details of the pirates' haunts in Madagascar, see Jan Rogozinski, *Honour Among Thieves: Captain Kidd, Henry Every and the Story of Pirate Island* (London: Conway Maritime Press, 2000), pp. 54–68 and David Cordingly, *Life Among the Pirates: The Romance and the Reality* (London: Little, Brown, 1995), pp. 173–5. The centre of their operations was St. Mary's Island [Isle Sainte Marie], off the northeast coast. Jacobsz and Cornelisz planned to sail there almost three-quarters of a century before Madagascar became the principal pirate base in the Indian Ocean. They would have used St. Mary's large natural harbour as an anchorage and sailed out from there to raid the shipping lanes that ran along the Indian coast. Two of the other possible bases they discussed, Mauritius and St. Helena, were then uninhabited, though both had been stocked with animals by passing sailors who visited infrequently and used the islands to rest and replenish their supplies of food and water.

'He would act, Ariaen predicted ...' Interrogation of Allert Janssen, JFP 19 Sep 1629 [DB 195].

'Terra Australis Incognita' De Jode's atlas, *Speculum Orbis Terrae,* notes: 'This region is even today almost unknown, because after the first and second voyages all have avoided sailing thither, so that it is doubtful until even today whether it is a continent or an island. The sailors call this region New Guinea, because its coasts, state and condition are similar in many respects to the African Guinea ... After this region the huge Australian land follows which – as soon as it is once known – will represent a fifth continent, so vast and

immense is it deemed …' Günter Schilder, *Australia Unveiled: The Share of Dutch Navigators in the Discovery of Australia* (Amsterdam: Theatrum Orbis Terrarum, 1976), pp. 268–9. The name 'Terra Australis Incognita' appears on Henricus Hondius's famous world map of 1630 (ibid. pp. 320–1). Abraham Ortelius's *Types Orbis Terrarum* (ca. 1600) gives 'Terra Australia Nondum Cognita' (ibid., pp. 266–7), and there were several other variants.

Early theories concerning the existence of the South-Land Ibid., pp. 7–10; Miriam Estensen, *Discovery: The Quest for the Great South Land* (Sydney: Allen & Unwin, 1998), pp. 5–9.

The discovery of Australia Aborigines arrived in Australia about 70,000 years ago, sailing rafts or crossing land bridges created by the last great Ice Age. The identity of the European discoverers of the continent remains a matter of dispute. Kenneth McIntyre, *The Secret Discovery of Australia: Portuguese Ventures 200 Years Before Captain Cook* (Medindie, South Australia: Souvenir Press, 1977), makes a case for the Portuguese, whose bases in Timor were only a few hundred miles to the north.

'Faulty interpretation of the works of Marco Polo' The Venetian had actually been describing Malaysia and Indochina.

Beach, Maletur and Lucach J. A. Heeres, *The Part Borne by the Dutch in the Discovery of Australia 1606–1765* (London: Luzac, 1899), p. iv; Schilder, op. cit., pp. 23, 78n; Estensen op. cit., pp. 9, 87.

The old route to the Indies Heeres, p. xiii; Estensen, p. 126.

Hendrik Brouwer Heeres, pp. xiii–xv; Estensen, pp. 126–7; Boxer, 'The Dutch East-Indiamen,' p. 91.

The new Dutch route Like the Portuguese before them, the Dutch attempted to keep their new route secret. As late as 1652, the *seynbriefen* – sailing instructions – issued to eastbound ships were handwritten rather than printed, in an attempt to keep control of this secret information. The instructions for this portion of the voyage were relatively bald – sail 1000 *mijlen* (about 4,600 miles) east of the Cape, and then turn north. Vessels passing close to Amsterdam or St. Paul received some intelligence of their position from the presence of seaweed in the water, but otherwise the decision as to when to make the turn was largely a matter of guesswork. The problem was exacerbated by the difficulties experienced by ships that turned north too early; those that did so found themselves on the coast of Sumatra, where the prevailing winds were easterlies that blew them away from their destination in Java. Bruijn et al., *Dutch-Asiatic Shipping*, I, p. 61; Boxer, 'The Dutch East-Indiamen,' p. 87; Boxer, *The Dutch Seaborne Empire*, p. 164; Jaap Bruijn, 'Between Batavia and the Cape: Shipping Patterns of the Dutch East India Company,' *Journal of Southeast Asian Studies* 11 (1980): 256–7; Jaap Bruijn and Femme S. Gaastra, 'The Dutch East India Company's Shipping, 1602–1795, in a Comparative Perspective,' in Bruijn and Gaastra (eds.), *Ships, Sailors and Spices: East India Companies and their Shipping in the 16th, 17th and 18th Centuries* (Amsterdam: NEHA, 1993), p. 188; Jeremy Green, *Australia's Oldest Shipwreck: the Loss of the Trial, 1622* (Oxford: British Archaeological Reports, 1977), p. 4.

The Eendracht She was skippered by Dirck Hartog of Amsterdam, who engraved a pewter plate commemorating his discovery and left it on a wooden post atop a cliff on the island at the north end of Shark Bay that now bears his name. The plate was rediscovered by a latter skipper, William de Vlamingh, in 1696, and taken to Batavia. It is still preserved today, in Amsterdam. Schilder, op. cit., pp. 60–1, 294–5.

The Zeewolf The skipper's name was Haeveck van Hillegom. Heeres, op. cit., pp. 10–13; Estensen, op. cit., p. 130.

'... *long before she could turn away*...' Dutch *retourschepen* had an estimated turning circle of about five and a half miles, could not use their rudder to manoeuvre, and were unable to steer more than six points off the wind. Phillip Playford, *Carpet of Silver: the Wreck of the Zuytdorp* (Nedlands, WA: University of Western Australia Press, 1996), pp. 69–70.

The Vianen Schilder, op. cit., p. 105; Estensen, op. cit., pp. 155–6.

The loss of the Tryall Brookes escaped blame for the *Tryall*'s loss and the death of the majority of the crew and was soon appointed to command another English East India Company ship, the *Moone*. He proved his dangerous incompetence by running her aground off Dover in 1625, and on this occasion was imprisoned for purposely wrecking his vessel.

The location of the *Tryall*'s wreck remains a matter of some dispute. Most historians and maritime archaeologists concur that she ran aground in the Monte Bello Islands, and in 1969 divers found 10 old anchors, five cannon, and some granite ballast from an old ship on Ritchie Reef, a little way to the northeast of the Monte Bellos. These were identified as coming from the *Tryall*. Recovery of the majority of the artifacts was rendered impossible by appalling local conditions, and more recently it has been suggested that the materials that were salvaged may not be consistent with an English East Indiaman of the 1620s. Green, *Australia's Oldest Shipwreck,* pp. 1, 16–17, 21, 48–51; Graeme Henderson, *Maritime Archaeology in Australia* (Nedlands, WA: University of Western Australia Press, 1986), pp. 20–1; J. A. Henderson, *Phantoms of the* Tryall (Perth: St. George Books, 1993), pp. 24–45, 76–92; Estensen, pp. 140–1.

Latitude The sun was shot with one of a variety of navigational instruments carried by East Indiamen – astrolabes, cross-staffs and back-staffs. A VOC equipment list of 1655 suggests that a wide variety of instruments would have been carried for the use of the skipper and the upper steersman. The manifest includes three round astrolabes, two semicircular astrolabes, a pair of *astrolabe catholicum* (the 'universal astrolabe,' used for solving problems of spherical geometry), a dozen pairs of compasses, four Jacob's Staffs, four Davis's quadrants and many charts and manuals.

The astrolabe, which was perfected by the Portuguese, was the most primitive of the three principal navigational tools. The *Batavia* carried at least four – the number that have been recovered from the wreck site. Almost certainly Ariaen Jacobsz would have taken another with him in the longboat for his voyage to Java. Green, *The Loss of the Verenigde Oostindische Compagnie Retourschip* Batavia, p. 83.

Navigational problems The skipper of an East Indiaman was primarily responsible for navigation, but as a document dated 1703 explained, he was supposed to cooperate with others in 'calculating the latitude, shooting the sun, checking the variation of the compass, altering the course, and in everything else concerning the navigation of the ship.' Boxer, 'The Dutch East Indiamen,' p. 87.

An additional problem lay in the fact that while lines of latitude run parallel, those of longitude get closer together the farther a ship sails from the equator. Navigating far to the south, along the borders of the Roaring Forties, the *Batavia* would traverse each degree of longitude considerably more quickly than would have been the case farther north. This made it even more easy to underestimate the distance run when sailing east across the Southern Ocean.

The *Batavia* would have carried four varieties of hourglass – a four-hour glass, for measuring the duration of watches, and one hour, 30 minute, and 30 second glasses. Later recalculation eventually revealed that in order to measure longitude correctly, the last-named glass should have contained 28 and not 30 seconds' worth of sand, so Jacobsz's calculations of longitude would have been 7 percent out even if he had been in possession of every other fact he needed. The only realistic option available at the time was to calculate longitude based on magnetic variation. The Dutch *savant* Petrus Plancius (1552–1622) developed a system of 'eastfinding' that used this principle and published a table of variations for the guidance of mariners, but his results were insufficiently precise to guarantee accuracy.

The Dutch prime meridian Playford, op. cit., p. 31. At the time, it was popularly supposed that this was the highest mountain in the world.

Logs The English system, which involved a piece of wood attached to a long line, was considerably more accurate. Knots on the line allowed English sailors to assess the distance travelled in any given time with a greater degree of certainty. Green, *The Loss of the VOC Retourship* Batavia, pp. 10–11.

'... it is in retrospect surprising...' One reason for the comparative excellence of Dutch navigation was the superiority of the VOC's charts. The Dutch made great efforts to pool all available information, and returning skippers were required to hand over their journals and charts to the Company's official mapmakers. The first mapmaker was appointed in the same year that the VOC was founded. Boxer, 'The Dutch East Indiamen', p. 87; Boxer, *The Dutch Seaborne Empire,* p. 164; W. F. J. Mörzer Bruyns, 'Navigation of Dutch East India Company Ships around the 1740s,' *The Mariner's Mirror* 78 (1992): 143–6.

Charts Dutch charts of this period were regularly updated to incorporate discoveries. A relatively complete map of the known South-Land coast by Hessel Gerritsz, the chief cartographer of the VOC, and dated 1618 (Schilder, op. cit., pp. 304–5), actually incorporates discoveries made off Australia up to 1628 and so could not have been available to Pelsaert when the *Batavia* sailed from Holland in the autumn of that year. Even this showed the Abrolhos as a long, thin string of islands and thus gave no real indication of their exact position or appearance.

Frederick de Houtman He came from Gouda, where he was born in 1571, and sailed with his brother in the first Dutch fleet to reach the Indies. Captured in battle in Sumatra, he learned Malay and on his release wrote the first Dutch-Malay dictionary. De Houtman was later governor of the Moluccas (1621–3). He died in Alkmaar in 1627.

Houtman's Abrolhos De Houtman's only comment was: 'One should stay clear of this shoal, for it lies most treacherously for ships that want to call in at this land. It is at least 10 *mijlen* [45 miles] long; lies at 28 degrees, 26 minutes.' J. P. Sigmond and L. H. Zuiderbaan, *Dutch Discoveries of Australia: Shipwrecks, Treasures and Early Voyages Off the West Coast* (Adelaide: Rigby, 1979), p. 39. See also Schilder, op. cit., pp. 75–6, 100, 112–3. The *seynbriefen* of the VOC did mention the existence of the islands and warned seamen to beware of them.

Chapter 5: The Tiger

The material in this chapter is based almost entirely on the surviving primary source material: Pelsaert's journal, the letters of various survivors, and the Harderwijck MS. The original material has, however, been supplemented with archaeological evidence. Almost all the important works on this subject have been produced under the auspices of the Western Australian Maritime Museum and the National Centre of Excellence for Marine Archaeology in Fremantle, but the unpublished BSc. Hons dissertation of Bernandine Hunneybun, *Skullduggery on Beacon Island* (University of Western Australia, 1995) and Sofia Boranga's work on the camps of the *Zeewijk* survivors in the southern Abrolhos, *The Identification of Social Organisation on Gun Island* (Post Graduate Diploma in Archaeology dissertation, University of Western Australia, 1998) also made interesting reading. Copies of both papers can be found in the library of the Western Australian Maritime Museum.

Weather conditions in the Abrolhos Jeremy Green, *The Loss of the Verenigde Oostindische Compagnie Retourschip* Batavia, *Western Australia 1629: An Excavation Report and Catalogue of Artefacts* (Oxford: British Archaeological Reports, 1989), p. 3, summarises the islands' weather as follows: in the summer the predominant wind is southerly, blowing at Force 5–6 40 percent of the time. There can be cyclones between January and March, and in winter the winds are variable, with occasional gales of up to Force 8–12. In spring the weather improves and the winds drop to become mild and variable. The climate is temperate and, except when it is raining, there is relatively little danger of exposure. See also Hugh Edwards, *The Wreck on the Half-Moon Reef* (New York: Charles Scribner's Sons, 1970), pp. 94–5; Boranga, *The Identification of Social Organisation on Gun Island*, p. 5; Hunneybun, *Skullduggery on Beacon Island*, pp. 1–5; Jeremy Green, Myra Stanbury, and Femme Gaastra (eds.), *The ANCODS Colloquium: Papers Presented at the Australia-Netherlands Colloquium on Maritime Archaeology and Maritime History* (Fremantle: Australian National Centre of Excellence for Maritime Archaeology, 1999), pp. 89–91.

'*... no real undergrowth*' Archaeologists are of the opinion that there would have been considerably less brush on the island in 1629 than there is now, the construction of fishermen's homes in the period from 1946 having created a set of windbreaks that allow more plants to grow.

The survivors as a group JFP 4 June 1629 [DB 124]. The breakdown of numbers is not actually given anywhere; mine is based on a thorough examination of all the references in Pelsaert's journals. Jeronimus Cornelisz implicitly commented on the early banding together of survivors into groups, writing that the oaths of loyalty his men swore to him 'cast away all previous promises ... including the secret comradeships, tent-ships and others.' Mutineers' oath of 20 Aug 1629, JFP 19 Sep 1629 [DB 148].

Proportion of foreigners This is the earliest proportion cited by Bruijn et al., *Dutch-Asiatic Shipping*, I, p. 155. It dates to 1637. No specific figures exist for the *Batavia* or the period before 1637, though from mentions in Pelsaert's journal it is possible to identify at least eight Frenchmen, an Englishman, a Dane, a Swiss, and seven Germans among the crew. The total number of foreigners would certainly have been higher than that, but it is disguised by the *commandeur*'s habit of putting all names into their Dutch form.

Frans Jansz Jansz's role as leader of the first survivors' council is conjecture on my part; the journals are quite silent on the subject. It seems likely he took leadership of the camp, both because his seniority would have made it natural and also because there are two minuscule hints in the journals that the surgeon's unpleasant fate (see chapter 7) was occasioned by an unresolved conflict with Jeronimus's principal lieutenant, Zevanck, whose nature is undisclosed, but which can only have been based on some claim, on Jansz's part, to a degree of authority over the survivors. Since the surgeon was never a member of Cornelisz's council, it seems most logical to assume that he had been, rather, the leader of the council that Jeronimus deposed.

VOC hierarchy See the salary scales (for 1645–1700) printed by C. R. Boxer, *The Dutch Seaborne Empire 1600–1800* (London: Hutchinson, 1965), pp. 300–2. Following these scales, and taking the lower estimates printed to allow for some inflation between 1629 and 1645, it would appear that relative seniority and the monthly rates of pay for the principals on the *Batavia* would have been roughly as follows:

NAME	RANK	MONTHLY PAY
Francisco Pelsaert	Upper-merchant	80–100 guilders
Araien Jacobsz	Skipper	60 guilders
Jeronimus Cornelisz	Under-merchant	36 guilders
Claes Gerritsz	Upper-steersman	36 guilders
Frans Jansz	Surgeon	36 guilders
?	Ship's carpenter	30 guilders
Jacob Jansz Hollert	Under-steersman	24 guilders
Aris Jansz	Surgeon's mate	24 guilders
?	Carpenter's mate	24 guilders
Jan Evertsz	High boatswain	22 guilders
Reyndert Hendricxsz	Steward	20 guilders
?	Constable	20 guilders

?	Cook	20 guilders
?	Sailmaker	18 guilders
David Zevanck	Assistant	16 guilders
Jan Willemsz Selyns	Upper-cooper	16 guilders
Pieter Jansz	Provost	14 guilders
Harman Nannings	Quartermaster	14 guilders
Gabriel Jacobszoon	Corporal	14 guilders
Jacop Pietersz Steenhouwer	Lance corporal	12 guilders
Rutger Fredricx	Locksmith	12 guilders
Coenraat van Huyssen	Cadet	10 guilders

Able seamen were paid about 10 guilders a month, ordinary seamen 7 guilders, private soldiers 9 guilders, and ship's boys 4 guilders a month. Among the sailors and craftsmen, the relative importance of carpenters – who were vital to the integrity of a *retourschip* in the course of the long voyage east – is particularly striking.

Councils V. D. Roeper, *De Schipbreuk van de Batavia, 1629* (Zutphen: Walburg Pers, 1994), pp. 30–1; Henrietta Drake-Brockman, *Voyage to Disaster* (Nedlands, WA: University of Western Australia Press, 1995), pp. 11–12.

Supply of water JFP 5 June 1629 [DB 125].

'Begun to coalesce...' This is supposition on my part, but based on the typical behaviour of survivors after a shipwreck. See, for example, the behaviour of the *Medusa* survivors – members of the crew of a French transport stranded off the coast of Mauritania in 1816 – described by Alexander McKee, *Death Raft: the Human Drama of the Medusa Shipwreck* (London: Souvenir Press, 1975), pp. 117–9.

Suffering caused by lack of water Harderwijk MS [R 22–4]; JFP 16 Sep 1629 [DB 145]; Nathaniel Philibrick, *In the Heart of the Sea: The Epic True Story That Inspired Moby Dick* (London: HarperCollins, 2000), pp. 127–9.

Deaths from thirst Harderwijk MS [R 22]; anonymous Letter of 11 Dec 1629, published in *Leyds Veer-Schuyts Praetjen, Tuschen een Koopman ende Borger van Leyden, Varende van Haarlem nae Leyden* (np [Amsterdam: Willem Jansz], 1630) [R 233]. The author says the dead consisted of nine children and one woman.

'Our own water...' LGB.

Wybrecht Claasen She presumably came from Dordrecht, like her employer. A very large proportion of people from the town earned a living from the sea, which may explain how the girl came to swim so well. Harderwijk MS [R 22–3].

The breakup of the wreck 'Declaration in short [of] the origin, reason, and towards what intention, Jeronimus Cornilissen, under-merchant, has resolved to murder all the people...,' JFP nd [DB251], anonymous letter of 11 December 1629, op. cit. [R 233].

'Taken by surprise' Letter of 11 December, op. cit. refers to people 'swimming naked through the surf.'

'... the wrecking went on ...' JFP 17 Sep 1629 [DB 145].

Jeronimus comes ashore JFP 17 Sep 1629; 'Declaration in Short,' op. cit. [DB 145, 158, 251].

Southeast wind JFP 12–14 June 1629 [DB 129].

The camp The position of the *Batavia* survivors' camp was revealed by test dig-
gings conducted in 1992. Green, Stanbury, and Gaastra, *The ANCODS
Colloquium*, p. 111.

There is little in the ship's journals to indicate how the survivors organised
themselves, but the campsites left by the crew of the *Zeewijk*, another
retourschip lost in the Abrolhos (see epilogue), have been excavated, and they
offer many clues as to how the *Batavia*'s men would have set up their camp.

One key feature of the *Zeewijk*'s camp was the way in which the officers
retained control of the supplies salvaged from the wreck of their ship and
kept their distance from the men. They pitched their tent on their island's
highest point and kept all the salvaged victuals there. The soldiers occupied a
separate site about 100 yards along the beach, but both the common sailors
and the petty officers were kept farther away, on the far side of the soldiers'
camp, apparently because they posed a significant threat to the officers'
authority and even their lives.

The example of the *Zeewijk* survivors also provides some clues as to what
happened next. Despite the presence of both the skipper and the upper-
merchant, the shortage of supplies meant that discipline was a constant
problem on the islands. The petty officers and the seamen sometimes refused
to accept their officers' authority to ration the supplies, and on at least three
occasions near-mutinies forced the distribution of stores that should really
have been rationed.

The *Zeewijk*'s officers and the VOC officials, who were outnumbered eight
to one by the rest of the survivors, seemed to have solved this problem by
forming a loose alliance with the soldiers. Analysis of the animal bones found
at the various sites suggests that the *retourschip*'s troops enjoyed significantly
better rations than the petty officers, whose main diet was sea lion. In
exchange for these privileges, the soldiers provided an armed guard for the
supply tent. Even so, the officers' authority over the sailors remained
extremely fragile. The petty officers retained control of the ship's boat, and
used it to roam freely around the islands. There is no sign that they stockpiled
food at their main camp site, and it seems likely that they used their superior
experience and skills to catch and eat a good deal of fresh food for
themselves.

It seems unlikely that the *Batavia* survivors' camp was even this well
ordered. The *Zeewijk* carried no women and no passengers, and the officers
stayed on the islands with the men. The *Batavia* survivors, on the other hand,
were a more disparate group and had no natural leaders. If the example of the
Zeewijk is any guide, discipline would quickly have broken down and the petty
officers would have become almost impossible to control.

The first of the near-mutinies referred to above occurred when the petty
officers and common hands forced the distribution of 1.5 *aums* of wine among
the men; on another, 'all the rabble as well as the petty officers' ordered an *aum*
of wine to be distributed equally among them, as well as five Edam cheeses, six
kegs of salted fish and some tobacco. On the third occasion, the high

boatswain, the gunner and the boatswain's mate took bread and pork barrels from the store and gave each of the petty officers 12 loaves. The officers themselves were not immune to such temptation; one day the longboat was seized by an officer and several petty officers and rowed to a distant point, where the men on board consumed a large quantity of food, drink, and tobacco rather than share it with their colleagues. Finally, when the *Zeewijk*'s longboat set out for Java, the composition of her crew was decided by the drawing of lots, a procedure insisted on by the men. Boranga, op. cit., pp. 6–9, 31–3, 93–104; Edwards, op. cit., pp. 107–8, 110–2, 118–9.

208 people on the island Anonymous letter of 11 Dec 1629 [R 232].

Water and wine from the wreck JFP 17 Sep 1629 [DB 145].

Store tent There is no mention of such a tent in the available sources, but as a store tent was a feature of practically every shipwreck survivors' camp, including that of the *Zeewijk*, it seems safe to assume that there would have been one on Batavia's Graveyard, too.

Water ration This estimate is calculated from the standard daily ration, which was 3 pints (1.5 litres) of water. R. van Gelder, *Het Oost-Indisch Avontuur: Duitsers in Dienst van de VOC, 1600–1800* (Nijmegen: SUN, 1997), p. 158.

Exhaustion of the food supplies Again, there is no explicit mention of this in the journals, but it is my impression that earlier authors have probably understated the effects of food shortages on Batavia's Graveyard. Even at the end of the mutiny, when the numbers of people on the island had been reduced to only 50 or so, strict rationing was still in force there (Interrogation of Jeronimus Cornelisz, JFP 17 Sep 1629 [DB 159]), and Wiebbe Hayes and his men were surprised at how gaunt their attackers were (anonymous letter of 11 Dec 1629 [R 233]). Shortages probably began within the first fortnight; the *Zeewijk* survivors wiped out the sea lion population on their much larger island within 10 days of coming ashore (Boranga, op. cit., p. 34). There were fewer than 100 of them (Edwards, op. cit., p. 103), and the position of the *Batavia* survivors was surely thus even more desperate. The 'seal's meat' noted as being present in the *predikant*'s tent six weeks later (Verdict on Andries Liebent, JFP 30 Nov 1629 [DB 244]) probably came from elsewhere, after the party's mobility had been restored by the construction of the rafts.

'... they deferred to him.' This is speculation on my part, but Jeronimus's outburst on 4 July, when the council defied him (see below), seems typical of a man who had come to expect that his proposals would be obeyed without question.

Cornelisz joins the Council Philippe Godard states (*The First and Last Voyage of the Batavia* (Perth: Abrolhos Publishing, nd, c. 1993), p. 132, that Jeronimus was never a member of the first ship's council, but Pelsaert, in his 'Declaration in Short,' op. cit. [DB 251], says specifically that the council was 'his' on 4 July, i.e., before the dismissal of the first set of councillors and the appointment of Zevanck, Van Huyssen, and Pietersz to the group. Bastiaensz, in LGB, wrote that the under-merchant was 'elected chief.' It would, indeed, have been remarkable – given his seniority – if the apothecary had not become the leader of the *raad*.

Pelsaert's clothing JFP 19 Sep 1629 [DB 146].

'He seemed to be everywhere...' This behaviour is inferred from Bastiaensz's statements and from modern insights into the psychopathic personality (see epilogue). Exactly what the under-merchant really did during this period was not recorded and cannot now be known.

'This merchant...' LGB.

Ryckert Woutersz 'Declaration in Short,' op. cit. [DB 251]. Jeronimus alleged that Woutersz had spoken up 'on the day that the ship *Batavia* was wrecked'; confession of Jeronimus Cornelisz, JFP 19 Sep 1629 [DB 162]. On the obscure fate of this mutineer, see chapter 9.

Hopes that Ariaen would dispose of Pelsaert and flee to Malacca Interrogation of Jan Hendricxsz, JFP 19 Sep 1629 [DB 164].

Cornelisz's estimate of the jacht*'s crew* Summary of the interrogation of Jeronimus Cornelisz, JFP 28 Sep 1629 [DB 153].

The plan to seize the rescue ship JFP 17 Sep 1629 [DB 143]; JFP 28 Sep 1629 [DB 152–3].

Seductive LGB.

Van Welderen's age Gÿsbert was younger than his brother, Olivier, who was 22. Verdict on Olivier van Welderen, JFP 30 Nov 1629 [DB 245]

Rutger Fredricx Interrogation of Rutger Fredricx, JFP 20 Sep 1629 [DB 205].

'Appear not to have been approached...' There is an evident discrepancy between the number of mutineers said to have been active on the *Batavia* (not more than 12–15) and the numbers who revealed themselves in the Abrolhos (25–35).

David Zevanck Unfortunately, nothing at all is known of Zevanck's background. He presumably came from Zevanck (modern Zevang), which is a rural area a little to the north of Amsterdam, but without more detailed information it would be useless – or at least extremely time-consuming – to try to trace his antecedents; nor has anyone yet found his name mentioned in the earlier records of the VOC. It is, indeed, quite possible that he was making his maiden voyage on the *Batavia*. That he came from a good family is almost certain – on several occasions he is referred to as 'Van Zevanck' in the journals, which suggests his family owned some property and had at least pretensions to being counted among the gentry of the Netherlands – but all that can be said with any certainty is that he must have been educated and was probably young.

'Acting very subtly...' 'Declaration in Short' [DB 251].

The mutineers' tents Ibid. [DB 252].

'Discouraged the ship's carpenters...' This is interpretation, but it is difficult to imagine what else Pelsaert might have meant by his passing reference to the under-merchant 'practising devilish shifts in such a manner as to prevent them going to Batavia.' 'Declaration in Short' [DB 251]. In 1727, the survivors of the *Zeewijk* built quite a large one-masted sloop, the *Slopje,* from the wreckage of their *retourschip* and successfully sailed her to Java.

'He said that the number...' LGB.

'Nothing but some biscuit barrels' There was also a note written by Pelsaert, which was found tucked beneath a barrel. From this, the survivors learned what they

had already guessed; that their *commandeur* had sailed on to the South-Land in search of water. JFP 6 June 1629 [DB 127].

The naming of Traitors' Island The derivation of the name is not actually explained in Pelsaert's journals. For the naming and the location of this island, see Green et al, *The ANCODS Colloquium,* pp. 99–100.

The Seals' Island party The actual figure is nowhere given in the journals but seems to have been 45; 18 men and boys died on the island on 15 July, and 16 women, boys, and children on 21 July, and we are told three boys were captured and about eight escaped. Another estimate does suggest the party was larger – perhaps 60 strong – but this has to be wrong; there must have been about 130 people left on Batavia's Graveyard when the killings began, if the account of the killings given in JFP is correct. For the larger estimate, see anonymous letter of 11 Dec 1629 [R 232].

Jeronimus's promise to the people of Traitors' Island Interrogation of Jan Hendricxsz, JFP 19 Sep 1629 [DB 179].

'Toward the end of the third week of June' Hayes and his men were on the islands about 20 days before finding water (JFP 20 Sep 1629 [DB 149]), landing first on what was later known as High Island and then, when they were unable to find wells, wading across the mudflats to what became Wiebbe Hayes's Island (LGB). Their signals appear to have been noticed on 9 July, when Pieter Jansz and his party abruptly left Traitors' Island for the high islands and had to be intercepted by Cornelisz's men (Verdict on Jan Hendricxsz, JFP 28 Sep 1629 [DB 183]). This would give an approximate date of 20 June for Hayes's arrival on the High Land itself.

'High Land' The phrase comes from LGB.

'Some of the boldest soldiers ...' Ibid.

Wiebbe Hayes The baptismal and marriage records of Winschoten, in the Provincial Archive of Groningen, date only to 1646, and the burial registers only begin in 1723; no traces of Hayes's early life have yet emerged. The files of Winschoten marriage contracts date to 1608, but Hayes's name does not appear among them. A check on signatures in the surviving solicitors' records for the period 1624–28 also produced nothing, but Hayes may simply have been too poor and insignificant to have had any need of solicitors. Alternatively, he may not have come from Groningen. 'Wiebbe' – pronounced 'Webb-uh' – is a Frisian name, which was unusual even for the time and is now obsolescent, so perhaps Hayes and Cornelisz had that origin in common. If he survived to return to the Netherlands, Hayes might have been rich enough to leave more trace of his activities, but no sign of him has yet emerged. There is, for example, no record in the local burial registers of a Wiebbe Hayes ever being buried in Amsterdam.

Hayes known to Cornelisz The under-merchant later wrote to the French mercenaries in Hayes's party that he had 'a particular liking for and trust in Wiebbe Hayes.' His letter was intended to split Hayes's Defenders, and Cornelisz would have found it important to have retained at least the veneer of truthfulness in setting out his case. It seems unlikely that he would simply have lied outright about their acquaintance, as this would have cast doubt on some of his other statements. Jeronimus to Jean Hongaar et al., 23 July 1629, in JFP 19 Sep 1629 [DB 149].

Jeronimus's plans for the rescue ship 'His procedures,' wrote Francisco Pelsaert, 'could neither exist nor be acceptable to God or Worldly Power.' But to Jeronimus they were merely common sense. JFP 3 Dec 1629 [DB 239]. For Cornelisz's thoughts, see JFP 17–28 Sep 1629 [DB 143, 153, 160]. On the number of men the *jacht* would carry, see JFP 28 Sep 1629 [DB 153].

Abraham Hendricx He was possibly, but not certainly, the same Hendricx who had taken part in the assault on Creesje Jans.

'On 4 July…' Pelsaert's 'Declaration in Short,' JFP nd [DB 251].

Appointment of the new council Ibid.

'He proved this point immediately…' Pelsaert gives 4 July as the date of the sentencing of these men (Verdict on Jeronimus Cornelisz, JFP 28 Sep 1629 [DB 173]), but 5 July as the date of their executions (Verdict on Daniel Cornelissen, JFP 30 Nov 1629 [DB 240]) and also as the day on which Zevanck and the others joined the council ('Declaration in Short' [DB 251]), while clearly implying that the carpenters were sentenced by Cornelisz's *raad*. One or other of these journal entries must be incorrect. See also verdict on Hans Frederick, JFP 30 Nov 1629 [DB 244].

The first covert drownings The date of this incident appears to have been 4 July, and not 3 July as Drake-Brockman suggests, which would have put the murders before Cornelisz ordered the execution of Hendricx and Ariaensz. Van Os's interrogation makes it clear that the murders were ordered on 3 July but not committed until the following day, which probably suggests that Jeronimus knew he was going to charge Hendricx and Ariaensz with theft well in advance. Jan Cornelis was the only Dutchman; he came from Amersfoort, in the province of Utrecht, while Liebent and Janssen, an ordinary private, were Germans and Wensel was a Dane. Interrogation of Lenert van Os, JFP 23 Sep 1629 [DB 186]; verdict on Mattys Beer, JFP 28 Sep 1629 [DB 192]; verdict on Rutger Fredrick, JFP 28 Sep 1629 [DB 206–7]; verdict on Daniel Cornelissen, 30 Nov 1629 [DB 240]. Pelsaert's various accounts of these killings are somewhat confused. Some state that the men were tied up on the raft, others that they were taken to Traitors' Island, tied up there, and dragged into the sea to drown.

Murder of Hans Radder and Jacop Groenwald Verdict on Jan Hendricxsz, JFP 28 Sep 1629 [DB 182–3]; verdict on Mattys Beer, JFP 28 Sep 1629 [DB 192–3]; interrogation of Rutger Fredrix, JFP 28 Sep 1629 [DB 205].

Andries de Vries is spared Verdict on Mattys Beer, JFP 28 Sep 1629 [DB 192–3]; interrogation of Rutger Fredrix, JFP 20 Sep 1629 [DB 205].

Signal beacons 'Declaration in Short,' JFP nd [DB 252]. Bastiaensz, in LGB, adds that Jeronimus 'affected not to see' the fires.

Massacre of the people from Traitors' Island I assume that Jansz's departure was caused by sight of Hayes's beacons, though this is not mentioned in the journals; Pelsaert is clear that the provost's party left the island before they were attacked, and it seems clear that they would not have departed unless they had indeed seen signals. The coincidence of the known date of the massacre – 9 July – and the statement that Hayes's men, who must have been put onto the High Land sometime around 20–30 June, had searched 'for 20 days' for water seems to fit this supposition. Exactly when the provost was killed is not stated, either, but I think the journals would have mentioned if he had been one of the otherwise anonymous men who jumped into the sea and drowned, and since he did not survive long enough to come ashore on Batavia's Graveyard I have assumed he met his death in the shallows in the manner described.

In general, the account of the massacre of Jansz's men is perhaps the most fragmented to be found anywhere in Pelsaert's journals. There is no single coherent account of the episode; instead, important details lie scattered throughout the transcripts of many separate interrogations and verdicts. See, chiefly, interrogation of Jeronimus Cornelisz, JFP 22 Sep 1629 [DB 167]; verdict on Jeronimus Cornelisz, JFP 28 Sep 1629 [DB 173]; interrogation of Jan Hendricxsz, JFP 19 Sep 1629 [DB 179]; verdict on Jan Hendricxsz, JFP 28 Sep 1629 [DB 183]; interrogation of Andries Jonas, JFP 24 Sep 1629 [DB 200]; verdict on Andries Jonas, JFP 28 Sep 1629 [DB 203]; interrogation of Rutger Fredricx, JFP 20 Sep 1629 [DB 205]; verdict on Rutger Fredricx, JFP 28 Sep 1629 [DB 207]; verdict on Lucas Gellisz, JFP 12 Nov 1629 [DB 233].

Andries Jonas Interrogation of Andries Jonas, JFP 24 Sep 1629 [DB 200].

The declarations of the minor mutineers It can hardly be argued that these men were anxious to become killers, since practically none of them took any part in the violence in the archipelago.

Frans Jansz changes loyalties Because Jansz never signed the mutineers' oaths (see chapter 7), his involvement with Cornelisz emerges only from vague hints in the journals and in his participation in the massacres on Seals' Island (below).

Hans Hardens and his family The murder of Hilletgie took place on 8 July. JFP 19 Sep 1629 [DB 146]; verdict on Jan Hendricxsz, JFP 28 Sep 1629 [DB 183]. Hardens played no active part in any of the events of the mutiny, and there is no record that he ever killed or wounded anyone. Yet he signed both the mutineers' oaths, in the first instance above Rutger Fredricx, Cornelis Pietersz, and Lucas Gellisz, and in the second behind Fredricx and Gellisz, but ahead of Pietersz, Olivier van Welderen, and Jan Pelgrom. His name is conspicuously absent from the list of the 'most innocent' minor mutineers that Jeronimus supplied to Pelsaert. Finally, he was one of the crew who attempted to capture the *Sardam* when the *jacht* eventually appeared in the Abrolhos (see chapter 8). From this it would appear that he was not only one of the earlier recruits to Cornelisz's cause, but also one of the more active. Pelsaert gave no interpretation of the reasons for Hilletgie Hardens's death; this is my own. Interrogation of Jeronimus Cornelisz, JFP 19 Sep 1629 [DB 146, 165, 166].

'Written unbreakable agreement…' This quotation comes directly from the text of the oath sworn by all the mutineers on 12 July 1629 (see chapter 7). JFP 19 Sep 1629 [DB 147].

'The whole day long it was their catch-call…' LGB.

Andries de Vries and the killing of the sick Interrogation of Jeronimus Cornelisz, JFP 22 Sep 1629 [DB 167]; verdict on Jeronimus Cornelisz, JFP 28 Sep 1629 [DB 173–4]; verdict on Allert Janssen, JFP 28 Sep 1629 [DB 198–9]. Little is known of how Jeronimus and his men solved the problem of disposing of these bodies. In the early seventeenth century, medical wisdom held that corpses produced a poisonous miasma capable of causing plague and fever, and the mutineers evidently made arrangements to bury at least some of their victims, scraping out grave pits in the middle of the island, where the soil was deepest. These shallow graves – none was more than about two feet deep – held up to seven or eight dead bodies. When men were killed close to the water, the mutineers may well have thrown their corpses into the sea. Interview with Dr. Alanah Buck, Western Australian Centre for Pathology and Medical Research, Perth, Australia, 13 June 2000.

Jan Pinten This murder took place on 10 July. Interrogation of Jan Hendricxsz, JFP 19 Sep 1629 [DB 179].

Sick cabin boy This murder took place at the same time as the killings of Van Den Ende and Drayer (below), with whom the sick boy shared a tent. Ibid. [DB 180].

Hendrick Claasz This murder took place on 14 July. In Janssen's recollection, 'Jeronimus himself came and called him out of his tent and has said, "Go get Hendrick Claasz of Apcou, carpenter, out of his tent and say he must come to me, and when he comes outside, you, with the help of De Vries, must cut his throat," which they have done.' Interrogation of Allert Janssen, JFP 19 Sep 1629 [DB 196].

Hans Frederick and Oliver van Welderen Verdicts on Frederick and Van Welderen, JFP 30 Nov 1629 [DB 244–5]. Frederick and Hendricxsz both came from Bremen.

Murder of Van den Ende and Drayer Interrogation of Jan Hendricxsz, JFP 19 Sep–28 Sep 1629 [DB 179–81]; verdict on Lucas Gellisz, JFP 12 Nov 1629 [DB 233].

'He, together with David Zevanck…' Interrogation of Jan Hendricxsz, JFP 19 Sep 1629 [DB 180].

'Have murdered or destroyed' Verdict on Jeronimus Cornelisz, JFP 28 Sep 1629 [DB 172–3].

Diet of the Batavia *survivors* Pelsaert's journals scarcely concern themselves with the survivors' diet. If the people from the *Batavia* were typical of Dutch sailors of the era, however, it would appear that, given the choice, they would eat their familiar preserved meats first, then sea lion and finally birds or fish. Clear distinctions seem to have existed between the diets of officers (for which, in the case of the *Batavia,* read 'mutineers') and those of the common people in the case of shipwreck. The diet of the *Zeewijk* survivors – as reconstructed by Boranga (op. cit., pp. 97, 103), who believed she was able to positively identify 76 percent of the animal bones recovered from the several camp sites on Pelsaert Island – indicates that the food consumption of the various groups stranded on the island after the *retourschip* went aground there in 1727 was as follows:

%	CASK BEEF	CASK PORK	SEA LION	BIRDS	FISH
Officers	60	17	22	1	-
Petty officers	12	12	72	3	1
Soldiers	24	17	49	9	1

This analysis no doubt understates the importance of fish in the diet of all three groups – their bones are less likely to be detected in an excavation – and a preference for familiar fare over fresh meat is apparent, but the general pattern is clear enough. The campsites of the common hands were not identified, and Boranga theorises that they were probably split into small groups and kept some distance from the main camp, in an area subsequently destroyed by guano mining. The archaeologists' discoveries contradict assertions in journals kept by two of the *Zeewijk*'s surviving officers that food was distributed equally to all parties on the island. However, these same journals mention that ordinary sailors – the 'common hands,' who were equivalent to the VOC loyalists on Batavia's Graveyard – were the first to catch and eat birds, which certainly suggests that their rations were the most meagre of all.

Freedom of movement All Pelsaert's notes concerning the men permitted to crew the makeshift rafts and yawls refer to men who had signed oaths of allegiance to Cornelisz.

Morning stars The remains of a weapon of this description were found early in 2001, during a metal detector search of Seals' Island conducted on behalf of a Perth-based TV production company called Prospero Productions. The nails and the rope were both long gone, but the deadly purpose of the carefully worked lump of lead could not be doubted. Interview with Ed Punchard of Prospero Productions, 7 May 2001.

Case of jewels 'List of cash and goods retrieved from the wreck,' ARA VOC 1098 fol. 529r–529v [R 218–9]. In various places in a single long letter written over several weeks, Antonio van Diemen valued the contents of the case at between 20,000 and 60,000 guilders, which has led to speculation that the jewel-studded golden frame was looted at some point. However, the estimates rise, rather than fall, in the course of the letter, so this theory looks untenable. The highest of the estimates appears the most reliable. Van Diemen to Pieter Carpentier, 30 Nov–10 Dec 1629 [DB 42, 49, 51]

The Great Cameo The Gentlemen XVII had to be content with sight of a sketch of the piece. For profit, see VOC contract with Boudaen, 18 Dec 1628 [DB 88]. The specified commission was 28 percent of the sale price. See also A. N. Zadoks-Josephus Jitta, 'De lotgevallen van den grooten camee in het Koninklijk Penningkabinet,' *Oud-Holland* 66 (1951): 191–211; Drake-Brockman, op. cit., pp. 84–93. Drake-Brockman also suggests that a valuable agate vase, the property of Peter Paul Rubens (and now in the Walters Art Gallery, Baltimore) was among Pelsaert's trade goods. Her interpretation of the rather obscure contemporary evidence for this assertion has been followed by later authors, but in my view it is not possible to state with any certainty that the Rubens vase was ever in the Abrolhos. For the known history of the vase, see Marvin Chauncey Ross, 'The Rubens Vase: Its History and Date,' *Journal of the Walters Art Gallery* 6 (1943): 9–39.

'For they were led to thinking...' Interrogation of Andries Jonas, JFP 27 Sep 1629 [DB 202].

Mutton birds Edwards, op. cit., p. 169. The term 'mutton bird' is actually an eighteenth-century colloquialism, which probably refers to the taste of the birds' flesh. It was invented by early British settlers on Norfolk Island. Other emigrants knew the birds as 'flying sheep.' In Western Australia the mutton bird is *Puffinus tenuirostris,* the short-tailed shearwater; in New Zealand, the phrase refers to *P. griseus,* the sooty shearwater.

The first wave of killings on Seals' Island Interrogation of Jan Hendricxsz, JFP 19 Sep 1629 [DB 180]; verdict on Jan Hendricxsz, JFP 28 Sep 1629 [DB 183–4]; interrogation of Lenert van Os, JFP 23 Sep 1629 [DB 187]; verdict on Abraham Gerritsz, JFP 12 Nov 1629 [DB 232]; verdict on Claas Harmansz, JFP 12 Nov 1629 [DB 233–4].

'Kill most of the people...' Verdict on Jan Hendricxsz, JFP 28 Sep 1629 [DB 183–4].

'Lenert, immediately after he arrived...' Interrogation of Lenert van Os, JFP 23 Sep 1629 [DB187]; verdict on Jan Hendricxsz, JFP 28 Sep 1629 [DB 183–4].

'Eight men...' Pelsaert names only five (Interrogation of Jan Hendricxsz, JFP 19 Sep 1629 [DB 180]), but the anonymous author of the letter of 11 December 1629, says 10, and he is probably closer to the truth. The numbers add up as follows: there were about 45 people on the island, it appears, and 18 were definitely killed in the first assault. During the second attack all four women were killed, and 12 of the 15 cabin boys; two of the other three were dealt with later (see below), leaving eight people unaccounted for.

The second wave of killings on Seals' Island Verdict on Mattys Beer, JFP 28 Sep 1629 [DB 193]; interrogation of Andries Jonas, JFP 24 Sep 1629 [DB 200–1]; verdict on Andries Jonas, JFP 28 Sep 1629 [DB 203]; verdict on Jan Pelgrom, JFP 28 Sep 1629 [DB 210].

Jan Pelgrom Pelgrom, a cabin boy, is variously referred to in Pelsaert's journals as 'Jan van Bemmel' and, more usually, 'Jan Pelgrom de Bye.' 'Bemmel' is Zaltbommel, on the River Waal, which was known simply as Bommel in the seventeenth century, and Jan of the *Batavia* seems to have been a minor member of a patrician family called Pelgrom de Bye, whose senior branch was based just to the south, in Bois-le-Duc, Northern Brabant. The first recorded member of this family came there from Bommel in 1375. Jan was a common name in the family (in our Jan Pelgrom's time one of the aldermen of Bois-le-Duc was named Jan Pietersz Pelgrom de Bye). The Jan of the *Batavia* may have been a member of a cadet branch, or perhaps a bastard son forced to seek his fortune in the East. See *Geschiedenis van het Geslacht Vaasen,* vol. 8 (unpublished MS, nd, twentieth century), Centraal Bureau voor Genealogie, The Hague, mainly fol. 141–52.

'On the 18 July...' Verdict on Andries Jonas, JFP 28 Sep 1629 [DB 203]. I have inserted the word *heavily* from Jonas's interrogation of 24 Sep 1629 [DB 201]; the two versions of the event are otherwise more or less identical.

The massacre of the cabin boys Interrogation of Mattys Beer, JFP 23 Sep 1629 [DB 190].

Gerritsz's killing The dead boy's name was Frans Fransz, and he came from Haarlem. Verdict on Abraham Gerritsz, JFP 12 Nov 1629 [DB 232].

Murder of the three surviving boys Verdict on Claes Harmansz, JFP 12 Nov 1629 [DB 233–4]; verdict on Isbrant Isbrantsz, JFP 30 Nov 1629 [DB 246]. Isbrantsz was unfortunate; two other unwilling mutineers – the steward, Reyndert Hendricx, and Gerrit Willemsz of Enkhuizen, a sailor – were with him in the yawl, but they were not required to participate in any killing and escaped unpunished when the mutiny was crushed.

'Like some Roman tyrant' Cornelisz's contemporaries compared him with Nero; his abandonment of the Seals' Island party was a deed 'as Nero or some other tyrant would have thought of' for the writer of the letter of 11 Dec 1629 [R 232].

Deschamps as a clerk In fact, Pelsaert's journals state in several places that Deschamps was not an assistant but an under-merchant (Verdict on Salomon Deschamps, JFP 12 Nov 1629 [DB 231]) – an unexplained anomaly, given that this was Jeronimus's rank, and *retourschepen* were supposed to carry only a single under-merchant.

Salomon Deschamps and Mayken Cardoes's child Ibid.

Number of deaths 'List of those on board the *Batavia*,' ARA VOC 1098, fol. 582r [R 220].

'To have murdered or destroyed…' Verdict on Jeronimus Cornelisz, JFP 28 Sep 1629 [DB 172–3].

Gijsbert Bastiaensz and his family LGB. Bastiaen: GAD baptismal registers 3 (1605–1619), June 1606; interrogation of Wouter Loos, JFP 24 Sep 1629 [DB 225]. Pieter: GAD baptismal registers 3, March 1610. Johannes: Ibid., December 1615. Roelant: GAD baptismal registers 4 (1619–41), May 1621. Judick: GAD baptismal registers 3, January 1608. Willemijntge: Ibid., October 1614. Agnete: Ibid., March 1618. For details of the family's early life in Dordrecht, see chapter 3. Father and children were temporarily separated after the wreck, but reunited on Batavia's Graveyard, LGB.

'… no more than three unmarried adult women…' The only other definite example who can be traced in Pelsaert's journals is Wybrecht Claasen, who as a servant would have been a much less attractive catch than Judick. One other women, Marretgie Louys, is not explicitly mentioned as having either a husband or children, but it may be presumed that to have come on board she probably was married to a member of the crew.

Judick's betrothal to Van Huyssen LGB. The precise chronology is very slightly unclear here, as the *predikant* does not say explicitly whether the betrothal took place before or after the murder of the remainder of the family. He does note that Judick and Van Huyssen were together 'for about five weeks' before the mutineer's death on 2 September (see chapter 7), which would place the couple's engagement on about 29 July, or a week after the murders, which took place on 21 July. It is evident, however, that the relationship between the two predated the killings.

'… a pleasant outing…' Confession of Andries Jonas, JFP 27 Sep 1629 [DB 204].

Murder of the predikant's *family* Ibid; sentence on Jeronimus Cornelisz, JFP 28 Sep 1629 [DB 174]; confession of Jan Hendricxsz, JFP 19 Sep 1629 [DB 180–1]; sentence on Jan Hendricxsz, JFP 28 Sep 1629 [DB 184]; confession of Mattys Beer, JFP 23–24 Sep 1629 [DB 190–1]; confession of Wouter Loos, 24 Sep 1629 [DB 224–5]; testimony of Judick Gijsbertsdr, JFP 27 Oct 1629 [DB 225–6]; sentence on Andries Liebent, JFP 30 Nov 1629 [DB 243–4].

Murder of Hendrick Denys Confession of Jan Hendricxsz, JFP 19 Sep 1629 [DB 181]. The skull of a *Batavia* victim, now in Geraldton Museum, has been identified as possibly that of Denys; see Juliëtte Pasveer, Alanah Buck, and Marit van Huystee, 'Victims of the *Batavia* Mutiny: Physical Anthropological and Forensic Studies of the Beacon Island skeletons,' *Bulletin of the Australian Institute for Maritime Archaeology* 22 (1998): 47–8. My description of the wounds is largely based on an interview with Dr. Alanah Buck of the Western Australian Centre for Pathology and Medical Research in Perth, 12 June 2000. This skull (the jaw is missing and the remainder of the body still lies buried under the foundations of a fisherman's house on Beacon Island), catalogue number BAT A16136, was originally excavated in 1964, during filming for a television reconstruction of the *Batavia* story (Hunneybun, op. cit., section 4.11), and in 2000 was the subject of detailed reconstruction by a forensic dentist, Dr. Stephen Knott. See the epilogue for additional details. The identification with Denys is conjectural; the wounds agree with the description given in the journals, but nothing definite is said about the disposal of the body. In general it may be stated that the sex, age, and wounds found on the bodies so far excavated on the island do not agree very well with the descriptions of the murders and burials listed in Pelsaert's journals, which casts some doubt on the accuracy of the survivors' recollections and the upper-merchant's record.

Murder of Mayken Cardoes Confession of Andries Jonas, JFP 24–27 Sep 1629 [DB 201–2]; sentence on Andries Jonas, JFP 28 Sept 1629 [DB 202–4]. Jonas denied repeatedly, even under torture, that he had entered the *predikant*'s tent that night, but admitted freely to murdering Mayken Cardoes.

Attempted murder of Aris Jansz Testimony of Aris Jansz, JFP 27 Sep 1629 [DB 196–7]; sentence on Allert Janssen, JFP 28 Sep 1629 [DB 199].

Chapter 6: Longboat

Phillip Playford's books provide the best description of the Western Australian coastline between the Abrolhos and Shark Bay. I found Jean Gelman Taylor, *The Social World of Batavia: European and Eurasian in Dutch Asia* (Madison, WI: University of Wisconsin Press, 1983) particularly useful in reconstructing early seventeenth-century Batavia, and R. Spruit, *Jan Pietersz Coen: Daden en Dagen in Dienst van de VOC* (Houten: De Haan, 1987), is the most up-to-date authority on the remarkable and controversial governor-general of the Indies. The only reasonably full account of the bizarre incident concerning Sara Specx and her lover, Pieter Cortenhoeff (which for its sheer awfulness deserves much more space than it has been possible to accord it here) that could be found is C. Gerretson, *Coen's Eerherstel* (Amsterdam: Van Kampen, 1944). The fact that Gerretson felt compelled to give his book this title – it means 'Coen's Rehabilitation' – says a good deal about twentieth-century historians' general disapproval of this most remarkable of Dutch empire builders.

Description of the longboat A reconstruction of the boat, based on contemporary plans, was completed in the Netherlands some years ago. I saw it in Sydney, where the full-size replica of the *Batavia* built in Lelystad (see epilogue) had gone as part of the 2000 Olympic celebrations; it seems tiny, and far too small ever to have held 48 people. A photo of the reconstructed longboat can be found in Philippe Godard, *The First and Last Voyage of the* Batavia (Perth: Abrolhos Publishing, nd, c. 1993), p. 150.

The plan Pelsaert's resolution of 8 June 1629, JFP [DB 127–8].

The crew Neither the bos'n's mate nor Nannings, both of whom were active mutineers, are mentioned among Jeronimus's band, so they must either have been on board the longboat or – less likely – have been among the dozen men who drowned when the *Batavia* was wrecked. For other members of the crew, see Antonio van Diemen to Pieter de Carpentier, 30 Nov–10 Dec 1629, ARA VOC 1009 [DB 42–3]; Pelsaert's resolution of 8 June 1629, JFP [DB 127–8].

The voyage up the coast JFP 8 June–7 July 1629 [DB 128–33]; Phillip Playford, *Carpet of Silver: The Wreck of the Zuytdorp* (Nedlands, WA: University of Western Australia Press, 1996), pp. 69–71; Godard, op. cit. pp. 149–56. De Vlamingh's views are quoted in Playford's *Voyage of Discovery to Terra Australis by Willem de Vlamingh in 1696–97* (Perth: Western Australian Museum, 1999), pp. 49–50.

The first landing JFP 14 June 1629 [DB 129–30]. The breakers were still far too fierce to permit a landing, but six sailors managed to swim ashore through the heavy surf. It did no good; they found no water and did not even see the Aborigines who were undoubtedly present in the area until the end of the day, when the *commandeur* noted a frightening incident: 'Saw four men creeping towards [our men] on hands and feet. When our folk, coming out of a hollow upon a height, approached them suddenly, they leapt to their feet and fled full speed, which was clearly seen by us in the boat; they were black savages, entirely naked, without any cover.'

The second landing JFP 15–16 June 1629 [DB 125n, 130].

The river of Jacop Remmessens It had been discovered by the boatswain of the VOC ship *Leeuwin*. JFP 16 June 1629 [DB 131]; Günter Schilder, *Australia Unveiled: The Share of Dutch Navigators in the Discovery of Australia* (Amsterdam: Theatrum Orbis Terrarum, 1976), p. 77.

Decision to head for Java JFP 16 June 1629 [DB 131].

Conditions in the longboat Survivor's letter, Dec 1629, published in anon., *Leyds Veer-Schuyts Praetjen, Tuschen een Koopman ende Borger van Leyden, Varende van Haarlem nae Leyden* (np [Amsterdam: Willem Jansz], 1630) [R 235-6]. For Bligh's voyage, see John Toohey, *Captain Bligh's Portable Nightmare* (London: Fourth Estate, 1999), pp. 62–4, 72–8. On psychological issues, see S.

Henderson and T. Bostock, 'Coping Behaviour After Shipwreck,' *British Journal of Psychiatry* 131 (1977): 15–20. Henderson and Bostock, who made a particular study of the case of 10 men cast adrift off the coast of Australia in 1973, are explicit concerning the importance of 'attachment ideation,' as they term it: 'Throughout the ordeal,' they write, 'the most conspicuous behaviour was the men's preoccupation with principal attachment figures such as wives, mothers, children and girl friends ... Every one of the survivors reported it as the most helpful content of consciousness which they experienced' (p. 16). In contrast, one man who died after five days adrift was said by the others to have 'given up.'

The mutineers' prediction that Jacobsz would go to Malacca JFP 17 Sep 1629 [DB 143–4].

One kannen of water left Pelsaert declaration, op. cit.

Making Sunda Strait JFP 3 Jul 1629 [DB 133].

Batavia Taylor, *The Social World of Batavia*, pp. 3–32; Jaap Bruijn et al., *Dutch-Asiatic Shipping in the 17th and 18th Centuries* (The Hague: Martinus Nijhoff, 3 vols., 1979–1987), I, pp. 123–4; C. R. Boxer, *The Dutch Seaborne Empire 1600–1800* (London: Hutchinson, 1965), pp. 189–93, 207; Bernard Vlekke, *The Story of the Dutch East Indies* (Cambridge, MA: Harvard University Press, 1946), pp. 87, 91–2; Spruit, *Jan Pietersz Coen*, pp. 48–58.

Jan Coen He was born in January 1587 and sent to Rome as a young merchant at the age of 13. Returning to the United Provinces six years later, he signed on with the VOC as an under-merchant, aged only 20. Revisiting the Netherlands in 1611, he presented the Gentlemen XVII with a caustic report on the incompetence he had witnessed among its servants in the East. Impressed, they promoted him to upper-merchant and sent him back east in 1612 in command of a flotilla of two ships. He improved efficiency by cutting down on the number of landfalls his vessels made, and kept his crews healthy by feeding them lemons and plums, thus reducing the incidence of scurvy. These actions further commended him to the Gentlemen XVII, who in 1613 named him director-general, the second most senior position available in the Indies. Six years later Coen succeeded Governor-General Reael, serving in the latter post until 1623, and again from September 1627 until his death in 1629. Coen was well rewarded for his work. In 1624, at the conclusion of his first term as governor-general, the Gentlemen XVII awarded him the unheard-of gratuity of 20,000 guilders – money enough to set their servant up for life and enable him to make an advantageous marriage. Spruit, op. cit., esp. pp. 9–10, 16–8, 41–4.

The expulsion of the English and the conquest of the Banda Islands Spruit, op. cit., pp. 47–50, 71–3; Jonathan Israel, *Dutch Primacy in World Trade, 1585–1740* (Oxford: Clarendon Press), pp. 172–6; Giles Milton, *Nathaniel's Nutmeg: How One Man's Courage Changed the Course of History* (London: Hodder & Stoughton, 1999), pp. 286–7, 298–314. The English retained a foothold in the Spiceries thanks largely to the so-called Treaty of Defence (July 1619) between the Dutch Republic and the English crown, which guaranteed the East India Company a third of the produce of the Indies. The treaty had been signed before the authorities in the United Provinces became fully aware of Coen's successes in the East. When news of the agreement at last reached Java, the governor-general was predictably apoplectic. Nevertheless, by 1628, when the English East India Company finally abandoned its foothold in Batavia, its only remaining factories in the Indies were in Bantam, Macassar, and Sumatra.

Coen and the attempted conquest of China Spruit, op. cit., pp. 74, 80–2.

The Amboina massacre The total armament available to the English contingent, it seems worth noting, consisted of three swords and two muskets. Ibid., pp. 89–92; John Keay, *The Honourable Company: A History of the English East India Company* (London: HarperCollins, 1993), pp. 47–51; Milton, op. cit., pp. 318–42.

'An oriental despotism of the traditional kind' Boxer, op. cit., p. 191.

Agung of Mataram Spruit, op. cit., pp. 92–105; Boxer, op. cit., pp. 190–2; Vlekke, op. cit., pp. 88–9, 94; Israel, op. cit., p. 181. The Mataramese war effort was covertly backed by the Portuguese. Mataram itself is nowadays known as Jogjakarta.

'... a small proportion of their ships ...' Not all that many. The Company had lost four vessels in the years 1602–24, and would lose another 16 (14 wrecked and two captured) in the next quarter of a century, about 3 for every hundred voyages made during the period 1602–49. Jaap Bruijn et al., op. cit., I, p. 75.

'could never forget misdeeds ...' The opinion of the historian Bernard Vlekke, cited by Drake-Brockman, op. cit., p. 45.

Sara Specx Coen's principal motive in prosecuting this case was to assuage the disgrace done to the reputation of the Dutch in the eyes of the Javanese; Sara's lover, a standard-bearer named Pieter Cortenhoeff, had bribed some slaves to allow him access to the girl's chamber, and news of their actions had thus spread to the native community. Sara Specx was the natural child of Jacques, the president of the fleet Pelsaert was supposed to have sailed in. She was half-Japanese and was born on the island of Hirado in 1617. Taylor, *The Social World of Batavia,* p. 16.

Pelsaert before the Council of the Indies Minutes of the Governor-General in council, 9 Jul 1629, cited by Drake-Brockman, op. cit., p. 44. During Pelsaert's time in Batavia, he was also interrogated by Anthonij Van den Heuvel, the *fiscaal,* as to the precise circumstances of the disaster. Pelsaert declaration, op. cit.

Coen's encounter with the South-Land J. A. Heeres, *The Part Borne by the Dutch in the Discovery of Australia 1606–1765* (London: Luzac, 1899), p. 52; Schilder, op. cit., p. 100; Miriam Estensen, *Discovery: the Quest for the Great South Land* (Sydney: Allen & Unwin, 1998), p. 152. Coen's estimates of distance are given here in English miles; his original account gives them in Dutch *mijlen,* each of which was approximately 4½ miles long.

'the other members of the council' Although the Council nominally had eight seats, there were in fact six vacancies at this time. Nor were the two remaining members in any real sense independent. Van Diemen was an undischarged bankrupt who had fled to the Indies, and Coen had shielded him from the Gentlemen XVII in spite of this because he recognised his great ability; he

thus owed his entire career to the governor-general. Vlack was Coen's brother-in-law. Gerretson, op. cit., p. 64.

Coen's orders Order of 15 July 1629, cited by Drake-Brockman, op. cit., pp. 257–8.

Arrest of Jacobsz and Evertsz Drake-Brockman, op. cit., pp. 46, 63.

'Because Ariaen Jacobsz ...' Governor-General in council, 13 July 1629, cited in ibid., p. 46.

Antonij van den Heuvel He had arrived in Batavia in June 1628 and three months later was appointed *fiscaal*. His principal task was to curb the excesses of the private trade, and in order to incentivise him the Gentlemen XVII had promised Van den Heuvel one-third of all the fines he imposed on those found guilty of the crime. The new *fiscaal* took to his job with enthusiasm, even fining members of the Council of the Indies for their activities. He quickly became the most hated man in Batavia as a result. Gerretson, op. cit., pp. 68–70.

The Sardam's *voyage* JFP 15 Jul–16 Sep [DB 134–141]; Drake-Brockman, op. cit., pp. 46–7. For Gerritsz, Hollert, and Claas Jansz, see ibid., pp. 46, 68.

Gerritsz, Jacob Jansz, and Claes Jansz OV; JFP 28 Sep 1629 [DB 157]; Drake-Brockman, op. cit., p. 68; Pelsaert's declaration, op. cit.

'Smoke on a long island ...' JFP 17 Sep 1629 [DB 141].

Chapter 7: 'Who Wants to Be Stabbed to Death?'

Gijsbert Bastiaensz's letter home, the only personal account of life on Batavia's Graveyard, was particularly important in compiling the information in this chapter. Information on the geography, geology, and archaeology of Wiebbe Hayes's Island has been drawn from the various publications of the Western Australian Maritime Museum, and my discussion of the events surrounding Pelsaert's return to the Abrolhos on the interpretations advanced in Jeremy Green, Myra Stanbury, and Femme Gaastra (eds.), *The ANCODS Colloquium: Papers Presented at the Australia-Netherlands Colloquium on Maritime Archaeology and Maritime History* (Fremantle: Australian National Centre of Excellence for Maritime Archaeology, 1999).

Gijsbert Bastiaensz LGB; J. Mooij, *Bouwstoffen voor de Geschiedenis der Protestantsche Kerk in Nederlands-Indië* (Weltevreden: Landsdrukkerij, 1927), I, 328.

Jeronimus preaches his views Verdict on Jan Hendricxsz, JFP 28 Sep 1629; interrogation of Jan Pelgrom, JFP 26 Sep 1629 [DB 184, 209]; Mooij, op. cit., p. 308.

'He tried to maintain ...' This summary was written by Salomon Deschamps, but presumably at Pelsaert's dictation. JFP 30 Sep 1629 [DB 212].

Spiritual Liberty and its views Norman Cohn, *The Pursuit of the Millennium: Revolutionary Millenarians and Mystical Anarchists of the Middle Ages* (Oxford: Oxford University Press, 1970), pp. 148–97.

'Bastiaensz was rarely allowed to preach' In his evidence to the Church Council in Batavia, Bastiaensz claimed that he had continued to preach in the Abrolhos.

It was certainly in his interests to assert this, since – as we will see – his perceived weakness during the *Batavia* episode had left him in danger of being prevented from taking up a post in the Indies. Since there are several references in the journals to a ban on religious services (cf. verdict on Andries Jonas, JFP 28 Sep 1629 [DB 204]), the *predikant* was probably referring to his time on Wiebbe Hayes's Islands, if he was telling the truth at all. There is, however, one reference in the Harderwijk MS to a religious ceremony on the island; see below. Mooij, op. cit., p. 328.

'Blaspheme and swear' Harderwijck MS [R 26].

'Let us sing' Ibid.

Severed seals' fins Ibid.

Oaths of loyalty Later on, when circumstances compelled Jeronimus to remove potential rivals from his band, 'he tore the Oath of agreement publicly, by which action he dismissed the same, and so those who had to die were murdered at night, and then a new agreement was made.' For this, and the oaths themselves, see JFP 19 Sep 1629; interrogation of Jeronimus Cornelisz, same date [DB 147–8, 166].

Those who signed Twenty-five men signed the first oath of loyalty, and 36 the second, not including Cornelisz himself. Their names are listed here; note the changes in the order of the names, which in certain cases seem to denote variations in status within the group. The original lists give occupations and places of origin for most of the men, which have had to be omitted here. Deschamps, who wrote out the documents, places himself at the bottom of each, no doubt to dissociate himself as far as possible from the mutineers, though his rank would have assured him of a higher place in the originals. Finally, note that Cornelisz signs as a member of the band on the first occasion, *primus inter pares*, while the second oath was sworn *to* him, as undisputed leader. From JFP 19 Sep 1629 [DB 165–7]. Additions to the ranks of the mutineers are marked* on the second list:

FIRST OATH, 16 JULY 1629	SECOND OATH, 20 AUGUST 1629
Hieronomus Cornelisz	Coenraat van Huyssen
Coenraat van Huyssen	David van Zevanck
Jacop Pietersz	Jacop Pietersz
David van Zevanck	Wouter Loos
Isbrant Isbrantsz	Gÿsbert van Welderen
Olivier van Welderen	Gijsbert Bastianesz*
Gÿsbert van Welderen	Reyndert Hendricx
Jan Pelgrom de Bye	Jan Hendricxsz
Jan Hendricxsz	Andries Jonas*
Lenert Michielsz van Os	Rutger Fredricx
Mattys Beer	Mattys Beer
Allert Janssen	Hans Frederick*
Hans Hardens	Jacques Pilman*
Rutger Fredricx	Lucas Gellisz
Gerrit Willemsz	Andries Liebent*

Cornelis Pietersz
Hans Jacob Heijlweck
Lucas Gellisz
Reyndert Hendricx
Daniel Cornelissen
Wouter Loos
Gerrit Haas
Jan Willemsz Selyns
Jeuriaen Jansz
Hendrick Jaspersz
Salomon Deschamps

Abraham Jansz*
Hans Hardens
Olivier van Welderen
Jeuriaen Jansz
Isbrant Isbrantsz
Jan Willemsz Selyns
Jan Egbertsz*
Cornelis Pietersz
Hendrick Jaspersz
Gillis Phillipsen*
Tewis Jansz*
Hans Jacob Heijlweck
Gerrit Haas
Claes Harmansz*
Allert Janssen
Rogier Decker*
Gerrit Willemsz
Abraham Gerritsz*
Jan Pelgrom de Bye
Lenert Michielsz van Os
Salomon Deschamps

The killers It would not do to suggest these men were too discriminating. Beer, for example, claimed never to have killed a woman, but in fact he slaughtered one of Bastiaensz's daughters and helped to kill his wife. Nor did he display any reluctance to murder children. Interrogation of Mattys Beer, JFP 23 Sep 1629 [DB 190].

Jan Hendricxsz's murders Upon Pelsaert's return to the Abrolhos, Hendricxsz immediately and openly confessed to this number of killings, almost as though he were boasting of his achievement. JFP 17 Sep 1629 [DB 143].

The women Mutineers' oath of 20 Aug 1629 [DB 147].

'*...for common service...*' JFP 19 Sep 1629 [DB 147].

Jan Hendricxsz's woman Verdict on Jan Hendricxsz, JFP 28 Sep 1629 [DB 184].

Mattys Beer's woman Verdict on Mattys Beer, JFP 2 Oct 1629 [DB 193].

Olivier van Welderen's woman Verdict on Olivier van Welderen, JFP 30 Nov 1629 [DB 245].

Loos's and Van Os's women Verdict on Wouter Loos, 24 Sep 1629; verdict on Lenert Michielsz van Os, JFP 28 Sep 1629 [DB 188–9, 225].

Jan Pelgrom's women Interrogation of Jan Pelgrom, JFP 26 Sep 1629 [DB 209].

'*My daughter...*' LGB.

'*Almost as soon as he took power*' The journals state that Cornelisz enjoyed Lucretia as his concubine 'for two months.' Since he was captured by Hayes's men on 2 September (see below), this implies that his relationship with her began early in July, though Zevanck's conversation with Creesje suggests she did not sleep with him before 22 July. Verdict on Jeronimus Cornelisz, JFP 28 Sep 1629 [DB 176].

Cornelisz's wooing The romantic expectations of the period are mapped by Simon Schama, *The Embarrassment of Riches: An Interpretation of Dutch Culture in the Golden Age* (London: Fontana, 1987), pp. 437, 439–40. In seeking to seduce Creesje, Cornelisz naturally ignored the inconvenient fact of his existing marriage; by now he must have realised that, whatever happened on the Abrolhos, he would never see Haarlem again.

'... in the end...' Testimony of Wiebbe Hayes et al., 2 Oct 1629, OV [DB 68-9]. This testimony does not feature in Pelsaert's journals, and was first published in Isaac Commelin's pamphlet of 1647. As Drake-Brockman point out, it might be a forgery designed to clear Creesje of the suspicion that she submitted too tamely to Cornelisz; but there is internal evidence, in its dating, that it was at least written when it is supposed to have been, on the day of the apothecary's execution.

Jan Pelgrom de Bye Interrogation of Jan Pelgrom, JFP 26–28 Sep 1629 [DB 209–11].

'Zevanck wanted to ensure...' It will be recalled that Stone-Cutter Pietersz was also present that night, but played no direct part in the massacre. Perhaps, as a member of Cornelisz's council, he was beyond suspicion; perhaps, as Zevanck's superior, he could not simply be ordered to take part in the killing.

Murder of Jan Gerritsz and Obbe Jansz Verdict on Jeronimus Cornelisz, JFP 28 Sep 1629 [DB 174].

Murder of Stoffel Stoffelsz Confession of Jeronimus Cornelisz, JFP 23 Sep 1629; verdict on Jan Hendricxsz, JFP 28 Sep 1629 [DB 169, 184]

Murder of Hendrick Jansz Statement of Jeronimus Cornelisz, JFP 24 Sep 1629; verdict on Rogier Decker, JFP 12 Nov 1629 [DB 169, 231–2] The date of this killing is variously given as 25 July and 10 August in the journals. Jansz was bound when Decker stabbed him and could not have put up much of a fight. Verdict on Jeronimus Cornelisz, JFP 28 Sep 1629 [DB 175].

Murder of Anneken Hardens Verdict on Jan Hendricxsz, JFP 28 Sep 1629; verdict on Jan Pelgrom, JFP 28 Sep 1629; verdict on Andries Liebent, JFP 30 Nov 1629 [DB 184, 210, 244]. The date of this killing is variously given as 28 and 30 July.

Murder of Cornelis Aldersz Confession of Jeronimus Cornelisz, 23 Sep 1629; interrogation of Jan Pelgrom, 23 Sep 1629; interrogation of Mattys Beer, 26 Sep 1629; verdict on Mattys Beer, JFP 28 Sep 1629, [DB 169, 190–1, 195, 208–11]. In writing up his interrogation of Pelgrom, Pelsaert tells this story twice in almost exactly the same words. My quotations have been pieced together from these two accounts. Further variants appear in the *commandeur*'s notes on Mattys Beer. Pelsaert says on four occasions that Aldersz was decapitated by Beer's single stroke, but another reference in the journals says merely that the soldier 'with one blow near enough struck off his head.'

The murder of Andries de Vries Verdict on Jeronimus Cornelisz, JFP 28 Sep 1629 [DB 174]; summary of the crimes of Rutger Fredricx, JFP 28 Sep 1629 [DB 156]; verdict on Rutger Fredricx, JFP 28 Sep 1629 [DB 207]; interrogation of Lenert van Os, JFP 23 Sep 1629 [DB 186–7]. The notion that Creesje and Andries shared a bond of friendship, and that De Vries was seen as an especial threat to the captain-general, arises from the fact that De Vries alone, rather than the mutineers in general, had sworn to forfeit his life if he ever talked to her.

The Selyns incident Confession of Wouter Loos, JFP 27 Oct 1629; verdict on Hans Jacob Heijlweck, 30 Nov 1629 [DB 226, 241].

Murder of Frans Jansz This incident took place on the High Island (Jansz was the only man to die there in the course of the mutiny), while Jeronimus and his principal lieutenants were negotiating with Wiebbe Hayes. A reserve body of mutineers stayed behind to act as reinforcements if required, and they had orders to dispose of Jansz while they were waiting for the others to return. Evidently Jeronimus had Hayes and his men firmly in mind at the time, and this must have help to crystallise his thought concerning the surgeon's possible defection. Verdict on Hans Jacob Heijlweck, 30 Nov 1629 [DB 241].

'… creatures of miraculous form …' This was Pelsaert's description of the tammar. The *commandeur* was the first Westerner ever to observe and describe marsupials, and his journal thus has considerable scientific as well as historical value. JFP 15 Nov 1629 [DB 235–6].

Wells According to one Defender, the wells were '50, 60 or even 100 *vademen* deep, being very sweet water.' Letter of 11 Dec 1629 in *Leyds Veer-Schuyts Praetjen, Tuschen een Koopman ende Borger van Leyden, Varende van Haarlem nae Leyden* (np [Amsterdam: Willem Jansz], 1630), pp. 15–8 [R 231]. The fact that two wells were discovered is mentioned by Pelsaert, JFP 20 Sep 1629 [DB 149]. Otherwise, see *The ANCODS Colloquium,* p. 99; Jeremy Green and Myra Stanbury, 'Even More Light on a Confusing Geographical Puzzle, Part 1: Wells, Cairns and Stone Structures on West Wallabi Island,' *Underwater Explorers' Club News* (January 1982): p. 2; Hugh Edwards, *Islands of Angry Ghosts* (New York: William Morrow & Co., 1966), pp. 174–5. Edwards comments that he finds it hard to believe it can have taken Hayes's men almost three weeks to find the larger cisterns; an unresolved mystery. In any case, we are told that the quality of the water was excellent; it tasted 'very sweet, like milk.' LGB.

Food Letter of 11 Dec 1629 in *Leyds Veer-Schuyts Praetjen, Tuschen een Koopman ende Borger van Leyden, Varende van Haarlem nae Leyden,* pp. 15–8 [R 231]. Shellfish were also available in abundance on the islands, but Dutchmen of the seventeenth century despised them as the poorest sort of food, and would have eaten oysters and mussels only *in extremis*. Gijsbert Bastiaensz, who spent some weeks on the island, commented on the fecundity of the island in very similar terms: 'Miraculously God has blessed the good ones … with Water, with fowls, with fish, with other Beasts, with eggs in basketfull; there were also some Beasts which they called Cats with as nice a flavour as I ever tasted.' LGB. Tammars *(Thylogale eugenii houtmani)* stand up to two feet tall, and lack the extremely well developed hind limbs of the kangaroo.

New arrivals For the escape of people from Batavia's Graveyard, see JFP 17 Sep 1629 [DB 143].

Improvised weapons Letter of 11 Dec 1629 [R 232]; LGB, which includes the reference to 'guns'; Edwards, pp. 52–4.

Hayes's dispositions For a full discussion of the coastal shelter and its inland counterpart, see chapter 10.

Location of Hayes's boats See the discussions in *The ANCODS Colloquium,* pp. 93, 100.

Allert Jansz According to OV, he was a corporal rather than a cadet. This seems less likely, as, whatever Hayes's qualities, an experienced corporal might have been expected to command the landing party, while a young cadet would not.

Jeronimus's plans Verdict on Jeronimus Cornelisz, JFP 28 Sep 1629 [DB 175]; Pelsaert's 'Declaration in short, [of] the origin, reason, and towards what intention, Jeronimus Cornelissen, undermerchant, has resolved to murder all the people ... ,' JFP nd [DB 252].

'... by exploiting the well-known antipathy ...' It is interesting, from this perspective, to note that when the mutineers signed their second oath of comradeship on 20 August, it included a clause that specified: 'Also that the ship's folk amongst us will not be called sailors any more, but will be reckoned on the same footing as the soldiers, under one company.' Oath of 20 August [DB 148].

Jeronimus's letter Letter of 23 July to the French soldiers on Wiebbe Hayes's Island [DB 148–9]. This letter was handed to Pelsaert by Hayes when the mutiny was over and was copied into the *commandeur*'s journals, together with the mutineers' oaths, to form part of the evidence against Cornelisz and his men.

Cornelissen captured Verdict on Daniel Cornelissen, JFP 30 Nov 1629 [DB 240].

Attacks on Wiebbe Hayes's island Pelsaert is inexact concerning the number and dates of these contacts. Drake-Brockman, op. cit., pp. 115–7, presents a chronology with the most likely dates. For the sources, see the *commandeur*'s 'Declaration in Short' [DB 252–3]; verdict on Jeronimus Cornelisz, JFP 28 Sep 1629 [DB 175]. Pelsaert's earlier account (JFP 17 Sep 1629 [DB 159]) of the same episodes is partial, since it was based on Jeronimus's original statement to him, and thus emphasised the roles of Zevank and Van Huyssen while minimising Cornelisz's own. The second attack coincided with the murder of Frans Jansz, from which it appears that the mutineers split their forces and for some unknown reason chose to leave at least five of their best fighting men on the High Island.

Van Huyssen and Liebent grumble JFP 17 Sep 1629 [DB 159]; verdict on Andries Liebent, JFP 30 Nov 1629 [DB 244].

'To come to an accord ...' Pelsaert, 'Declaration in Short' [DB 253].

Clogs LGB. When he arrived on the island (see below), the Defenders gave Bastiaensz a pair of these homemade shoes, a gesture that touched him so deeply that he wrote that he would keep them for the rest of his life.

'... under cover, as friends ...' JFP 17 Sep 1629 [DB 142].

Bastiaensz and the treaty of peace This occurred on 1 September, during a reconnaissance. Jeronimus was also present, and, according to the *predikant,* 'Our Merchant offered them Peace, but [tried] to deceive them.' It would appear that Cornelisz was planning some sort of surprise attack, but two musketeers, who had instructions to pick off the Defenders when they came to the beach, found that their weapons persistently misfired, and Hayes had again emerged unscathed. Ibid.

'Saying joyfully ...' 'Declaration in Short' [DB 253].

'Very skinny ...' Letter of 11 Dec 1629 [R233].

'Deceiving them with many lies ...' LGB. Negotiations seems to have been conducted through Gijsbert Bastiaensz, who acted as go-between. JFP 17 Sep 1629 [DB 142]

'Hither and thither ...' LGB.

Capture of Cornelisz and execution of his lieutenants JFP 17 Sep 1629 [DB 159]; 'Declaration in Short' [DB 253]; LGB.

Jeronimus in the pit Harderwijk MS [R 28].

Election of Wouter Loos Verdict on Wouter Loos, JFP 13 Nov 1629 [DB 226-7]; 'Declaration in Short' [DB 253].

Loos and Creesje Interrogation of Wouter Loos, JFP 24 Sep 1629 [DB 225].

Loos and Judick LGB.

New council Bastiaensz, ibid., refers to the setting up of a 'new government' on the island.

Loos's motives for attacking Francisco Pelsaert, in interrogating Loos, suggested that the attack was launched 'on the pretext that they wanted to be Master of the Water,' but adds, remarkably, 'but on the contrary no water ever was refused to them.' Verdict on Wouter Loos, JFP 13 Nov 1629 [DB 228].

... 'at least some military experience ...' I would count Wouter Loos, Jan Hendricxsz, Stone-Cutter Pietersz, Lenert van Os, Mattys Beer, Andries Jonas, Hans Jacob Heijlweck, Lucas Gellisz, and perhaps Hans Frederick (who was often ill) among the soldiers, and Rutger Fredricx, Jan Willemsz Selyns, Allert Janssen, Andries Liebent, and Cornelis Janssen among the sailors. Of the boys, Jan Pelgrom, Rogier Decker, Abraham Gerritsz, and Claes Harmansz Hooploper might have been relied on to fight, taking the mutineers' maximum fighting strength to 18 men. The other signatories to Loos's oath – there would have been 15 of them, if the numbers of the mutineers' party had remained unchanged since the men had signed Cornelisz's second oath of 20 August – had played no part in the earlier attacks or killings, even though there were four or five soldiers and a similar number of sailors among them. A couple, including Olivier van Welderen, were not well enough to fight, but plainly the rest had no appetite for the killing.

Two muskets 'Declaration in Short' JFP nd [DB 253]. It took some time to get these weapons into action; according to Jan Hendricxsz, 'had we shot them [Hayes's men] immediately, we should certainly have got them, but the gunpowder burned away 3 to 4 time from the pan.' Cornelisz, told of this later when they were all under guard, admonished Hendricxsz, saying, 'If you had used some cunning you would have got it all ready on the water, and then we should have been ready.' JFP 19 Sep 1629 [DB 160].

The final attack JFP 17 Sept–13 Nov 1629 [DB 142, 222, 227–8]; LGB. Pelsaert and Bastiaensz give conflicting accounts as to how the action ended; the *predikant* writes that Loos ordered a retreat before the rescue ship appeared, but Pelsaert implies that the attack was still continuing when the *Sardam* hove into view: '[The mutineers] apparently would have caused even more disasters if it had not pleased God that we arrived here with the Yacht at the same time, or in the very hour, when they were fighting, and thus all their design has been destroyed.' Verdict on Wouter Loos, JFP 13 Nov 1629 [DB 227]. Jan Hendricxsz confirmed this account, noting that 'while they were fighting with the other party, they suddenly saw the ship.' Confession of Jan Hendricxsz, JFP 17 Sep 1629 [DB 178].

Chapter 8: Condemned

Pelsaert's *Batavia* journals contain detailed summaries of the interrogations of all the major mutineers, together with the sentences passed on them. These, with the commentaries of Henrietta Drake-Brockman (*Voyage to Disaster* [Nedlands, WA: University of Western Australia Press, 1995]) and V. D. Roeper (*De Schipbreuk van de* Batavia, *1629* [Zutphen: Walburg Pers, 1994]), have been my principal sources for this chapter.

Pelsaert's initial actions JFP 17 Sep 1629 [DB 141–2].

The Sardam's *anchorage* Hugh Edwards, 'Where Is Batavia's Graveyard?,' in *The ANCODS Colloquium,* pp. 91–3; Jeremy Green, 'The *Batavia* Incident: The Sites,' in ibid., p. 100.

'Frantic relief' 'The pious ones jumped for joy,' wrote Bastiaensz, 'and immediately went in their little boat to the *jacht* to warn them.' LGB.

Loos and Pelgrom Verdict on Jan Pelgrom, JFP 28 Sep 1629 [DB 209–10].

Hayes's anchorage Edwards, 'Where Is Batavia's Graveyard?' p. 93, persuasively advocates this as the most likely explanation for Hayes's appearance 'round the northerly point,' as mentioned in Pelsaert's journals.

'Thick with nettles…' H. Edwards, *Islands of Angry Ghosts* (New York: William Morrow & Co., 1966), p. 174.

The crew of the mutineers' boat JFP 19 Sep 1629 [DB 146] lists the 11 members of the crew as Stone-Cutter Pietersz, Jan Hendricxsz, Rutger Fredricx, Hans Jacob Heijlweck, Lucas Gellisz, Hans Frederick, Jan Willensz Selyns, Hendrick Jaspersz Cloet, Hans Hardens, Jacques Pilman, and Gerrit Haas. It is interesting to note that the last four were very minor figures, who had committed no specific crimes and who were in fact never actually punished for their involvement in the mutiny. Probably at this point all those who had signed Jeronimus's oaths expected nothing but death as a result.

The 'boat race' Philippe Godard, *The First and Last Voyage of the* Batavia (Perth: Abrolhos Publishing, nd, c. 1993), p. 174n. It should be pointed out that neither party seems to have been aware that the 'race' was going on; both were simply trying to reach Pelsaert and the *jacht* as rapidly as possible.

Crew of the Sardam Drake-Brockman, *Voyage to Disaster,* p. 153n.

Encounter with Wiebbe Hayes JFP 17–28 Sep 1629 [DB 142–3, 152].

Swivel guns These were small cannons, on pivots, which were generally loaded with grapeshot, nails, or other antipersonnel devices and mounted on the poop rail to deter boarders. When Pelsaert, in JFP 17 Sep 1629 [DB 143] says that he and his men 'made all preparations to capture the scoundrels,' he surely meant that he had these pieces loaded and prepared to fire; at least, the anonymous Defender implies as much when he writes that the commandeur 'pointed his guns' at the men in the boat. Letter of 11 Dec 1629, *Leyds Veer-Schuyts Praetjen, Tuschen een Koopman ende Borger van Leyden, Varende van Haarlem nae Leyden* (np [Amsterdam: Willem Jansz], 1630), pp. 15–18 [R 321].

The arrival and arrest of the mutineers JFP 28 Sep 1629 [DB 152].

'They answered me…' JFP 17 Sep 1629 [DB 143].

'We learned from their own confessions…' JFP 28 Sep 1629 [DB 152].

'I looked at him with great sorrow…' JFP 17 Sep 1629 [DB 144].

'Where the rest of the scoundrels were…' JFP 18 Sep 1629 [DB 144–5].

'These have all been found…' Ibid. [DB 145].

'We found that the ship was lying in many pieces…' Ibid.

Pelsaert legally obliged to administer justice swiftly Roeper, *De Schipbreuk van de Batavia, 1629,* pp. 30–2.

Jan Willemsz Visch Drake-Brockman, in *Voyage to Disaster,* p. 157n, speculates that he was a sailor, but on no good evidence. My identification of him as the *Sardam*'s provost, or – given the small size of the crew – simply the man deputed to fill that role is also guesswork, but it fits the typical composition of a shipboard *raad* rather better. He was certainly illiterate, signing the various interrogations only with a mark.

Dutch law on confessions and evidence Roeper, op. cit., pp. 31–2.

Water torture Ibid., p. 32; Drake-Brockman, op. cit., pp. 101–2; Giles Milton, *Nathaniel's Nutmeg: How One Man's Courage Changed the Course of History* (London: Hodder & Stoughton, 1999), pp. 328–9.

'Forcing all his inward parts…' Cited by John Keay, *The Honourable Company: A History of the English East India Company* (London: Harper Collins, 1993), p. 49.

Cornelisz's testimony Interrogation of Jeronimus Cornelisz, JFP 19 Sep 1629 [DB 160–70].

'Saying they are lying…' Interrogation of Jeronimus Cornelisz, JFP 28 Sep 1629 [DB 170].

'On account of his unsteady and variable confessions…' Ibid.

'In order to speak again to his wife…' Ibid.

'Something was in it…' Ibid. Janssen and Hendricxsz indignantly denied the suggestion of their captain-general, calling out 'as one Man that they would die on it, on the salvation of their souls, not to have lied in the least in the things heretofore confessed.'

'Mocked the Council…' Ibid.

'Confesses at last… He well knows…' Ibid.

Hendricxsz put to the torture Interrogation of Jan Hendricxsz, JFP 17 Sep 1629 [DB 177].

Torture of Andries Jonas Interrogation of Andries Jonas, JFP 24 Sep 1629 [DB 201].

Cornelisz betrays his followers Interrogation of Rutger Fredricx, JFP 20 Sep 1629 [DB 205–6]; interrogation of Lenert van Os, JFP 23 Sep 1629 [DB 168–9]; interrogation of Rogier Decker, JFP 24 Sep 1629 [DB 169]; interrogation of Mattys Beer, JFP 23 Sep 1629 [DB 189–90].

Jonas's contrition Interrogation of Andries Jonas, JFP 27 Sep 1629 [DB 202].

Verdict on Cornelisz Sentence on Jeronimus Cornelisz, JFP 28 Sep 1629 [DB 172–7].

Verdicts on the major mutineers JFP 28 Sep 1629 [DB 154–6].

Men held and released JFP 28 Sep 1629 [DB 156–7]; list of mutineers, 20 Aug, JFP 19 Sep 1629 [DB 166–7].

Hayes's promotion JFP 28 Sep 1629 [DB 157].

'Who had been without a commanding officer...' Gabriel Jacobszoon, the corporal, was dead, and Pietersz, the lance corporal, in prison.

'Keep his men supplied with food and water' The main wells on Wiebbe Hayes's Island had begun to run dry, and it was only after careful searching that new sources of fresh water were at last uncovered on the High Island.

'The only goods recovered...' JFP 25 Sep 1629 [DB 150].

'It would not be without danger...' JFP 28 Sep 1629 [DB 151].

Executions set for 29 September This is the only date Pelsaert can have had in mind, since it must have been almost dark when sentences were passed on the 28th, and he states (JFP 28 Sep 1629 [DB 211]) that the executions would be 'postponed' to 1 October. It would have been proper to have carried them out on the Sunday, 30 September.

Cornelisz requests a delay Ibid.

'The predikant put him at ease...' Ibid.

Jeronimus again begged to know... JFP 29 Sep 1629 [DB 211–2].

'Tut – nothing more?' Ibid.

Jeronimus's letters JFP 29 Sep 1629 [DB 171].

Jacob Jansz Hollert The journals actually have 'Jacop Jacopsz Holloch' at this point, an apparent error since no one of this name is referred to anywhere else in the text. Drake-Brockman interprets the name as a probable reference to 'Jacob Jacobsz Houtenman,' the skipper of the *Sardam;* but the name as given actually seems closer to Jacob Jansz Hollert, the *Batavia*'s under-steersman, who had returned with Pelsaert; and this man does seem a much more probable recipient of the letters, since he would actually have known Cornelisz. Given that Ariaen Jacobsz is said to have stated [Interrogation of Jeronimus Cornelisz, JFP 19 Sep 1629, DB 164] that he mistrusted both Claes Gerritsz and 'the under-steersman, my brother in law,' this reading would imply that Gillis Fransz Halffwaack was the skipper's relative, but that Fransz's colleague, Jacob Jansz, was – at least in Jeronimus's eyes – more sympathetic to the mutineers. Before condemning Hollert as a crypto-mutineer, however, it is worth recalling that by this stage in the story, the under-merchant had wiped out all but a tiny handful of the people he had got to know in the *retourship*'s stern; of his immediate peer group, only Pelsaert, Claes Gerritsz, Bastiaensz, and Creesje were both alive and present in the archipelago. Since Gerritsz seems to have been kept busy on the Council and at the wreck, and neither the *predikant* nor Creesje were at all likely to act willingly as messengers, Hollert may have been nothing more than a last, despairing hope. For a more conspiracy-oriented perspective, see Philip Tyler, 'The *Batavia* Mutineers: Evidence of an Anabaptist "Fifth Column" within 17th Century Dutch Colonialism?' *Westerly* (December 1970): 36–7.

'Was, perhaps, a remnant of the batch ...' The other possibility is that the poison was obtained from the *Sardam*'s apothecary's chest. (Frans Jansz's chest had evidently been lost with the *Batavia*, as the eventual rediscovery of some of its contents at the wreck site showed. Jeremy Green, *The Loss of the Verenigde Oostindische Compagnie Retourschip Batavia, Western Australia 1629: An Excavation Report and Catalogue of Artefacts* (Oxford: British Archaeological Reports, 1989), pp. 95–6, 99–101. This catalogue lists two different sets of ointment jars; in excess of 24 jars, or about one-eighth of the original contents of the chest, were recovered from the seabed. It is however possible that the remainder of the jars were recovered by the mutineers.

The suicide attempt JFP 29 Sep 1629 [DB 211–2].

Pelsaert confronts Jeronimus's religious views JFP 30 Sep 1629 [DB 212].

'Godless' Verdict on Andries Jonas, JFP 28 Sep 1629 [DB 203].

'Evil-minded' Ibid.

'Innately corrupt' Pelsaert to the Gentlemen XVII of Amsterdam, 12 Dec 1629, ARA VOC 1630 [DB259].

'See how miraculously ...' JFP 30 Sep 1629 [DB 212].

Site of the gallows Edwards, op. cit., p. 177.

Creesje and Cornelisz Testimony of Wiebbe Hayes, Claes Jansz Hooft et al, 2 Oct 1629, OV, pp. 59–60 [G pt. 2, p. 37]. As Drake-Brockman points out (op. cit., pp. 67–9), this testimony does not appear in JFP and there are no places in Pelsaert's journal from which it could reasonably have been excised. Its first appearance was in Jan Jansz's *Batavia* pamphlet of 1647. Drake-Brockman adds that it may [1] be a genuine addition to the record, which the pamphleteer somehow got hold of (it is in the first, rather than the third person, unlike JFP, but its content is consistent with the unpublished records of the VOC, making outright forgery unlikely) or [2] a fake, invented by someone who wished to make quite certain that Creesje Jans was cleared of any imputation that she submitted willingly to Cornelisz. Both modern editors of Pelsaert's journals – Drake-Brockman and Roeper (op. cit., p. 210) tend to favour its authenticity.

'So that their eyes could see ...' JFP 2 Oct 1629 [DB 213].

Amputation of hands OV [G pt. 2, p. 37]. There is some uncertainty as to whether the full sentence was carried out, as Bastiaensz, in LGB, mentions the amputation of only Cornelisz's right hand. I tend to think the *predikant* was simply being inexact in what was not, after all, an official account.

'They all shouted ...' JFP 2 Oct 1629 [DB 213]

'If ever there had been a Godless Man ...' LGB.

Chapter 9: To Be Broken on the Wheel

Henrietta Drake-Brockman did invaluable work, in the 1950s and 1960s, on the aftermath of the *Batavia* mutiny, and her *Voyage to Disaster,* while inaccurate in some small details, includes almost all that is known about the later history of Pelsaert, Gijsbert Bastiaensz and his daughter, Ariaen Jacobsz, and Creesje Jans. My own research has added only a little to

Drake-Brockman's findings. The archives of Dordrecht, Haarlem, and Amsterdam did provide some fresh information, and the massive early Dutch histories of the Indies also proved invaluable – in particular the first volume of J. Mooij's *Bouwstoffen voor de Geschiedenis der Protestantsche Kerk in Nederlands-Indië* (Weltevreden: Landsdrukkerij, 1927), which translates as 'Building Blocks for the History of the Protestant Church in the Netherlands Indies' and contains additional details concerning the fates of the *predikant* and his daughter.

Death by hanging John Laurence, *A History of Capital Punishment* (New York: Citadel Press, 1960), pp. 41–5.

'He could not reconcile himself...' JFP 2 Oct 1629 [DB 213].

'Dying as he had lived...' Anonymous *Batavia* survivor's letter, December 1629, in anon., *Leyds Veer-Schuyts Praetjen, Tuschen een Koopman ende Borger van Leyden, Varende van Haarlem nae Leyden* (np [Amsterdam: Willem Jansz], 1630), pp. 19–20 [R 236]. For the identification of the author, see the general comments at the beginning of the notes.

Final confessions of the Batavia *mutineers* JFP 2 Oct 1629 [DB 213].

Display of executed prisoners at Haarlem William Brereton, *Travels in Holland, the United Provinces etc... 1634–1635* (London: Chetham Society, 1844), p. 49.

Salvage operations JFP 25–26 Sep, 3 Oct–14 Nov 1629 [DB 150–1, 213–22]. Pelsaert indicates, and other writers have assumed, that only one chest remained unsalvaged. However, the numismatist S. J. Wilson, in *Doits to Ducatoons: The Coins of the Dutch East India Company Ship* Batavia, *Lost on the Western Australian Coast 1629* (Perth: Western Australian Museum, 1989), p. 9, reports that salvage operations undertaken in the period from 1963 brought up so much money – in excess of 10,000 coins – that the cash seems to have once filled two chests rather than one.

'With heart's regret' JFP 12 Oct 1629 [DB 215].

'... well in excess of 150,000 guilders...' The *Batavia* herself had cost about 100,000 guilders, and the cash in the missing money chests totalled another 45,000 guilders. The value of the ship's miscellaneous trade goods, particularly some of Pelsaert's silver, must have totalled at least 5,000 guilders more. Wilson, op. cit., p. 9.

Loss of the Sardam*'s boat* JFP 12–13 Oct, 15 Nov 1629 [DB 215–16, 234]. Drake-Brockman's translation is a little confusing at this point. As printed, it gives the distance from the *Sardam* to the yawl as 'two miles' as though they were English units of measurement, but the original manuscript reads '2 mijlen,' seventeenth-century Dutch miles, each of which was equivalent to about 4.6 English statute miles.

The possibility of a second mutiny Allert Janssen had, indeed, warned Pelsaert on the way to the gallows that the *commandeur* should 'watch very well on the Ship because quite many traitors remained alive who would seize an opportunity to execute that which they had intended; without naming anyone, saying that he did not wish to be called an informer after his death.' JFP 28 Sep–2 Oct 1629 [DB 157, 213].

Leniency shown to Wouter Loos Pelsaert's moderation in this case still seems remarkable today. It was not until the end of October, when Judick Gijsbertsdr belatedly came forward to testify against him, that the mutineers' last leader was closely questioned about his activities on Batavia's Graveyard, and though he finally confessed, under repeated torture, to the murders he had previously denied, there was never any talk of increasing his sentence. Testimony of Judick Gijsbertsdr, 27 Oct 1629 [DB 225–6].

The trials on board the Sardam Sentences on Daniel Cornelissen, Hans Jacob Heijlweck, Cornelis Janssen, Jean Thirion, Andries Liebent, Hans Frederick, Olivier van Welderen, Jan Renou, and Isbrant Isbrantsz, JFP 24 Sep–20 Nov 1629; [DB 240-6].

Numbers of Batavia *survivors* Pelsaert to the Gentlemen XVII, 12 Dec 1629, ARA VOC 1630 [DB 259–61]. The names of the survivors are nowhere given, but Pelsaert seems definite that only seven women survived the disaster. Two of them – Zwaantie Hendricxsz and her companion – had reached *Batavia* in the longboat, so it would appear that either Anneken Bosschieters or Marretgie Louys, two of the women kept for 'common service,' must have died on the islands. Neither is mentioned among Cornelisz's victims, and both survived the wreck and the initial days without supplies, so presumably the death can be attributed to injury or disease.

The return to Batavia JFP 15 Nov–5 Dec [DB 234–9, 247].

The marooning The exact spot where the two mutineers were put ashore is still debated. Henrietta Drake-Brockman favoured the mouth of the Hutt River. Most modern authors identify the location as a cove just north of Red Bluff, which stands at one end of Wittecara Gully. The Red Bluff site is several miles to the north of Drake-Brockman's preferred location. Today a small memorial marks the spot. JFP 16 Nov 1629 [DB 237]; Phillip Playford, *Carpet of Silver: The Wreck of the Zuytdorp* (Nedlands, WA: University of Western Australia Press, 1996), pp. 237–42.

The Sardam's *council* Thanks to the loss of Jacob Jacobsz, the council numbered only five on this occasion. The principal members were Pelsaert, Claes Gerritsz, Sijmon Yopzoon, and Jan Willemsz Visch. For some reason Gijsbert Bastiaensz and Jacob Jansz did not sit in judgment on the mutineers; possibly they were ill. Remarkably, however, Salomon Deschamps retained his place even though he had been sentenced to be keelhauled and flogged only a fortnight earlier. Once again, the only likely explanation is that he alone among those on board had the clerical skills needed to keep the necessary records.

Sentences passed on board the Sardam JFP 30 Nov 1629 [DB 239–47]. Daniel Cornelissen was sentenced to receive 200 strokes, twice the number meted out to Deschamps and the other minor mutineers who had been sentenced in the Abrolhos. Cornelis Janssen received 150 strokes and the fine of 18 months' wages (the larger fine may simply represent a longer service with the VOC) and Hans Jacob Heijlweck was sentenced to 100 strokes and the loss of six months' wages. The lightest flogging was meted out to Isbrant Isbrantsz, who received only 50 strokes.

'in order not to trouble...' Ibid. [DB 239].

Zussie Fredericx As we have seen, the unfortunate Zussie had already been made to sleep with Jan Hendricxsz, who had kept her as his concubine for two months, as well as with Mattys Beer and Jan Pelgrom (Sentence on Jan Hendricxsz, 28 Sep 1629 [DB 184]; sentence on Mattys Beer, 28 Sep 1629 [DB 193]; interrogation of Jan Pelgrom, 26 Sep 1629 [DB209]), so the allegation, if true, would take to at least six the number of men she had intercourse with in the Abrolhos.

The second siege of Batavia Bernard Vlekke, *The Story of the Dutch East Indies* (Cambridge, MA: Harvard University Press, 1946), pp. 93–4; Drake-Brockman op. cit., pp. 71–2; R. Spruit, *Jan Pietersz Coen: Daden en Dagen in Dienst van de VOC* (Houten: De Haan, 1987), pp. 103–7.

The death of Jan Coen Spruit, op. cit., pp. 106–10; F. W. Stapel (ed.), *Beschryvinge van de Oostindische Compagnie,* vol. 3 (The Hague: Martinus Nijhoff, 1939), p. 456.

The elevation of Jacques Specx Specx had not actually left the Dutch Republic until 25 January 1629, two months after Pelsaert had sailed. His election was merely provisional, as the appointment was made by the Council of the Indies and not by the Gentlemen XVII, but it was later made permanent and he served in the position for three years. F. W. Stapel, *De Gouveneurs-Generaal van Nederlandsch-Indië in Beeld en Woord* (The Hague: Van Stockum, 1941), p. 19.

Execution of justice on the Sardam Drake-Brockman draws attention to the fact that Deschamps was back on the *Sardam's* council by 30 November, a fortnight after he was supposedly keelhauled and flogged – apparently because she doubted that he could have recovered from his punishment so quickly. Gijsbert Bastiaensz, the only witness to have left any sort of account, says merely that 'of the others, some were punished on the Ship, some were brought to Batavia.' The last comment may simply refer to Jacop Pietersz, but since the reference to people is in the plural, I think it more probable that none of the sentences actually passed on the *Sardam* eight were actually carried out in the five days between the delivery of the verdicts and the ship's arrival in Batavia. There is reason to assume that the five prisoners sentenced earlier did receive their punishments, since Pelsaert was quite definite, in his summing up, that they would take place 'tomorrow,' i.e., on 13 November. It is certainly not impossible that Deschamps had recovered sufficiently to act as Pelsaert's clerk again by the end of the month; much would depend on the actual severity of the flogging he received. It is beyond question that naval men who received a flogging were expected back at their posts more quickly than that. Sentences on Salomon Deschamps, Rogier Decker, Abraham Gerritsz, and Claes Harmansz, JFP 12 Nov 1629 [DB 231–4]; LGB; Drake-Brockman, op. cit., p. 247n.

Specx's sentences 'Final sentences on men already examined and sentenced aboard *Sardam,'* ARA VOC 1011 [DB 270–1].

Stone-Cutter Pietersz The *Batavia* journals contain no details of any interrogation of Pietersz, which makes ascertaining his part in the mutiny unusually difficult. See, however, the confession of Jan Hendricxsz, JFP 19 Sep 1629 [DB 178] for Pietersz's role in the Traitors' Island killings.

Breaking on the wheel Philippe Godard, *The First and Last Voyage of the* Batavia (Perth: Abrolhos Publishing, nd, c. 1993), p. 215; Laurence, op. cit., pp. 224–5. An executioner was typically paid three guilders for performing such an execution.

The proportion of casualties Francisco Pelsaert left the following note regarding the fate of the people embarked on board the *Batavia* (ARA VOC 1098, fol. 582r [R 220]; Godard, op. cit., pp. 205–8):

VOC PERSONNEL AND SOLDIERS

Men of little worth who deserted before departure by running away through the dunes	6
Transferred to the *Galiasse* and the *Sardam*, two consorts, on the eve of departure	3
Died from illness, especially scurvy, during the voyage	10
Drowned during shipwreck, trying to swim ashore	40
Died on the island where the *Batavia* was wrecked, either from illness or from drinking seawater	20
Reached the East Indies with the *Batavia* longboat	45
Murdered by Jeronimus Cornelisz by drowning, strangling, decapitation, or butchery by axe	96
Executed by Wiebbe Hayes after being captured in their attack against his positions on the Cats' Island	4
Condemned to death and hanged on Seals' Island	7
Condemned to death, then reprieved and abandoned on the continent	2
Died accidentally on board the *Sardam* during the return to Batavia	2
Arrived safely at Batavia on board the *Sardam*	68
Total	303

PASSENGERS OF BOTH SEXES

Died of illness or thirst on Batavia's Graveyard	9 children, 1 woman
Killed by the mutineers	7 children, 12 women
Reached Batavia safe and sound on board the *Sardam*	2 children, 7 women
Total	38

Giving a total complement of 341, of whom 329 were apparently on board when the ship sailed. At least two babies are known to have been born on the ship, and a boy, Abraham Gerritsz, was picked up in Sierra Leone, while 10 other people died of illness during the voyage itself. This gave the *Batavia* a total complement of 332, which had been reduced to 322 by the time she was wrecked. Of these, a minimum of 110 were killed by Cornelisz's men (in his journals Pelsaert puts this figure as 'more than 120,' and on one occasion '124'), 82 died of accident and illness, 13 were executed or marooned, and the remainder survived to reach Batavia in either the *retourschip*'s longboat or the *Sardam*. In addition, however, Jan Evertsz at least, and probably Ariaen Jacobsz and Zwaantie Hendricx, died as a direct result of the events on board the ship, and five more mutineers were executed after their arrival at Batavia, taking the number of deaths associated with the mutiny and the shipwreck to as many as 218. There is still some possibility of error here, since accounts written in the Indies suggest that the longboat carried 48 people and not the 45 mentioned by the *commandeur*. Taking Pelsaert's own estimates, however, 36.7 percent of the *Batavia*'s actual complement survived, and if Evertsz and the five minor mutineers executed in the Indies are excluded from those figures, and Jacobsz and his paramour included, on the grounds that their true fate remains unknown, the proportion falls to the figure cited: 116 survivors from the total complement of 332, or 34.9 percent.

Perhaps remarkably, no definitive list of the passengers and crew of the *Titanic* actually exists, but best estimates suggest that the total number of people on board was 1,284 passengers and 884 crew, a total of 2,168. Lists compiled of the survivors give from 703 (Board of Trade enquiry) to 803 people (consolidated list). My calculation assumes that the consolidated list favoured by most researchers is correct, and that 37 percent of the liner's complement therefore survived.

Travails of the year 1629 Jeremy Green, *The Loss of the Verenigde Oostindische Compagnie Retourship* Batavia, *Western Australia 1629: An Excavation Report and Catalogue of Artefacts* (Oxford: British Archaeological Reports, 1989), p. 1; Malcolm Uren, *Sailormen's Ghosts: The Abrolhos Islands in Three Hundred Years of Romance, History and Adventure* (Melbourne: Robertson & Mullens, 1944), pp. 218–9. The apparent discrepancy between Van Diemen's total of 74 survivors and Pelsaert's figure of 77 is explained by the fact that three men – Pelsaert, Gerritsz, and Holloch – had originally escaped in the longboat and then returned in the *Sardam*.

Van Diemen's letter Van Diemen to Pieter de Carpentier, 10 December 1629, ARA VOC 1009, cited by Henrietta Drake-Brockman, *Voyage to Disaster* (Nedlands, WA: University of Western Australia Press, 1995), pp. 49–50.

Goods salvaged from the wreck 'Notice of the retrieved cash and goods taken with the *Sardam* to Batavia,' ARA VOC 1098, fol. 529r–529v, [R 218]. In an enclosure, Van Diemen listed all goods retrieved from the wreck with the scrupulous thoroughness expected by the VOC. *Realen* were pieces of eight, valued at rather more than two guilders each, and a *rijksdaalder,* or riksdollar, was worth two and a half guilders:

'Nine chests with *realen,* with one chest No. 3 ? with nine bags of ducatons and 41 bags of double and single stuivers. Some of the stuivers have fallen out of the chest, and are missing.

One chest, retrieved broken, without lid, the money being stuck together by rust, in total 5,400 *rijksdaalders* in 27 bags, 400 *rijksdaalders* in two small bags, found on the island and taken from the crew.

One small case of jewellery, with four small boxes belonging to the VOC, worth 58,671 guilders 15 stuivers, from which is missing one small necklace worth 70 guilders nine stuivers. In total 58,601 guilders and six stuivers.

In the same case is a jewel belonging to Caspar Boudaen, which the VOC allowed him to sell in India.

One small case containing 75 silver *marcken*, consisting of four Moorish fruit dishes, two small eating dishes, one Moorish wash-basin, and some broken silver plate. In this case there is also some silver and gold braid, but most of it is spoiled.

Three small casks with cochenille, of which one has been very wet, each cask weighing 52 Brabant pounds.

Two cases with various sorts of linen, many spoilt.

One chest with various kinds of linen, most of them spoilt.

One small case with some linen.

Various *rijksdaalders* retrieved by the Gujerati divers.

Two small cases with thin copper, each case containing some smaller ones, but most of it having gone black.

Two pieces of artillery, that is, one weighing 3310 pounds and one iron one weighing 3300 pounds.

Some ironwork.

Two small casks of Spanish wine.

One filled with oil.

One filled with vinegar.

Two casks of beer.

One pack of old linen.'

Torrentius A. Bredius, *Johannes Torrentius* (The Hague: Martinus Nijhoff, 1909), pp. 54–69; A. J. Rehorst, *Torrentius* (Rotterdam: WL & J Brusse NV, 1939), pp. 65–6; Govert Snoek, *De Rosenkruizers in Nederland, Voornamelijk in de Eerste Helft van de 17de Eeuw. Een Inventarisatie* (Ph.D. thesis, University of Utrecht, 1997), pp. 75–6.

The surviving painting It was identified by being matched to the description of a piece acquired for Charles in 1628, and by the discovery of the King's mark on the reverse. Rehorst, op. cit., pp. 73–8. It is the work described by Zbigniew Herbert in his *Still Life With a Bridle: Essays and Apocryphas* (London: Jonathan Cape, 1993).

Specx's later career and death Stapel, *De Gouverneurs-Generaal*, p. 19; M. A. van Rhede van der Kloot, *De Gouverneurs-Generaal en Commissarissen-Generaal van Nederlandsch-Indië, 1610–1888* (The Hague: Van Stockum, 1891), pp. 41; W. Ph. Coolhaas, 'Aanvullingen en Verbeteringen op Van Rhede van der Kloot's *De Gouveneurs-Generall en Commissarissen-Generaal van Nederlandsch-Indië (1610-1888),*' *De Nederlandsche Leeuw* 73 (1956): 341; J. R. Bruijn et al., *Dutch-Asiatic Shipping in the 17th and 18th Centuries* (The Hague: Martinus Nijhoff, 1987), I, p. 88.

The fate of Sara Specx On the aftermath of the Specx affair, see C. Gerretson, *Coen's Eerherstel* (Amsterdam: Van Kampen, 1944), pp. 58–70; Coolhaas, op. cit., p. 342; Van Rhede van der Kloot, op. cit., p. 41.

Escape of the minor mutineers The fate of Nannings, Gerritsz, and Jan Jansz Purmer is conjecture on my part. Although ne'er-do-wells at best, and most likely active mutineers, their names do not appear on the lists of Jeronimus's band found in the captain-general's tent after Pelsaert's return. It is certainly possible that one or more of them drowned on board the *Batavia* or died of thirst on Batavia's Graveyard before the mutiny began; but all three were experienced sailors and I think it much more likely they were with Ariaen Jacobsz in the longboat.

Ryckert Woutersz's fate is nowhere mentioned in the journals, but the likelihood is that he was dead by 12 July, when his name was conspicuously absent from the first list of those swearing loyalty to Jeronimus. It was Hugh Edwards who first suggested that he was murdered by his confederates, which is entirely plausible, though one might expect to find some reference to it in the interrogations. Edwards, *Islands of Angry Ghosts* (New York: William Morrow & Co., 1966), p. 37.

Jan Willemsz Selyns JFP 28 Sep 1629 [DB 157]; sentence on Mattys Beer, JFP 28 Sep 1629 [DB 193]; confession of Wouter Loos, 27 Oct 1629 [DB 226].

Pelsaert's later career and death The renewed onset of the illness can probably be dated to some time shortly before 14 June, on which day Pelsaert made his will. Drake-Brockman, pp. 52–60, 259–61; Roeper, op. cit., pp. 39–41; D. H. A. Kolff and H. W. van Santen (eds.), *De Geschriften van Francisco Pelsaert over Mughal Indië, 1627: Kroniek en Remonstrantie* (The Hague: Martinus Nijhoff, 1979), p. 41.

Pelsaert's affair with Pieterge Mooij, p. 330; Kolff and van Santen, op. cit., p. 33.

Jambi Today the town is called Telanaipura. It lies on the northern side of the island, more than 50 miles up the River Hari. The Dutch expeditionary force, which Pelsaert joined, was so substantial that the Portuguese fled when it appeared, and the siege was lifted without the necessity of firing a shot.

'...wholly ill...' Pelsaert to the Gentlemen XVII of Amsterdam, 12 December 1629, ARA VOC 1630 [DB 258–60]. This is apparently the only letter known to have been written by Pelsaert still extant. It was the *commandeur's* covering note to the journals containing his account of the disaster.

Council of the Indies Neither Specx nor Pelsaert seems to have been aware that Pelsaert himself had been nominated to the Council as a 'councillor extraordinary,' or supernumerary, at a salary of 200 guilders per month. The letter noting this appointment was written in the Netherlands at the end of August 1629, when the *commandeur* was still searching for the Abrolhos in the *Sardam,* and would not have arrived until some time in the spring of 1630. By then Pelsaert had been posted to Sumatra, and there is no record that he ever took up the seat or even learned that he had received the honour. Drake-Brockman, op. cit., pp. 36–7. Pelsaert's new salary is mentioned in a letter from the Gentlemen XVII to Jan Coen, governor-general of the Indies, cited in ibid.

The fate of the cameo A. N. Zadoks-Josephus Jitta, 'De lotgevallen van den grooten camee in het Koninklijk Penningkabinet,' *Oud-Holland* 66 (1951): 191, 200–4; Roeper, op. cit., pp. 40–1; Kolff and Van Santen, op. cit., p. 42.

Pelsaert's private trade Roeper, op. cit., pp. 41, 59; Drake-Brockman, op. cit., pp. 56–9.

Pelsaert's mother Roeper, op. cit., pp. 41, 59; Kolff and Van Santen, op. cit., p. 42. Roeper points out that the payment of any compensation at all implies that the Company could not entirely substantiate its allegations of private trading, as it would certainly have confiscated the entire amount had the case been thoroughly clear-cut.

Wiebbe Hayes and the Defenders' rewards Drake-Brockman, op. cit., pp. 270–1; Roeper, op. cit., pp. 38, 59.

Records of Winschoten As noted above, only the town's judicial records (in the Provincial Archive at Groningen) survive from this period, and no signature of a Wiebbe Hayes can be found in them – not even among the marriage contracts. There are no notarial records from Winschoten, either.

Hayes's fate Mortality rates for soldiers in the Indies ran to 25–33 percent over the course of a commission. C. R. Boxer, 'The Dutch East-Indiamen: Their Sailors, Their Navigators and Life on Board, 1602–1795,' *The Mariner's Mirror* 49 (1963): 85.

The fate of Gijsbert Bastiaensz LGB; Mooij, op. cit., pp. 328, 331–2, 339–42, 344–5, 347, 359, 366–8, 380–1, 446, 456; Drake-Brockman, op. cit., pp. 79–80.

The fate of Judick Gijsbertsdr The 600-guilder payment comprised 300 guilders to which she was entitled as the widow of a Company *predikant,* and the unusual *ex gratia* sum of 300 more, paid in recognition of her tribulations in the Abrolhos. Will of Judick Gijsbertsdr, ONAD 58, fol. 817v–819; CAL van Troostenburg de Bruijn, *Biographisch Woordenboek van Oost-Indische Predikanten* (Nijmegen: np, 1893), pp. 176–7; Drake-Brockman, op. cit., pp. 80–1.

'... like roasted pears...' L. Blussé, 'The Caryatids of Batavia: Reproduction, Religion and Acculturation under the VOC,' *Itinerario* 7 (1983): 64, citing the eighteenth-century Dutch historian Valentijn.

The later life of Creesje Jans Drake-Brockman, op. cit., pp. 63–71. A search of the surviving records of Leyden seems to confirm that Drake-Brockman was wrong in assuming Creesje and her husband went to live in the city. No burial records can be found for the couple and they have left no trace in Leyden's church or solicitors' records, with the exception of the two occasions on which they stood as godparents. Furthermore, Cuick's name does not appear in the Leyden *Poorterbooks,* which scrupulously list every full citizen of the town. Finally, it defies belief that a couple with some money – and we know that Creesje was reasonably well-off – could have lived for more than 15 years in a city without once requiring the services of a solicitor. Had they dwelled in Leyden, in short, they would surely have left more record of their presence.

Creesje's husband Cuick was a widower, having been the husband of Catharina Bernardi of Groningen. Drake-Brockman notes, from the records of Amsterdam's Orphans' Court, that Creesje may have taken a third husband between the other two – a certain Johannes Hilkes, of whom nothing else is known. No other records exist to prove the case either way, but the church records of Batavia record that when Creesje married Cuick, she did so as the widow of Boudewijn van der Mijlen and not of Johannes Hilkes. The Orphans' Court papers may therefore be in error. If Hilkes did marry Lucretia Jans, he must have done so almost immediately after she arrived in Batavia, and died perhaps as rapidly as Judick's Pieter van der Heuven. Even if that was the case, Lucretia could not have completed the appropriate period of mourning either for Boudewijn or Johannes before marrying Jacob van Cuick. Drake-Brockman, op. cit., pp. 64n, 71.

Creesje Jans as godmother On the first occasion, 4 September 1637, Creesje alone stood as godparent to twins named Willem and Dirck; on the second, 3 December 1641, she and her husband both became godparents to another pair – this one a boy and a girl – who were christened Willem and Neeltje; presumably the first Willem must have died in the interim. Some years earlier, in Batavia, Jans had also stood as godmother to two other infants baptised in the Dutch Church there. Ibid. pp. 70n–71n.

It also seems worth noting that the first husband of Creesje's sister, Sara, was called Jacob Kuyk (ibid. p. 67). The tangled interfamily relationship between the Janses, the Cuicks, and the Dircxes may thus have been even more complicated than it first appears.

Lucreseija van Kuijck GAA, burial registers 1069, fol. 38.

The further interrogation of Ariaen Jacobsz Drake-Brockman, op. cit., pp. 46, 62–3. As has already been noted, a good deal of paperwork concerning Jacobsz's case went missing somewhere between Batavia and the VOC record office. In its absence, it is impossible to say for certain how good or bad the evidence against the skipper was.

'The skipper was very much suspected...' Specx to the Gentlemen XVII, 15 Dec 1629, ARA VOC 1009, cited in Drake-Brockman, op. cit., p. 63.

'Jacobsz... is still imprisoned...' Van Diemen to the Gentlemen XVII, 5 June 1631, in ibid., p. 58.

The fate of Belijtgen Jacobsdr ONAH 132, fol. 157v; GAH, rood 215, burgomasters' decisions 1628–32, fol. 94v; for the significance of the burgomasters' memorials, see Gabrielle Dorren, 'Burgers en hun besognes. Burgemeestersmemorialen en hun Bruikbaarheid als bron voor Zeventiende-Eeuws Haarlem,' *Jaarboeck Haarlem* (1995): 53–5; for the social status of the Cornelissteeg, see Dorren, *Het Soet Vergaren: Haarlems Buurtleven in de Zeventiende Eeuw* (Haarlem: Arcadia, 1998), p. 17; for the date of the arrival of the news of the *Batavia* mutiny in the Republic, see Roeper, op. cit., pp. 42, 47, 61.

Decomposition of the bodies and the blooming of Batavia's Graveyard Archaeological excavation has revealed that many of the *Batavia* corpses lie partially buried in a dense black mass. Analysis of this substance has shown it is composed almost entirely of decayed plant roots, with a 1 percent trace of human fat. The explanation appears to be that plants were tapping into the nutrients offered by the decomposing bodies; food of any sort was so scarce on the island that competition for such resources must have been fierce. Author's interview with Juliëtte Pasveer and Marit van Huystee, Western Australian Maritime Museum, 12 June 2000.

Epilogue: On the Shores of the Great South-Land

It is impossible to say with any certainty what became of the Dutch sur-
vivors thrown up on the Western Australian coast. The most important
sources, which are archaeological, are well summarised by Phillip
Playford, the rediscoverer of the *Zuytdorp* wreck, in his *Carpet of Silver: the
Wreck of the Zuytdorp* (Nedlands, WA: University of Western Australia
Press, 1996), which is probably the most interesting and best-researched
contribution to the subject yet published. The case for survival is put by
Rupert Gerritsen in *And Their Ghosts May Be Heard...* (South Fremantle,
WA: Fremantle Arts Centre Press, 1994), though many of his most
important points have subsequently been rebutted. For the archaeology
of the *Batavia* victims' skeletons, I turned mainly to Myra Stanbury (ed.),
Abrolhos Islands Archaeological Sites: Interim Report (Fremantle: Australian
National Centre of Excellence for Maritime Archaeology, 2000), Juliëtte
Pasveer, Alanah Buck, and Marit van Huystee, 'Victims of the *Batavia*
Mutiny: Physical Anthropological and Forensic Studies of the Beacon
Island Skeletons,' *Bulletin of the Australian Institute for Maritime Archaeology*
22 (1998), and Bernandine Hunneybun, *Skullduggery on Beacon Island* (BSc
Hons dissertation, University of Western Australia, 1995).

The fate of the two mutineers 'Instructions to Wouter Loos and Jan Pelgrom de By
van Bemel,' JFP 16 Nov 1629 [DB 229–30]; J. A. Heeres, *The Part Borne by the
Dutch in the Discovery of Australia 1606–1765* (London: Luzac, 1899), pp. 64–7;
Henrietta Drake-Brockman, *Voyage to Disaster* (Nedlands, WA: University of
Western Australia Press, 1995), pp. 81–3; Gerritsen, pp. 64–8, 224–32;
Playford, pp. 237–42.

The champan As Drake-Brockman points out (op. cit., pp. 123n, 229n), Pelsaert
nowhere else uses the word *champan* in his journals. Normal ship's boats are
referred to throughout as *boot* – a longboat or yawl – or *schuijt* – a small jolly-
boat or dinghy. It defies belief that the *commandeur* would have supplied the
two mutineers with a VOC boat, which he would certainly have had to
account for on his return to Batavia, particularly as it would have meant
leaving himself and the people on the *Sardam* without a single boat of their
own.

Wittecarra spring The spring could be seen in its original state as late as 1967, but
by 1996 it had dried up due to the extraction of groundwater from a nearby
bore. Phillip Playford, *Voyage of Discovery to Terra Australis by Willem de Vlamingh
in 1696–97* (Perth: Western Australian Museum, 1998), p. 47.

'*... the first western vessel...*' The identity of the first Westerners to discover the
fifth continent remains a matter of dispute. George Collingridge, author of
*The Discovery of Australia: a Critical, Documentary and Historical Investigation
Concerning the Priority of Discovery in Australasia Before the Arrival of Lieut. James
Cook in the Endeavour in the Year 1770* (Sydney: Hayes Brothers, 1895), and
Kenneth McIntyre, in *The Secret Discovery of Australia: Portuguese Ventures 200
Years Before Captain Cook* (Medindie, South Australia: Souvenir Press, 1977),

have both argued for the primacy of the Portuguese, and a date somewhere in the sixteenth century. This is not unlikely, although some of the specific evidence these authors advance – early maps, and, in particular, the discovery of 'Portuguese' cannon off the northwest coast – has since been called into question. There is, in addition, a tradition on the southern Australian coast of a so-called mahogany ship, popularly supposed to be of Spanish origin, aground on a beach near Warrnambool, Victoria, and discovered sometime between 1836 and 1841. This vessel, if it ever existed, is supposed to have vanished subsequently beneath the sands and has never been rediscovered. See 'Notes on Proceedings of the First Australian Symposium on the Mahogany Ship: Relic or Legend?,' *Regional Journal of Social Issues,* monograph series, no.1 (copy in the library of the Western Australian Maritime Museum). A balanced, popular view of the controversy is provided by Miriam Estensen, *Discovery: the Quest for the Great South Land* (Sydney: Allen & Unwin, 1998), pp. 47–50, 52–81. The latter book also mentions the alleged salvage of a 'Spanish helmet' dating to ca. 1580 from Wellington harbour, New Zealand, around 1904 (p. 97).

The Duyfken, *the* Arnem, *and the* Pera *on the northern coast* James Henderson, *Sent Forth a Dove: Discovery of the* Duyfken (Nedlands, WA: University of Western Australia Press, 1999), pp. 32–42, 212n; Heeres, op. cit., pp. 4–6, 22–5; Günter Schilder, *Australia Unveiled: The Share of Dutch Navigators in the Discovery of Australia* (Amsterdam: Theatrum Orbis Terrarum, 1976), pp. 43–53, 80–98; J. P. Sigmond and L. H. Zuiderbaan, *Dutch Discoveries of Australia: Shipwrecks, Treasures and Early Voyages off the West Coast* (Adelaide: Rigby, 1979), pp. 20–1, 47–9. Records of the *Duyfken*'s voyage are, however, so incomplete that it is uncertain whether her men were killed on the shores of Australia or New Guinea, though most authorities argue that at least one was lost on a riverbank somewhere on the Cape York Peninsula.

Early Dutch-Aboriginal relations Noel Loos, 'Aboriginal-Dutch Relations in North Queensland, 1606–1756,' in Jeremy Green, Myra Stanbury, and Femme Gaastra (eds.), *The ANCODS Colloquium: Papers Presented at the Australia-Netherlands Colloquium on Maritime Archaeology and Maritime History* (Fremantle: Australian National Centre of Excellence for Maritime Archaeology, 1999), pp. 8–13.

'… look out keenly…' 'Instructions to Wouter Loos and Jan Pelgrom de By van Bemel,' JFP 16 Nov 1629 [DB 229–30].

Gerrit Thomasz Pool Heeres, op. cit., p. 66; Schilder, op. cit., pp. 129–37.

Abel Tasman The relevant portion of Tasman's instructions read as follows: '… Continue your course along the land of d'eendracht as far as Houtman's Abrolhos, and come to anchor there at the most convenient place, in order to make efforts to bring up from the bottom the chest in which eight thousand rixdollars, sunk with the lost ship *Batavia* in 1629, owing to half a brass cannon having fallen upon it… and so save the same together with the said gun, which would be good service done to the Company, on which account you will not fail diligently to attend to this business. You will likewise make search on the mainland to ascertain whether the two Netherlanders who, having forfeited their lives, were put ashore here by the *commandeur* Francisco Pelsaert at the same period, are still alive, in which case you will from them ask information touching the country, and, if they should wish it, allow them to take passage hither with you.' Drake-Brockman, op. cit., pp. 81–2; Schilder, op. cit., pp. 139–94.

'... *circumnavigating the continent...*' In 1642–3 Tasman actually sailed south from Mauritius, east across the Roaring Forties until he came across Tasmania, east again to New Zealand, and then north through Polynesia, reaching the Indies via the north coast of New Guinea. He saw no part of the Australian mainland throughout the voyage. In 1644, he explored the northern coast and sailed down the west coast to about latitude 23½ south. Beacon Island (Batavia's Graveyard) lies at lat. 28' 28', about 350 miles further to the south. Cf. Schilder, op. cit., p. 154; Sigmond and Zuiderbaan, op. cit., pp. 72–85.

'*The "mutineers' hut"* De Vlamingh's landing party found five huts in all, but this was the only one regarded as worthy of description – implying it was probably noticeably superior in construction and design to the other four. Gerritsen, op. cit., p. 227; Playford, *Voyage of Discovery,* pp. 46–7. Gerritsen fails to identify this structure with the two mutineers, whom he believes were marooned a little further south at Hutt River, preferring to suggest it was built by Jacob Jacobsz, the skipper of the *Sardam,* and the crew of the boat apparently lost in the Abrolhos on 12 October 1629. In any case, there is no real reason to suppose it was not built by the Nanda people.

VOC losses J. R. Bruijn et al., *Dutch-Asiatic Shipping in the 17th and 18th Centuries* (The Hague: Martinus Nijhoff, 3 vols., 1979–1987), I, pp. 75, 91.

The wreck of the Vergulde Draeck James Henderson, *Marooned* (Perth: St. George Books, 1982), pp. 42–155. The wreck site was rediscovered in 1963 by Graeme Henderson, who is now the director of the Western Australian Maritime Museum; he was then a schoolboy on a fishing expedition.

The three rescuers R. H. Major, *Early Voyages to Terra Australis, Now Called Australia* (Adelaide: Australian Heritage Press, 1963), p. 58. The real total may have been higher than this – a second party of eight sailors sent after the first three also vanished; their boat was found smashed to pieces on a beach, and it remains a matter of some doubt whether the crew ever got ashore. The VOC nearly lost a third boatload two years later, when another effort at rescue and salvage was made. Fourteen men from a *fluyt,* the *Waeckende Boey,* led by the steersman Abraham Leeman, were abandoned on the coast and had to sail their small boat back to the Indies. Most of them survived the voyage, but landed on the southern coast of Java many miles from Batavia. Only Leeman and three other men eventually reached the city alive. Henderson, *Marooned,* pp. 95–155.

Evidence of survival Ibid., p. 96; Gerritsen, op. cit., pp. 48–63.

'... *followed by the* Zuytdorp...' Two other ships, the *Ridderschap van Holland* (1694) and the *Concordia* (1708) may have been lost on the Australian coast before this date. C. Halls, 'The Loss of the *Ridderschap van Holland,*' *The Annual Dog Watch* 22 (1965): 36–43; Playford, *Voyage of Discovery,* pp. 4, 71n; Femme Gaastra, 'The Dutch East India Company: A Reluctant Discoverer,' *The Great*

Circle 19 (1997): 118–20. Halls's view, that the *Ridderschap van Holland* sprung her mast, limped north to Madagascar, and fell victim to the pirate leader Abraham Samuel at Fort Dauphin on the southern coast, cannot be correct; Samuel did not arrive at the port until some time after July 1697. There certainly was a rumour that he had captured a Dutch ship and killed all her crew, but contemporary documents date this supposed event to January 1699; the vessel concerned was probably a small slaver. There were, however, plenty of pirate ships on the northern coast of Madagascar, based on St. Mary's, that could perhaps have accounted for a wounded *retourship*. Jan Rogozinski, *Honour Among Thieves: Captain Kidd, Henry Every and the Story of Pirate Island* (London: Conway Maritime Press, 2000), pp. 67–8.

The fate of the Zuytdorp Without a boat – the *Zuytdorp*'s pair must surely have been reduced to matchwood by the surf – their only real hope of rescue was to attract the attention of another Dutch ship as she passed along the coast. The cliffs offered good vantage points, and they had gone aground close to the spot where VOC ships normally made their Australian landfall, but any experienced hands among the survivors would have known that although fires were often seen along the shoreline, they were routinely attributed to the local Aborigines and ignored. It must have been for this reason that the *Zuytdorp*'s men went to the effort of hauling ashore eight bronze breech blocks for the swivel guns mounted on the poop. In the right circumstances these could have been loaded with shot and used to signal to passing ships. Unfortunately for the survivors, however, none of the guns could be got out of the stern before it broke up and drifted away. The breech blocks were then abandoned at the foot of the cliffs, where they were eventually rediscovered more than 200 years later.

There was plenty of driftwood about, however, and the survivors evidently did gather large quantities of it and built at least one huge bonfire on the cliffs immediately above the wreck site. Up to seven other East Indiamen would have made their way along the coast during the next two months, beginning with a ship called the *Kockenge,* which apparently passed the *Zuytdorp* survivors' position only a week after they came ashore, and the discovery of what appears to be the remains of a signal fire next to the wreck site – a substantial layer of charcoal mixed with melted hinges, barrel rings, and clasps – suggests that at least one of them came within view of the shipwrecked sailors and that the *Zuytdorp*'s survivors hurriedly lit their beacon and piled everything they had onto the fire – sea chests and barrels as well as driftwood – in the desperate hope of being noticed. That they received no response is suggested by another modern discovery along the cliffs: the smashed remains of many old Dutch bottles that had once been filled with wine or spirits, which appear to have been drained by men determined to drink themselves into oblivion.

The ship had run aground early in the southern winter, and there would have been sufficient fresh water about to sustain a small group of survivors for some months. The men could have collected large quantities of shellfish from along the cliffs, and if they were able to salvage any firearms from the ship, it would have been possible for them to hunt for kangaroos. In these circumstances, it seems likely that they stayed close to the wreck site for as long as they could in the hope that rescue ships might be sent from Java when their failure to arrive was noticed. By September or October, however, the rains would have ceased, and any survivors would have had to move inland in search of water. The only supplies available for miles in any direction were Aboriginal soaks – areas of low ground where water ran and collected during the wet season, and which the local Malgana tribe 'farmed' by digging them out and covering them with stones to keep wildlife away and prevent evaporation.

The *Zuytdorp*'s men would have required the help of the Malgana to have located these rare spots, but there is some evidence that Dutch sailors did receive assistance from the local Aborigines. The Malgana were certainly aware of the wreck; the event made such an impact on them that 120 years later, when British colonists arrived in the area, it was still talked of as though it had been a recent happening. Aboriginal tradition suggested that the survivors had lived along the cliffs in two large and three small 'houses' made of wood and canvas, and exchanged food for spears and shields. Playford, *Carpet of Silver,* pp. 68–77, 78–82, 115, 200–4; *The ANCODS Colloquium,* p. 49; Fiona Weaver, *Report of the Excavation of Previously Undisturbed Land Sites Associated with the VOC Ship* Zuytdorp, *Wrecked 1712, Zuytdorp Cliffs, Western Australia* (Fremantle: Western Australian Maritime Museum, 1994); Mike McCarthy, '*Zuytdorp* Far from Home,' *Bulletin of the Australian Institute for Maritime Archaeology* 22 (1998): 52. The *Zuytdorp,* incidentally, was the same ship that lost a large proportion of her crew in the Gulf of Guinea on the voyage out; see chapter 3.

The tobacco tin Playford, *Carpet of Silver,* pp. 214–5; McCarthy, op. cit., p. 53. It has also been argued that the lid could have been carried to Wale from the *Zuytdorp* wreck site by an Aboriginal farm hand in more recent years; no definite resolution of this conundrum is likely.

'*The third and last...*' Two other *retourschepen* – the *Fortuyn* (1724) and the *Aagtekerke* (1726), the former from Amsterdam and the latter a ship of the Zeeland chamber, both on their maiden voyages – disappeared between Batavia and the Cape just before the loss of the *Zeewijk,* and may possibly have deposited survivors on the Australian coast. C. Halls, 'The Loss of the Dutch East Indiaman *Aagtekerke,*' *The Annual Dog Watch* 23 (1966): 101–7; Graeme Henderson, 'The Mysterious Fate of the Dutch East Indiaman *Aagtekerke,*' *Westerly* (June 1978): 71–8; Playford, *Carpet of Silver,* pp. 28–9.

The Zeewijk and her survivors Hugh Edwards, *The Wreck on the Half-Moon Reef* (New York: Charles Scribner's Sons, 1970).

'*...from New South Wales to China...*' David Levell, 'China Syndrome,' *Fortean Times* 123 (June 1999): 28–31. The distance between the two territories was supposed by these prisoners to be about 150 miles (it is actually 5,565 miles from Sydney to Beijing). The first recorded attempt was made by 20 men and one pregnant woman in November 1791; the last around 1827.

Evidence of survival Gerritsen, op. cit., pp. 70–81; Playford, *Carpet of Silver,* pp. 217–32. Gregory's recollection may not be entirely reliable, as he recorded it only in 1885. Much of other evidence advanced by Gerritsen, such as the presence of what appear to be Dutch loan words in Aboriginal languages, have been subject to considerable criticism by specialists.

Unfortunately for the Aborigines of the western coast, the great majority died out soon after the first Europeans arrived with their guns, diseases, and modern agricultural practices, and evidence of the sort supplied by Daisy Bates and her contemporaries can never be more than merely anecdotal. It is also true that relations with passing sealers or the earliest settlers, or genetic mutation, could account for the light-skinned individuals found in the areas where the *Zuytdorp* survivors and the *Batavia* mutineers came ashore. Only genetic evidence is likely to prove at all conclusive; but since old Aboriginal skeletons are sometimes exposed by wind and water throughout Western Australia, it may eventually be found.

One clue that intermarriage between Dutch and Aboriginals did actually occur may already have emerged. In 1988 Phillip Playford, one of Australia's leading experts on the *Zuytdorp,* was approached by a woman whose part-Aboriginal husband apparently suffered from porphyria variegata, a condition that can cause rashes, blisters, and sensitive skin. This disease is an inherited one and can be passed to children of either sex. It is also relatively rare, except among the white population of South Africa, where an estimated 30,000 people carry the gene for the condition.

Geoffrey Dean, a British doctor based in Port Elizabeth, South Africa, became aware of the unusual incidence of porphyria in the region in 1949 and devoted years to researching the family trees of all the sufferers he treated. He claimed to have traced all known cases of the disease to a single Dutch couple, Gerrit Jansz van Deventer and Ariaantje van den Berg, who were married at the Cape in 1688. Van Deventer had settled there in 1685, and his bride was one of eight orphans sent out to provide wives for the early burghers three years later. The couple had eight children, half of whom Dean showed must have carried the gene for porphyria variegata. Dean and Playford have suggested that the disease may have been introduced to Australia by an Afrikaner signed on to the *Zuytdorp* at the Cape to help make good the extensive losses among the crew that had occurred on the passage from the Netherlands, who survived the wreck and lived long enough to join an Aboriginal community.

A good deal of work remains to be done if this disease is to be traced to the arrival of Dutch mariners on the western Australian coast in the seventeenth and eighteenth centuries. It remains entirely possible that it was introduced at a much later date, and its appearance in Australia cannot be regarded as definite evidence for the long-term survival of Loos and Pelgrom and their compatriots. Nevertheless, evidence of interaction between VOC sailors and the Aborigines continues to emerge occasionally, and it is not impossible that a definite link will be established one day. Interview with Dr. F. W. M de Rooij, Erasmus University, Rotterdam, 26 June 2000. De Rooij's work in South Africa has confirmed Dean's thesis that most South African porphyriacs can trace the source of their disease to their kinship with Ariaantje van der Berg. Playford, *Carpet of Silver,* pp. 227–32; Geoffrey Dean,

The Porphyrias: A Story of Inheritance and Environment (London: Pitman Medical, 1971), pp. 114–30; *The ANCODS Colloquium,* pp. 50–1; 'First Europeans in Australia,' *History Today* (June 1999): 3–4. A second condition – Ellis van Creveld syndrome, which results in children being born with short limbs, extra fingers or toes, and heart defects – exists among the Aborigines of Western Australia and has also been tentatively linked to the arrival of ship-wrecked Dutchmen. It has been calculated that about one Aborigine in 40 carries the recessive Ellis van Creveld gene – the second-highest incidence of the disease among any community in the world. The highest incidence, tellingly enough, occurs among the Amish people of Pennsylvania, a Mennonite sect whose ancestors emigrated from the Netherlands in 1683.

'... *purely anecdotal evidence* ...' Even today, speculation as to the existence of Dutch survivors has not entirely died away, and the most recent discovery is, in fact, also one of the strangest. It concerns reports of an expedition into the interior of Australia that set out from Raffles Bay, at the end of the Coburg Peninsula in the Northern Territories, some time prior to 1834. (Raffles Bay was the site of a British military outpost established in 1818 and abandoned in 1829, which may date the expedition more precisely.) This party included a Lieutenant Nixon, and it was on his private journals that newspaper reports concerning what appeared to be a whole colony of white people living in the interior were eventually based.

Nixon and his colleagues, it appears, explored the interior of the Northern Territories for two months. One day, to their considerable surprise, they reached a spot quite different from the untamed wilderness they had been traversing: 'a low and level country, laid out as it were in plantations, with straight rows of trees.' Exploring further, Nixon then encountered 'a human being, whose face was so fair, and dress so white, that I was for a moment staggered with terror, and thought I was looking at an apparition.'

The 'apparition' spoke in broken Dutch, which – remarkably enough – was understood by Nixon, who had spent time in the Netherlands in his youth. It thus emerged that the local people believed they were descended from the survivors – 80 men and 10 women – of a Dutch ship that had been wrecked on the coast many years earlier. This group had been forced by famine to go inland, where they had established their colony and lived off maize and fish from a nearby river. They were now led by a man who claimed descent from a Dutchman named Van Baerle, and 'did not have books or paper, nor any schools; their marriages were performed without any ceremony, they retained a certain observance of the Sabbath by refraining from daily labours and performing some sort of superstitious ceremony on that day all together.' Evidently they had refrained from mixing with the local Aborigines.

This tale could be a nineteenth-century hoax, and it would be unwise to accept it at face value without any supporting evidence. However, research by Femme Gaastra, the noted Dutch historian of the VOC, has discovered that an assistant named Constantijn van Baerle was indeed lost, with 129 others, on the ship *Concordia,* which vanished in the Indian Ocean some time in 1708.

Van Baerle is not a particularly common surname in the Netherlands; just possibly, then, this discovery corroborates Lieutenant Nixon's original report. Femme Gaastra, 'The Dutch East India Company: A Reluctant Discoverer,' *The Great Circle* 19 (1997): 117–20, citing the *Leeds Mercury* of 25 Jan 1834, p. 7 col. a. The sponsors and the purpose of the expedition remain a mystery. Its members are reported to have been conveyed back to Singapore on a merchant ship, which may suggest it was not naval in origin. From an examination of the map, it would appear that the Coburg Peninsula – which lies 700 miles to the east of Batavia – and the interior of Arnhem Land generally are far from the first places one would look for the survivors of a ship that had sailed west from Java and was apparently last heard of near Mauritius.

Lort Stokes John Lort Stokes entered the Royal Navy in 1826 and served in South American waters, joining Darwin's *Beagle* as a midshipman, and rising to command the ship from 1841 to 1843 (this was after the naturalist had left her). In addition to his work in the Abrolhos, Stokes conducted the first survey of New Zealand since Cook's day, and was the author of *Discoveries in Australia 1837–1843*. Despite a lifetime in the hydrographical service, he was passed over for the position of Hydrographer of the Navy in 1863 in favour of Captain (later Vice Admiral Sir) George Richards, the pioneer oceanographer. See G. S. Ritchie, *The Admiralty Chart: British Naval Hydrography in the Nineteenth Century* (London: Hollis & Carter, 1967), pp. 180, 190, 307, 313.

Stokes in the Abrolhos Malcolm Uren, *Sailormen's Ghosts: the Abrolhos Islands in Three Hundred Years of Romance, History and Adventure* (Melbourne: Robertson & Mullens, 1944), pp. 238–43; Drake-Brockman, op. cit., pp. 278–9. He conducted the survey under the orders of Commander John Wickham.

'…published by a Perth newspaper…' It appeared in the Christmas 1897 edition of the Perth *Western Mail*. The translation was by Willem Siebenhaar; it has since been reprinted by Philippe Godard as part of his *The First and Last Voyage of the* Batavia (Perth: Abrolhos Publishing, nd, c. 1993).

Gun island as Batavia's Graveyard Uren, op. cit., pp. 244–5.

Identity of the wreckage The debris was described by the *Zeewijk*'s crew as noticeably old, while the *Aagtekerke* had vanished only the previous year and the *Fortuyn* three years earlier. This seems to make an identification with the *Ridderschap van Holland,* lost in 1694, at least possible. See also Graeme Henderson, *Maritime Archaeology in Australia* (Nedlands, WA: University of Western Australia Press, 1986), pp. 26–7.

Drake-Brockman and the Broadhurst collection Hugh Edwards, *Islands of Angry Ghosts* (New York: William Morrow & Co., 1966), pp. 93–5; *The ANCODS Colloquium*, pp. 106–7; Drake-Brockman, pp. xxi–xxii; 279n. The Broadhurst Collection is now in the Western Australian Maritime Museum, Fremantle. Henrietta Drake-Brockman was the author of a historical novel, *The Wicked and the Fair* (Sydney: Angus & Roberston, 1957), which was based on the *Batavia*'s story and identified present-day Goss Island as Batavia's Graveyard. She died, in her mid-60s, in 1968.

'…an article published in 1955…' Henrietta Drake-Brockman, 'The Wreck of the *Batavia*,' *Walkabout Magazine* 21, no. 1 (1955).

The first artifacts Edwards, *Islands of Angry Ghosts,* pp. 98–101; *The ANCODS Colloquium,* pp. 107–8.

Discovery by Johnson and Cramer Edwards, *Islands of Angry Ghosts,* pp. 111–2, 116–7.

'*The sea had dug a grave …*' Ibid., pp. 134–5.

The Batavia artefacts Jeremy Green, *The Loss of the Verenigde Oostindische Compagnie Retourschip* Batavia, *Western Australia 1629: An Excavation Report and Catalogue of Artefacts* (Oxford: British Archaeological Reports, 1989), pp. 37, 45, 55–60, 83, 90–1, 95–6, 99–101, 178, 183–5, 197–200; Edwards, *Islands of Angry Ghosts,* pp. 149–51. The mortar bears the – in the circumstances ironic – inscription AMOR VINCIT OMNIA: 'Love conquers all.'

Wiebbe Hayes's dwellings Robert Bevacqua, 'Archaeological Survey of Sites Relating to the *Batavia* Shipwreck,' *Early Days Journal* 7 (1974): 64–9; Jeremy Green and Myra Stanbury, 'Even More Light on a Confusing Geographical Puzzle, Part 1: Wells, Cairns and Stone Structures on West Wallabi Island,' *Underwater Explorers' Club News* (January 1982): 1–6; *The ANCODS Colloquium,* p. 10. There is considerable doubt that these structures are now as they would have been several hundred years ago. There is anecdotal evidence of extensive reconstruction, as well as general 'tidying,' particularly by film crews filming reconstructions of the events of 1629.

The Batavia reconstruction The ship can be seen at the Bataviawerf in Lelystad, to the east of Amsterdam. Philippe Godard, *The First and Last Voyage of the* Batavia (Perth: Abrolhos Publishing, nd, c. 1993), pp. 246–73; J. R. Bruijn et al., *Dutch-Asiatic Shipping in the 17th and 18th Centuries* (The Hague: Martinus Nijhoff, 3 vols., 1979–87), I, pp. 37–40, 42–44.

Skeletons Hunneybun, pp. 1.4a, 3.14, 4.2–4.13, 5.2–5.7; Myra Stanbury (ed.), *Abrolhos Islands Archaeological Sites: Interim Report* (Fremantle: Australian National Centre of Excellence for Maritime Archaeology, 2000), pp. 5–10; *The ANCODS Colloquium,* pp. 159–61; Juliëtte Pasveer, Alanah Buck, and Marit van Huystee, 'Victims of the *Batavia* Mutiny: Physical Anthropological and Forensic Studies of the Beacon Island skeletons,' *Bulletin of the Australian Institute for Maritime Archaeology* 22 (1998): 45–50; Edwards, op. cit., pp. 3–7, 165–6; author's interviews with Juliëtte Pasveer, Alanah Buck, and Stephen Knott, 12–13 June 2000. The seven bodies in the grave pit consist of five partial skeletons and two separate sets of teeth. In the case of 'Jan Dircx,' who was exhumed by Max Cramer in 1963, the musket ball has been separated from the body and now lies mounted as part of a display in the dining room of the Batavia Motor Inn motel in Geraldton. 'Dircx,' if that is who he was, suffered from rickets and was so physically immature he must have made a poor sort of soldier. His body (catalogued as BAT A15508) has no skull, but a similarly weathered skull, BAT A15831, may belong to it. The two relics have been attributed ages of 16–18 and 18–23, respectively, which is how I have arrived at an estimated age of 18 for this body.

Death of Jacop Hendricxen Drayer Sentence on Jan Hendricxsz, JFP 28 Sep 1629 [DB 183]. Buck's reexamination of this body has revealed no trace of the broken shoulder that some early writers on the subject say the skeleton displays.

The death toll in the islands Pelsaert to the Gentlemen XVII of Amsterdam, 12 Dec 1629 ARA VOC 1630 [DB 259]; 'Note regarding the fate of the people embarked on board the Batavia,' ARA VOC 1098, fol. 582r [R 220]. It is hard to know what Pelsaert meant by 'children.' Certainly the *Batavia*'s cabin boys must have been included among the 96 'employees of the VOC,' but when the offspring of Pieter Jansz, Claudine Patoys, Hans and Anneken Hardens, and Mayken Cardoes are added to the six children of the *predikant,* the number of children definitely known to have been killed in the archipelago rises to at least 10. Conversely, if we take 'children' to mean those under the age of, say, 10, and count Bastiaensz's three daughters as 'women,' thus correcting the number of children who died to the number given by the *commandeur,* the number of female deaths cannot be less than 14. Bernandine Hunneybun, in *Skullduggery on Beacon Island* (BSc Hons dissertation, University of Western Australia, 1995), section 5-5, suggests a total death toll of 137 in the archipelago, including the 11 mutineers who died on Seals' and Wiebbe Hayes's Islands.

'*... more than 120*' 'Declaration in Short,' JFP nd [DB 248].

'*... all but two of the children ...*' The exceptions were one child who was among those who fled to Wiebbe Hayes, and the babe in arms who reached Batavia in the longboat.

'*... almost two-thirds of the women ...*' There were seven survivors among the 20 women on the ship: Creesje Jans, Zwaantie Hendricx, Judick Bastiaens, Zussie and Tryntgien Fredricx, either Anneken Bosschieter or Marretgie Louys, and the unnamed mother who sailed on the longboat.

Pelsaert on Jacobsz's responsibility 'Declaration in Short,' op. cit.; see also Drake-Brockman, op. cit., p. 61.

'*Torrentian*' JFP 30 Sep 1629 [DB 212] (where the word is spelled phonetically, '*torrentiænschen,*' an indication of its rarity).

'*Epicurean*' Ibid.; verdict on Andries Jonas, JFP 28 Sep 1629 [DB 203].

'*Following the beliefs of Torrentius*' Van Diemen to Pieter de Carpentier, 10 Dec 1629, ARA VOC 1009 [DB 50].

Anonymous sailor Letter of December 1629, published in *Leyds Veer-Schuyts Praetjen, Tuschen een Koopman ende Borger van Leyden, Varende van Haarlem nae Leyden* (np [Amsterdam: Willem Jansz], 1630), pp. 19–20 [R 235]. It has been suggested that the author was the upper-steersman, Claes Gerritsz, and certainly the man, whoever he was, seems to have returned to the Abrolhos with the *Sardam,* judging from the details in his letter.

Torrentius's views Govert Snoek, *De Rosenkruizers in Nederland, Voornamelijk in de Eerste Helft van de 17de Eeuw. Een Inventarisatie* (Ph.D. thesis, University of Utrecht, 1997), pp. 80–7.

Jeronimus and Torrentius How, then, it might be asked, did the word *Torrentian* find its way into Pelsaert's journals? Torrentius's trial had been such a cause célèbre that it is certainly possible the upper-merchant used it as a label for something he hardly understood. But Pelsaert was not in Holland when Van der Beeck was arraigned, and there is no sign that he was familiar with the minutiae of the charges or the trial. On the whole it seems more likely that it was indeed Jeronimus who brought up the painter's name.

If so, Cornelisz's reasoning remains obscure. Admitting that he had known such a notorious heretic was hardly likely to help his case, and it may be that Van der Beeck's name was dragged from him under torture. However, it is perhaps more likely that Jeronimus volunteered it freely, perhaps with the intention of using it in mitigation – presenting himself as the painter's dupe. Such an effort would be in keeping with his earlier attempt to place the blame for all the murders on his dead councillors, and it would have been equally characteristic for the under-merchant to assimilate a few of Torrentius's beliefs into his own warped world view, while ignoring any that did not fit his preconceived opinions.

'Well spoken' 'Declaration in Short,' op. cit.

The psychology of Jeronimus Cornelisz Theodore Milton, Erik Simonsen, Morton Birek-Smith, and Roger Davis (eds.), *Psychopathy: Antisocial, Criminal and Violent Behaviour* (New York: Guildford Press, 1998), pp. 34–6, 161–9; Robert Hare, *Without Conscience: The Disturbing World of the Psychopaths Among Us* (New York: Guildford Press, 1999), pp. 12–4, 18, 34–5, 38, 40, 44, 46, 52, 135–6, 158, 166–70, 195–200; Hare, *Psychopathy: Theory and Research* (New York: John Wiley & Sons, 1970), pp. 95–109.

'Most clinicians and researchers…' Hare, *Without Conscience,* p. 22.

'Rebel without a cause' Cited in ibid., p. 81. In 1944, Lindner wrote a well-regarded study of criminal psychopathy titled *Rebel Without a Cause,* which was later turned – with extensive modifications – into the famous film of the same name.

'Psychopaths have a narcissistic view…' Hare, *Without Conscience,* p. 38.

'Careful observers…' Ibid., p. 52.

Psychopathy has no cure Ibid., pp. 195–7.

Source of Chapter Heading Quotes

Opening quote	JFP 17 Sep 1629 – Resolution of Francisco Pelsaert, JFP 28 Sep 1629 (DB 144, 153)
Prologue	From Francisco Pelsaert's last letter to the Gentlemen XVII of Amsterdam, 12 Dec 1629, ARA 1098, fol. 583–4 [DB 259–61]
Chapter 1	JFP 17 Sep 1629 [DB 158]
Chapter 2	John Keay, *The Honourable Company: A History of the English East India Company* (London: HarperCollins, 1993), p. 34.
Chapter 3	Jacques Specx to the Gentlemen XVII, ARA VOC 1009 [DB 77]
Chapter 4	JFP 19 Sep 1629 [DB 164]
Chapter 5	JFP 17 Sep 1629 [DB 158]
Chapter 6	Letter by an anonymous sailor, published in *Leyds Veer-schuyts…* [R235]
Chapter 7	JFP 19 Sep 1629 [DB 146]
Chapter 8	LGB
Chapter 9	JFP 2 Oct 1629 [DB 213]
Epilogue	JFP 13–16 Nov 1629 [DB 222–37]

Bibliography

1. Archival material

[a] Amsterdam
Gemeente Archief [Municipal Archive]
Baptismal registers
Marriage registers
Burial registers
Records of the Classis of Amsterdam

[b] Dordrecht
Gemeente Archief [Municipal Archive]
Baptismal registers
Marriage registers
Burial registers
Family Archive Balen
Records of the Church Council of Dordrecht
Transportregisters [Registers of transfers of ownership]

Oud-Notarieel Archief [Old Solicitors' Archive]
Solicitors' acts

[c] The Hague
Algemeen RijksArchief [General State Archive]
General correspondence, letters, and resolutions of the VOC

Centraal Bureau voor Genealogie
Van Welderen collection
Anonymous MS entitled *Geschiedenis van het Geslacht Vaassen,* vol. 8 (nd, twentieth century)

[d] Haarlem
Gemeente Archief [Municipal Archive]
Burial registers
Memorialen [Burgomasters' records]

Oud-Notarieel Archief [Old Solicitors' Archive]
Solicitors' acts

[e] Leeuwarden
Gemeente Archief [Municipal Archive]
Authorisation books
Certificate books
Mortgage books

RijksArchief in Friesland [State Archive of Frisia]
Hypotheekboeken Tietjerksteradeel [Tietjerksteradeel mortgage
books]

2. Unpublished dissertations, theses, and typescripts

Boranga, Sofia. *The Identification of Social Organisation on Gun Island* (Post
   Graduate Diploma in Archaeology dissertation, University of
   Western Australia, 1998).
Hunneybun, Bernandine. *Skullduggery on Beacon Island* (BSc Hons
   dissertation, University of Western Australia, 1995).
Huystee, Marit van. *The Lost Gateway of Jakarta* (Fremantle: Western
   Australian Maritime Museum, 1994).
Snoek, Govert. *De Rosenkruizers in Nederland, Voornamelijk in de Eerste
   Helft van de 17de Eeuw. Een Inventarisatie* (PhD thesis, University of
   Utrecht, 1997).
Zuiderbaan, Louis. 'Translation of a journal by an unknown person from
   the Dutch East Indiaman *Zeewijk,* foundered on Half Moon Reef in
   the Southern Abrolhos, on 9 June, 1727' (typescript, nd, copy in
   Western Australian Maritime Museum).

3. Published material

Ablaing van Giessenburg, WJ d'. *De Ridderschap van het Kwartier van
   Nijmegen* (The Hague: Van Stockum, 1899).
———. *De Ridderschap van de Veluwe* (The Hague: Martinus Nijhoff,
   1859).
Acda, G. M. W. *Voor en Achter de Mast: Het Leven van de Zeeman in de 17de
   en 18de Eeuw* (Bussum: De Boer Maritiem, 1976).
Aerts, R., and H. te Velde (eds.). *De Stijl van de Burger: Over Nederlandse
   Burgerlijke Cultuur vanaf de Middeleeuwen* (Kampen: Kok Agora, 1998).
Alie, Joe. *A New History of Sierra Leone* (London: Macmillan, 1990).
Anon. *Droevighe Tijdinghe van de Aldergrouwelykste Moordery, Geschiet door
   Eenighe Matrosen op 't Schip* Batavia (Rotterdam: Cornelis Fransz, 1630).
———. *Leyds Veer-Schuyts Praetjen, Tuschen een Koopman ende Borger van
   Leyden, Varende van Haarlem nae Leyden* (np [Amsterdam: Willem
   Jansz], 1630).

————. *Wonderlijck Verhael van het Leven en Gevoelen van Jan Symensz Torrentius* (Haarlem: Louwerens Jansz, 1630).

Anon. [Isaac Commelin] *Ongeluckige Voyagie, Van 't Schip* Batavia, *Nae de Oost-Indien. Gebleven op de Abrolhos van Frederick Houtman, op de Hooghte van 28 ⅓ Graet, by-Zuden de Linie Æquinoctiael. Uytgevaren Onder den E. Francoys Pelsaert …* (Amsterdam: Jan Jansz, 1647; expanded edn., Amsterdam: De Vries, 1649; third edn., Utrecht: Lucas de Vries, 1652).

Barend-van Haeften, M. *Op Reis met de VOC: De Openhartige Dagboeken van de Zusters Lammens en Swellengrebel* (Zutphen: Walburg Pers, 1996).

Barend-van Haeften, M., and A. J. Gelderblom (eds.). *Buyten Gaets: Twee Burleske Reisbrieven van Aernout van Overbeke* (Hilversum: Verloren, 1998).

Bevacqua, Robert. 'Archaeological Survey of Sites Relating to the *Batavia* Shipwreck.' *Early Days Journal* 7 (1974).

Blussé, L. 'The Caryatids of Batavia: Reproduction, Religion and Acculturation under the VOC.' *Itinerario* 7 (1983).

Boucher, M. 'The Cape Passage: Some Observations on Health Hazards Aboard Dutch East Indiamen Outward-bound.' *Historia* 26 (1981).

Boxer, C. R. 'The Dutch East-Indiamen: Their Sailors, Their Navigators and Life on Board, 1602–1795.' *The Mariner's Mirror* 49 (1963).

————. *The Dutch Seaborne Empire 1600–1800* (London: Hutchinson, 1963).

————. *Dutch Merchants and Mariners in Asia 1602–1795* (London: Variorum Reprints, 1988).

Bredius, Abraham. *Johannes Torrentius* (The Hague: Martinus Nijhoff, 1909).

Brereton, William. *Travels in Holland, the United Provinces etc … 1634–1635* (London: Chetham Society, 1844).

Breuker, P. H., and A. Janse (eds.). *Negen Eeuwen Friesland-Holland: Geschiedenis van een Haat-Liefdeverhouding* (Zutphen: Walburg Pers, 1997).

Brockliss, Laurence, and Colin Jones. *The Medical World of Early Modern France* (Oxford: Clarendon Press, 1997).

Bruijn, Iris. 'The Health Care Organisation of the Dutch East India Company at Home.' *Social History of Medicine* 7 (1994).

Bruijn, Jaap. 'Between Batavia and the Cape: Shipping Patterns of the Dutch East India Company.' *Journal of Southeast Asian Studies* 11 (1980).

————. *The Dutch Navy in the 17th and 18th Centuries* (Columbia, SC: University of South Carolina Press, 1993).

Bruijn, Jaap, and E. S. van Eyck van Heslinga. *Muiterij, Oproer en Berechting op de Schepen van de VOC* (Haarlem: De Boer Maritiem, 1980).

————. 'Seamen's Employment in the Netherlands, 1600–1800.' *The Mariner's Mirror* 70 (1984).

Bruijn, Jaap, and Femme S. Gaastra (eds.). *Ships, Sailors and Spices: East India Companies and Their Shipping in the 16th, 17th and 18th Centuries* (Amsterdam: NEHA, 1993).

Bruijn, Jaap, F. S. Gaastra, and I. Schöffer. *Dutch-Asiatic Shipping in the 17th and 18th Centuries* (The Hague: Martinus Nijhoff, 3 vols., 1979–1987).

Bruyns, W. F. J. 'Navigation of Dutch East India Company Ships Around the 1740s.' *The Mariner's Mirror* 78 (1992).

Buist, M. G., et al. (eds.). *Historisch Bewogen: Opstellen over de Radicale Reformatie in de 16e en 17e Eeuw* (Groningen: Wolters-Noordhoff, 1984).

Cohn, Norman. *The Pursuit of the Millennium: Revolutionary Millenarians and Mystical Anarchists of the Middle Ages* (Oxford: Oxford University Press, 1970).

Collingridge, George. *The Discovery of Australia: a Critical, Documentary and Historical Investigation Concerning the Priority of Discovery in Australasia Before the Arrival of Lieut. James Cook in the* Endeavour *in the Year 1770* (Sydney: Hayes Brothers, 1895).

Cook, Harold. *The Decline of the Old Medical Regime in Stuart London* (Ithaca, NY: Cornell University Press, 1986).

Coolhaas, W. Ph. 'Aanvullingen en Verbeteringen op Van Rhede van der Kloot's "De Gouveneurs-General en Commissarissen-Generaal van Nederlandsch-Indië (1610-1888)." *De Nederlandsche Leeuw* 73 (1956).

———— (ed.). *Pieter van den Broecke in Azië* (The Hague: Martinus Nijhoff, 1962).

Cotterell, Geoffrey. *Amsterdam: The Life of a City* (Farnborough: DC Heath, 1973).

Dam, P van. *Beschryvinge van de Oostindische Compagnie,* vol. 3 (The Hague: Martinus Nijhoff, 1943).

Davies, Ralph. *The Rise of the English Shipping Industry in the Seventeenth and Eighteenth Centuries* (Newton Abbot: David & Charles, 1971).

Dean, Geoffrey. *The Porphyrias: a Story of Inheritance and Environment* (London: Pitman Medical, 1971).

Deursen, A. T. van. *Plain Lives in a Golden Age: Popular Culture, Religion and Society in Seventeenth Century Holland* (Cambridge: Cambridge University Press, 1991).

Dorren, Gabrielle. 'Burgers en Hun Besognes. Burgemeestersmemorialen en Hun Bruikbaarheid als Bron Voor Zeventiende-Eeuws Haarlem.' *Jaarboeck Haarlem* (1995).

————. *Het Soet Vergaren: Haarlems Buurtleven in de Zeventiende Eeuw* (Haarlem: Arcadia, 1998).

————. 'Communities Within the Community: Aspects of Neighbourhood in Seventeenth Century Haarlem.' *Urban History* 25 (1998).

————. *Eenheid en Verscheidenheid: De Burgers van Haarlem in de Gouden Eeuw* (Amsterdam: Prometheus/Bert Bakker, 2001).

Drake-Brockman, Henrietta. *Voyage to Disaster* (Nedlands, WA: University of Western Australia Press, 1995).

Edwards, Hugh. *Islands of Angry Ghosts* (New York: William Morrow, 1966).

————. *The Wreck on the Half-Moon Reef* (New York: Charles Scribner's Sons, 1970).

Eisenberg, A. F. Plotke, and A. Baker. 'Asexual Syphilis in Children.' *Journal of Venereal Diseases Information* 30 (1949).

Estensen, Miriam. *Discovery: The Quest for the Great South Land* (Sydney: Allen & Unwin, 1998).

Estep, William. *The Anabaptist Story: An Introduction to Sixteenth-Century Anabaptism* (Grand Rapids, MI: William B. Eerdmans, 1996).

Gaastra, Femme. 'The Dutch East India Company: A Reluctant Discoverer.' *The Great Circle* 19 (1997).

Gelder, R. van. *Het Oost-Indisch Avontuur: Duitsers in Dienst van de VOC, 1600–1800* (Nijmegen: SUN, 1997).

Gerretson, C. *Coen's Eerherstel* (Amsterdam: Van Kampen, 1944).

Gerritsen, Rupert. *And Their Ghosts May Be Heard...* (South Fremantle, WA: Fremantle Arts Centre Press, 1994).

Glamann, Kristoff. *Dutch-Asiatic Trade 1620–1740* (Copenhagen: Danish Science Press, 1958).

Godard, Philippe. *The First and Last Voyage of the* Batavia (Perth: Abrolhos Publishing, nd, c. 1993).

Green, Jeremy. *Australia's Oldest Shipwreck: The Loss of the* Trial, *1622* (Oxford: British Archaeological Reports, 1977).

————. *The Loss of the Verenigde Oostindische Compagnie Retourschip* Batavia, *Western Australia 1629: An Excavation Report and Catalogue of Artefacts* (Oxford: British Archaeological Reports, 1989).

Green, Jeremy, and Myra Stanbury. 'Even More Light on a Confusing Geographical Puzzle, Part 1: Wells, Cairns and Stone Structures on West Wallabi Island.' *Underwater Explorers' Club News* (January 1982).

Green, Jeremy, Myra Stanbury, and Femme Gaastra (eds.). *The ANCODS Colloquium: Papers Presented at the Australia-Netherlands Colloquium on Maritime Archaeology and Maritime History* (Fremantle: Australian National Centre of Excellence for Maritime Archaeology, 1999).

Halls, C. 'The Loss of the *Ridderschap van Holland*.' *The Annual Dog Watch* 22 (1965).

————. 'The Loss of the Dutch East Indiaman *Aagtekerke*.' *The Annual Dog Watch* 23 (1966).

Hare, Robert. *Psychopathy: Theory and Research* (New York: John Wiley & Sons, 1970).

————. *Without Conscience: The Disturbing World of the Psychopaths Among Us* (New York: The Guildford Press, 1999).

Heeres, J. A. *The Part Borne by the Dutch in the Discovery of Australia 1606–1765* (London: Luzac, 1899).

Henderson, Graeme. *Maritime Archaeology in Australia* (Nedlands, WA: University of Western Australia Press, 1986).

————. 'The Mysterious Fate of the Dutch East Indiaman *Aagtekerke*.' *Westerly* (June 1978).

Henderson, JA. *Marooned* (Perth: St. George Books, 1982).

———. *Phantoms of the* Tryall (Perth: St. George Books, 1993).

———. *Sent Forth a Dove: Discovery of the* Duyfken (Nedlands, WA: University of Western Australia Press, 1999).

Henderson, S., and T. Bostock. 'Coping Behaviour after Shipwreck.' *British Journal of Psychiatry* 131 (1977).

Herbert, Zbigniew. *Still Life With a Bridle: Essays and Apocryphas* (London: Jonathan Cape 1993).

Israel, Jonathan. *Dutch Primacy in World Trade, 1585–1740* (Oxford: Clarendon Press, 1989).

———. *The Dutch Republic: Its Rise, Greatness and Fall, 1477–1806* (Oxford: Oxford University Press, 1998).

Jansma, L. G. *Melchiorieten, Münstersen en Batenburgers: Een Sociologische Analyse van een Millennistische Beweging uit de 16e Eeuw* (Buitenpost: np, 1977).

Jones, Adam (ed.). *West Africa in the Mid-Seventeenth Century: An Anonymous Dutch Manuscript* (London: African Studies Association, 1994).

Kamer, H. N. *Het VOC-Retourschip: Een Panorama van de 17de-en 18de-Eeuwse Scheepsbouw* (Amsterdam: De Bataafsche Leeuw, 1995).

Keay, John. *The Honourable Company: A History of the English East India Company* (London: HarperCollins, 1993).

Keevil, J. J., C. S. Lloyd, and J. L. S. Coulter. *Medicine and the Navy, 1200–1900* (4 vols., Edinburgh, 1957–1963).

Kindleberger, Charles. 'The Economic Crisis of 1619 to 1623.' *Journal of Economic History* 51 (1991).

Kolff, D. H. A., and H. W. van Santen (eds.). *De Geschriften van Francisco Pelsaert over Mughal Indië, 1627: Kroniek en Remonstrantie* (The Hague: Martinus Nijhoff, 1979).

Krahn, Cornelis. *Dutch Anabaptism: Origin, Spread, Life and Thought, 1450–1600* (The Hague: Martinus Nijhoff, 1968).

Laurence, John. *A History of Capital Punishment* (New York: Citadel Press, 1960).

LaWall, Charles. *Four Thousand Years of Pharmacy: An Outline History of Pharmacy and the Allied Sciences* (Philadelphia: JB Lippincott, 1927).

Leslie, Edward. *Desperate Journeys, Abandoned Souls: True Stories of Castaways and Other Survivors* (London: Papermac, 1991).

Luger, A. 'Non-Venereally Transmitted "Endemic" Syphilis in Vienna.' *British Journal of Venereal Diseases* 48 (1972).

McCarthy, Mike. '*Zuytdorp* far from home.' *Bulletin of the Australian Institute for Maritime Archaeology* 22 (1998).

McIntosh, Christopher. *The Rosy Cross Unveiled: The History, Mythology and Rituals of an Occult Order* (Wellingborough: The Aquarian Press, 1980).

McIntyre, Kenneth. *The Secret Discovery of Australia: Portuguese Ventures 200 Years Before Captain Cook* (Medindie, South Australia: Souvenir Press, 1977).

Macco, H. F. *Geschichte und Genealogie der Familie Peltzer* (Aachen: np, 1901).

Major, R. H. *Early Voyages to Terra Australis, Now Called Australia* (Adelaide: Australian Heritage Press, 1963).

Milton, Giles. *Nathaniel's Nutmeg: How One Man's Courage Changed the Course of History* (London: Hodder & Stoughton, 1999).

Milton, Theodore, Erik Simonsen, Morton Birek-Smith, and Roger Davis (eds.). *Psychopathy: Antisocial, Criminal and Violent Behaviour* (New York: Guildford Press, 1998).

Mooij, J. *Bouwstoffen voor de Geschiedenis der Protestantsche Kerk in Nederlands-Indië* (Weltevreden: Landsdrukkerij, 3 vols., 1927–31).

Mout, M. E. H. N. 'Spiritualisten in de Nederlandse Reformatie van de Zestiende Eeuw.' *Bijdragen en Mededelingen Betreffende de Geschiedenis der Nederlanden* 111 (1996).

Mundy, Peter. *The Travels of Peter Mundy* (London: Hakluyt Society, 4 vols., 1907–24).

O'Malley, C. D. (ed.). *The History of Medical Education* (Berkeley, CA: University of California Press, 1970).

Parr, Charles McKew. *Jan van Linschoten: The Dutch Marco Polo* (New York: Thomas Y. Cromwell, 1964).

Parthesius, R. (ed.). Batavia *Cahier 2: De Herbouw van een Oostindiëvaarder* (Lelystad: np, 1990).

———. Batavia *Cahier 3: De Herbouw van een Oostindiëvaarder* (Lelystad: np, 1990).

Pasveer, Juliëtte, Alanah Buck, and Marit van Huystee. 'Victims of the *Batavia* Mutiny: Physical Anthropological and Forensic Studies of the Beacon Island Skeletons.' *Bulletin of the Australian Institute for Maritime Archaeology* 22 (1998).

Pérez-Mallaína, Pablo. *Spain's Men of the Sea: Daily Life on the Indies Fleets in the Sixteenth Century* (Baltimore: Johns Hopkins University Press, 1998).

Philbrick, Nathaniel. *In the Heart of the Sea: The Epic True Story That Inspired Moby Dick* (London: HarperCollins, 2000).

Playford, Phillip. *Carpet of Silver: The Wreck of the Zuytdorp* (Nedlands, WA: University of Western Australia Press, 1996).

———. *Voyage of Discovery to Terra Australis by Willem de Vlamingh in 1696–97* (Perth: Western Australian Museum, 1999).

Ratelband, K. (ed.). *Reizen naar West-Africa van Pieter van den Broecke, 1605–1614* (The Hague: Martinus Nijhoff, 1950).

Rathblum, K. 'Congenital syphilis.' *Sexually Transmitted Diseases* 10 (1983).

Raven-Hart, R. *Before Van Riebeeck: Callers at South Africa from 1488-1652* (Cape Town: C. Struik, 1967).

Rehorst, A. J. *Torrentius* (Rotterdam: WL & J Brusse NV, 1939).

Rhede van der Kloot, M. A. van. *De Gouverneurs-Generaal en Commissarissen-Generaal van Nederlandsch-Indië, 1610–1888* (The Hague: Van Stockum, 1891).

Ritchie, G. S. *The Admiralty Chart: British Naval Hydrography in the Nineteenth Century* (London: Hollis & Carter, 1967).

Rodger, N. A. M. *The Wooden World* (London: Fontana, 1988).

———. *The Safeguard of the Sea* (London: HarperCollins, 1997).

Roeper, V. D. (ed.). *De Schipbreuk van de* Batavia, *1629* (Zutphen: Walburg Pers, 1994).

Rogozinski, Jan. *Honour Among Thieves: Captain Kidd, Henry Every and the Story of Pirate Island* (London: Conway Maritime Press, 2000).

Ross, Marvin Chauncey. 'The Rubens Vase: Its History and Date.' *Journal of the Walters Art Gallery* 6 (1943).

Schama, Simon. *The Embarrassment of Riches: An Interpretation of Dutch Culture in the Golden Age* (London: Fontana, 1987).

Schilder, Günter. *Australia Unveiled: The Share of Dutch Navigators in the Discovery of Australia* (Amsterdam: Theatrum Orbis Terrarum, 1976).

Schilfgaarde, A. P. van. *Register op de Leenen van het Huis Bergh* (Arnhem: Gouda Quint, 1929).

Shephard, Sue. *Pickled, Potted and Canned: The Story of Food Preserving* (London: Headline, 2000).

Sigmond, J. P., and L. H. Zuiderbaan. *Dutch Discoveries of Australia: Shipwrecks, Treasures and Early Voyages off the West Coast* (Adelaide: Rigby, 1979).

Sprengard, Karl, and Roderich Ptak (eds.). *Maritime Asia: Profit Maximisation, Ethics and Trade Structure c. 1300–1800* (Wiesbaden: Harrassowitz, 1994).

Spruit, R. *Jan Pietersz Coen: Daden en Dagen in Dienst van de VOC* (Houten: De Haan, 1987).

Stanbury, Myra (ed.). *Abrolhos Islands Archaeological Sites: Interim Report* (Fremantle: Australian National Centre of Excellence for Maritime Archaeology, 2000).

Stapel, F. W. (ed.). *Beschryvinge van de Oostindische Compagnie* vol. 3 (The Hague: Martinus Nijhoff, 1939).

———. *De Gouveneurs-Generaal van Nederlandsch-Indië in Beeld en Woord* (The Hague: Van Stockum, 1941).

Stayer, James. *Anabaptists and the Sword* (Lawrence, KA: Coronado Press, 1972).

Taylor, Jean Gelman. *The Social World of Batavia: European and Eurasian in Dutch Asia* (Madison, WI: University of Wisconsin Press, 1983).

Tickner, F. J., and V. C. Medvei. 'Scurvy and the Health of European Crews in the Indian Ocean in the Seventeenth Century.' *Medical History* 2 (1958).

Toohey, John. *Captain Bligh's Portable Nightmare* (London: Fourth Estate, 1999).

Troostenburg de Bruijn, C. A. L. van. *Biographisch Woordenboek van Oost-Indische Preidikanten* (Nijmegen, npj 1893).

Tyler, Philip. 'The *Batavia* Mutineers: Evidence of an Anabaptist "Fifth

Column" Within 17th Century Dutch Colonialism?' *Westerly* (December 1970).

Uren, Malcolm. *Sailormen's Ghosts: The Abrolhos Islands in Three Hundred Years of Romance, History and Adventure* (Melbourne: Robertson & Mullens, 1944).

Vlekke, Bernard. *The Story of the Dutch East Indies* (Cambridge, MA: Harvard University Press, 1946).

Vos, Willem. Batavia *Cahier 1: De Herbouw van een Oostindiëvaarder: Bestek en Beschrijving van een Retourschip* (Lelystad: np, 1990).

————. Batavia *Cahier 4: Een Rondleiding door een Oostindiëvaarder* (Lelystad: np, 1993).

Watson, Gilbert. *Theriac and Mithridatium: A Study in Therapeutics* (London: The Wellcome Historical Medical Library, 1966).

Weaver, Fiona. *Report of the Excavation of Previously Undisturbed Land Sites Associated with the VOC Ship* Zuytdorp, *Wrecked 1712, Zuytdorp Cliffs, Western Australia* (Fremantle: Western Australian Maritime Museum, 1990).

Wilson, Stan. *Doits to Ducatoons: The Coins of the Dutch East India Company Ship* Batavia, *Lost on the Western Australian Coast 1629* (Perth: Western Australian Museum, 1989).

Wittop Koning, D. A. *Compendium voor de Geschiedenis van de Pharmacie in Nederland* (Lochem: De Tijdstroom, 1986).

Zadoks-Josephus Jitta, A. N. 'De Lotgevallen van den Grooten Camee in het Koninklijk Penningkabinet.' *Oud-Holland* 6 (1951).

Zumthor, Paul. *Daily Life in Rembrandt's Holland* (London: Weidenfeld & Nicholson, 1962).

Dutch Pronunciation Guide

CHRISTIAN NAMES	PHONETIC	ENGLISH EQUIVALENT
Belijtgen	bel-LIGHT-ren	Mabel
Coenraat	CORN-rat	Conrad
Cornelis	cor-NAY-lee-us	Cornelius
Hilletgie	HILL-et-treen	Gilberta
Gijsbert/Gÿsbert	GUYZ-bert	Gilbert
Gillis	HILL-is	Giles
Jan	YANN	John
Janneken	YONN-a-kun	Jane
Jeurian	YOOR-ee-an	George
Mayken	MY-ken	Mary, Maria
Mattys	MATT-ayz	Matthew
Marretgie	MARR-et-heuh	Margaret
Roelant	ROO-lant	Roland
Teunis	TERN-is	Anthony
Tryntgien	TRENT-ee-en	Catherine
Wiebbe	webb-UH	[Frisian name]
Willemijntgie	will-em-EEN-tee-ah	Wilhelmina
Wouter	VOW-ter	Walter
Wybrecht	VY-brecht	'Glittering Strife'
Zwaantie	SVAAN-tee-ah	'Little swan'

NB 'ken' and 'ie' are Dutch diminutives meaning 'small' or 'little'

SURNAMES

Cardoes	kar-DOOS	
Cornelisz	cor-NAY-lee-us (-zoon)	
Loos	LOW-se	

PLACES

Hoorn	horn
Houtman's Abrolhos	HOWT-man's ab-ROL-hoss
Leeuwarden	loo-WAH-den
Monnickendam	MON-ik-an-dam
Texel	TESS-el

VOC SHIPS	PHONETIC	MEANING
Aagtekerke	AHG-te-kerk-eh	Named after a village in Zeeland
Batavia	BAT-ah-fee-uh	Named for the VOC's main base in the East Indies
Duyfken	DYFE-ken	Little Dove
Fortuyn	FOR-town	Fortune
's Gravenhage	SCHRAR-vun-har-chen	The Hague
Meeuwtje	MAY-oot-chee-ah	Little Seagull
Ridderschap van Holland	RIDD-er-schap	Knighthood of Holland
Vergulde Draeck	fer-HOOL-duh DRAAK	Gilt Dragon
Zeewijk	ZAY-vayk	Named after a village in Zeeland
Zuytdorp	ZOWT-dorp	Named after a village in Zeeland

Acknowledgements

The writing of *Batavia's Graveyard* involved considerable research and would never have been possible without the help – freely offered and gratefully received – of a large number of people.

I owe particular thanks to my research assistant, drs Henk Looijesteijn of Amsterdam, who carried out extensive original research on my behalf in archives the length and breadth of the Netherlands, and whose discoveries have added immeasurably to our knowledge of the *Batavia* and her passengers and crew.

I have also been fortunate enough to receive valuable assistance from many other sources. In Australia, drs Marit van Huystee and drs Juliëtte Pasveer of the Western Australian Maritime Museum, Fremantle, generously shared the results of their recent archaeological work on Beacon Island; Marit was also kind enough to read and comment on the manuscript. Ed Punchard of Prospero Productions told me a good deal about conditions in the Abrolhos Islands. Dr. Alanah Buck and Dr. Stephen Knott of the Western Australian Centre for Pathology and Medical Research in Perth explained what the skeletons of Cornelisz's victims, dug up on the island, can tell us about the *Batavia* mutineers and their bloody methods; and Max Cramer and the staff of Abrolhos Helicopters in Geraldton helped during my flying visit to the site of the tragedy.

In the Netherlands, Professor Femme Gaastra of the University of Leiden described his research into the possible survival of shipwrecked Dutch mariners in the Australian interior, and Dr. F. W.

M. de Rooij of Erasmus University, Rotterdam discussed the implications of the existence of porphyria in Australia and the possibility that shipwrecked Dutchmen might have been integrated into aboriginal society. Paul van Dam of the Gemeente Archief, Haarlem, and Gabrielle Dorren were especially helpful during research in Cornelisz's old stamping ground.

My agent, Patrick Walsh, had enormous belief in this book from the start and was a great support during the final stages of writing. My remarkable editor, Rachel Kahan, shared Patrick's faith in the project and was a valued source of inspiration and advice.

As for Penny and Ffion, who had to see things through to the very end, what can I say but thank you, and I hope that it was worth it.

Index